TRAGIC ENCOUNTERS

TRAGIC ENCOUNTERS

THE PEOPLE'S HISTORY OF NATIVE AMERICANS

PAGE SMITH

COUNTERPOINT

Library of Congress Cataloging-in-Publication Data is available.
ISBN 978-1-61902-574-5

Cover design by Faceout Studio
Interior design by Domini Dragoone

COUNTERPOINT
2560 Ninth Street, Suite 318
Berkeley, CA 94710
www.counterpointpress.com

Printed in the United States of America
Distributed by Publishers Group West

10 9 8 7 6 5 4 3 2 1

This book is dedicated to Page's grandchildren and great-grandchildren: Cary, Page, Levi, Noah, Sara, Robert, Matthew, Samantha, Gavin, Logan, Reef, and Isa

CONTENTS

EDITOR'S
NOTE

Publishing posthumous work presents unusual challenges. Lacking entirely, of course, is the dialogue between the author and his or her editors. On a few occasions, the author has finished a complete and final draft, and the book is for all intents and purposes ready to go. We can then proceed concerned only with making certain that through copyediting and proofreading we have accomplished what the author would have wished.

On other occasions a manuscript is discovered left in an earlier draft, in a form showing clearly that the author would have wished to revise further and had not completed his or her own necessary work. A few of these are so far from being other than fragmentary first drafts as to discourage even the best editorial intentions from going forward. But in the case of Page Smith's *Tragic Encounters*, the great American historian obviously had devoted considerable time and effort into assembling this manuscript. It shows evidence of revision that suggests he was readying a version for a new typescript, and the version left behind lacks sources and his bibliography. And knowing a bit of his working habits one can easily imagine this text being only a draft away from something he would have submitted to his publisher.

We know too that he was a willing participant in the editorial process and we might have had exchanges that would have led to smoothing out a bit of the prose and eliminating some of the repetition that remains. Out of respect for Professor Smith, we have kept these editorial alterations to a minimum.

All books are products of the time of their composition, and this one is no different. Some readers may find a few words or characterizations offensive and for that we apologize. But it is our belief that Page Smith has here made a wonderful contribution to the story of the European contact with the Native peoples of North America, and together with the surviving members of Smith's family we are proud to see it into print.

PREFACE

In a striking, and to me somewhat mysterious manner, those aboriginal or tribal people, whom we have chosen, rather misleadingly, to call Indians, have emerged in the last two decades from the obscurity into which they fell at the end of the Indian Wars, circa 1890, to become once more a major preoccupation of white Americans. Their champions have claimed a new name for them, Native Americans, on the grounds that they were here long before the white man invaded "their" continent. The white invaders are now often called Euro-Americans, presumably to emphasize that they (we) were the intruders and conquerors of the original, real Americans. Seen in this light the latecomers appear as false claimants, bogus Americans (ironically, a substantial majority of Indians when polled as to their preference indicated that they preferred the name "Indian," to "Native American").

The reasons for the sudden prominence of Indians are undoubtedly related in part to a re-awakened "environmental ethic," to admonitions to love and preserve the land. The Indians, we are told, are a model for us. They had an intimate relationship to the natural world that we should try to emulate. Contributing to the elevation of the Indian is, doubtless, a kind of modern primitivism, a weariness with a world of technological wonders; a desire to return to a womb of innocence, to recapture the instinctual life of the "natural" man and woman.

In addition, we now have a "men's movement," represented most conspicuously by the aging poet, Robert Bly, who tells middle-class, middle-aged white American males that they need to assert their "warrior selves"; that they need to revive the primitive rituals of initiation, to drum and make spears and dance primitive dances.

Finally, the strange, tragic story of the encounter of white Europeans with darker-skinned aborigines has proved to be a convenient stick for angry critics of everything American to beat the "corrupt," "criminal, "genocidal" United States with. That encounter is offered as irrefutable evidence of our national depravity.

It seems to me that the most sensible way to address the issue of Euro-Americans versus Native Americans is to eschew polemics and tell the story as simply and directly as possible in the classic form of narrative history. In each volume of my *People's History of the United States* I have discussed the relations between "Indians" and "Settlers" from the days of colonization to the end of the nineteenth century. I have collected chapters from each volume to constitute a chronological account of those relationships and I have added an additional chapter to bring the story more or less up to the present.

This work is not offered in any sense as a history of the American Indians or even a comprehensive account of white–Indian relations. It is, rather, an effort to suggest the nature of that interchange, of its inherent drama and abiding human interest; and to trace the hold that Indian culture has had on the imagination of the European settlers who ventured to the part of the New World that became in time the United States.

CHAPTER I

EARLY
ENCOUNTERS

The encounter between the English colonists and the American aborigines, to whom the English gave the general name of "Indians" because of the darkness of their skin, was one of the most dramatic meetings between different cultures in all of history. The Indians were divided into innumerable tribes that spoke some five hundred different tongues and dialects. (This was one of the facts about the native Americans that led to the speculation of the colonists that the Indians might be the Lost Tribes of Israel—once a single people, but now cursed by God for their presumption in seeking to build the Tower of Babel and condemned to be divided and to speak in a multitude of strange tongues.) Many of these tribes were constantly at war with each other. With few exceptions, the culture of those Indians encountered by settlers from the Old World was based upon a perpetual state of war. Fierce courage in battle and stoic endurance under horrible tortures were the highest ideals of tribal life. In almost every respect, colonists and the Indians represented radically different patterns of culture. In the eastern part of the North American continent most of the aborigines were warrior-hunters, people of extraordinary physical hardihood and stamina. Roaming over vast territories, they had no notion of landed property and no idea of abstract justice. Cruelty, violence, and constant warfare were the facts of daily life. Yet the European mind was captivated by the idea of the noble savage as it has been by few ideas in its history. Both Voltaire and Rousseau, philosophers who nurtured the Enlightenment, saw society as corrupt and decadent, far removed from the wholesomeness and simplicity of the natural man. They romanticized the savage man, whom they saw as being close to nature, his intelligence unclouded by priestly superstition, by social conventions, fashion, greed, and ambition. Voltaire wrote a novel called *L'Ingenu*, about an Indian who came to France and everywhere encountered and saw through the superficiality and falseness of French life. Religion, government, philosophy, the haut monde—all were revealed as empty and meretricious.

This was an eighteenth-century phenomenon. The planters or original settlers in the preceding century had a somewhat different perception of the Indian. For them he was alternately a poor heathen soul to be saved for the greater glory of God, or a figure of startling exoticism and terrible menace. Most of the English adventurers and planters in the New World were entirely sincere in their desire to bring to the savages of America the benefits of European Christianity. The task simply proved inordinately difficult.

Quite typically, Captain John Smith, who had his hands full contending with the deceitful Powhatan, was constantly exhorted by the officers of the Virginia Company to make more progress in converting the Indians to Christianity. To one such admonition, the captain replied testily that he needed some soldiers to force the Indians to pay attention to the preachers. It was difficult to convert an Indian who was shooting arrows at you or was plainly intent on trying to scalp you. If the settler's Christian faith had not inclined them to try to make peace with various tribes of aborigines they encountered, simple prudence would have. Outnumbered and untrained, with a few exceptions, in the art of warfare—and

2

certainly unfamiliar with the Indian guerrilla tactics of stealth and cunning—they did their best to avoid conflict. But the problem of maintaining peace was complicated by the constant state of warfare among the various tribes, conflicts that the settlers could only avoid with the greatest difficulty. In addition, the prolonged cold war between France and England for possession of North America, which smoldered for one hundred years before it burst into open flames in the French and Indian War or the Seven Years' War starting in 1754, was profoundly demoralizing to Indians and settlers alike. Neither the French nor the English could forbear using the tribes as pawns in their struggle for the dominance of the continent. The French repeatedly encouraged their Indian allies to make forays against English settlements, while the English played the same unscrupulous game.

In Virginia, where the first meeting of planters and aborigines took place, we had the inexhaustibly romantic encounter of Captain John Smith with the Indian chief Powhatan and his daughter Pocahontas. People will believe or disbelieve according to their own disposition the story of Pocahontas saving John Smith's life when her bad-tempered and wily old father was about to have Smith's brains bashed out. We have only the captain's word for it, and some historians have said he was a notorious liar (though others, as is the way with historians, have defended him very resourcefully). What is quite clear is that there was a close and affectionate relationship between the grizzled English captain, half-suitor, half-father, and the Indian princess. And she must have been a charming girl, running naked through the square at Jamestown with her bacchanalian troop of Indian girls. The problems of Indian diplomacy were pointed up by the fact that as soon as John Smith left the colony, Powhatan began to harass the settlers. The response of the colonists was to seize Pocahontas and hold her as hostage for her father's good behavior. While she was being held at Jamestown, John Rolfe, who perhaps first observed her turning cartwheels in the square, fell in love with her and went through a profound struggle with his conscience to decide whether or not to marry her. He wished to be sure that he was "called hereunto by the spirit of God." And he protested that he was not led, as he put it, "with the unbridled desire of carnal affection; but for the good of this plantation for the honour of our countries, for the glory of God, for my own salvation and for converting to the true knowledge of God and Jesus Christ, an unbelieving creature." That combination proved, as might have been expected, irresistible. Rolfe married Pocahontas and took his Indian princess, now called Rebecca Rolfe and dressed in English finery, to England to be introduced to the queen and stared at as a seven-day wonder.

Rebecca Rolfe died on the voyage back to Virginia. She left an infant son from whom—the romantics say—many present-day inhabitants of Virginia descend. The story symbolizes the romance and the tragedy of the white–Indian relationship, which started out so promisingly in the marriage of John Rolfe and Pocahontas and came at last, after innumerable colorful and often bloody episodes, to such a dismal end.

In 1622, several years after the death of Pocahontas, the Virginia Indians turned on the whites and massacred almost the entire colony. Those who survived did so only because of a warning from an Indian woman. And this fact points up one of the most striking aspects of the relations between the whites and the Indians: Time and again, groups of settlers were saved from surprise attack and extermination by an Indian woman who, at the risk of her own life, warned them of an impending raid.

> John Lawson, a gentleman and a surveyor, who was well acquainted with the Indians of North Carolina, was particularly charmed by the Indian women, who were in his opinion as fine shaped Creatures, (take them generally) as any in the Universe. They are of a tawny Complexion, their eyes very brisk and amorous, their Smiles afford the finest Composure a Face can possess, their Hands are of the finest Make, with small, long Fingers, and as soft as their Cheeks, and their whole Bodies of a smooth Nature. They are not so uncouth or unlikely as we suppose them, nor are they . . . not Proficients in the soft Passion.

4

The "trading girls" were young unmarried women who would sleep with white traders for a price if their families and the sachem agreed on the arrangement and the sachem got a portion of the price (frequently a bottle of brandy). Such women, without any stigma attaching to them, usually married Indian warriors after a time and made good wives. Those white men who traded with the Indians "commonly have their Indian Wives," Lawson noted, "whereby they soon learn the Indian Tongue, keep a friendship with the Savages; and, besides the Satisfaction of a She-Bed-Fellow, they find these Indian girls very serviceable to them, on account of dressing their Victuals, and instructing them in the Affairs and Customs of the Country."

One of the unhappy consequences of these relationships, at least from Lawson's point of view, was that the children of such unions grew up as Indians. Nevertheless, "we often find, that English Men, and other Europeans that have been accustomed to the Conversation of these Savage Women and their Way of Living, have been so allured with that careless sort of Life, as to be constant to their Indian Wife, and her Relations, so long as they lived, without ever desiring to return again amongst the English. . . ." By the same token, it was Lawson's observation that "the Indian Men are not so vigorous and impatient in their Love as we are." The Indian girls were thoroughly independent, and "those . . . that have conversed with the English and other European, never care for the Conversation of their own Countrymen afterwards."

The word "conversation" or "conversing" as used by Lawson means living with, including sexual relations. The hint of a particularly close relationship between Indian women and white men is a fascinating one, borne out by numerous other bits of evidence, equally fragmentary. It seems apparent that one of the aspects of Indian life that appealed most to the white man was the Indian woman. This was probably the result, in part, of the easy accessibility of Indian women, and of the simplicity and naturalness of the relationship. Moreover, Indian women were strong-minded and independent, but gentle, loving, and loyal to their white "husbands."

To the Indian woman, the white man evinced the power, the complexity, and the exoticism that women of all races and ages seem to have found attractive in man. A special poignancy in the relationship between the settlers and the Indians was this evident tie between the white men and the Indian woman, a tie that was often the means of saving a frontier settlement from extermination.

Unfortunately, few colonists followed the example of John Rolfe. William Byrd, in *The History of the Dividing Line*, lamented the fact: "for after all," he wrote, with more facetiousness than wisdom, " . . . a sprightly lover is the most prevailing missionary that can be sent among these, or any other infidels. . . . Nor would the shade of skin have been reproached at this day; for if a Moor may be washed white in three generations, surely an Indian might have been blanched in two." Byrd was of the opinion that the Indian women "would have made altogether as honest wives for the first planters, as the damsels they used to purchase from aboard ships. . . . It is strange, therefore, that any good Christian should have refused a wholesome, straight bedfellow, when he might have had so fair a portion with her a claim to some of the Indian lands, as [well] as the merit of saving her soul."

If the colonists did not marry Indians in any substantial numbers, they nevertheless extended hospitality to them. When William Durand attended a Virginia wedding in the 1690s a company of Indians came to visit. Durand described the women as wearing "some kind of petticoats, others wore some piece of shabby blue cloth from which were made the blankets they had traded on some ships in exchange for deer skins. They had made a hole in the center to put their heads through and fastened it around their body with deer-thongs." They mixed freely with the guests and added a colorful note to the ceremonies.

Members of tribes who were on friendly terms with a particular colony did not hesitate to visit individuals or to claim to be guests of the colony itself, as in the case of Pennsylvania, which maintained apartments in the State House for the use of visiting sachems. In Virginia, the tradition of hospitality to passing Indians lingered on as the residue of the days when reciprocal hospitality was quite common. Thomas Jefferson recalled that they came often, and in considerable numbers, to Williamsburg. The Virginian spent much time with them and was a friend of the great Cherokee warrior and orator Outacity, who always stayed with Jefferson's father on his trips to and from the colonial capital. John Adams likewise recalled from his childhood frequent visits by the priest and the king of the Punkapog and Neponset tribes, named, respectively, Aaron and Moses, "the tallest and stoutest Indians I have ever seen." In turn, Adams on his rambles would often stop at the wigwam of an Indian family who lived nearby, where, he wrote, "I never failed to be treated with Whortle Berries, Blackberries, Strawberries, or Apples, Plumbs, Peaches, etc., for they had planted a variety of fruit trees about them."

Unfortunately, to befriend one tribe was to make inveterate enemies of *their* enemies. The Indian ethic allowed of no compromise on this score. If you were the friend of a particular tribe, you were of necessity an ally against its enemies. Anything else was the darkest treachery. Weak tribes or tributary tribes often tried to form an alliance with settlers in the hope of defeating a tribe to whom they had been tributary. The French in Canada, by forming an alliance with the Hurons, incurred the enmity of the Iroquois, the most powerful and warlike tribe in the northeast. Thus the traditional opponents of the Hurons became English allies when the great European powers brought their war to America. In Connecticut, settlers were invited to establish themselves on Indian lands, apparently in hopes that they would strengthen a particular tribe against its enemies. When Connecticut settlers under John Mason and John Underhill exterminated the Pequot tribe in 1637, they were assisted by the Narragansetts and the Mohegans, the two most powerful tribes in the area, with whom the Connecticut settlers managed, on the whole, to maintain friendly relations.

When the Massachusetts Bay colony was founded, John Eliot translated the Bible into the Indian tongue. But Eliot was only the most famous of a number of missionaries who labored to improve the lot of the Indians and to convert them to Christianity. Harvard erected a building especially for the instruction of Indians and Caleb Cheeshateaumuck, an Indian, obtained an early bachelor's degree. When the College of William & Mary was founded at Williamsburg in 1693, it included an Indian school, as, of course, did Dartmouth. The Dartmouth school produced Samson Occom, the noted Indian preacher and scholar.

All such efforts were ultimately unavailing. The white man's perception of the Indian was too limited. He wanted in effect to turn the Indian into a "white Protestant"—to which project the Indian was stubbornly resistant. The problem was vastly complicated by the fact that in a real sense there was no such thing as an Indian. There were members of tribes of frequently very different speech, customs, and manners, whose consciousness was a tribal consciousness. These did not and could not fully exist outside of the tribe of which they were members. The white man's ways and culture were as unfathomably strange to the so-called Indian as his ways were to the white man.

In any event, despite all efforts by enlightened spirits on both sides, the white settlers and the Indians were periodically involved in bitter warfare. The warfare was invariably, after the early years, to the Indians' disadvantage, because it provided opportunities for whites to take possession of Indian lands secured by treaties that could not be readily broken.

Through all the contacts between the Indian and the white man there runs a fascinating doubleness or ambiguity. There was much that was attractive in Indian life to the bearer of the Protestant ethic. White society was organized around the notion of contractual relationship, around predictable behavior. The Indian would have understood a medieval knight better than a sober Puritan, and vice versa. The Reformation, which made its adherents into "individuals," also made them hopelessly alien to a people who still lived in a tribal consciousness. And yet, to the white settler with his psychological burdens, the most basic of which was the sense that he must always behave as he was expected to behave, the free and, indeed, capricious life of the Indians had a sometimes irresistible attraction.

Observing the Indians, who "have few but natural wants and those easily supplied," Benjamin Franklin was inclined to propose a whole new theory of human development. If man could be so content in a state of nature, he asked himself, how had civilization ever arisen? It must have been as a consequence of a condition of scarcity, where some peoples, driven from lands that afforded an easy living, were forced to create a more complex and varied economic and social life. Franklin wrote to a friend: "They are not deficient in natural understanding and yet they have never shown any inclination to change their manner of life for ours, or to learn any of our Arts."

Even when an Indian child had been brought up among whites, "taught our language and habituated to our Customs," if "he goes to see his relations and makes one Indian ramble with them there is no persuading him ever to return. . . ." Indeed, when whites of either sex who had been taken prisoner at a tender age and had lived for a time among the Indians were returned to white society, "in a Short time they become disgusted with our manner of life . . . and take the first good Opportunity of escaping again into the woods, from whence there is no reclaiming them."

William Penn gave a vivid account of his initial meeting with the Indians of Pennsylvania, and a close account of their appearance and customs:

> For their persons, they are generally tall, straight, well-built and
> of singular proportion. They tread strong, and clever, and mostly
> walk with a lofty chin. Of complexion black, but by design as
> the gypsies in England. They grease themselves with bears-fat
> clarified, and using no defence against sun or weather, their skins
> must need be swarthy. Their eye is little and black, not unlike a
> straight-look't Jew. The thick lip and flat nose so frequent with
> East-Indians and blacks are not common among them; for I have
> seen as comely European-like faces among them of both sexes, as
> on your side the sea. . . . Their language is lofty, yet narrow, but
> like the Hebrew . . . one word serves in the place of three . . . I
> must say that I know not a language spoken in Europe that hath

9

words of more sweetness or greatness in accent and emphasis than theirs; for instance Octorockon, Rancoros, Ozicton, Shakamacon . . . all of which are names of places and have grandeur in them.

As soon as Indian children were born, they were washed and plunged into cold water to harden them.

Having wrapped them in a clout they lay them on a straight thin board, a little more than the length and breadth of the child and swaddle it fast upon the board; wherefore all Indians have flat heads; and thus they carry them on their backs. . . . When the young women are fit for marriage, they wear something upon their heads for an advertisement, but so as their faces are hardly to be seen but when they please. The age they marry at, if women, is about thirteen and fourteen, if men seventeen and eighteen; they are rarely elder.

Their diet is maze, or Indian corn, divers ways prepared; sometimes roasted in the ashes, sometimes beaten and boiled with water which they call homine; they also make cakes not unpleasant to eat. They have likewise several sorts of beans and peas that are good nourishment and the woods and rivers are their larder. . . . They are great concealers of their own resentments, brought to it, I believe, by the revenge that hath been practised among them; in either of these, they are not exceeded by the Italians.

But in liberality they excel, nothing is too good for their friend: give them a fine gun, coat, or other thing, it may pass twenty hands, before it sticks; light of heart, strong affections, but soon spent; the most merry creatures that live, feast, and dance perpetually; they never have much; nor want much. Wealth circulateth like the blood, all parts partake. . . . If they are ignorant of our pleasures, they are also free from our pains. They are not disquieted with bills of lading and exchange, nor perplexed with chancery-suits and exchequer-reckonings. We sweat and toil to live; their pleasure feeds them; I mean their hunting, fishing and fowling. . . . They eat twice a day, morning and evening; their seats and table are on the ground. Since the European came into these parts, they are grown great lovers of strong liquors, rum especially. If they are heated with liquors, they are restless till they have enough to sleep, that is their cry—some more and I will go to sleep; but when drunk, one of the most wretchedst spectacles in the world.

The justice they have is pecuniary: In case of any wrong or evil fact, be it murder itself, they atone by feasts and presents of their wampum, which is proportion to the quality of the offense or person injured, or of the sex they are of: For in case they kill a woman, they pay double, and the reason they give is, "That she breedeth children which men cannot do."

Penn's formula for Indian negotiations was simple.

Don't abuse them, but let them have justice, and you win them. The worst is that they are the worse for the Christians who have propagated their vices and yielded them tradition for ill, and not for good things. . . . I beseech God to incline the hearts of all that come into these parts, to out-live the knowledge of the natives by a fixt obedience to their greater Knowledge of the will of God, for it were miserable indeed for us to fall under the just censure of the poor Indian conscience, while we make profession of things so far transcending.

The Reverend John Heckewelder, a Moravian missionary, expressed the same admiration for Indian life. They think

that [God] made the earth and all it contains for the common good of mankind . . . it was not for the benefit of a few, but of all. Everything was given in common to the sons of man. Whatever liveth on the land, whatsoever groweth out of the earth, and all that is in the rivers and waters flowing through

11

the same, was given jointly to all, and every one is entitled
to his share. From this principle, hospitality flows as from its
source. . . . They give and are hospitable to all, without exception,
and will always share with each other and often with a stranger,
even to their last morsel.

"Yours" and "mine," "ours," "his," "hers," were not the deter-
minative words for the Indians that they were for the white man.
The Indian did not think that the land was "his" in the sense that
the white man insisted that it was his property. The whole notion
of buying and selling land was so alien to the Indian that while he
could understand driving an enemy off a hunting range or general
territory, he had no notion of marking off a specific area as belonging in perpetuity to some individual tribe, and certainly not to an
individual Indian. Thus he often "sold" the same land to several
English purchasers, thereby causing vast confusion and misunder-
standing, if not bloody skirmishes.

Franklin's classic account of the effort to interest the Indians in
the white man's education suggests some of the difficulties involved
in trying to reconcile the two cultures. According to Franklin, in
a treaty meeting between the Six Nations and the authorities of
one of the colonies, the Indian commissioners told the Indians that
as a special gesture of friendship and goodwill, "a particular foun-
dation in favour of the Indians" would "defray the expense of the
Education of any of their sons who should desire to take the benefit
of it." If the Indians were agreeable, the English would take half-a-
dozen of their brightest young men "and bring them up in the Best
manner." The response of the Indians was, in effect, that a college
education was impractical. "Some of their Youths had formerly been
educated in that College, but it had been observed that for a long
time after they returned to their Friends, they were absolutely good
for nothing being neither acquainted with the true methods of killing deer, catching beaver or surprising an enemy." However, the
chiefs, impressed by the evident kindness in the proposal, offered
in return "if the English Gentlemen would send a dozen or two of

their Children to (the Indian settlement at) Onondago," they would undertake to bring them up in what really was the best manner and make men of them. The story is probably apocryphal—just the kind of moral-making yarn Franklin was forever spinning—but it does make the point, and the fact is that the purported answer of the Indians was typical of their sense of humor.

Much of the conflict between white and Indian revolved around the Protestant "work ethic" of the settlers, especially those of New England. For the whites, a man who was not working or who would not work was, as a matter of course, a weak and foolish, if not a wicked man. Not to work, and to drink as well, was vagabondage and a certain damnation. The Indian did both—he was resistant to work and drank himself into insensibility whenever he had the chance. Josiah Cotton's *Vocabulary of the Massachusetts (or Natick) Indian language*, which was written for the Christianized "praying Indians" who lived at Natick as wards of the colony, reveals white attitudes quite clearly. The most striking phrases in the dictionary have to do with work and drink: "Why don't you work hard?" (*Kah tohawal mat menukanakausean.*); "So I would with all my heart, but I am sickly." "But it might be work will cure you, if you would leave off drinking too." And again, "Idleness is the root of much evil."

The numerous treaty meetings with the Indians were always colorful and dramatic affairs. There the Indians appeared at their noblest and most striking. Merciless and cruel in warfare, they were magnanimous in peace. When a site for the powwow had been agreed upon, the Indian tribe or tribes would begin to assemble. With none of the white man's preoccupation with being "on time," they were often maddeningly slow to appear, days or weeks late by English time. They came in full panoply, in a bizarre combination of English and Indian finery, a beaded buckskin shirt set off by a plumed beaver hat festooned with shells, or a headdress with a blue broadcloth coat with tarnished silver buckles. The Indian orations were lengthy and extraordinarily eloquent, woven with rich metaphorical figures and conceits. Agreements were bound by smoking the calumet, or pipe of peace.

The colonists were clearly much impressed by Indian oratory, and some historians have suggested that the "stem-winding," "spread-eagle" oratory much favored by American politicians of the nineteenth century had its origin in the treaty speeches of Indian chiefs. Treaty meetings were usually accompanied by much drinking and revelry, especially after a treaty had been agreed upon, since a keg of rum was not infrequently part of the treaty settlement, and the Indians might linger on for days of celebration.

A typical treaty meeting was one that took place at Albany in 1754 between the governor of the province of New York and the Onondagas and Cayugas.

> Brother: You are a mighty sachem and we but a small people. When
> the English first came to New York, to Virginia and Maryland,
> they were but a small people and we a large nation, and we finding
> they were good people gave them land and dealt civilly with them.
> Now that you are grown numerous and we decreased you must
> protect us from the French, which if you don't we shall lose all our
> hunting and beavers. The French want all the beavers and are angry
> that we bring any to the English. We have put all our land and our
> persons under the protection of the Great Duke of York, brother
> to your mighty sachem. The Susquehanna River which we won by
> our sweat, we have given to this government. And we desire that it
> may be a branch of that great tree which is planted here, whose top
> reaches to the sun and under whose branches we shelter ourselves
> from the French or any other enemy. Our fire burns in your houses.
> Your fire in our houses and we desire it may ever so continue. . . .
>
> We have submitted ourselves to the Great Sachem Charles who
> liveth on the other side of the Great Lake and now we give you in
> token thereof two white buckskins to be sent to him.

Then came the presentation of wampum and skins by the Indians and of presents by the white men—needles, cloth, lace, shirts, beads, mirrors, guns, etc.

Jefferson, who, like Franklin and indeed most American intellectuals, was fascinated by Indian life, was present in the camp of Outacity, a chief of the Cherokees, when he made his farewell oration to his people on the evening of his departure for England. As Jefferson recalled the scene many years later: "The moon was in full splendor, and to her he seemed to address himself in his prayers for his own safety on the voyage, and that of his people during his absence. His sounding voice, distinct articulation, animated action, and the solemn silence of his people at their several fires, filled me with awe and veneration, altho' I did not understand a word he uttered."

As Wilcomb Washburn has put it:

The white man as officeholder is, in many ways, a more perplexing and perverse figure to the Indian than the individual conqueror, or fur trapper, or explorer. Under the panoply of European formality the government representative communicated with the Indian leaders, but too often the form and spirit were not in close juxtaposition. The Indian, valuing the spirit rather than the recorded form, which in his letterless society was, for the most part, superfluous, could not cope with the legalisms of the white man.

Nor could an alien government sympathize with, let alone understand, the plight of a race organized into categories that had no parallels in the white bureaucratic machinery.

This was certainly the case in those constant negotiations between the white man and the Indian that began when John Smith seized Powhatan by the hair of his head and quite literally wrung concessions from him. A famous instance of hard bargaining by whites at Indian expense was the so-called Walking Purchase of Indian lands in Pennsylvania. The Indians sold, at a reasonable price, that area of land that a man could walk around in one day, from sunup to sunset. This was for a moderately fast walker, let us say, some twenty square miles. However, the white purchasers arranged for relays of runners to cover a vastly larger territory and thus claim several times the extent of land the Indians intended to sell. To the Indians this was simple deceit and chicanery. To the whites, it was a clever ruse. It is small wonder that to Pocahontas it was a plain truth that Englishmen "lied much," or that later generations of Indians took it for granted that the white man spoke with a forked tongue. The irony of the situation was that the society of nascent capitalism that was developing out of the Protestant passion was based on contractual relationships and, above all, on a man's word being as good as his bond. Thus "English honor" came to be a synonym for fair dealing. However, in time the burden of personal honesty was shifted to the contract. Whatever could be negotiated into the contract (or treaty) was fair enough. Deviousness was part of the game. People who live without or outside of conventional bureaucratic structures are inevitably thrown back on the requirement of personal integrity and oftentimes appear naive to sophisticated negotiators.

Whether the aborigines of North America were "squalid savages" or nature's noblemen; whether the English settlers were ruthless exploiters or pious Christians anxious to save heathen souls, it is hard to imagine how the two cultures could have coexisted on the same continent without the bitter conflicts that marked their historic encounters.

The so-called Indians taught the colonists how to plant corn and tobacco, peas, beans, pumpkins and squash, melons and cucumbers; how to harvest maple sugar; how to use fish for fertilizer; how to hunt and trap; how to make canoes. They supplied them with innumerable place names and, finally, with the ubiquitous barbecue. But of far greater importance, they stirred the deepest levels of the white imagination. Did they represent a freer and more spontaneous life, a new vista of human possibilities? Or did they by their cruelties and violence awaken in the souls of "civilized" men the savage passions that they had struggled to repress? However one might approach that unanswerable question, the fact was that white man and red man were locked in a strange and terrible embrace that degraded the white and ultimately destroyed the Indian's tribal life.

CHAPTER II

THE AMERICAN REVOLUTION

The French and Indian War began in America with the British effort to oust the French from the land along the Ohio River, an area claimed by Virginia. The royal governor of Virginia, Robert Dinwiddie, sent an ambitious young militia officer named George Washington to drive the French out of the area. When Washington built Fort Necessity at Great Meadows, a much larger French force surrounded it and forced the defenders to surrender. The outbreak of hostilities prompted the calling of the Albany Congress, instructed by the British government to discuss the conduct of Indian affairs. The hope was to prevail upon the various Indian tribes to abandon their allegiance to the French, or, better, to aid the colonists. Delegates met with representatives of the Iroquois Confederacy, the most powerful alliance of tribes on the northern frontier. Benjamin Franklin, a delegate from Pennsylvania with a reputation as a friend of the Indians, arrived armed with a "Plan of Union" that called for a "general government" of all the colonies gathered in a "Grand Council" to be chosen by "representatives of the people of the several colonies. . . ." Its ostensible purpose was "to hold or direct all Indian treaties in which the general interest of the colonies may be concerned; and make peace or declare war against Indian nations." Franklin's Albany Plan of Union is taken as the first tentative step toward at least a degree of intra-colonial rule and although it was promptly squelched by the British government (it indeed went much further than most of the colonies themselves were willing to go), it may be said that the seed of colonial union was planted as a response to the need for a common Indian policy. Without such a policy individual tribes could play one colony off against another much as they played the French off against the British. It was none-theless a notable effort and it demonstrated the importance of the "Indian problem" to the colonists.

The failure of the Albany Plan was underlined by the role that Indian allies of the French played in General Braddock's disastrous defeat at Fort Duquesne in July, 1755. In the campaigns that followed, culminating in General Wolfe's spectacular victory over the French general Montcalm, Indians were involved with both the French and British forces, operating as irregular troops and as scouts and raiders. Wolfe's victory was followed by the ceding of Canada to the British crown. The Indian allies of France suffered from having chosen the wrong party; many of them transferred their alliance to Great Britain with the consequence that when the War of Independence broke out in 1776, Great Britain was able to call upon a formidable array of Indian cohorts. The colonists were not without Indian allies of their own but these were in the main "domiciled" Indians, converted to Christianity and living as farmers, tribes like the Stockbridge Indians of Massachusetts who were organized into a company of Minutemen along with a troop of Mohawk warriors. When the Stockbridge Indians were placed under the command of white officers, their chief promptly protested. "Brothers," he wrote to the Massachusetts Provincial Congress, "one thing I ask of you, that you will let me fight in my own Indian way. I am not used to fight English fashion, there-fore you must not expect I can train like your men. Only point out where your enemies keep, and that is all I shall want to know." The "domiciled" Indians were thought to be much less fearsome than the "savages" who maintained their nomadic, tribal ways. Their principal assignment was to frighten the British by, in effect, pretending to be their fiercer rivals. They enjoyed that game, coming dangerously close to the British lines where they would "flourish their scalping knives, and yell by Way of Insult." But they were not well-suited to camp life. As one militia officer put it, "They were too fond of Liquor; they grew troublesome . . . there was no Bush fighting to employ them in; and they were dismissed."

With the warrior tribes the matter was different. The initial policy of Congress was to do all possible to keep the Indian tribes neutral, especially the fearsome Iroquois Confederacy. "The Indians are known to conduct their wars so entirely without Faith and humanity," John Adams wrote to his friend, James Warren, "that it will bring eternal infamy on the Ministry throughout Europe if they should incite the Savages to War. The French disgraced themselves last war by employing them. To let loose those blood Hounds to scalp Men and to butcher Women and Children is horrid."

Congress took special pains with the speech that was to be delivered with much wampum to the chiefs of the Six Nations:

> You Indians know how things are proportioned in a family— between the father and the son—the child carries a little pack— England we regard as the father—this island may be compared to the son. The father . . . appoints a great number of servants. . . . Some of his servants grow proud and ill-natured—they were displeased to see the boy so alert and walk so nimbly with his pack. They tell the father, and advise him to enlarge the child's pack— they prevail. . . . Those proud and wicked servants . . . laughed to see the boy sweat and stagger under his increased load. By and by, they apply to the father to double the boy's pack, because they heard him complain. . . .

The boy implores the father with "tears and entreaties"; the father gives no answer and, staggering under the crushing load, the boy "gives one struggle and throws off the pack. . . . Upon this, those servants . . . bring a great cudgel to the father, asking him to take it in his hand and strike the child." The speech concluded: "This is a family quarrel between us and old England. You Indians are not concerned in it. We don't wish you to take up the hatchet against the King's troops. We desire you to remain at home, and not join on either side, but keep the hatchet buried deep. . . . What is it we have asked of you? Nothing but peace."

Although the British had made sporadic use of Indian allies early in the war, the ministers in England, like the British commanders in the field, were deeply divided in their feelings about employing Indians against the American rebels. Most of them viewed the Indians as the colonists did: as savages who, once turned loose, could not easily be kept within the bounds of civilized warfare. The Indian propensity for massacre and pillage was well known. Especially in the early stages of the war, when British hopes of reconciliation were stronger, there was a disinclination to employ methods of warfare that might alienate the Americans. In addition, there was the simple fact that the Indians, like most partisan or guerrilla fighters, were unreliable in prolonged and arduous campaigns. It was, first of all, not the Indians' fight; secondly, their concept of warfare was that of stealthy raids, with a brief explosion of fierce fighting and a rich harvest of loot. They had no stomach for long-drawn-out engagements, and their undisciplined methods of fighting were not easily coordinated with the white man's rather formal and cumbersome tactics. On the other hand, the Indians were superb scouts and raiders, and the psychological effects of their use were often more devastating than the practical effects. Americans, particularly those who inhabited isolated frontier settlements, lived in constant fear of Indian attacks. Their dreams were haunted by images of painted savages sweeping out of the forest to murder, burn, scalp, and rape. In such sudden assaults, the fortunate were those who were tomahawked where they lay; the unfortunate survived to be tortured to death. White feelings are perhaps best indicated by the fact that New Hampshire in 1776 offered seventy pounds for each scalp of a hostile male Indian, and thirty-seven pounds, ten shillings for each scalp of a woman or of a child over twelve years old.

In New York and "the Old Northwest," the region north of the Ohio River, there was a close alliance between the Tories and the Indians, most notably various tribes of the Iroquois Confederacy. The Tories' bitter hatred drove them to stir up the Indians against the patriots whenever possible and to try to persuade the British to make full use of the capacity of the Indians for spreading terror and demoralization in the white settlements.

Massachusetts had enrolled the Stockbridge Indians in the Minutemen, but that was rather a special case, and the Indians, during the siege of Boston, had become restless and unhappy with the routines of camp life and army training.

Congress had the subject of the Indians constantly in mind. Various measures were proposed to keep the Indians neutral. In July, 1775, not long after the Battle of Bunker Hill, Congress had divided the colonies into three departments—northern, middle, and southern—and had appointed eleven commissioners to supervise Indian affairs in the three areas. The commissioners were to have "power to treat with the Indians in their respective departments, in the name, and on behalf of the united colonies, in order to preserve peace and friendship with the said Indians, and to prevent their taking any part in the present commotions."

James Duane, a New York delegate, saw the hostility of the Onondagas as justifying the seizure of their lands after the Revolution ended. The Indian tribes, he advised the commissioners of the Northern Department, should be notified that if they engaged in hostilities against the Americans, the result would be the confiscation of their lands. Duane added,

> The Indians are sufficiently sensible of the value of their lands. No other consideration will keep them within the bounds of humanity or good faith . . . I flatter myself that the venal and disgraceful system hitherto practiced, of courting and bribing

them to lay down their arms after the most wanton barbarities will never be revived. Let justice be done to them as reasonable beings; but let them know that they shall not injure us with impunity. This alone can secure our future tranquility; especially if Britain should retain Canada on a pacification.

Every colony had had a different experience with the Indians; each one had its own interest in exploiting them, and often these interests were in sharp conflict. South Carolina, which profited from a rich trade in deerskins with the Indians, was fearful that Congress might try to regulate or impede her commerce with the Indians. Georgia, exposed to the raids of the Southern tribes, was anxious to have all possible help from Congress.

James Wilson, a Pennsylvania delegate and a large land speculator, insisted on the autonomy of Congress in dealing with the Indians. There could be no peace with the Indians -unless that peace was made by one body. "No such language as this ought to be held out to the Indians. 'We are stronger, we are better, we treat you better than another colony.' No power ought to treat with the Indians, but the United States." The Indians knew firsthand the "striking benefits of confederation"; they had an extraordinary example in the union of the Six Nations. "None should trade with the Indians," Wilson concluded, "without a license from Congress. A perpetual war would be unavoidable, if everyone was allowed to trade with them."

In October, 1775, the commissioners for the Middle Department met at Fort Pitt with a number of Indian chiefs— Silver Heels; Blue Jacket, a famous warrior; Cornstalk, chief of the Shawnees and one of the most noted Indians in America; Kilbuck, a Delaware chief; and Kyashota of the Senecas.

The Indians agreed to remain neutral, and White Eyes, a principal Delaware chief, returned to Philadelphia to meet the members of Congress and assure them of the friendship of his tribe. Congress, for its part, undertook to support several young Indians at the College of New Jersey at Princeton, but the experiment was somewhat less than a success. When one of the Indians made a white girl pregnant, her indignant father applied to Congress for compensation.

Treaty discussions also were carried on between Congressional commissioners and Indians in the Northern Department. When the commissioners arrived at the site of the council they found the "Chiefs all in one House to receive us," as the secretary, Tench Tilghman wrote, "and the men all seated in a Circle in an adjoining Orchard the Women & Children standing at a little distance. Seats were set for us in the area of the Circle. When we entered there was a mutual solemn salutation of How do you do or something of that kind and then a profound silence." Interpreters informed the assembled chiefs of the business on which the commissioners had come, but nothing could be done since the Mohawk chiefs had not arrived. On word that they would be provided with drink and tobacco, the chiefs brightened up "and assured us in general," Tilghman wrote "that their Brothers the Americans should find them fast friends." Tilghman continued, "The Behaviour of the poor Savages at a public meeting ought to put us civilized people to the Blush. The most profound silence is observed, no interruption of a speaker. When any one speaks the rest are attentive." The Indians smoked the tobacco that the commissioners gave them with a quiet, deliberate air.

> When drink was served round it was in the same manner, no Man seemed anxious for the Cup. One of them made a speech and set forth the bad effects of drinking at a time of Business and desired that the White people might not have liberty to sell rum to their Young Men."

> An Indian Treaty, by the by . . . is but dull entertainment owing to the delay and difficulty of getting what you say, delivered properly to the Indians. The Speech is first delivered in short sentences by one of the Commissioners, then an Interpreter tells an Indian what the Commissioner has been saying. After this has been repeated to the Indian he speaks it to the six nations, so that

> a speech that would not take up twenty minutes in the delivery
> will from the necessary delays employ us two or three hours.

An additional difficulty was that the formal language of Congress had to be altered and amended "and put . . . into such mode & Figure as would make intelligible to the Indians for in its original form, you might almost as well have read them a Chapter out of Locke or any of your most learned reasoners."

In the evening the commissioners turned a bull loose for the "young Indians to hunt and kill after their manner, with arrows, knives and hatchettes. The Beast," Tilghman added, "was not of the furious Spanish breed for he suffered himself to be despatched in a very few minutes without ever turning upon his assailants." Then there was a foot race run for "two laced Hats." The Indians entertained the commissioners by singing, but Tilghman found the voices of the women too shrill. The Stockbridge Indian girls, Christianized and trained in hymn singing by the missionaries, Tilghman found "pretty and extremely cleanly they speak tolerable English too. . . ."

After several days of parleying, the negotiations were transferred to Albany for the convenience of the Indians, but Tilghman found that town uncomfortably and dangerously crowded with soldiers and Indians. "It is hard to say which is the most irregular and Savage," he noted. "The former are mutinous for want of liquor the latter for want of pay, without which they refuse to march. The troops raised in and about New York are a sad pack. They are mostly old disbanded Regulars and low lived foreigners."

After an interval of several days, the Indians replied to the proclamations of Congress that had been delivered by the commissioners. "It is amazing," Tilghman wrote, "with what exactness these people recollect all that has been said to them. The speech which delivered took up nine or ten pages of folio Paper, when they came to answer they did not omit a single head and on most of them repeated our own words. . . . They are thoroughbred politicians. They know the proper time of making demands.

"It was soon evident that the most influential Indian in the council was Molly, the squaw or mistress of the famous and beloved Sir William Johnson, now deceased, British Commissioner for the Northern Indians." A woman of noble bearing, "she saluted us," Tilghman wrote, "with an air of ease and politeness, she was dressed after the Indian Manner, but her linen and other Cloathes the finest of their kind." She reproached Kirkland, an Oneida missionary present at the meeting, for not having visited her since her husband's death—"the poor and unfortunate were always neglected." Tilghman guessed that she would be the principal impediment to a treaty with the assembled tribes. She had thrown her considerable weight, it was rumored, with Guy Johnson and the British. "It is plain," Tilghman wrote at the end of the treaty meeting, "that the Indians understand their game, which is to play into both hands."

In the Southern Department a similar meeting with the chiefs of local tribes took place, at which presents were distributed and promises of neutrality exacted in return.

As the war dragged on month after month and as the British sense of frustration increased, their policy of employing Indians cautiously and for primarily military ends was gradually replaced by one of using them to punish and frighten the Americans. In the fall of 1776, Lord George Germain wrote to the British Indian agent in the South, John Stuart, urging him to press on in his negotiations with the Creeks and Choctaws and to try to get them to join with the Cherokee in raiding the Carolina and Virginia frontier. At the outbreak of hostilities it was rumored that the South Carolina assembly had offered bounties for Indian scalps and had stated that Indian children "of a certain age which may be taken prisoners [shall be] the slaves of their captors. . . ." Such policy, Germain assured Stuart, would help to recruit the Indian tribes to fight against the American rebels.

Six months later the Tory Governor William Tryon of New York was urging the British ministry to "loose the savages against the miserable Rebels in order to impose a reign of terror on the frontiers. . . ." Indeed, his proposal soon became government policy. When North tried to defend it in Parliament on the grounds that the British were obliged to use such means as "God and nature put into our hands," Chatham was stirred to one of his most eloquent flights of rhetoric. He was, he declared,

> astonished to hear such principles confessed! . . . Principles equally unconstitutional, inhuman, and unchristian! . . . What! to attribute the sacred sanction of God and nature to the massacres of the Indian scalping knife? to the cannibal savage, torturing, murdering, roasting and eating; literally, my lords, *eating* the mangled victims of his barbarous battles! Such horrible notions shock every precept of religion, divine or natural and every generous feeling of humanity . . . they shock me as a lover of honorable war, and a detester of murderous barbarity. . . . We turn loose these savage hellhounds against our brethren and countrymen in America, of the same language, laws, liberty and religion, endeared to us by every tie that should sanctify humanity.

Washington, who had his own problems, wrote to the commissioners of Indian affairs, in the name of Congress, asking them to enlist a "body of four hundred Indians, if they can be procured upon proper terms. Divesting them of the Savage customs exercised in their Wars against each other, I think they may be made of excellent use, as scouts and light troops, mixed with our own Parties."

While such matters of policy were debated, small-scale but bitter fighting between patriots and those Indians who were willing to throw in their lot with the British broke out along the American frontier. It was a time of settlers murdered in their beds, of frontier cabins and lean-tos put to the torch, of children abducted, and of reprisals as savage as the raids that provoked them.

The most devastating of these raids was directed at the Wyoming Valley, which lay along the Susquehanna near Wilkes-Barre. The area, which made up roughly the northern quarter of Pennsylvania was claimed by Connecticut also, and every effort by

Pennsylvania to oust the Connecticut settlers had resulted in open warfare. The valley settlers were strong patriots and most of the able-bodied men had enlisted in the Connecticut Line.

Major John Butler's Tory Rangers and their Indian allies chose the Wyoming Valley as the object of an attack designed to wreak vengeance and provide a rich haul of plunder. Led by Butler, a combined force of over twelve hundred Indians and Tories set out from Niagara. The march to western Pennsylvania was marked by looting and murder. In the words of Hector St. John de Crèvecoeur, who lived near the plundered towns, "it was easy to surprise defenseless isolated families who fell an easy prey to their enemies. . . . Many families were locked up in their houses and consumed with their furniture. Dreadful scenes were transacted which I know not how to retrace."

The raiders took the settlements of the Wyoming Valley by surprise. The only defense was provided by Colonel Zebulon Butler, who with some three hundred boys and old men occupied Forty Fort. On the morning of June 28, 1778, the Tories and Indians, principally Senecas and White Eyes' Delawares, came, in the words of a Tory carpenter, Richard McGinnis, "to a mill belonging to the Rebels. The Savages burnt the mill and took 3 prisoners, two white men and a Negro whom they afterwards murdered in their own camp." The hungry raiders were supplied by local Tories, the Wintermots, who brought fourteen head of fat cattle into their camp. The Wintermots told Sir John Butler they came from a fort that bore their name, which was ready to surrender if given assurance that the women and children would be safe from the Indians. Butler then sent a flag of truce to Forty Fort and Jenkins' Fort calling for their capitulation on the same terms. Jenkins' Fort followed the example of Wintermot, but the defenders of Forty Fort, under Zeb Butler, sent word that they never "would give it over to Tories and savages but stand it out to the last and defend it to the last extremity."

The Tories and Indians surrounded the fort and waited. Finally, on July 3 at five o'clock in the afternoon, Sir John Butler ordered his men to set fire to Wintermot's Fort, intending to give the impression that he and his raiders were retreating. Zeb Butler took the bait, the patriots issued from Forty Fort in hot pursuit, calling to the enemy, concealed in the woods, "Come out, ye villainous Tories! Come out, if ye dare and show your heads, if ye durst, to the brave Continental Sons of Liberty!" With the patriots dispersed in pursuit, the Tories and Indians sprang their trap. At first the patriots held their ground, but after they had fired their muskets, the Indians rushed on them with spears and tomahawks, and the inexperienced men turned and fled for their lives. Many of them jumped into the Susquehanna, where the Indians, naked and better swimmers, overtook them and killed them in the water, "and for a long time afterwards the carcasses became offensive, floated and infested the banks of the Susquehanna as low as Shamokin," Crèvecoeur wrote. "The other party, who had taken their flight towards their forts, were all either taken or killed. It is said that those who were then made prisoners were tied to small trees and burnt the evening of the same day." Crèvecoeur, who was no sympathizer with the Revolution, added, "Thus the ill-judged policy of these ignorant people and the general calamities of the times overtook them and extirpated them even out of that wilderness which they had come twelve years before to possess and embellish. Thus the grand contest entered into by these colonies with the mother-country has spread everywhere, even from the sea-shores to the last cottages of the frontiers." The losses to the raiders were given as one Indian killed and two white men wounded. "Thus," a Tory wrote, "did loyalty and good order that day triumph over confusion and treason, the goodness of our cause aided and assisted by the blessing of Divine Providence. . . ." The defenders of Forty Fort paid for their temerity with their property as well as, in many instances, their lives. There was, again in Richard McGinnis's words, "a total confiscation of property, such as oxen, cows, horses, hogs, sheep and every thing of that kind. Thus did Rebellion get a severe shock."

The Wyoming Valley Massacre, as it was immediately called, aroused a storm of fury against the Indians and the Tories. The ruthless destruction carried out by the attackers was grist for the patriot press. There were enough atrocity stories, many of them true, many not, to keep printer's devils busy for weeks setting type. The fort had been set on fire, it was said, and the captured prisoners thrown into the flames, or pinned down with pitchforks and slaughtered by the tomahawk of an Indian queen of notorious cruelty. At dark, it was said, fires had been kindled and those prisoners who had survived were chased, naked, through the flames until they dropped from exhaustion. Thus the Wyoming Valley Massacre became a byword for Tory and Indian brutality. They made, indeed, an ugly combination. As we have seen, the Tories were apt to be particularly vindictive. Their sense of outrage at the actions of the patriots in resisting the authority of the mother country were, for the most part, not tempered by any respect for the rules of warfare. The Tories usually neither gave nor expected any quarter, and when this vengeful spirit was augmented by the Indian propensity for total war, the results were almost invariably grim.

The Mohawk Valley and western New York north to Michilimackinac was soon largely emptied of its inhabitants, becoming a wasteland of charred houses whose desolate chimneys marked spots where villages and farmhouses had once stood. Settlers of English, Irish, and French Huguenot descent had occupied the area in the decades prior to the outbreak of the war. Goshen, Minisink, and Wawarsing had become thriving communities, even though they were situated in the middle of Indian country; Indians and settlers had lived in a kind of armed and wary peace. The Revolution turned the area into a battleground, a center of British power. Tory and Indian irregulars from Canada swept through the Mohawk Valley in endless raids. Strongly built houses were used as forts, and the residents of the area kept their muskets nearby day and night. The premier Indian chief of the region was Joseph Brant, or Thayendanegea, a Mohawk who had been educated at Eleazar Wheelock's Indian Charity School and had then become secretary to Guy Johnson, the Indian superintendent. Brant, who had been in England in the spring of 1776, became a friend of James Boswell, had his portrait painted by Romney, and returned to fight against the Americans in the home territory he knew so well.

Brant chose as his objective a cluster of villages in the Cherry Valley, an area of western New York. The valley had first been settled by the family of a New Yorker, John Lindsay, in 1740. From the spring of 1778 on, rumors circulated that Brant and his Mohawks intended to raid the valley, which was protected primarily by a fortified house belonging to Colonel Samuel Campbell. In July Colonel Ichabod Alden and his Seventh Massachusetts Regiment, consisting of some two hundred and fifty soldiers, arrived to provide for the defense of the valley and speed the building of an adequate fort. Alden was an inefficient martinet who paid little attention to the advice or the needs of the inhabitants of the region. He was warned by friendly Indians in November that a "great meeting of Indians and Tories" had taken place on the Tioga River and that a decision had been made to attack Cherry Valley. With a new fort finished, the settlers, who had also heard reports of the projected raid, requested permission from Alden to move into it with their families or at least to store their most important possessions there. Alden refused on the strange grounds that his soldiers would be tempted to steal the settlers' goods.

Meanwhile Brant, hearing that the officers of the Seventh Massachusetts Regiment were quartered outside the fort, made plans for a surprise attack on the morning of November 11. He was aided by a heavy fog that shrouded the fort and concealed the approach of his force. Just as he was ready to launch an assault, a farmer came jogging by on his way to the fort. He saw Brant's silent warriors just as they spied him. The Indians fired and wounded him, but he galloped off in time to give a few minutes' warning to the sleepy garrison. Close on his heels came a party of Senecas, who were auxiliaries to Brant's Mohawks. Their mission was to seize the Wells house, some four hundred yards from the fort. Alden, asleep in the Wells house, awoke and ran for the fort, but he was killed as he ran. His second-in-command was captured, and other officers and men of Alden's staff who tried to put up some resistance were quickly struck down.

After four or five hours spent in skirmishing, it became clear to Brant that there was little chance of reducing the fort, and he withdrew his men. Baffled in their primary object, the Indians in Brant's force then turned on the defenseless inhabitants, burning and pillaging the nearby settlements. There were some forty farmhouses in the area, and in six of these the occupants, mostly women and children, were killed without mercy. Captain Walter Butler, whose name was anathema because of his father's role in the Wyoming Valley Massacre, was held accountable for the atrocities, and Joseph Brant's biographers have been at pains to depict him as rushing about to check the Senecas' slaughter of the innocent. Timothy Dwight, when he visited the valley years later, was told the story of Butler's men entering a house where a women had just given birth to a child and ordering both mother and child to be killed. At that moment Brant, coming up, cried out, "What, kill a woman and child! No, that child is not an enemy to the King, nor a friend to Congress. Long before he is big enough to do any mischief, the dispute will be settled." A guard was set at the door and the child and mother saved.

At the height of the destruction, Captain McDonnell led some of his men out of the fort and rescued a number of terror-stricken settlers who had taken refuge in the woods. Besides the thirty-some settlers killed, seventy-one prisoners were taken by Brant and Butler. They spent the night in fear of their lives, but most were released the next day. Butler kept two women and seven children as hostages to exchange for his own mother and wife, who were prisoners in Albany, and also took with him some twenty slaves, who doubtless went willingly.

The wanton killing of unarmed residents and the methodical pillaging of the Cherry Valley settlements added to the bitter indignation over the Wyoming Valley Massacre and increased the pressure for a campaign that would crush the Indians and Tories once and for all. Thus began the tedious work of collecting and equipping an expeditionary force to sweep the Indian country. While it was being assembled, Brant struck again, this time at the little town of Minisink in the Mohawk Valley, which had been left defenseless when Count Pulaski was ordered south to reinforce

General Lincoln at Charles Town. Brant, with a force of sixty Indians and twenty-seven Tories disguised as Indians, attacked the little settlement on July 22, 1779, setting fire to several buildings while most of the settlers were still sound asleep. The first warning of the attack came from the howls of the Indians and Tories and the explosions of dry and burning wood. The inhabitants, mostly women and children and males too young or old to be recruited into the army, fled for the woods. The small fort, the mill, and twelve houses were fired, a few people were killed or taken prisoner, the orchards were chopped down, the farms were laid waste, and the livestock were driven off.

When word of the raid reached Goshen twelve miles away, Colonel Tustin, head of the local militia, sent word to the officers of his regiment scattered through the adjacent communities to collect as many volunteers as they could and meet him the following day at Minisink. The next morning Tustin counted 149 boys and men, "many of these . . . principal gentlemen of the vicinity." A council of war decided, over the objections of Tustin, to pursue Brant, and while the colonel was still expostulating, his second-in-command, a Major Meeker, mounted his horse, flourished his sword, and called out the kind of challenge no group of raw and inexperienced solders could resist: "Let the *brave* men follow me; the *cowards* may stay behind!" The first day the little force made seventeen miles and gained on the enemy, encumbered by their loot. The next morning, the pursuers came on the still-smoldering ashes of the Indian campfires. There were indications that the force was a large one, and Tustin again urged the men to turn back, but he was once more overruled. By nine the advance scouts came to the ridge overlooking the Delaware River near the Lackawaxen. Below they could see the Indians, genuine and bogus, moving toward a ford on the river. Colonel Hathorn, a militia officer senior to Tustin who had arrived with a detachment of militia and taken command of the combined forces, decided to ambush the Indians and cut off their line of retreat. He disposed his men beside the trail, but Brant had observed the maneuver and, slipping through a ravine, he brought his force behind the Americans, thus in effect ambushing the ambush. When the Indians failed to appear at the point where the militia expected them, they went to search them out, and a battle ensued. Hathorn's party was completely outmaneuvered and surrounded. The Indians had the advantage of high ground and kept up a constant, harassing fire during the whole day, while the ammunition of the militia dwindled away and their casualties mounted. At dusk the Indians attacked and broke the crude square that the defenders had formed. The militia fled for their lives with the Indians in close pursuit. Tustin, who was a doctor as well as a militia officer, had set up a primitive field hospital to care for the wounded. There seventeen of his patients were cut down and scalped. Some of the militia tried to escape by swimming the Delaware, and the Indians shot them in the water like ducks.

Of the group of something more than 170 men, only thirty returned to the settlements from which they had set out so boldly. The nineteenth-century historian Benson Lossing says that they were heavily outnumbered, but the only figures we have for Brant's force are sixty Indians and twenty-seven Tories for a total of eighty-seven, while the militia had almost twice as many. The Indian and Tory force, moreover, suffered only a handful of casualties.

During the battle Major Wood, a militia officer from Goshen, inadvertently made, according to Lossing, the sign of the Masonic order. Brant, who was a Mason, took special care after the American lines were broken to see that Wood's life was spared and that he was well treated as a prisoner. When the Indian leader questioned Wood and discovered that he was not a Mason, he thought that Wood had given the sign as a ruse to save his life and was furious at this betrayal of the order. He spared the terrified officer's life, however, and as soon as Wood was exchanged the major lost no time in becoming a Mason.

CHAPTER III

FRONTIER WARFARE

The most important Western theater of military operations was in the area known as the Old Northwest, an area that was to contain the future states of Ohio, Illinois, Michigan, and Indiana. It was a region of vast forests, open plains, mighty rivers, and of course, over it all, the seemingly endless expanse of the Great Lakes. It was a region interlaced with rivers that ran out from the spine of the Ohio like the ribs of a skeleton. (From east to west, on the north of the Ohio are the Allegheny, the Muskingum, the Scioto, the Little and Great Miami, the Wabash [with the White River angling off from it to the east] and the Little Wabash, and then, of course, the Mississippi. On the south side of the Ohio are the Monongahela, forming a juncture with the Allegheny, the Kanawha [pointing at western Virginia], the Big Sandy, the Licking, the Kentucky, the Green, the Cumberland, and the Tennessee.) That great country had been the preserve of the western Indians: the Ottawas and Hurons in Michigan; the Potawatomis in western Ohio and Indiana; the Mascoutens, Kickapoos, and

Illinois in what was to become Illinois; in later-day Wisconsin the Winnebagos; to the northwest, near the headwaters of the Mississippi River, the Ojibwas or Chippewas; and south and west of them the Sioux (or Dakotas), whom the Ojibwas had driven out of their homeland with the help of the French. South of the Sioux were the Sauks and the Foxes. This enormous area had first been explored by LaSalle and other great seventeenth-century French adventurers and had then become the terrain of the *courier de bois*, the tough and enterprising French fur traders who roamed far into Indian country in search of beaver pelts. The Treaty of Paris, in 1763, had given control of the region, along with Canada proper to the British, but at the outbreak of the Revolution, French settlers still lived at the old French posts of Vincennes on the Watash and Kaskaskia and Cahokia on the Mississippi. There were other scattered posts—Fort St. Joseph at the southeastern end of Lake Michigan, Fort Miami on the Maumee, and most important of all, Fort Detroit, near the northwest tip of Lake Erie.

That splendid country, filled with sparkling lakes, broad rivers, and verdant forests, was seen by most Americans as a dark and perpetual menace. In a series of "intercolonial wars" stretching back into the preceding century, the French and their Indian allies had time and again emerged from the Northwest to ravage the border settlements.

The Indians of the Northwest, now allied with the British, posed a threat to all the Western settlements as far east as Pittsburgh. George Rogers Clark's dream was to take possession of the Northwest Territory, an area almost the size of the entire continent of Europe. The first priority was the defense of the Kentucky country against Indian raids, especially against the attacks of the Shawnees and the Cherokees. Clark visited Williamsburg in 1776 to get help from Virginia and took an active part himself in organizing militia for the defense of the area. Almost from the beginning of hostilities, there had been schemes for an attack on Detroit. Daniel Morgan, Edward Hand, and Lachlan McIntosh had all tried to mount expeditions. Clark became convinced that the middle and upper Southern frontier could never be defended as long as the Indian sanctuary in the Northwest was inviolate. From Detroit, Lieutenant Colonel Henry Hamilton, the "Hair Buyer," incited the Indians by blandishments and bribery to undertake forays against the Americans, and from that post came a constant stream of supplies and gifts for the Indians.

If Detroit was the ultimate objective, it was also the remotest and best defended. Attacks on Kaskaskia and Vincennes would do much to neutralize that post and check Indian raids. While Clark pressed his campaign to win official approval and support for such an expedition, he sent two of the most experienced and hardy woodsmen of the frontier on a risky mission to assay the condition of Vincennes and Kaskaskia. Clark had originally picked four, but it was decided that two men could accomplish the task better. Simon Kenton, Si Harland, Ben Lyon, and Sam Moore drew lots. Moore and Lyon won and set out for the juncture of the Ohio and the Mississippi. Meanwhile, Clark rallied support for his plan. There was general approval in the Virginia assembly, but the state's resources were too meager to provide support for such an ambitious undertaking. There was also uneasiness at the idea of Virginia initiating a venture that was much more properly the business of Congress. Yet the primary reason for going to the Virginia authorities for backing was that Virginia claimed virtually the whole of the present-day United States west of the Alleghenies, including the Northwest. Thus leading Virginians, especially those involved in land speculation (and those who hoped to be) were by no means disinterested parties. As Jefferson saw it, having a Virginian capture the territory under the auspices, formal or informal, of his home state "would have an important bearing ultimately in establishing our western boundary," that is to say, the western boundary of the United States and the western boundary of Virginia. By late summer Lyon and Moore were back with encouraging news. The British garrison at Kaskaskia had been withdrawn to Detroit. Kaskaskia and the little, dependent, largely French towns near it—Misère, Ste. Geneviève, Fort de Chartres, Prairie du Rocher, and even Cahokia, farther up the Mississippi—were virtually defenseless. Moreover their inhabitants had no great love for the British.

Clark wrote promptly to Governor Patrick Henry, describing the situation of the country and his plans for seizing control of it. There were, he told Henry, about one hundred French and English families at Kaskaskia, most of them engaged in trade with the Indians. In addition, he said, there were a number of Negroes who constituted a kind of militia force and worked in the fields that surrounded the town. The fort, which was a short distance below the town, was built of logs and stood some ten feet high with blockhouses at each corner, defended by several cannon. The commander at Kaskaskia, Rocheblave, had encouraged the Wabash Indians to "invade the frontiers of Kentucky; was daily treating with other nations, giving large presents and offering them great rewards for scalps." After describing the advantages that accrued to the British by possessing Kaskaskia, Clark added, "If it was in our possession it would distress the garrison at Detroit for provisions, it would fling the command of the two great rivers into our hands, which would enable us to get supplies of goods from the Spaniards [who controlled the lower Mississippi] and to carry on a trade with the Indians. . . ."

Clark got the uneasy support of Governor Patrick Henry and the Virginia assembly. His ostensible orders were to defend the Kentucky country. It was not felt to be necessary to let many people know that this was to be done by capturing Kaskaskia, a hundred and fifty miles northwest of the Kentucky River, and, if possible, Detroit, several hundred miles farther on.

The extraordinary story of Clark's expedition to and capture of Kaskaskia lies beyond the scope of this narrative. What is relevant to our story is that Henry Hamilton, the British lieutenant governor of Canada, managed to enlist some of the principal tribes of his area, thereby involving them in the war, much to their subsequent misfortune.

The Indian allies of the British were called on to assemble at L'Arbre Croche, in Michigan country, to join forces with Hamilton.

When the Indians held back, fearful of Clark's reputation and reluctant to undertake an arduous campaign in Illinois, Hamilton sent Charles de Langlade, a French officer serving with the British army, to try to persuade them to go on the warpath. When Langlade's arguments were unavailing, he drew on his intimate knowledge of the customs and superstitions of the Indians. He built a lodge with a door at each end in the middle of the Indian village. He had several dogs killed for the dog feast that was very popular with the Indians. He then placed the still warm hearts of the dogs on sticks at each door to the lodge and invited the warriors to the banquet. At the end he sang a war song and went around the lodge from one door to the other, tasting, at each entrance, a piece of the dog's heart. The challenge was inescapable. If the Indians present were not to appear as cowards they must follow his example, taste the dogs' hearts, and follow him to war. They dared not dishonor an ancient custom of the tribe. They joined in the war chant and took up their arms to follow Langlade into the Illinois country.

ALTHOUGH THE MAJOR THEATER OF operations on the frontier— the so-called Western Department—was in the area north of the Ohio and south and east of Lakes Erie and Ontario, the Southern frontier was the scene of intermittent warfare during the years from 1775 to 1783. What distinguished this region was the fact that the fighting was, in large part, a continuation of border conflicts that went back to the colonial wars.

As early as the mid-1760s, settlers and land speculators had pushed westward along the Watauga and Kentucky rivers. In 1771 James Robertson came into the Watauga Valley with his family and a small band of settlers. A year later he was joined by John "Nolichucky Jack" Sevier. Strikingly handsome, tall and fair with bright blue eyes, Sevier was a member of a prosperous Huguenot family, a literate and intelligent man, charming and gracious in his manners. When enough settlers had filtered into the area so that the need was felt for some form of government, the inhabitants met

and formed the Watauga Association and elected five commissioners to govern the settlements. In August, 1776, they had addressed
the North Carolina assembly thusly:

> Finding ourselves on the frontiers, and being apprehensive that
> for want of proper legislature we might become a shelter for such
> as endeavored to defraud their creditors; considering the neces-
> sity of recording deeds, wills, and doing other public business; we,
> by consent of the people, formed a court for the purposes above
> mentioned taking, by desire of our constituents, the Virginia laws
> as our guide, so near as the situation of affairs would permit. This
> was intended for ourselves, and was done by consent of every
> individual. . . . We pray your mature and deliberate consideration
> on our behalf, and that you may annex us to your Province . . . in
> such manner as may enable us to share in the glorious cause of lib-
> erty; enforce our laws under authority and in every respect become
> the best members of society. . . .

In 1775, near the Kentucky River, James Harrod established the first permanent settlement in what was to be Kentucky,
and the same year Daniel Boone started the little community of
Boonesborough not many miles away. Logan's Station and Boiling
Spring were also founded in 1775, and Richard Henderson, a North
Carolina land speculator, tried to organize the settlements into the
state of Transylvania. Such pressure was bound to bring a reaction from the Indians of the region. As early as 1769 a Shawnee
chief, Captain Will, had warned Daniel Boone, "Now, brothers . . .
go home and stay there. Don't come here any more, for this is the
Indians' hunting ground, and all the animals, skins and furs are
ours; and if you are so foolish as to venture here again you may be
sure the wasps and yellow-jackets will sting you severely."

At the outbreak of the Revolution the Cherokees, the most
powerful tribe in the South, were still smarting from a crushing defeat during the French and Indian War. In that campaign,
Amherst had sent twelve hundred regulars along with provincial

auxiliaries to break Cherokee resistance and destroy fifteen of their settlements. Thus when the war began the Cherokees, urged on by the Shawnees, with whom they had close ties, seized the opportunity to attack the frontier settlements of Georgia and South Carolina. The British agents in this instance advised against such forays and advised wisely. After the Cherokees had raided the settlements on the Watauga and the Holston and been beaten off, a counteroffensive was mounted from Georgia, the Carolinas, and Virginia. In August, 1776, General Andrew Williamson at the head of eighteen hundred troops, guided by Catawba scouts, struck at the Indian villages and cornfields. In September he was joined by General Griffith Rutherford from North Carolina with twenty-five hundred militia. The combined force pushed on, driving the Indians toward Florida, wiping out the Middle Cherokee villages and driving them westward to the Overhills. A third column of two thousand Virginia and North Carolina militia under Colonel William Christian came down the Holston River and advanced deep into the territory of the Overhill Cherokees. The Cherokees' hope for aid from the Creeks and the British proved groundless, and from May to July, 1777, the Cherokees signed treaties ceding all their lands east of the Blue Ridge and north of the Nolichucky River.

That campaign, the largest and most ambitious mounted against the Indians during the Revolution, marked the effective end of Cherokee participation on the side of the British. James Robertson was appointed Indian agent for North Carolina. He established himself at the leading Cherokee town of Echota, and much credit goes to him for keeping the Cherokees off the warpath. A small group of irreconcilables moved to the Chickamauga Creek area, where, aided by the Creeks, they conducted raids against the frontier throughout the war. When Robertson left Echota in 1779, the Cherokees there joined the Chickamaugas and the Creeks in extensive forays. But after frontier militia defeated a Tory force at Kings Mountain, South Carolina, on October 7, 1780, John Sevier and Isaac Shelby once more laid waste to the Indian settlements.

In the summer of 1779, Spain threw in its lot with France and America against Great Britain. Spain had, if it was possible, even less interest in American independence than France, but she could not resist the notion of scooping up some loot from the beleaguered British lion, who seemed plainly on the run. The hope of recapturing Gibraltar, in which France encouraged her, was perhaps the principal incentive. In America, Spain had a strong interest in the British posts on the lower Mississippi, and Spanish troops advanced from New Orleans to seize Baton Rouge, Natchez, Mobile, and Pensacola. Patrick Sinclair, the British governor of Fort Michilimackinac (now Mackinaw City, Michigan), was determined to try to retrieve the posts and push the Spanish back to New Orleans by means of an expedition down the Mississippi. Governor Sinclair's chief reliance was on a British trader named Emmanuel Hesse. Hesse persuaded Sinclair, who was anxious to win military laurels, that a large number of Indians could be recruited for an expedition that would depart from the confluence of the Mississippi and the Wisconsin, float down the Mississippi, and seize St. Louis, thereby controlling the rich fur trade up the Missouri and establishing a base for a further thrust to Natchez and, eventually, to New Orleans itself. Sinclair's strategic imagination far outran his resources. Hesse was dispatched on his ambitious project with three hundred regular troops and nine hundred Indians, the latter consisting of Menominees, Sauks, Foxes, Winnebagos, Ottawas, and Sioux.

The Spanish commander at St. Louis was Captain Don Fernando de Leyba. Hearing that Hesse was on the move, de Leyba strengthened the fortifications of St. Louis with a wooden tower holding five cannons. He had in his command twenty-nine Spanish regulars and 281 residents of the town. Hesse's attack on St. Louis was to have been accompanied by an attack from Detroit into the Kentucky country and an expedition against New Orleans from Florida. As Hesse was approaching St. Louis, Captain Henry Bird, a brilliant British partisan leader, was on his way down the Maumee and Miami rivers with six hundred Indians and Tory irregulars, picking up another six hundred as he went. Bird's most notable accomplishment was to carry with him six artillery pieces. When he struck at the forts at Ruddle's and Martin's Station, which defended the Kentucky region between the Kentucky and Licking rivers, those forts quickly surrendered in the face of cannon fire. Captain Ruddle surrendered with Bird's assurance that the settlers crowded into his stockaded fort would not become prisoners of the Indians. It turned out that Bird was unable to keep his promise; the Indians refused to be deprived of their human booty, but Bird extracted an agreement that all future prisoners should be in the charge of the white men in the expedition. After the capitulation of Martin's Station, the Indians, delighted with their loot, were anxious to press on against Lexington, but Bird, only too well aware that a reversal of the fortunes of war might scatter his army far and wide, prevailed on them to withdraw, taking three hundred and fifty prisoners and much plunder.

George Rogers Clark, who still hoped to be able to attack Detroit, was forced to drop such plans for the moment and try to intercept Bird. Indeed, most of the credit for the collapse of the British plan must go to Clark. Bird avoided him, and Hesse, after a short skirmish with Clark's forces at Cahokia, turned back. Part of the speed with which Bird withdrew after taking Ruddle's and Martin's Station was undoubtedly due to his uneasiness about rumors of Clark's activities. His caution was well founded. As soon as Clark had learned of Bird's general plan of campaign, he had started for Fort Jefferson, and from there with two other men, for Harrodsburg. There he recruited men to counter Bird's maneuvers. In a few weeks he had collected a thousand volunteers at the mouth of the Licking. The men came not only armed but with their own rations. As we have seen, Bird evaded him, and Clark, disappointed, decided to use his newly recruited force to attack the Shawnees in their home country.

Burdened with artillery, Clark's men made only seventy miles in four days. Indian scouts kept a constant check on their movements, and when they reached the first large Shawnee settlement at Old

Chillicothe, they found it abandoned. It was clear to Clark that the Indians were drawing them deeper and deeper into their own territory, waiting simply for an appropriate moment to attack. Clark's men destroyed the buildings and crops at Chillicothe and pressed on to the Pickaway settlements, which were guarded by a fort. There the Indians attacked, and a fierce battle ensued. Gradually, the superior tactical skill and discipline of the Americans began to tell. The Indians—Shawnees, Mingoes, Wyandots, and Delawares—were repeatedly outflanked and forced to fall back until they were finally penned in a small wood and in an adjacent fort. Now Clark's artillery could be used with effect, and by dark the Indians were completely routed. The Americans had lost fourteen killed and thirteen wounded (a very high ratio of killed to wounded, incidentally), and the Indians, by Clark's estimate, three times as many.

In thirty-one days Clark and his men had marched 480 miles and destroyed eight hundred acres of corn in addition to large quantities of vegetables. The heat and lack of provisions made it impossible to carry the campaign further. For the remainder of the year the Kentucky settlements were undisturbed, and Clark once more revived his scheme to capture Detroit, the source of all the infection.

Rumors of Clark's plan to attack Detroit caused anxiety to the British, who spent much of the winter trying to prevail on the Northwest tribes to stand fast. Rumor had it that twenty-seven of the tribes were prepared to treat with Clark, but the British spared no efforts and no money to enlist the Shawnees, Wyandots, and Delawares "to prevent the inroads of the Virginians." The Indians must be "delicately managed, to prevent their favouring those rebels," an English officer wrote.

The Indians were informed that the British planned a major offensive in the spring that would capture Fort Nelson and devastate the whole frontier. Meanwhile raids were renewed against the Kentucky and Virginia settlements.

CHAPTER IV

SULLIVAN'S EXPEDITION

The Wyoming Valley and Cherry Valley massacres and Brant's attack on Minisink, less than fifty miles from West Point and Morristown, speeded the launching of an expedition under General Sullivan against the Indians of the region. The plan of the campaign called for a three-pronged invasion of the Indian stronghold. Sullivan, in command of twenty-five hundred men, would move up the Susquehanna to the southern border of New York. General James Clinton, with fifteen hundred soldiers, would drive into the Mohawk Valley to Lake Otsego, at the head of the Susquehanna, and then proceed down that river, while six hundred men under the command of Colonel Daniel Brodhead would move from Fort Pitt up the Allegheny River. Sullivan and Clinton were to join forces at Tioga (now Athens, Pennsylvania) and then move north to Niagara, joining Brodhead at Genesee, near Cuylerville.

Sullivan's mission, assigned by Washington, was "the total destruction and devastation" of the Iroquois settlements and "the capture of as many prisoners of every age and sex as possible. It will be essential to ruin their crops now in the ground and prevent their planting more."

The Indians, well informed of Sullivan's expedition, slipped away. When the Americans arrived at the Indian village, they found it abandoned. "Finding it impossible to bring them to an engagement," Sullivan wrote, "I directed their Town to be burnt, which consumed between 30 and 40 Houses some of them large and neatly finish'd; particularly a Chapel and Council House. I also caus'd their Fields of Corn which were of a considerable extent, and all their Gardens which were repleted with Herbiage to be destroy'd . . ." along with "great quantities of potatoes, pumpkins, squashes. . . ." In the desultory fighting that followed the evacuation of the Indians and Tories from Chemung, seven Americans were killed and thirteen wounded.

Sullivan's next target was an Indian settlement at Newtown. It was so large that the whole army spent the better part of a day destroying the "extensive fields of the best corn and beans." It appeared to Sullivan that Newtown was the principal supply center of the Indians. Twenty houses were burned there, and two miles east another thirty were discovered and destroyed, bringing the number of Indian villages that had been burned down by Sullivan since the beginning of the campaign to some fourteen, "some of them considerable, others inconsiderable."

After Sullivan's success at Newtown, he made an effort to form an alliance with the Oneidas. His message hinted at some doubts as to their loyalty to the Americans. These doubts could only be removed if the warriors of the Oneidas were to join his expedition, especially such as "have a perfect knowledge of the country through which I am to pass." If he received such proof of their "attachment to the American cause . . . the army which I have the honor to command will be able totally to extirpate our common enemy [the Iroquois], and leave you in a perfect state of tranquility, enable you to enjoy your possessions and carry on with the Americans a commerce which will tend to the mutual advantage of both." The Oneidas, thus threatened, offered cautious assistance.

Everywhere, as Sullivan advanced, he found abandoned villages and no sign of Indians. At Catherinestown, the Americans found two old women of the Cayuga tribe, one of whom had been shot by an advance party of Americans. Sullivan ordered that a keg of pork and some biscuits be left "for the old creature to subsist on, although," as an officer noted resentfully, "it [the pork] was so scarce an article that no officer under the rank of a field officer had tasted any since leaving Tioga. . . ." The squaw was glad to tell whatever she knew. The morning after the fight at Newtown the warriors had arrived there. She heard them "tell their women they were conquered & must fly, that they had a great many killed & vast numbers wounded. . . . They kept runners on every mountain to observe the march of our army. . . ." At word of the approach of the American force, "all those who had not been before sent off, fled with precipitation leaving her without any possible means of escape." Brant had taken the wounded up the Tioga in canoes. Estimates of the number of the Indians and Tories varied from eight hundred to fifteen hundred, the latter being Sullivan's own estimate and undoubtedly somewhat too generous.

At another abandoned Indian town, Kendaia, Sullivan found one of the survivors of the Wyoming Valley Massacre, who had escaped from his captors and who gave a graphic account of the demoralization of the Indians. Here, again, the army spent almost a day destroying cornfields and ancient fruit trees, "of which there was a great abundance." Pushing on to Canadasaga on Seneca Lake, they found a white child about three years old and carried it along with the army. Canadasaga consisted of fifty houses and a great number of fruit trees that were, once again, destroyed with the town. Another town, Canandaigua, was unusual among the Indian villages in that it contained twenty-three "very elegant houses, mostly framed" after the white man's style. The fields of corn and groves of fruit trees were so extensive that two days were required to complete the work of destruction.

Genesee, "the grand capital" of the Indian country, was the final objective. Because it was the most remote of the villages, it had been chosen as the central Indian granary. The Indians of all nations had spent the spring there planting the crops that would nourish them through the winter and enable them to carry out raids against the white border settlements. Even the Tory rangers and some British troops, the story went, had been active in helping to plant corn and squash.

Sullivan's force reached the vicinity of Genesee on the 14th of September. It had been a strange march; everywhere the Indians hovered about, but they were unwilling to attempt another organized stand against Sullivan's force, which was certainly larger than any collection of warriors and Tories that could be rallied to oppose it. They thus had to watch as their villages and fields were obliterated and the food that they depended on to carry them through a long, bitter winter was systematically destroyed. The Indians received, of course, no substantial help from their British friends.

But the Indians and Tories had one dramatic success. Lieutenant Thomas Boyd, with a scouting party of twenty-six men, including several Indians, surprised some enemy Indians near Genesee and killed two. But while Boyd's men argued over who should have the right to scalp the Indians they had just killed, Walter Butler and several hundred Indians and Tories rose out of an ambush. They killed or captured twenty-two of the party. Boyd, who had been wounded in the fighting, was questioned by Butler and then turned over to the Indians, who tortured him to death. Along with Boyd was an Oneida Indian, Han Yerry, a famous marksman, who was "literally hewn to pieces" by his captors.

When Sullivan's men found Boyd's body, it was apparent that he had been mercilessly whipped, and that his fingernails had been pulled out, his nose and tongue cut off, one of his eyes put out, and his body pierced with spears in various places. His genitals had been cut off, and there had been other tortures, Sullivan wrote, "which decency will not permit me to mention." As the *coup de grâce*, he had been skinned alive and his head had been cut off.

Genesee was an impressive town of 128 houses, "most very large and elegant." The village, in Sullivan's words, "was beautifully situated almost encircled with a clear flat, which extends for a number of miles, where the most extensive fields of corn were and every kind of vegetable that can be conceived." Once again the work of destruction went on: "apples, peaches, cucumbers, watermelons, fowls, etc." A white woman appeared who had been hiding outside the village. She also had been captured at Wyoming, and she had interesting information for Sullivan. There was, understandably, much bitterness between the Indians and their Tory leaders. Some Indians, she reported, had attempted to shoot Colonel Guy Johnson "for the falsehoods by which he had deceived and ruined them." She had overheard Butler telling Johnson that it was impossible to keep the Indians together after the Newtown battle; their crops were being destroyed and they could not count on Canada to supply them with food. For his own part, Butler declared that he would not even try to get the warriors together to assist in the defense of Niagara, which, in his opinion, would be the final objective of Sullivan's march.

But Sullivan had less ambitious notions. Complaining regularly of a shortage of food (though never explaining why his soldiers were not dining like lords on the pillage of the Indian villages), Sullivan declared that his supplies were too meager to press on to Niagara. Instead he turned northeast along the southern shore of Lake Ontario to wreck havoc in the Cayuga country. The Oneidas, apparently at the behest of the Cayugas, who had often been their enemies, tried to persuade Sullivan to spare the Cayuga villages, but Sullivan insisted it was too late. There were too many black marks against the Cayugas. Sullivan detached Lieutenant Colonel Peter Gansevoort, Lieutenant Colonel William Butler, and Colonel Henry Dearborn to systematically destroy the Cayuga towns. Dearborn burned six and took an Indian boy and three women prisoners, "one of the women being very ancient & the Lad a cripple"—hardly a very impressive haul. The officer in command ordered that one house be left to provide shelter for them, but after the troops had begun to move out, "some of the soldiers taking an opportunity when not observed set the house on fire, after securing and making the door fast . . . and . . . the house was consumed together with the savages. . . ."

Colonel Philip Van Cortlandt on a similar mission "destroyed several fields of corn, & burnt several houses." Lieutenant Colonel William Butler destroyed five principal towns "and a number of scattering houses, the whole making about one hundred in number, exceedingly large & well built," along with "two hundred acres of excellent corn, with a number of orchards, one of which, had in it 1500 fruit trees." Sullivan estimated that forty towns had been destroyed and a hundred and sixty thousand bushels of corn, "with a vast quantity of vegetables of every kind. . . . I am well persuaded," Sullivan wrote to Congress after his return to Tioga, "that except for one Town . . . there is not a single Town left in the Country of the five nations."

This had all been accomplished, Sullivan pointed out, with the loss of only forty men. He had moved his army without adequate maps or experienced guides over a country "abounding in woods, creeks, rivers, mountains, morasses & defiles," hacking out roads as they went. Yet they had managed to average ten to fifteen miles a day, "when not detained by rains, or employed in destroying settlements."

Sullivan's campaign was the most ruthless application of a scorched-earth policy in American history. It bears comparison with Sherman's march to the sea or the search-and-destroy missions of American soldiers in the Vietnam War. The Iroquois Confederacy was the most advanced Indian federation in the New World. It had made a territory that embraced the central quarter of New York State into an area of flourishing farms with well-cultivated fields and orchards and sturdy houses. Indeed, I believe it could be argued that the Iroquois had carried cooperative agriculture far beyond anything the white settlers had achieved. In a little more than a month all of this had been wiped out, the work of several generations of loving attention to the soil, which promised a new kind of Indian society, one not dependent on nomadic wandering or exclusively on hunting, but one that, while preserving the rich Indian culture virtually intact, also created a stable and orderly society able to hold its own against white encroachments. The Iroquois never recovered from that blow.

It must be pointed out, however, that ruthless as the action of the Americans was, it had been provoked by numerous incidents of Indian savagery, most dramatically, of course, the episodes in the Wyoming Valley and Cherry Valley. The Americans conceived themselves to be fighting for their lives as well as their liberties. They had taken, out of self-interest to be sure, substantial steps to try to keep the border Indians neutral, and they had, for the most part also out of self-interest, avoided trying to make allies of those tribes who were the traditional enemies of the nations that made up the Iroquois Confederacy. Despite the skill and enterprise with which the Iroquois embraced agricultural life, they retained their warlike tradition. Indeed, without it their whole culture would have collapsed. So they were more than a constant threat to the Americans; they resisted the efforts of the more responsible British officials like Sir Guy Carleton to keep them neutral and listened instead to the blandishments of Tory leaders like the Butlers, who were both ruthless and shortsighted.

The fallaciousness of the British policy was well expressed by Edward Abbott, lieutenant governor of Canada and in command at Detroit, who wrote to Sir Guy Carleton in June, 1778:

> Your Excellency will plainly perceive the employing Indians
> on the Rebel frontiers has been of great hurt to the cause, for
> many hundreds would have put themselves under His Majesty's
> protection was there a possibility; that not being the case, these
> poor unhappy people are forced to take up arms against their
> Sovereign or be pillages & left to starve; cruel alternative. This is
> too shocking a subject to dwell upon; Your Excellency's known
> humanity will certainly put a stop if possible to such proceed-
> ings as it is not people in arms that Indians will ever daringly
> attack, but the poor inoffensive families who fly to the deserts
> to be out of trouble, & who are inhumanly butchered sparing
> neither women or children.

When the major raids at Wyoming and Cherry valleys—which were largely punitive and had no real military purpose and which, without Tory initiative, would hardly have been attempted—provoked retaliation, neither the Tories nor the British regular army could, or took the trouble to, do anything to protect the Indian country from the devastation that Sullivan's army visited upon it. Haldimand, commander in chief in Canada, had ample warning of the projected campaign and chose to ignore that warning, in part at least because it came from the Indians (and was thus presumptively unreliable); beyond that, one cannot help feeling that he did not really care about the fate of the Indians. They were a convenience and were to be used when it was clearly expedient to do so, but they were not, after all, Englishmen. So, having been ruthlessly exploited, they were abandoned to their fate. British strategic plans did not include defending the country of their Indian allies.

As for the Sullivan campaign itself, one is astonished at the facility of it; a territory almost as large as the state of New Hampshire and occupied by people famous for their warlike qualities was ravaged in a few weeks by a motley army, operating in unfamiliar terrain and led by a general not notable for skill or resolution. The truth is that Sullivan's expedition revealed most dramatically the basic weakness in the Indians' tribal organization, at least as it related to sustained warfare. The Indians, warlike as they were, were not prepared for protracted campaigning. Their "wars" were wars of stealthy raids and individual acts of heroism that expressed their warrior skills and validated them as brave men. They did not intend to inflict heavy casualties; or at least they were unwilling to sustain heavy casualties themselves. As warfare was an almost constant state with them, fighting that resulted in many warriors being killed or disabled would destroy a tribe in which virtually every male member was a warrior. The Indians certainly displayed great personal bravery—that was at the heart of their "ethic"; but they did not have the will to persist in the face of unfavorable odds or to sustain heavy casualties. They fought for glory and spoils, not for "victory" in the white man's terms. At the same time, they were volatile and naive and were, in consequence, constantly manipulated by white men who played skillfully upon their baser emotions of greed, hate, and fear. Beyond this, Indians with few exceptions were capable of just one form of military action—attack. In an attack, especially at night or at daybreak, their terrifying appearance, their speed and agility, their paralyzing howls, their strength and the ferocity with which they fought in close combat, their skill with tomahawk and knife made them highly effective auxiliaries. But as we have seen on numerous occasions, the difficulty of restraining or controlling them once they were aroused made them difficult allies in any conventional military operation.

In defensive situations they were virtually useless. There were few if any engagements where substantial bodies of Indians stood fast in the face of sustained attacks by superior forces. The only instances were when they were surrounded and were faced with death or surrender. Then, almost invariably, they chose death. Again, it was not a matter of courage but of the fact that their temperament, their mode of warfare, and even their "consciousness" made them incapable of the particular kind of discipline, or effort of will, required to defend a position against enemy attack. Part of the problem was that the Indians, not having or being used to artillery, could not withstand its fire. Thus one cannon would be enough to put a large force of Indians to flight. It is only by taking into account these aspects of Indian culture that we can understand why it was that the Iroquois nations stood by and saw their "country" destroyed without being able to muster any effective opposition to the invader. Any resolutely led force of whites, fighting in its own territory, could almost certainly have delayed Sullivan's cumbersome army for months until it was finally immobilized by winter. While it is true that the Indians were heavily outnumbered, they could certainly have put up more of a defense than they did. Their casualties at Newtown, despite Sullivan's optimistic calculations, were apparently not very heavy. Had any substantial number of them decided to die in defense of their "homeland," the outcome of Sullivan's campaign might have been very different.

Describing the expedition, Major Jeremiah Fogg wrote: "Not a single gun was fired for eighty miles on our march out or an Indian seen on our return. Then we expected the greatest harassment—a hundred might have saved half their country by retarding us until our provisions were spent; and a like number hanging on our rear in the return would have occasioned the loss of much baggage and taught us an Indian dance."

Weather had also favored the expedition to a remarkable degree, Fogg noted. He ended his account of the expedition on what proved a prophetic note: "The question will naturally arise, What have you to show for your exploits? Where are your prisoners? To which I reply that the rags and emaciated bodies of our soldiers must speak for our fatigue, and when the querist will point out a mode to tame a partridge, or the expediency of hunting wild turkeys with light horses, I will show them our prisoners. The nests are destroyed, but the birds are still on the wing."

Sullivan concluded his report to Congress on the expedition with the following observation: "It would have been very pleasing to this army to have drawn the enemy to a second engagement, but such panic seized them after the first action that it was impossible as they never ventured themselves in reach of the Army, nor have they fired a single gun at it, on its march or in quarters, tho, in a Country exceeding well calculated for ambushcades."

On the third of October, Washington wrote to Sullivan ordering him to march "with all possible dispatch" to join him for, hopefully, a joint operation against New York with the fleet of the Count D'Estaing. The campaign against the Indian country was over. The Iroquois, their homes and fields laid waste, had to depend on the British at Niagara for sufficient food to keep them from starving. They huddled miserably through the winter in makeshift camps, thirsting for revenge.

In retrospect, Washington must bear a part of the blame for the inept Indian policy. Sullivan's, Clinton's, and Brodhead's campaigns kept almost five thousand men, a number as large as the entire army of the Southern Department and more than half the size of the Continental Army under Washington, tied up from April to early October, 1779, a period of almost six months. The only tangible result of the scorched-earth policy that Washington ordered Sullivan to undertake was the destruction of the Iroquois society, but without doing serious damage to the warlike potential of those embittered Indians. The expedition also ensured, of course, a winter on the frontier free from Indian attacks.

Two other lines of action certainly would have produced better results. A mobile force of some five hundred experienced Indian fighters (one-tenth of the force mobilized for Sullivan's campaign), led by an officer who knew his business and headquartered at Tioga, could have made periodic raids into the edges of the Indian country—on such towns as Chemung and Newtown—and done a great deal to neutralize the Indians and Tories of the area.

Once the decision had been made to raise a force the size of Sullivan's, a far better strategy than the one employed would have been to penetrate deep into Indian territory to Genesee, destroy it, move on to invest Niagara, and then, having impressed the Indians with American strength and the impotence of their British allies, try to bring the Iroquois to a peace meeting. Sullivan's campaign was simply a vengeful, punishing reaction to the raids on the Wyoming and Cherry valleys; and as we have argued elsewhere, punitive actions are always self-defeating. The Iroquois were left with a sense of grievance that could not be assuaged, with wounds that would, quite literally, never heal. The poisonous combination (poisonous to frontier and to Indian alike) of Tory and Indian remained intact; indeed, by forcing the Indians to depend on the British for their survival, the Indian–Tory–British alliance was sealed beyond undoing. All that Sullivan's expedition accomplished was to let loose a storm of Indian vengeance on the frontier come spring. Acting under Washington's instructions, Sullivan had sown the wind and left the settlers to reap the whirlwind.

* * *

THE HEADQUARTERS OF THE WESTERN Department were at Pittsburgh, and the command there was in the hands of a Scottish-born officer, General Lachlan McIntosh, from Charles Town, South Carolina. McIntosh, who was contentious and quarrelsome and not notably efficient, had a dreary tale to tell Washington of Indian raids against the frontier settlements of western Pennsylvania that his fort was supposed to protect. Simon Girty, an American soldier turned renegade, had led a small party of Mingoes or Senecas in an ambush of Captain Clark and fifteen men of the Eighth Pennsylvania Regiment who were returning from Fort Laurens. Clark was driven back to the fort in the fighting that ensued, and two of his men were killed and one captured. A few weeks later a scalping party killed or carried off eighteen men, women, and children from Turtle Creek, a little settlement only twenty miles from Pittsburgh. Word came also from Fort Laurens that a wagoner who had been sent out of the fort to haul wood with an escort of eighteen men was attacked by Indians who killed and scalped the entire party within sight of the fort and then laid siege to the post.

Much the same disheartening story was repeated throughout the spring and summer, while Colonel Daniel Brodhead, who relieved McIntosh, struggled to recruit and equip a force large enough to carry the war to the enemy. Brodhead, who had joined Sullivan in his raids against the Iroquois settlements, was an experienced officer of the Pennsylvania Line and a veteran of the Battle of Long Island. He was a martinet, impervious and overbearing, but he had the drive and energy that were lacking in McIntosh, and he launched his little force of five or six hundred men in an expedition into Indian country.

Marching in single file along the banks of the Allegheny, Lieutenant Harding, commanding an advance party of fifteen whites dressed and painted to look like Indians, and eight Delawares, came on twice as many hostile Indians landing from their canoes in a clearing ahead of them. Harding quickly formed his men into a crude semicircle, and with tomahawks in their hands they dashed to the attack "with such irresistible fury . . . that the savages could not long sustain the charge, but fled with the utmost horror and precipitation, some plunging themselves into the river, and others, favored by the thickness of the bushes, made their escape on the main, leaving five dead. . . ." Three of the attackers were slightly wounded; the dead Indians were promptly scalped.

That was the only engagement of the campaign, although in the course of thirty-three days, Brodhead's force marched almost four hundred miles. In the words of one soldier, the men advanced

> through a country almost impassable by reason of stupendous heights and frightful declivities with a continued range of craggy hills, overspread with fallen timbers, thorns and underwood . . . Brodhead's little army "burnt ten of the Mingo, Munsey and Senecca towns . . . containing one hundred and sixty-five houses, and destroyed fields of corn, computed to be five hundred acres."

Back at Pittsburgh, the Wyandot chief, Doonyontat, came to treat with Brodhead. The Indian declared,

> *Brother,* it grieves me to see you with tears in your eyes. I know it is the fault of the British. *Brother,* I wipe away all those tears, and smooth down your hair, which the English and the folly of my young men has ruffled. . . . *Brother,* I see your heart twisted, and neck and throat turned to one side, with the grief and vexation which my young men have caused, all which disagreeable sensations I now remove, and restore you to your former tranquility, so that now you may breathe with ease, and enjoy the benefit of your food and nourishment, . . . *Brother,* I gather up the bones of all our young men on both sides, in this dispute, without any distinction of party. *Brother,* I now look up to where our Maker is, and think there is still some darkness over our heads, so that God can hardly see us, on account of the evil doings of the King over the great waters. All these thick clouds, which have been raised on account of that bad

King, I now entirely remove, that God may look and see in our treaty of friendship, and be a witness to the truth and sincerity of our intentions.

The speech, a long ritual interspersed with the solemn presentation of wampum, was answered by Brodhead the next day. "*Brother*, the Chiefs of the Wyandot have lived too long with the English to see things as they ought to do. They must have expected when they were counciling that the Chief they sent to this council fire would find the Americans asleep. But the sun which the Great Spirit has set to light this island discovers to me that they are much mistaken." The Americans were not to be taken in by easy promises and smooth words. What Brodhead wished as pledges of good faith were hostages from Hurons. He continued,

> As I said before, unless they have killed and taken as many
> from the English and their allies as they have killed and taken
> from the Americans, and return whatever they have stolen from
> their brothers, together with their flesh and blood, and on every
> occasion join us against their enemies—upon these terms. . . .
> They and their posterity may live in peace and enjoy their prop-
> erty without disturbance from their brethren of this island, so
> long as the sun shines or the waters run. *Brothers*, I have spoken
> from my heart. I am a warrior as well as a councillor; my words
> are few, but what I say I will perform. And I must tell you that
> if the Nations will not do justice, they will not be able, after the
> English are driven from this island, to enjoy peace or prosperity.

They were hard words, but they were spoken in desperate times.

The Americans, who, in the words of Governor Clinton of New York, waited for "the overtures of peace which we had some reason to expect from them [the Indians]," heard instead disturbing rumors that the Indians were planning new attacks on the border settlements. The Oneidas, whose cooperation Sullivan had enlisted, felt the full force of the initial onslaught. Supported by

British regulars and Tories, the Mohawks, Senecas, and Cayugas destroyed the Oneida settlements and drove them down the Mohawk Valley. Most of them gathered near Schenectady, where they were no longer able to function as a kind of early warning line for raids on the frontier.

In March the militiamen garrisoning the fort at Skenesborough, near Lake George, were captured. Harpersfield, a little town twenty miles south of Cherry Valley, was hit by Brant a few weeks later. Most of the inhabitants had decamped, but several of those who remained were killed, and Captain Alexander Harper, after whom the village had been named, was captured along with eighteen men and women. Hearing Brant speaking about his intention of attacking Lower Fort, Harper gave him the false information that three hundred Continental soldiers were there. That stratagem must have been cold comfort to the battered survivors at Minisink, for Brant and his men returned to that village and plundered whatever was left after their earlier raid the previous spring.

It was soon evident that hostile Indians were ranging the whole length of the country from Canajoharie to the northern end of the Wyoming Valley. A blockhouse at Sacandaga was attacked by seven Indian warriors, who were all killed by the defenders of the fort. At the end of April a party of seventy-nine Indians attacked Cherry Valley again and killed and scalped several whites, but this time the settlers and the soldiers in the fort gave a good account of themselves and fought off the marauders.

In this first phase, aside from Brant's raid on Harpersfield, the attacks were largely carried out by "small unorganized parties of starving men." Much worse was to come. By May, Sir John Johnson was ready to strike at the network of small forts and blockhouses that offered at least some protection to the settlers in the Mohawk Valley. Coming down the Lake Champlain route to Crown Point with a force of four hundred Tories and two hundred Indians, Johnson reached the Johnstown settlements at the north end of the valley on May 21. From there he marched to the Sacandaga River and sent Brant to burn Caughnawaga. Two days later he burned

Johnstown and rounded up forty prisoners, as well as collecting a number of the families of his Tory officers and soldiers who had been held more or less as hostages by the patriots. On the first and second of August, Brant with five hundred Tories and Indians pillaged Canajoharie, burned most of its buildings, killed a number of the inhabitants, and captured others.

Then Brant started down the Ohio, where he captured part of an advance party bringing word to George Rogers Clark that Colonel Archibald Lochry was on his way down the Ohio with a picked company of a hundred Pennsylvania volunteers to join Clark in an attack on Kaskaskia. Brant got his force across Lochry's path, and when the Pennsylvanian landed with his men below the Great Miami River, Brant sprang his ambush and virtually annihilated Lochry's detachment. Five officers and thirty-six privates were killed and forty-eight privates and twelve officers captured. Lochry, who was captured, was tortured to death along with several other prisoners, but more than half of those captured eventually made their way back to Pennsylvania. The battle, if it could be called that, was a brilliantly executed maneuver by Brant and the worst defeat suffered by Americans in the border warfare.

From the forks of the Ohio, Brant and his party, loaded with scalps, booty, and prisoners, turned back north and by forced marches joined Johnson for another expedition into Tryon County, New York, the area of the Mohawk Valley that had already seen so much bitter fighting. Haldimand explained the purpose of the campaign to Germain in a letter written on September 17, 1780. He wished, he wrote, "to divide the strength that may be brought against Sir H. Clinton, or to favor any operations his present situation may induce him to carry on and to give His Majesty's loyal subjects an opportunity of retiring from the Province. . . ." For this purpose he had fitted out "two parties of about 600 men each, besides Indians, to penetrate into the enemy's territory by the Mohawk River and Lake George." One of the minor objectives of the campaign was Johnson Hall, the home of the famous superintendent of the Indians, Sir William Johnson, father of Sir John. At Johnson Hall, north of the conjunction of the Mohawk and Schoharie rivers, Sir John Johnson found the family silver and papers where they had been hidden when he had earlier escaped his patriot pursuers.

In September, 1780, Johnson left Oswego and advanced to Unadilla, where he met Brant, back from his brilliant victory over Lochry, and Cornplanter, son of a white trader and a Seneca woman, and now one of the most famous fighting chieftains. With Brant's and Cornplanter's men, Johnson commanded a force of over a thousand Tories and Indians. He also had with him a brass three-pounder, called a "grasshopper." He slipped undetected into the Schoharie Valley, devastated that area on the fifteenth of October, then destroyed all the rebel property near Fort Hunter and marched up the Mohawk, leaving a trail of burning buildings and ruined fields on both sides of the river as far north as Canajoharie. A lieutenant colonel of militia reported to General Robert Van Rensselaer that "the enemy have burnt the whole of Schohary . . . they have fired two swivel shoots thro' the roof of the church."

By the time Van Rensselaer started in pursuit with a much smaller force, Johnson had already crossed the Mohawk River. "Harassed and fatigued as my force is by a long march," Van Rensselaer wrote, "I am apprehensive I shall not be able to pursue them with that dispatch which is necessary to overtake them. No exertion, however, shall be wanting on my part to effect it. . . ."

Behind the simple recital of villages and farms burnt lies a story of terror, suffering, and death impossible to recount. "The panic that has seized the people is incredible," General Schuyler wrote to Governor Clinton, "with all my efforts I cannot prevent numbers from deserting their habitations, and I am very apprehensive that the whole will move, unless the militia will remain above until a permanent relief can be procured."

Meanwhile Schuyler did his best to help Van Rensselaer collect a force to do battle with Johnson's invading army. Some four or five hundred militia were assembled on the lower end of the Mohawk Valley, while Clinton left his headquarters in Albany with a small, hastily gathered force to join in pursuit of Johnson. From Fort Paris, near Stone Arabia, Colonel John Brown, assured by Van Rensselaer that the latter would arrive in time to support him, came out to attack Johnson's vastly superior force with 130 men. It was a sentence of death for many of Brown's militia. He overtook Johnson at the abandoned Fort Keyser, and in savage fighting that lasted the better part of the day, his little force was badly mauled; forty of his men were killed and the rest scattered far and wide. Johnson then looted and burned the village of Stone Arabia.

A battle like that of Fort Keyser has a very modest place in the history of the Revolution, but such casualties were devastating in a sparsely settled region where every soldier was the father or son of a family living in the area. The militiamen in Brown's company, who fought so bravely against heavy odds, fought quite literally for their lives, families, and property, and the forty dead men made up perhaps a fourth or fifth of the ablebodied men of the immediate vicinity. Like the partisan contests in the South, such fighting showed the grimmest face of war.

Van Rensselaer arrived too late to save Brown's men, but, reinforced by four hundred militia and sixty Oneidas under Colonel Lewis DuBois, he pressed so hard on Johnson's heels that the Tory leader was forced at sunset on the nineteenth to turn and fight at Fox Mills. Van Rensselaer's men needed no exhortation to attack. The fighting was intense before Johnson's force gave way and fled under cover of darkness, "leaving behind them," as Clinton reported to Washington, "their baggage, provisions and a three-pounder with its ammunition."

The Americans, who had marched thirty miles the day before without halting, were too exhausted to continue the pursuit, and Clinton's men, who arrived the following morning, were, in his words, "so beat out with fatigue, having marched at least 50 miles in less than 24 hours, as to be unable to proceed any further." The statistics that Clinton cited to Washington had an ironic echo: Johnson's raiders had "destroyed, on a moderate computation, 200 dwellings and 150,000 bushels of wheat, with a proportion of other grain and forage." Sullivan, in his monthlong raid through Indian country the year before, had claimed 160,000 bushels of corn and forty villages destroyed. Johnson had accomplished almost as much damage in a raid that lasted five days. His raid was the whirlwind that Sullivan had sown. There were two conspicuous differences. Johnson had been opposed at Fort Keyser and caught at Fox Mills. He could not have continued his raid another week without having been overwhelmed by patriot militia, collected from a hundred miles around. While he spread fear among the inhabitants of the region and inflicted heavy damage, as soon as he was gone families, recovering their nerve, began to filter back to their ruined farms and villages. By the following spring, a traveler in the area reported that "there is a prospect of as plentiful crops as has been in the memory of man."

In addition to Johnson's raid, a detachment of the British Fifty-third Regiment hit the upper Connecticut Valley and burned some houses at Royalton, while another small force marched down the line of the Hudson and attacked Ball's Town, twelve miles north of Schenectady.

In the early months of the new year, 1781, Brant, who had been wounded at Klock's Field and put out of action for four or five months, traversed the upper Mohawk Valley with impunity. So many families had fled from the valley that there was no militia to oppose him. Cherry Valley was attacked in April, and two detachments of the Second New York Continentals were captured trying to get supplies to the hungry garrison at Fort Stanwix, which lived in a state of virtual siege.

In May, Fort Stanwix, badly damaged by fire and floodwaters and almost impossible to supply, was abandoned. The decision seemed a symbol of the low estate of the American cause. Since 1776, Fort Stanwix had guarded the principal line of access from Oswego on Lake Ontario to the upper Hudson, Tryon County, the heart of New England, and the headwaters of the Mohawk River. The friendly Oneidas in whose territory the fort was located had, as we have seen, been driven into the vicinity of Schenectady.

But American fortunes, as it turned out, soon took a turn for the better. Colonel Marinus Willett was sent to take command of the defense of the region. Willett was a forty-year-old graduate of King's College in New York, a successful merchant who had served as a lieutenant in the French and Indian War; he had been with Washington on Braddock's campaign. One of the leaders of the Sons of Liberty, he had taken part in the raid on the British arsenal at New York in 1775 and had been made a captain in Alexander McDougall's First New York Regiment. He had distinguished himself at the Battle of Monmouth. Three times married and the father of at least one illegitimate child, Willett was a military leader in the classic mold. When he took charge of the defense of western New York and the Mohawk Valley, he assumed responsibility for some five thousand square miles of territory inhabited by roughly two thousand hardy settlers who had resisted all efforts to drive them from their land. He established his principal posts at Ball's Town, Catskill, and Fort Herkimer in German Flats; some hundred and twenty or thirty Continentals were scattered about these three posts. The main force was made up of a hundred and twenty men at Canajoharie, where Willett made his own headquarters. Because Willett had been with Sullivan in the campaign through the Indian country two years before, he knew the land and the nature of his adversaries well. Willett estimated that the country had suffered so heavily from repeated raids by Indians and Tories that its original muster of militia had shrunk from twenty five hundred at the beginning of the Revolution to a total of less than half as many "classible inhabitants" (males above sixteen years of age). Of these, not more than two-thirds (or some eight hundred) were eligible for the militia rolls. Thus, by Willett's calculations, the number of militia had diminished, during the course of the war, by two-thirds. Of the number lost, it was Willett's estimate that "one third of them have been killed, or carried captive by the enemy; one third have removed to the interior parts of the country; and one third deserted to the enemy."

Those inhabitants who remained relied mainly on crude forts, each giving shelter of a kind to between ten and fifty families. There were twenty-four such forts in the country that Willett was charged with defending. From them the farmers sallied forth every day to till their fields, with their muskets loaded and close at hand, and to them they returned in the evening. Hardly a week passed that marauding Indians did not surprise a farmer in his fields and kill and scalp him.

Willett's first move was to rotate his soldiers among the four main posts. This would enable him to get to know them all, it would keep them fit and alert, and the appearance of activity would improve morale among the settlers themselves. Willett was well aware of the fact that nothing deteriorates so fast as a soldier in garrison. "Having troops constantly marching backwards and for- wards through the country," he wrote Washington on July 6, "and frequently changing their route, will answer several purposes such as will easily be perceived by you, sir, without my mentioning them." In addition, Willett intended to personally visit every part of the region to make himself familiar with the state of the garrisons and to "observe the condition of the militia, upon whose aid I shall be under the necessity of placing considerable reliance." Willett's strat- egy was not to try to defend every post, but "in case the enemy should again appear this way with anything of force, to collect all the strength we can get to a point, and endeavour to beat them in the field." This meant an effective warning system and a high degree of readiness and mobility in the soldiers, regular and militia, under his command.

Shortly after his arrival at Canajoharie, Willett received a report that smoke was visible to the southeast in the direction of Corey's Town. Thirty-five Continentals had already set off on a patrol. Willett sent after them to turn them toward Corey's Town. Sixteen regulars with as many militia as they could round up were sent to the town, eleven miles away, and made such good time that they were able to extinguish some of the fires. Willett meantime rounded up a hundred more militia who, with the regu- lars, brought his little force to a hundred and seventy. A scout had brought him word of where the enemy encampment was located, and Willett, assuming that they would return there, headed for the spot under cover of darkness, covering eighteen miles over rough and unmapped country and arriving at six o'clock in the morning. In the daylight the element of surprise was lost, but Willett pushed ahead. The leader of the raiders, perhaps aware that his men were far more effective in offensive actions than in defensive ones, ordered an attack on Willett's force, and the Indians and Tories advanced, yelling and shouting and firing their muskets. "This," Willett wrote, "was the fury of the Indians and nothing more; for upon the huzzas and advance of the front line, they soon gave way." At the same time the Americans were attacked on their right, but they counterattacked so vigorously that the Indians broke and fled.

The battle had lasted for an hour and a half. Willett's force had lost five killed and nine wounded. Out of a force of some hundred, by Willett's calculations, the enemy had lost not less than forty, among them the notorious Tory raider, Donald McDonald. It was a severe setback for the Indians and Tories. They were not able to sustain such heavy losses, and for most of the summer the country round about was free of further incursions. Equally important, the one-sided victory gave a tremendous boost to patriot morale. Willett was voted the freedom of Albany by the grateful council of that city, and every settler slept a little better for it. It was a striking demonstration of what inspired leadership can accomplish.

The fall brought a resurgence of enemy activity, however. Later in October, Willett got word that a considerable force of the enemy had appeared at Warrens Bush, some twenty miles from Canajoharie. Willett moved at once, taking all the men he dared from Fort Rensselaer and sending orders to all the regulars and militia "in the contiguous posts and settlements, to follow." He marched all night, arriving in the morning at Fort Hunter, where he learned that the enemy had crossed the river and moved on Johnstown. An exhausted British soldier, who had fallen by the roadside, told Willett that the raiding expedition consisted of some eight hundred seasoned Tories and British regulars with a hundred and twenty Indians under the command of Walter Butler. At Fort Hunter, the other contingents that Willett had ordered to that rendezvous came in, giving him a force of slightly more than four hundred men, the majority of them militia, with which to oppose a force more than twice as large. Willett got his men across the river in bateaux by afternoon and began the march to Johnstown. Two miles outside the town Willett got word that the enemy were busy slaughtering cattle. He decided to attack at once and split his force into two divisions, one to attack in front on the line of march; the other to slip around and take the enemy in the rear. Willett, in command of the right wing of the attacking echelon, moved into a field adjacent to the one where Butler's force was camped and pressed the enemy so hard that they fell back into the cover provided by nearby woods. He then ordered his men to form a skirmish line, advance, and fire, but one of those unreasoning moments of panic that we are by now so familiar with seized the soldiers, and they turned and fled despite all their furious commander could do to rally them. At this juncture, with defeat apparently certain, Major Rowley, a Massachusetts officer in command of the encircling movement, attacked with his division, composed almost entirely of militia except for some sixty regulars. This force pressed the action so resolutely that the British were finally broken and driven from the field, leaving most of their packs and baggage behind them. It was dark by this time, and the Americans by the light of torches collected the wounded of both sides and the abandoned packs. They rounded up a bag of some fifty prisoners, who, in addition to those killed, brought the enemy toll to nearly a hundred. Willett lost some forty men killed or badly wounded.

Unable to determine the enemy intentions, Willett withdrew his troops to German Flats, thereby placing them between Butler's force and their boats that they had left at Oneida Creek. Here sixty Oneida warriors joined him, together with some more militia, bringing his small army to almost five hundred men. Two days later, when it was clear that Butler had given up hope of regaining his boats and had probably started overland for Oswego, Willett, with a picked body of four hundred men equipped with five days' rations, started after Butler. After two days of forced marches, the second through a heavy snowstorm, they discovered that they were on the heels of the enemy. Willett overtook a foraging detachment of forty soldiers and a few Indians. Some were killed or wounded, some captured, and the rest scattered in every direction. Again Willett pressed on and came up with the main body, which was by this time thoroughly demoralized by exhaustion and lack of food. There were plain signs of disorganization and confusion, and after a brief, halfhearted resistance the enemy left the field trotting in single file. It was a strange flight and pursuit. Butler must have realized that he could not flee forever. His men were at the limit of their endurance. The weather was bitter, and the snow, turning to icy slush, impeded their march. The pursuers, spurred on by the hope of vengeance on their tormentors, were almost as weary as those they pursued. Late in the afternoon, after fording Canada Creek, Butler stopped and made preparations for a battle. In the first skirmish, he was severely wounded, and twenty of his men were killed. The rest fled once more and when Willett's force made camp to get some desperately needed sleep, the British staggered on without food or blankets, determined to put as much distance as they could between themselves and the Americans. Their situation seemed hopeless. They had seven days' march to Oswego ahead of them, without provisions or blankets to protect them from the increasingly bitter nights. Reluctantly, Willett broke off the pursuit and left the British to the mercies of the wilderness. His men had only five days' rations and would soon have been as depleted as the enemy.

The invaders' most impressive accomplishment was their flight. On a ration of half a pound of horsemeat a day, after four days of grueling campaigning, the British, Tories, and Indians had moved, often at a trot, thirty miles before they stopped. Willett wrote Clinton that the wounded Butler was found by "one of our Indians, who finished his business for him and got considerable booty." The raiders were left (Willett's words) "in a fair way of receiving a punishment better suited to their merit than a musquet ball, a tomahawk or captivity . . ."—starvation in the forest.

The most important gain for the Americans was the death of Walter Butler, who with his father and Joseph Brant had been the scourge of the frontier for years. He was bitterly hated for his depredations and for his ruthlessness and cruelty. Historians have attempted to exonerate him from the worst charges against him. Trained in Albany as a lawyer, he was a handsome, graceful man. There had never been any doubt that he would cast his lot with His Majesty's forces. His father, as an Indian agent, had been a friend of the great Sir William Johnson and a faithful servant of the Crown; the son, joining forces with Sir William's son, Sir John, was true to that tradition. Four years before, Butler had been caught trying to recruit settlers to the Tory cause in Tryon County and had been sentenced to be hanged as a spy by a military court of which, ironically, Willett had been judge advocate. Butler had escaped. It was the opinion of Colonel Willett's son that Butler "had exhibited more instances of enterprise, had done more injury, and committed more murder, than any other man on the frontiers." To the patriot inhabitants of the Mohawk Valley his death was of greater moment and hailed with greater delight than Washington's defeat of Cornwallis.

Although small bands of Indians continued to roam the frontier and made occasional raids on isolated settlements and farmhouses, Willett's victory at Johnstown marked the end of large-scale attacks on the northern frontier. What Sullivan with five thousand men could not accomplish (indeed it could be argued he stimulated the border raids), Willett achieved with a tenth the number of troops.

CHAPTER V

SANDUSKY

In the early spring of 1782 an episode took place that disgraced American arms and brought severe retribution from the Indians.

David Zeisberger and John Heckewelder, two Moravian missionaries to the Delaware Indians, had Christianized a substantial number of that tribe and had prevailed on them to adopt a settled agricultural life in western Pennsylvania. Several years before the outbreak of the Revolution, the two missionaries had, in response to pleas by the Delawares, migrated to a site on the upper Tuscarawas River some one hundred miles from Fort Pitt. There they founded three prosperous little settlements: Schönbrunn, Gnadenhütten, and Salem. At the beginning of the Revolution, the missionaries and their Indian followers declared themselves neutral. In consequence they were suspected of treachery by both the British and the Americans. Because of the Moravian Indians' kinship with the Delawares—who were among the tribes most loyal to the British—they were under constant pressure to favor the British side, and some of their bolder young braves joined war parties of British Indians. Finally, a party of fifty British and Indians forced them in the fall of 1781 to move from their villages to the upper Sandusky River. When they satisfied the British authorities in Detroit that they were innocent of charges of having aided the Americans, a hundred of them were allowed to return to their settlements on the Tuscarawas to harvest the corn standing in the fields.

In the meantime, a series of particularly vicious Indian atrocities on the Pennsylvania frontier aroused bitter resentment among the white settlers there. When a rumor circulated that hostile Indians had occupied the deserted villages of the Moravian Indians, a force of three hundred militia was dispatched to attack them. Conscious of their own innocence and doubtless anxious to protect their towns from being destroyed, the Christian Indians who had returned home stood their ground and took no measures for defense. The militia arrived first at Gnadenhütten. A mile from the town they met a young Indian, Schebosh, whom they killed and scalped. Two other peaceful and unarmed Indians met a similar fate. The rest were rounded up with assurances that "no harm should befall them" and were taken to the center of town, where they were all bound, "the men being put into one house, the women into another."

By now the Indians realized that they were to become sacrifices to the Americans' thirst for vengeance. The men began to pray and sing hymns "and spoke words of encouragement and consolation to one another until they were all slain." It was the turn of the women next. Christina, a Mohegan woman who knew German and English, begged for her life and those of her sisters, but to no avail.

There was an added bitter irony. On the arrival of the militia at Gnadenhütten, one of the missionaries went on to Salem to inform the Indians there. Not knowing of the fate of their fellows, they too resolved not to flee, which would have suggested that they were guilty. The next day, a party of militia arrived in Salem, disarmed the Indians, and led them back to Gnadenhütten. There they bound them and took their knives. In Zeisberger's words, "They made our Indians bring all their hidden goods out of the bush, and then took them away; they had to tell them where in the bush the bees were, help get the honey out; other [things] they also had to do for them before they were killed. . . . They prayed and sang until the tomahawks struck into their heads. . . . They burned the dead bodies, together with the houses. . . ."

The militia knew very well that the Indians were "good Indians," that is to say, Indians who had not taken hostile action against the American settlements and who were not allied with the enemy. They knew, moreover, that they were Christians, and it is hard to believe that some of them were not moved by their victims' martyr-like courage in the face of certain death. What unappeasable hatreds lay in their hearts we cannot fathom. Like the soldiers of My Lai, the militia at Gnadenhütten destroyed unarmed men, women, and children and did so out of some strange reflex of fear and resentment toward people they felt were not quite human. The massacre aroused a storm of protest. The leading figures in the frontier settlements were virtually unanimous in denouncing it as an act of unparalleled barbarity. Punishment of the perpetrators was demanded. The Pennsylvania assembly investigated the episode and condemned it. And there the matter rested.

A month or so later, on May 25, an expedition under Colonel William Crawford set out from Fort Pitt for the Wyandot and Shawnee towns on the upper Sandusky, charged with destroying them "with fire and sword if practicable . . . by which we hope to give ease and safety to the inhabitants of this country . . ." as the Pennsylvanian, General William Irvine, wrote Washington. Among the 465 Pennsylvania and Virginia frontiersmen who had signed on with Crawford were some of the men who had participated in the massacre at Gnadenhütten.

The little force made its way through thickets and open woods, across huckleberry bushes and swamps, always alert for any sign of Indians. Approaching the settlements of the Moravian Indians on the trail to the Sandusky, scouts observed the tracks of some sixty Indians and saw in the distance three mounted warriors shadowing the American force. At various spots the Indians had set fire to the woods to detain the soldiers. The ground became increasingly rugged, with deep ravines and muddy creeks across their line of march. Losing a number of their horses to exhaustion and accidents along the trail, the party pushed on, making as much as twenty miles a day despite the terrain.

By the first of June, Crawford's band was clearly in trouble. The Indians had discovered their movements, and it was logical to assume that they were gathering their scattered forces. Supplies were running low, and there was murmuring among the men, who were disheartened by the difficulties of the march and the sense that Indians were all around them, though few could be seen. Crawford held a council of war the same day. If they reached the Sandusky, how would they find their way back through a territory filled with hostile Indians? How would they carry out the sick or wounded, and where would they get fresh food when they had exhausted their dwindling supply? But the decision was to press on; to turn back would almost be as dangerous as to continue. Nearing the Indian town on the Sandusky that was their objective, the Americans found numerous tracks. Soon they came under attack. Fighting from the cover of a small wood, the militia kept the Indians at bay until sunset. A hasty inventory the next morning showed that two men had been killed instantly. Three more had died during the night, their groans and cries doing little to improve the morale of their companions. Nineteen more had been wounded, and of these, three had wounds that were plainly mortal. One of the Americans had been scalped, and two Indian scalps had been taken. On the fifth of June, the Indians circled the beleaguered little force, apparently trying to draw their fire and keep them pinned down until further reinforcements might arrive. At evening a body of some hundred and fifty Shawnees appeared, advancing openly in three columns and carrying a red flag. Delawares were also identified among the Indians who encircled Crawford's force. The Indians began to erect primitive defenses across the American line of retreat. Crawford and most of his officers decided to try to fight their way out, under cover of darkness. The horses were quietly saddled and the men prepared to march in two columns. But one unit, unwilling to fall in with the general plan, took another route, and so the detachment was badly split at the beginning. In the darkness confusion was compounded, one group trying to fight its way back along the trail it had advanced over two days before, the other taking a path that brought it near the Indian town. The goal was a spring where the men had camped before encountering the Indians. Crawford disappeared in the confusion, and another officer assumed command of the men.

Many of the men deserted by two and threes, believing they had a better chance to get away on their own. Resting briefly and then pushing on in their flight, they heard the bloodcurdling "Scalp Halloo" from time to time, which told them that the Indians had caught a straggler or deserter and taken his scalp. Gradually, as the party got farther from the Shawnee towns, it picked up some of those who had made their way singly or in groups. Some 380 of the original 465 militia escaped. For so many of the party to have found their way back was a remarkable testimony to their skill as woodsmen and, equally, to the inability of the Indians to maintain a sustained pursuit. The final tally was between forty and fifty officers and men killed and missing and twenty-eight wounded. The escape of the Americans was undoubtedly facilitated by the capture of Crawford and the doctor of the expedition, along with a number of other Americans. Many of the Indians withdrew to one of their towns to entertain themselves with their prisoners.

First Crawford and Dr. John Knight were stripped of their clothes and daubed black; then they were made to run the gauntlet between two long lines of men, women, and children who beat them with clubs, sticks, and fists. The next day they were again blackened. Their hands were tied behind them, and Colonel Crawford was led to a stake surrounded by red hot coals; he was forced to walk in the hot coals while his torturers fired powder at his body at close range and prodded his body with burning sticks. This continued for two hours; when Crawford pled with Simon Girty, the American turncoat, who stood watching the spectacle, to shoot him, Girty replied, "Don't you see I have no gun?"

Finally Crawford was scalped, and with the blood pouring from the wound in his head, he fell down on the live coals while the Indian women heaped shovelfuls of coals on his body. Knight was forced to watch his friend's death, and when Crawford was scalped, the Indians "slapped the scalp over the Doctor's face, saying, 'This is your great captain's scalp; tomorrow we will serve you so.'"

Knight was to be tortured to death in another village. A single Indian was put in charge of him, and on the way to the other spot the savage, wishing a fire, untied Knight and ordered him to collect wood. With a good-sized chunk, Knight struck the Indian on the head, knocked him down, and seized his gun. When the Indian ran, Knight escaped through the woods and traveled for twenty days before he got back to Fort Pitt with his gruesome tale. The only prisoners who had been tortured were those captured by the Delawares, "who," a member of the expedition wrote a friend, "say they will shew no mercy to any white man, as they would shew none to their friends and relations, the religious Moravians."

The defeat of Crawford brought in its wake an outburst of Indian raids along the upper Ohio. The volatile Indians, cast down by defeat, were correspondingly excited by victory. Hannastown, some thirty miles beyond Pittsburgh, was surprised and burned, and twenty settlers who could not reach the fort were murdered or carried off as prisoners. All along the frontier the cry was raised for retribution for Crawford's defeat and torture and for the raids against Hannastown and other isolated settlements. If General Irvine would lead them, the settlers declared, they would raise and equip six or seven hundred men for an expedition against the Sandusky villages. Once more the machinery was set in motion to raise a force of a thousand men, stiffened by a hundred regulars, to clear out the Sandusky region and then join forces with Clark in an attack against the Shawnee.

Joseph Brant had been planning an attack against Wheeling, West Virginia, and the frontier settlements to the south. He had been joined by Simon Girty and a Captain William Caldwell, a bold and enterprising Tory officer. Brant's combined force consisted of over eleven hundred Indians, perhaps the largest Indian force assembled during the Revolution. While they were on the march word came of Clark's expedition against the Shawnee villages, and Brant was asked to turn back to help defend them. Most of the warriors wished to return, but their leaders were determined not to abandon the campaign without a foray into Kentucky country. Three hundred Wyandots and some Tory rangers thus crossed the Ohio on August 15, 1782, and surrounded Bryan's Station, five miles north of Lexington. Bryan's Station was a compound two hundred yards long and forty yards wide, containing forty cabins occupied by ninety men, women, and children. Each corner had a blockhouse two stories high; the palisades that surrounded the fort were twelve feet high. The residents of the fort soon got word that a large party of Indians was waiting to attack. The only water for the fort came from a spring at the foot of the hill below the fort, close to the point where the Indians lay in hiding. The fort's defenders decided to send the women down the hill with buckets to fetch water for cooking and washing, as though they had no suspicion that there were hostile Indians about. It was an extraordinary drama. Laughing and talking, the little band of women and young girls trooped down to the spring and filled their pails. The Wyandots, taking the expedition as clear evidence that no one in the fort suspected their presence, let the women carry out their task unmolested.

Soon after the women returned, the Indians sent a small party to try to decoy the settlers out of the fort. The defenders pretended to take the bait. A small group rushed out in pursuit of the Indians, but they were careful to stay close enough to the fort to be able to quickly return to it. Girty and his warriors, confident that their ruse had worked, rushed out of the woods in an attack on the other side of the fort, only to be met by a heavy fire that drove them back in disorder. Girty then began intermittent fire on the fort and called for its surrender, promising to protect its occupants from the Indians. Young Aaron Reynolds shouted back to Girty that he was a known scoundrel and dog who was despised by every honest man. If he and his mongrel followers got inside the fort, they would be driven out with switches rather than guns. And if he remained another day, Reynolds added, a relief party would nail his dirty hide to a tree. The Indians howled with fury at Reynolds's taunts. Bullets spattered against the palisades, and frequent efforts were made to set fire to it. But next day, convinced that the siege was hopeless, Girty withdrew after destroying the crops in the field, killing the cattle, sheep, and hogs, and carrying off the horses.

Girty fell back slowly to Blue Licks on the Licking River, inviting pursuit. Soon after Girty's retreat from Bryan's Station, volunteers had arrived from Lexington, Harrodsburg, and Boonesborough, with a hundred and thirty-five militia from Lincoln County and a contingent from Fayette County, led by Daniel Boone. It was decided to pursue Girty's party at once, and a picked group of 180 mounted riflemen started off after the Indians. At lower Blue Licks, they saw a few Indians moving along a rocky ridge less than a mile away. Some of the riflemen, Boone among them, suspected a trap and urged the party to wait until it was properly reinforced. Others were anxious to attack at once; Major Hugh McGary, a hotheaded Kentuckian, settled the debate by putting spurs to his horse and calling out, "Delay is dastardly! Let all who are not cowards follow me, and I will show them the Indians." The party, following McGary's lead, crossed a small stream and formed a line of attack with Boone in command of the left, McGary of the center. They rode to within sixty yards of the Wyandots and Tories who lay waiting for them, dismounted, and opened fire. Boone drove the Indians back on the left, but the American right gave way under the threat of being outflanked, and McGary found himself attacked on the right and from the rear. His men retreated against Boone's right, and the whole American line broke and ran for the ford. "He that could remount a horse was well off," one of the officers wrote, "and he that could not saw no time for delay." At the river they were partially intercepted by a detachment of Indians, and many were tomahawked as they tried to swim across the stream. One of the officers saved a number of lives by rallying the men who had gotten across to cover those of their fellows who were struggling to get over. Once across, what was left of the original force continued to retreat until they met reinforcements. At that point the Indians withdrew, and the action was broken off.

The battle of Blue Licks was the worst defeat suffered by the Kentuckians at the hands of the British Indians. Seventy were killed—more than a third of the force engaged—and twenty more captured or badly wounded. When the reinforcements reached the ford at Blue Licks, they found a number of Americans tied to trees and "butchered with knives and spears." Andrew Steele, one of the members of the relief party, wrote to Governor Benjamin Harrison of Virginia:

> Through the continued series of seven years vicessitudes, nothing has happened so alarming, fatal and injurious to the interest of the Kanetuckians. . . . To express the feelings of the inhabitants of both the counties at this rueful scene of hitherto unparalleled barbarities barre all words and cuts description short. . . . Forty seven of our brave Kanetuckians were found in the field, the matchless massacred victims of their [Indians] unprecedented cruelty. . . . The balance stand upon an equilibrium and one stroke more will cause it to preponderate to our irretrievable wo. . . .

Steele wrote to Harrison again a few weeks later, describing the condition of the frontier.

> The frequent Incursions & Hostile Depredations of a Savage Enemy upon our Exterior Posts, our Despersed Legions, our veteran army defeated, our Widows Tears & orphans cries grate strongly on the Ear . . . I beg leave to inform you that annually since the seventeen Hund'd & seventy eight an army of not less than three Hund'd Savages Infested our Territories & since seventy six, Eight hundred & sixty Effective men fell, the matchless massacred victims of unprecedented Cruelty [Steele plainly liked the phrase].

If Harrison would show some concern for the frontier settlers, "the Indigent Offspring of an opulent father," they would celebrate him as "the Illustrious Patron & Protector of our Lives, Laws & Religious Liberties," and the "annals of History will rank your name among the Bravest Patriots & Wisest Politicians & Gratitude like Torrent will flow from the Heart of every Kanetuckian. . . ."

For a time it seemed as if the whole Kentucky frontier would have to be abandoned. Clark, criticized for not protecting the Kentucky region, replied that the tragedy at Blue Licks was due to the "Extreamly Reprihensible" behavior of the officers in command, who acted recklessly in attacking before reinforcements had arrived.

The effect of Blue Licks, like the effect of similar setbacks, stirred the frontier to still another effort. By a herculean effort twelve hundred militia and regulars were collected to march under Irvine against the Indian stronghold on the Sandusky. "I am now preparing for an excursion into the Indian country," Irvine wrote to Harrison. "My troops are chiefly to be volunteer militia, who propose not only to equip & feed themselves, but also such Continental troops as I can take with me. If we succeed in burning the Shawnee, Delaware & Wyandot towns, it will put an end to the Indian war in this quarter."

Clark, with a similar force drawn from Kentucky, was to attack the Shawnee villages centered at Chillicothe, and nearly a thousand men were to be dispatched against the Indian towns in the Genesee area that Sullivan had destroyed three years before.

Early in November, 1782, weeks before Irvine's troops were ready to march, a force of a thousand and fifty mounted men under Clark's leadership set out from the mouth of the Licking to strike into Shawnee territory. Clark, characteristically, maintained strict discipline during the six days' march, but the Indians were on the alert and escaped with only ten killed and ten captured. Chillicothe and five other towns were put to the torch and ten thousand bushels of corn destroyed. Unable to bring on a general engagement with the Indians, Clark returned reluctantly to the mouth of the Licking, confident that he had at least thrown the Indians off balance and made the frontier settlements safe from raids for some months to come. The winter supplies of the Indians were wiped out, but more important, the effect of the victory at Blue Licks was negated, and the Indians once more were reminded of the American capacity for retaliation. In the words of Daniel Boone, "The spirits of the Indians were damped, their connections dissolved, their armies scattered & a future invasion entirely out of their power."

A British officer wrote to Abraham de Peyster, a Loyalist officer, to the same effect: "I am endeavoring to assemble the Indians, but I find I shall not be able to collect a number sufficient to oppose them, the chiefs are now met here upon that business who desire me to inform you of their Situation requesting you will communicate it by the inclosed strings to their Brethren the Lake Indians, without speedy assistance they must be drove off from their country, the Enemy being too powerful for them."

Before Irvine could mount his more cumbersome attack on the Sandusky towns, word came from Washington that the British had assured him that all hostilities were suspended in anticipation of a treaty of peace and that the Indians had been ordered to carry out no further raids. But in the Northwest, where fear gave wings to rumor, the declared intention of Clark to attack the other enemy Indians as he had done the Shawnees kept the British-allied tribes in continual ferment. The efforts of the British to restrain their raids made them restless and uneasy, as did the sharp decline in the presents usually provided for them by the British authorities at Detroit and Niagara. Clark urged a general offensive into the Indian stronghold at the head of the Wabash and the strengthening of Fort Nelson and Vincennes to convince the Indians "that they were inferior to us, that the British assertions of our weakness was false, and that we could at all times penetrate into their Country at Pleasure. . . ." By the middle of April, 1783, word reached the frontier of the signing of preliminary peace articles at Paris. By the terms of the definitive treaty, the Old Northwest was ceded to the United States. Governor Benjamin Harrison wrote to Clark in July informing him that his services would no longer be needed. "Before I take leave of you," he added, "I feel called on in the most forciable Manner to return to you my Thanks and those of my Council for the very great and singular services you have rendered your Country, in wresting so great and valuable a Territory out of the Hands of the

British Enemy, repelling the attacks of their Savage Allies and carrying on successful war in the Heart of their Country. . . ."

The war in the West, or the border war as it is sometimes called, often seems a kind of footnote or addendum to the Revolution, and for good reason. It was, in a real sense, another war, a war between Indians and Americans, with the Indians aided, abetted, and egged on by the British. It had begun well before the Revolution in the numerous "Indian wars" of the colonial era, and it continued well after the end of the fighting in the east (that is, essentially, after Yorktown) and, indeed, after the Treaty of Paris in 1783, which marked the formal end of the Revolution.

In many ways the most disastrous legacy of the Revolution could be found in the permanently embittered relations between the Western settlers and the Indians who confronted them. That confrontation was a difficult and dangerous one at best. The British, as we have seen, at first sporadically and then systematically promoted Indian raids on the frontier from upper New York State to Georgia. Most of these raids had only tenuous military objectives; increasingly they were punitive, a means of punishing those Americans who were most remote from any military support or reinforcement, for their presumption in revolting against the mother country. It was primarily an Indian war; without Indian allies the activity of the British in the West would have been confined to a few minor expeditions by British regulars and Tories, the latter mostly from the Mohawk Valley of New York. With the involvement of the Indians, the frontier was devastated by a ruthless and barbarous total war. Indeed, the frontier settlers suffered, in the course of the raids and counterraids of the border war, more casualties than Washington's Continental Army suffered in all its major engagements. The settler who had laboriously cleared a small patch of land in the wilderness, erected a simple cabin and some crude sheds, fenced a vegetable plot, and collected, at considerable effort and expense, a horse and a few domestic animals, and who then saw the buildings put to the torch and the animals slaughtered, nursed an understandable hatred of the British and their Indian auxiliaries. If, in addition, he saw the livid crimson skull of a friend or relative who had been scalped by Indians, the lust of vengeance burned in him as long as he lived. Not only had the Indians turned on the Americans when, in a sense, they were down and fighting for their lives; they were, in practical fact, British mercenaries, to be distinguished from the Hessians only by their savage waging of total war. The British paid the Indians, with an endless stream of gifts and presents, to murder Americans. Or at least that was the American view of the matter.

Of all the policies pursued by the British in the Revolutionary era, their employment of Indians to kill Americans is the least excusable. As we have pointed out, in the case of the devastation of the lands of the Iroquois Confederacy by General Sullivan, the British policy was as cruel and exploitive to the Indians as it was bloody and ruthless to the Americans. When the British departed, they left behind them a legacy of bitterness that could never be alleviated. From the Revolution on, those Americans who lived in the frontier settlements, which moved constantly westward, viewed the Indian as *the* enemy, cruel, deceitful, merciless; and they judged it a simple rule of self-preservation to match him in cunning and savagery, terror for terror, life for life, scalp for scalp, settler and savage caught in a terrible ritual of violence. At first there were distinctions made between "good" Indians and "bad" Indians, between "hostile" and "friendly" Indians. But the distinctions were crude ones and frequently not observed, and one corollary of these distinctions was that the traditional animosities between certain tribes were exacerbated, so that tribes warred with each other with a ferocity that had been rare in earlier days. They had learned the warfare of extermination from the white man.

The irony of the British policy, as Clark himself pointed out, was that most frontiersmen felt little identification with the Revolutionary "cause." They had moved to the frontier because they wished to be "free and independent" of governments, whether British or American. The prosperous lawyer of Boston or the wealthy patriot merchant or landlord of New York were to the frontier settlers as uncongenial figures as Lord North and his haughty emissaries. From the first the frontiersmen showed strong "separatist" tendencies; they wished, as in Vermont and Kentucky, Watauga, or the infant state of Franklin, to form separate states, and they were willing, in most instances, to ally themselves with any power that would grant them the independence they wished for. A group of Western settlers, for example, called for a meeting at Wheeling early in 1782, to make plans for acquiring lands on the Muskingum River and establishing a new state to come eventually under British authority. Had the British thus restrained the Indians and cultivated the separatist tendencies so evident on the frontier, they would in all probability have created far more trouble for the "United States" than they could ever have caused by promoting border raids. As it was, their strategy seemed designed to drive the frontier settlers into the not especially hospitable arms of Congress or of the particular states. To the harassed delegates in Congress, the bloody events that kept the frontier in an uproar seemed almost as remote as if they had happened on the moon. In general, Congress had little knowledge of the frontier or little sympathy with it. When they thought of the settlers at all, they thought of them as congeries of lower-class individuals, resistant to authority, not much better in their habits and manners than the "savages" themselves—men and women who, by their inability to get along with their Indian neighbors and their constant pressure on Indian hunting grounds, created endless problems for Congress, which already had problems enough.

Howard Swiggett, a close student of the warfare of the Northern Indians and their Tory allies, wrote thusly of the British use of the Indians:

> The irony of it all is that the Indians as fighters were worthless
> and the British high command were early sick of them. Time
> and again . . . their fighting qualities proved lower than the most
> worthless militia. . . . The problem of feeding them was terrific.
> They poured into the northwestern posts from Oswego to beyond
> Detroit, cold and hungry and the £17,000 spent on them by Sir
> William Johnson in thirteen months was to be quintupled in a few

months, and all for naught. They brought disgrace on the British arms and confusion to the management of the war.

Swiggett certainly overstates the case. While the British employment of the Indians was one of the most serious of many strategic mistakes they made, the Indians, under the proper conditions, were formidable fighters. The point is that they could not be controlled or disciplined, and they fought erratically when used with regular troops. If the Revolution could have been won by a war of attrition (as the British clearly thought it could be), then the use of the Indians was an astute, if immoral, policy (immoral, as we have said, as much because of the reckless exploitation of the Indians as because of the terrible devastation and suffering that the Indians caused in the frontier settlements). "The employing of the Indians," the Marquis de Chastellux wrote in 1783, ". . . it is now pretty generally admitted, produced consequences directly opposite to the interest of Great-Britain; uniting the inhabitants of all the countries liable to their incursions as one man against them and their allies, and producing such bloody scenes of inveterate animosity and vengeance as make human nature shudder."

While exploitation of the Indians and hostility between Indians and settlers were as old as the beginnings of the colonies, there had always been men like Roger Williams, William Penn, and John Eliot—leading settlers who labored sincerely to protect the rights of the Indians and to preserve peace with them. And while there were numerous Indian wars, massacres, and counter-massacres, the Indians, in large part, had managed to preserve their tribal integrity. Where they were forced out of heavily settled areas, they gave a good account of themselves in battle, fought a determined rearguard action, and withdrew to areas where they were safe, at least for the moment, from the intrusion of the whites. Some like the Stockbridge Indians, became "civilized" and settled down in peaceful proximity to the whites. Thus in 1775 it was possible to believe that there might be a "solution" to the Indian problem; that colonists and Indians, despite the cultural gulf that separated them, might learn to live together in this vast country. But the Revolution changed all that. The wounds made in that unrelenting contest never healed. From the time of the Revolution to the end of the nineteenth century there was, for the inhabitant of the frontier, only one good Indian, and that was a dead Indian.

If the war for independence ended with the Treaty of Paris, conflicts with the various tribes allied with Great Britain continued.

CHAPTER VI

INDIANS AND THE NEW NATION

The members of the new Congress had to deal with the problem of white–Indian relations in the first months of the new nation. The complexity of the issue was pointed up by the difference in the two problems that confronted them. In one, the Wabash Indians and their allies in the Old Northwest were killing settlers who infringed on their territory. That was a relatively simple problem. It required a military expedition to drive off the Indians and secure the new settlements. The other involved a treaty negotiated between the United States and the Creek Indians, whose traditional homelands were in southwestern Georgia. The treaty was designed to secure the rights of the Indians to their lands. It brought forth bitter declamations from the Georgia representatives in Congress. James Jackson, a Georgia member, declared: "That treaty has spread alarm among the people of Georgia. It has ceded away, without any compensation whatever, three millions of acres of land guaranteed to Georgia by the Constitution. . . . Has the Government recognized the rights of Georgia? No. It has given away her land, invited a savage of the Creek nation to the seat of Government, caressed him in a most extraordinary manner, and sent him home loaded with favors."

It was widely reported that the Creek Treaty contained secret clauses inimical to Georgia. "Good God! are there to be secret articles between the United States and any nation under heaven? . . . Will Congress suffer the laws of the United States . . . to be placed where no man can read them, and then punish the people for disobeying them? The people, sir, will never submit to be bound by secret articles." Jackson's outburst suggests the difficulties of the matter. Not surprisingly, the treaty was to have an unhappy aftermath.

The most immediate issue involved the Indians of the Northwest, who as we have noted, were emboldened by the British retention of the posts in the region north of the Ohio. The Delaware, the Shawnee, the Miami, the Wyandot, and the Ottawa tribes made common cause against the frontier. The Confederation Congress had taken the attitude that all these tribes had forfeited their rights to the land by their support of the British during the war. Nonetheless, Congress went to considerable pains to placate the Indians with treaties and presents. The Fort Stanwix Treaty in 1784 was designed to extinguish the claims of the Iroquois to the area of present-day Ohio, Illinois, and Indiana. The Wyandot, Chippewa, and Delaware accepted similar terms, and the Shawnee fell in line a year later. But the Miami, the Kickapoo, and the Potawatomi refused to enter treaty negotiations. It was a familiar problem in dealing with the Indians. The Potawatomi belonged to the Algonquian language group. They had been traditional enemies of the Iroquois and had cast their lot with the French. The very fact that the Iroquois had concluded a treaty with Congress disposed the Potawatomi to hold out.

The situation was much the same with the Miami. They had been at war intermittently with the Iroquois for a hundred years and had lost many braves to them and to the Sioux. Now they prepared to go on the warpath against any white settlers north of the Ohio:

some thousand at the old French settlement of Vincennes, thirteen hundred on what was known as Symmes Purchase, and another thousand on land claimed by the Ohio Company. The rest were scattered in small settlements, the most prominent of which were Clarkesville and Kaskaskia.

All during the spring and summer reports came in of Indian attacks. In the revealing words of a nineteenth-century historian, "At first they were supposed to be merely accounts of such barbariti as the Indians had always perpetrated on the settlers of a new country from the days of John Smith and Miles Standish on down," casual massacres, the interception of a boatload of emigrants on the Ohio, burned-out cabins, kidnapped women and children. Arthur St. Clair, the Revolutionary veteran who was more politician than general, had been appointed governor of the Northwest Territory. He fixed the seat of his administration in Cincinnati, which he named after the Society of the Cincinnati of which he was then president, an act that brought bitter criticism from the enemies of the fraternal order. St. Clair dispatched Major John Hamtramck to discover the intentions of the Indians, and Hamtramck in turn engaged a French trader at Vincennes to visit the tribes and report on their mood.

The trader's account was alarming. There was no doubt in his mind that at least three of the tribes were preparing for war. St. Clair immediately began to gather a ragtag force to strike at the Indian strongholds along the Wabash River. The expedition he scraped together was placed under the command of Colonels John Hardin and James Trotter. A hint of the fate of the little force of 1,453 men might have been read in the fact that although Hardin was the senior officer, he was disliked for his strict discipline. The men thus refused to accept him as a commander, and he was forced to give way to the more amiable Trotter. The clashes with the British-allied Indians during the Revolution had made it clear that in no military operations was march discipline more important than in campaigns against the Indians. Silence, mobility, and speed were essential if an enemy were to be taken by surprise.

The march to the Wabash turned out to be as close to low comedy as the ill-fated Sandusky expedition nine years earlier. The invading force was made up of a tatterdemalion militia band composed largely of old men and boys, since few husbands and fathers could be spared from their frontier farms. These gathered with a motley collection of arms, some with broken muskets and others with nothing better than a rusty sword. Quarrels broke out immediately between the untrained militia and the regulars, who were little better prepared for such an expedition. Their first objective was a cluster of Miami villages some thirty miles away. Hardin was given command of the strike force, whose mission was to surprise the Indians in their wigwams and prevent their escape until the main body of troops arrived. He and his men spent a day and a half crashing through the forest to reach the village.

Not surprisingly, they found it deserted. It was another two days before Trotter arrived with the main body and four days were then consumed destroying the villages and burning the fields. At night, security was so slipshod that Indians were able to steal into the American camp and drive off most of the pack and artillery horses thus making further pursuit impossible.

Hoping to salvage something from the ill-fated foray, General Josiah Harmar, who was military commander of the territory under St. Clair's jurisdiction, dispatched Trotter with three hundred men to round up any Indians in the vicinity. One Indian was chased and killed; another was sighted at a distance, and the four officers in Trotter's command, including the colonel himself, set off in pursuit and were gone for half an hour while their troops roamed about leaderless.

With Trotter in disgrace, Hardin was given his turn. Dispatched on a similar raid, he and his force discovered the remains of a recently abandoned Indian campground. Hardin deployed his men in a line of advance and pressed farther into the forest. One of the companies, failing to receive orders to move, remained at the point of departure. Without scouts to his front or outriders to protect his flanks, Hardin stumbled into an ambush. Finding themselves under fire, the militia abandoned their arms and ran, with their commander in the lead. The officer commanding the little detachment of regulars swore later that he and his men had stood their ground until all but himself were killed and that he had then made his escape. Whatever the particular circumstances, the operation was a fiasco. When the militia and the humiliated Hardin found their way back to the destroyed Indian villages, Harmar ordered a general withdrawal to Cincinnati.

Hardin, anxious to redeem himself, persuaded Harmar to place him in command of 350 men to trap the Indians when they returned to their villages. He set out on a night march, hoping to surprise the Indians at dawn, but the sun was well up before the little party reached the villages. Scouts reported that the Indians had returned and might still be surprised. Hardin deployed his force in three divisions. Two were to advance directly on the villages, and the third was to circle behind the villages to cut off the Indians' retreat. The maneuver proceeded smoothly enough until the troops flushed an Indian and fired at him, thus alerting the rest, who fled with the militia in pursuit. When the Indians finally turned on their pursuers, the militia once more panicked and fled back to the general's main force. Harmar now adopted a strategy not unknown to generals dispatched against the Indians. He announced that the expedition had been a great success: the Indians had been scattered and demoralized, and five Indian villages and winter supplies of corn in the amount of twenty thousand bushels had been destroyed. He then set out on a triumphal return to Fort Washington. In fact, the expedition had, like other such ventures, exactly the opposite of its intended effect. The inept conduct of the Americans had emboldened the Indians, and the destruction of their villages had infuriated them. Wavering clans were encouraged to take the warpath. Meanwhile, settlers, heartened by Harmar's account of his success, pressed farther into the Ohio country. Marietta grew to eighty houses and a small stockade.

Belle Prairie, at the juncture of the Kanawha and Ohio rivers, was another busy settlement. Sawmills and a mill for grinding corn were built on convenient streams, Duck Creek and Wolf Creek.

The most exposed settlement was at Big Bottom, forty miles farther upriver. There twelve families had begun the process described by Benjamin Rush of carving their primitive farms out of the uncongenial forest. On January 2, 1791, Indians attacked at dusk, killed all the settlers—men, women, and children—and burned their houses and barns to the ground.

The news of the Big Bottom Massacre sent rumors flying along the frontier from one isolated settlement to another. The most alarming rumor was that the great Joseph Brant was at the head of a large force made up of Miami and Wabash Indians, bent on driving the whites out of the whole Northwest Territory. Settlements too small to think of defending themselves successfully packed up what they could carry and, driving their animals ahead of them, headed for the fort at Marietta, which was manned by twenty regulars.

Rufus Putnam, cousin of General Israel Putnam who had commanded the American forces at the Battle of Bunker Hill, had founded, or refounded, the town of Marietta where he served as territorial judge. He wrote imploringly to General Washington, his father's old commander in chief, describing the Big Bottom Massacre, the exposed situation of the Americans, and the desperate need for help, adding, "Unless Government speedily sends a body of troops for our protection, we are a ruined people."

The Big Bottom Massacre called for a strong government response. Washington appointed St. Clair commander of a force with the task of pacifying the Indians by seeking them out and defeating them in battle and then building a chain of forts from Cincinnati to the confluence of the St. Mary and St. Joseph rivers. St. Clair set about accumulating men and supplies for his expedition. The summer months, best suited for campaigning, were lost as the general painstakingly collected and equipped his army. Finally, late in September, he set out for Indian territory with twenty-thee hundred regulars and a number of militia. On the banks of the Great Miami River where it entered the Ohio, he built Fort Hamilton. From there he advanced forty-four miles down the Ohio and constructed Fort Jefferson. Leaving Fort Jefferson, a crude and

hastily constructed palisade, he and his army resumed their tortuous progress west and south along the river. The fall air was sharp,
and the mists that hung over the water gave the soldiers chills and
fevers. The militia were poorly prepared for an extended campaign.
Many of them fell ill; food supplies ran short; and it was forbidden to kill game along the line of march for fear of alerting the
Indians. St. Clair himself fell ill and had to be carried for miles on
a stretcher. The commander's sickness further undermined morale,
and the militia began to desert, fifty or sixty at a time.

After a ten-day march, during the course of which St. Clair
lost more than half of his force through attrition, fourteen hundred thoroughly demoralized men reached what St. Clair thought
was the western terminus of his expedition, the St. Mary. In fact,
it was a branch of the Wabash, a creek some fifty feet wide. St.
Clair placed his troops in two lines along the creek. He situated
the militia encampment on the far side of the creek a quarter of a
mile away. A mile beyond the militia, a force of regulars formed an
advance guard whose mission was to search the woods for Indians.
They soon realized that the woods around them were alive with the
enemy, and they hastily withdrew to the main body to alert St. Clair.

St. Clair took no action to warn the members of his command,
and at dawn the Indians attacked and routed the militia, apparently taking them by surprise. Those who were not killed in the
first encounter fled across the creek with the Indians in pursuit. A
handful of regulars lined the bank to cover their crossing. St. Clair
then formed the remainder into a square around the artillery. It was
a strange formation to take up in the face of an Indian attack.

During the Revolution it had taken almost five years to train
soldiers of the Continental Army to stand and fire in close formation rather than in the extended skirmish lines they had learned
from the Indians, taking advantage of every tree and fold in the
terrain for protection and concealment. The British, meanwhile,
had learned to employ the tactics the Americans had abandoned;
and at the Battle of Green Spring, a few months before Yorktown,
American soldiers, advancing through the woods in close formation,

had encountered the British spread out and fighting Indian fashion. Now St. Clair behaved as though he were fighting a conventional European war. Standing in line, firing, and dropping back, exposed to the musket fire of Indians hidden behind tree trunks and rocks, the Americans suffered heavy casualties. The regulars demonstrated their superior discipline by making bayonet charges, but they might as well have been chasing shadows; the Indians slipped away with hoots of derision, and when the soldiers returned to their lines the Indians renewed their fire. Those regulars who fell in the bayonet charges were scalped in sight of their comrades.

The fight continued for four hours with the Americans getting the worst of it. The officers in their bright uniforms were the special targets of the Indians, as British officers had so often been of American marksmen. Five officers were killed and scalped, and five more were severely wounded. St. Clair decided to make a desperate effort to break through to the trail over which he and his men had traveled. Another bayonet charge drove the Indians back long enough for the panic-stricken militia to gain the path. They threw away their guns and packs, stripped off their heavy boots, and fled for their lives. The regulars followed in hardly better order, leaving wagons, artillery, horses, tents, and supplies behind and abandoning the wounded to the scalping knife and torture by fire. Some six hundred regulars and perhaps half as many militia made their way to Fort Jefferson, a distance of twenty-nine miles that had just taken them ten days to traverse. Spurred on by terror, they returned in less than ten hours.

As was almost invariably the case, the triumphant Indians, filling the woods with their wild cries, fell on the plunder, fighting and squabbling among themselves as to the apportionment of the loot. Distracted by the spoils of war, they failed to pursue St. Clair's shattered force. Although Little Turtle, a Miami chieftain famous for his skill in battle and wisdom in council, was in command (it had been Little Turtle who had been most instrumental in the defeat of Harmar's expedition a year earlier) and apparently responsible for the tenacity with which the Indians fought, he could not control his warriors after the Americans had fled. They entered enthusiastically into the post-battle ritual of torture. Wounded soldiers had their arms and legs torn off. Others were disemboweled or castrated. Women who had accompanied the army and were abandoned in the rout had stakes driven through their bodies.

At the beginning of the battle the American force had outnumbered the Indians, who, it has been estimated, brought less than a thousand warriors to the fray. The brilliant victory of Little Turtle and his braves sent shock waves along the entire frontier. Had the Indians had the capacity for concerted and coordinated action, they might have followed up their success with forays that would have devastated the frontier settlements as far east as Pittsburgh and killed or driven out most of the white settlers in the Northwest Territory. But such a massive rollback of white settlement would, at best, have offered the Indians only a temporary respite. Indian councils were seriously divided. While many of Little Turtle's braves wished to wage a war of extermination against the frontier settlements, the chieftain felt that persistent warlike acts on their part would lead to their own extermination. He therefore counseled negotiations for peace.

When word was brought to Washington of St. Clair's defeat by the Miami, he was at the dining table, as he had been when the news arrived of Arnold's betrayal of West Point. At the insistence of the officer who brought the message, Washington's secretary, Tobias Lear, whispered the news to him. Washington's face never changed expression. When the meal was over and the guests had departed, Washington abandoned himself to one of his terrible rages, cursing St. Clair and railing against the cowardice of the soldiers.

The Anti-Federalists showed considerable ingenuity in laying the blame for the debacle on the Federalists. It was, they argued, Federalist speculators, intent on robbing the Indians of their lands to fatten their own purses, who had promoted settlement in the Northwest and thereby provoked the Indians into defending their homes. Now they would reap a political dividend by calling for a large and expensive army to put down the Indians and save the settlers. To supply the army they would impose more ruinous taxes and then doubtless employ the army to collect them. Finally, the army would be used to suppress all honest Republicans.

General St. Clair bore the brunt of popular displeasure, and as he made his way eastward to give an accounting to his commander in chief, people lined the streets of the towns through which he passed to jeer and hoot at him.

The defeat of St. Clair could not go unavenged. It fell to General Anthony Wayne to repair the damage. Wayne, a meticulous planner and organizer, had completed the recruitment of his force by late autumn of 1793. He then marched his men, under the strictest discipline, into Indian Territory and went into winter camp at Greenville. There he engaged his men in rigorous training exercises and toughened them by sending them on scouting forays through the surrounding forests. He built Fort Recovery on the site, garrisoned it, and, as soon as the snows of winter had melted, pushed on to the Maumee Rover where it met the Au Glaize, and constructed Fort Defiance. At St. Mary's River his soldiers erected Fort Adams. It was August before Wayne had penetrated, with some three thousand men, to the heart of the Indian country near the British post of Fort Miami on the Maumee. There he sent scouts under a flag of parley to offer to negotiate with the Indians. Encouraged by their victory over St. Clair and by the support of the British who provided them with arms and ammunition, the Indian spokesmen asked for ten days to consider Wayne's proposal. "If you advance," they declared, "we will give you battle." Wayne, convinced that the tribes were determined to fight and simply wanted the ten days to augment their forces, refused and ordered his troops to move forward in battle order.

The area where the Indians had chosen to make their stand had suffered from the effects of a hurricane. Thousands of trees had been blown down—fallen timbers—and formed an almost impenetrable tangle, ideally suited for the Indian style of fighting. It was into this natural defensive position that Wayne's tough, disciplined soldiers forced their way. Wayne had deployed them in two extended skirmish lines, the first to advance and engage the Indians behind stumps and fallen trees, the second to remain in reserve and attack through the forward line as the battle developed. The second line was never committed. Faced with the skillful and determined attack of the first line, the Indians broke and fled after less than an hour's engagement, leaving the field to Wayne. The Battle of Fallen Timbers demonstrated dramatically the weakness of Indians in any extended military campaign against the whites. Usually fighting individually, without any overall plan or battle leadership, they could seldom sustain a protracted engagement, especially if the tide of battle appeared to be going against them. Under such circumstances, they could not effect that most difficult of military maneuvers, a retreat. They were brave and agile and demonstrated remarkable stamina, but they lacked any order or cohesiveness.

Little Turtle, who had led the Indians in the attack on St. Clair, was present at Fallen Timbers and understood quite well the respective strengths and weaknesses of the two opposing forces.

He knew Indians had little chance against white soldiers properly led. In defense, or in warfare of position or maneuver, the Indians were almost invariably routed. From the news that Indian scouts brought of Wayne's painstaking preparations, Little Turtle concluded that the Indian cause was doomed. He had urged his fellows to negotiate the best terms they could with the "General-Who-Never-Sleeps." The appellation was the greatest compliment he could have paid to Wayne. With characteristic Indian economy of language he had epitomized the general's most essential quality and anticipated the outcome of the battle.

After the Indians were routed, Wayne destroyed their villages, cut down their crops in the fields, and carried off or destroyed their corn, the precious staple of the Indian diet, leaving them largely dependent on the charity of the British. What was most demoralizing to the impressionable Indians was that Wayne carried out his "scorched-earth" policy almost within sight of the British fort to which the Indians looked for protection. The message was unmistakable: "Your avowed friends, the English, are the agents of your misfortune. They have equipped you with arms and encouraged you to resist the advance of our settlers into your country, but now you see they are quite powerless to protect you from the consequences of your mistaken deeds."

Wayne now moved unimpeded up the Maumee to the juncture of the St. Mary's and St. Joseph's, where he built a stout fortification he named Fort Wayne. The army then returned to Greenville and went once more into winter quarters.

The next summer the warriors and chiefs of tribes of the Northwest began to collect at Greenville to negotiate with the U.S. commissioners. For weeks they came in, a few dozen or a few hundred at a time—Kickapoo, Miami, Chippewa, Ottawa, Potawatomi, Wyandot, and Shawnee. They had, collectively, a vast amount of experience with the white man. They had roamed over a wide extent of territory, the Kickapoo being undoubtedly the most peripatetic, moving from the Tennessee River in the South through the present states of Wisconsin, Illinois, Indiana, Ohio, Pennsylvania, and New York. They would go as far again before they were assigned a "home." The same was true in varying degrees of the other tribes. Their great chiefs were present, including Little Turtle and an as yet unknown young Shawnee warrior, Tecumseh, who had fought well at Fallen Timbers, and other warriors who had led their braves in notable victories over the whites.

While they waited for the treaty negotiations to begin, the Indians entertained themselves with games and feasts. Yet the occasion had about it an inescapable atmosphere of gloom. The tribes were aware that their efforts to check the encroachment of whites had failed. They were meeting to acknowledge and seal that failure. They could not know what was ahead for them, but they were keenly aware that their life was no longer to be what it had been.

At the end of several weeks of negotiations, marked by the well-established formalities that characterized treaty meetings, an agreement was reached by which the Indians surrendered their claim to some twenty-five thousand square miles of territory, an enormous expanse of land. In return they received twenty thousand dollars in presents and were promised an allowance of ten thousand dollars a year to be distributed among the tribes who accepted the treaty, a kind of annual prize for good behavior.

At the end of the council, General Wayne addressed the Indians:

> Brothers, I now fervently pray to the Great Spirit that the peace
> now established may be permanent, and that it will hold us
> together in the bonds of friendship until time shall be no more.
> I also pray that the Great Spirit above may enlighten your minds,
> and open your eyes to your true happiness, that your children
> may learn to cultivate the earth and enjoy the fruits of peace
> and industry.

The tide of westering emigrants, whose pressure had precipitated the "Indian troubles" resolved by Fallen Timbers and the Treaty of Greenville and whose progress west had been only slightly interrupted by the "war," now resumed their irresistible movement, for the most part following the rivers flowing toward the Mississippi.

CHAPTER VII

THE
WESTERING
IMPULSE

While Congress undertook the arduous task of establishing a Republican government, events of some moment took place on the vast and poorly defined frontier. The Treaty of Paris (1783) that concluded the Revolution had provided for compensation to the Loyalists for confiscated property and, among other things, the British abandonment of the posts they had held in the Old Northwest. In defiance of the treaty, the British had held on to the posts, giving as their excuse the fact that the American states had refused to honor their treaty obligations in regard to the Loyalists. As we have seen, British retention of the posts had encouraged the Indian tribes in the region to persist in their raids against the frontier settlers, leading to the successive expeditions of St. Clair and Wayne.

The move westward was to be, in some ways, the major theme of American history. Pamphleteers, theorists, and politicians spoke confidently of occupying the continent, although they assumed that would occur in the distant future. Centuries must pass, they assumed, before this vast land, thinly populated by aborigines, would be covered with farms, towns, and great cities. The notion that it might happen in a few generations, even decades, seems to have occurred to no one but a few half-mad visionaries.

In fact, the persistent and relentless pressure of westward migration was one of the most remarkable phenomena in history. It was already very much in evidence before the Revolution. It continued during the Revolution, most notably in the South and in the Watauga settlements, and did so in the face of devastating Indian raids. After the war it increased very substantially in volume, doubtless encouraged by the illusion that the Indians had been intimidated by the defeat of their British supporters.

There was about the westward movement a quality of the instinct that put the thoughtful observer in mind of the migration of lemmings into the sea. It involved legendary hardships and dangers, and mortality rates that would turn an actuary pale. It was the most striking manifestation of the new man that Hector St. John de Crèvecoeur had speculated about in his *Letters from an American Farmer.* The "American experience," that odd mixture of Calvinist dogma and frontier living, had created a human type that the Revolution confirmed or "set," an individual to whom it seemed as natural as breathing to start a new community, carrying with him—"internalized," as we say today—all the values and institutions needed to set up stable communities in the wilderness.

From the beginning, the movement had its fascinated observers, amateur sociologists, and anthropologists who studied it, described it, and pondered its significance. They perceived it as having successive stages. Benjamin Rush wrote to an English doctor friend giving a detailed analysis of "the manner of settling a new country," based on his own observations.

> The *first* settler in the woods is generally a man who has outlived his credit or fortune in the cultivated parts of the state. His time for migrating is in the month of April. His first object is to build a small cabin of rough logs for himself and family. The floor of his cabin is of earth, the roof of split logs; the light is received

through the door and, in some instances, through a small window made of greased paper. A coarser building adjoining this cabin affords a shelter to a cow and a pair of poor horses. The labor of erecting these buildings is succeeded by killing the trees on a few acres of ground near his cabin; this is done by cutting a circle around the trees two or three feet from the ground.

Corn is then planted and the lone settler lives during the summer on fish and wild game—squirrels, rabbits, partridge, and turkeys. His animals feed in the woods, and

for the first year he endures a great deal of distress from hunger, cold and a variety of accidental causes, but he seldom complains or sinks under them. As he lives in the neighborhood of Indians, he soon acquires a strong tincture of their manners. His exertions, while they continue, are violent, but they are succeeded by long intervals of rest. His pleasures consist chiefly of fishing and hunting. He loves spirituous liquors, and he eats, drinks, and sleeps in dirt and rags in his little cabin.

Such a settler remains two or three years on the crude farm he has hacked out of the wilderness. Then, "in proportion as population increases around him, he becomes uneasy and dissatisfied. Formerly his cattle ranged at large, but now his neighbors call on him to confine them within fences to prevent their trespassing upon their fields of grain." The arrival of other settlers drives off the game. "Above all, he revolts against the operation of laws. He cannot surrender up a single natural right for all the benefits of government, and therefore, he abandons his little settlement, and seeks a retreat in the woods, where he again submits to all the toils which have been mentioned."

Sometimes the original tenant simply abandoned his crude farm and moved westward. More often he sold it with its "small improvements . . . to a *second* species of settler." This was "Generally a man of some property." He would pay down a third or fourth of the cost of three or four hundred acres of land, twenty-five or fifty dollars, and the rest in installments. His first object would be to enlarge the cabin and make it more comfortable, and he would typically do this with planks instead of logs, "as sawmills generally follow settlements." His roof would be clapboards—coarse shingles split out of short oak logs. He would have "a board floor as well, a second floor or sleeping loft and a cellar, an orchard of fruit trees, and, in a year or so, a stout log barn." The trees his predecessor killed and left standing, he would cut down and burn or root out the stumps. He would diversify his crops, adding rye to wheat. He would distill the rye into whiskey, which would be his cash crop. Although he would be more stable and industrious than the first settler, "his house as well as his farm bears many marks of a weak tone of mind." While he has windows in his house, they are

> unglazed, or, if they have had glass in them, the ruins of it are supplied by old hats or pillows. He has little use for the institutions of civilized life, schools or churches, and he is equally indisposed to support civil government; with high ideas of liberty, he refuses to bear his proportion of the debt contracted by its establishment in our country. He delights, chiefly, in company— sometimes drinks spirituous liquors to excess—will spend a day or two in attending political meetings; and thus he contracts debts which (if he cannot discharge in depreciated currency) compel him to sell his plantation . . . to the *third* and last species of settler.

This last type is clearly Rush's ideal: he is a substantial man of "good character" not addicted to "spirituous liquors." A neat, tidy man with a strong sense of social responsibility, a churchgoer and school supporter, pious, hardworking, ingenious in building up his farm. He ditches water from a stream or river, builds a solid stone barn "100 feet in front and 40 in depth." He has sturdy fences, a house garden for vegetables. He improves his stock by careful breeding. He builds a smokehouse. His wife weaves, tends the garden, and milks the cows. His sons work with him in the fields. He builds a house large, convenient, and filled with useful and substantial furniture. "We do not," Rush wrote, "pretend to offer immigrants the pleasures of Arcadia. It is enough if affluence, independence, and happiness are ensured to patience, industry, and labor." The cheapness of land, Rush added, "render[s] the blessings which I have described objects within the reach of every man."

Having described the process, Rush could not forbear from adding some reflections upon it.

> This passion for migration . . . will appear strange to a European. To see men turn their backs upon the houses in which they drew their first breath—upon the churches in which they were dedicated to God . . . upon the friends and companions of their youth—and upon all the pleasures of cultivated society . . . must strike a philosopher on your side of the water as a picture of human nature that runs counter to the usual habits and principles of action in man. But this passion, strange and new as it appears, is wisely calculated for the extension of population in America.

Timothy Dwight, former president of Yale College, took a tour through New England almost a generation later and described the stages of settlement in words that echoed Rush's. He, too, was moved and awed by the westward migration. He saw it as "a novelty in the history of man," of the implications of which his countrymen were only dimly aware. "The colonization of a wilderness by civilized men, where a regular government, mild manners, arts, learning, science, and Christianity have been interwoven from the beginning, is a state of things of which the eastern continent and the records of past ages furnish neither an example, nor a resemblance."

Like Rush, Dwight described this new class of

> the more restless, idle, roving inhabitants, who, as the state of society in these countries [Western territories] advance[s] toward order and stability, will leave them for the same reasons which induced them to quit the places of their nativity. Such men cannot

continue in any regular society, but quit it, of course, for places where they may indulge their own idle and licentious dispositions. Like a company of pioneers, they always go forward in the front of regular settlers and seem to be of no other use than to remove the difficulties which might discourage the attempts of better and more quiet men. Accordingly, they have constantly preceded the real, substantial farmers in every course of emigration and will probably precede them until the New England colonization shall be stopped by the Pacific Ocean.

These would be the plainsmen, the hunters and trappers and guides of the midcontinent and the mountain men of the Rockies, a classic American breed whom we shall encounter throughout every stage of this history.

In truth, both their detractors—men like Gouverneur Morris who believed that "the Busy haunts of men and not the remote wilderness, was the proper school of political talents"—and their defenders, Madison, James Wilson, and George Mason among them, had only the vaguest notion of the character, needs, or motives of the men and women who pushed westward like an irresistible tide. They and the land they inhabited had the dimmest reality to the vast majority of those who guided the affairs of the new Republic. A few of the more enterprising had traveled to the western boundaries of their own states, but that was their farthest range.

The handful of Easterners who traveled to the frontier found that life there had a very different character from that in the seacoast states. Young William Preston, a South Carolinian whose father sent him off on a three-thousand-mile tour of the frontier, noted that in nearby Kentucky even aristocratic families that had migrated from Virginia "had lost a portion of Virginia caste and assumed something of Kentucky esteem, an absence of reticence and a presence of presumptuousness." (It is perhaps worth noting that in London, Washington Irving, a New Yorker with whom Preston became close friends, chided the young South Carolinian for being too informal and open.) Preston wrote:

Amongst persons my own age . . . there was a self-dependence not to say self-assertion, and ostentatious suppression of the smaller courtesies of life and minute observance of convention, which was not pleasant. When emigration to a new country takes place even in masses, civilization is not transported or preserved. New physical circumstances induce new developments, and a fermentation of a society must take place. An old state of society cannot be propagated in a new country. A certain loss of civilization is inevitable. Stranger and hardier qualities may be super-induced, but they supplant the gentler and more refined.

Talleyrand, a French refugee visiting a colony of his countrymen in Ohio Territory, took a dim view of the frontiersman. He wrote:

He is interested in nothing. Every sentimental idea is banished from him. Those branches so elegantly thrown by nature—a fine foliage, a brilliant hue which marks one part of the forest, a deeper green which darkens another—all these are nothing in his eye. He has no recollections associated with anything around him. His only thought is the number of strokes which are necessary to level this or that tree. He has never planted [a tree]; he is a stranger to the pleasure of that process. Were he to plant a tree, it never would become an object of gratification to him, because he could not live to cut it down. He lives only to destroy. He is surrounded by destruction. He does not watch the destiny of what he produces. He does not love the field where he has expended his labor, because his labor is merely fatigue, and has no pleasurable sentiment attached to it.

Henry Tuckerman, an indefatigable traveler, wrote of the frontier as an area completely lacking "that vital and vivid connection between the past and present," having instead "the painful sense of newness; the savage triumph, as it were, of nature, however beautiful, over humanity."

Among the most vivid accounts we have of frontier life is that of the Reverend Doctor Joseph Doddridge, whose family had moved from Maryland to the western border of Pennsylvania when he was four years old. Doddridge, an Episcopal minister who had studied medicine under Benjamin Rush, entitled his account, modestly enough, *Notes on the Settlement and Indian Wars of the Western Parts of Virginia and Pennsylvania, from 1763 to 1783, Inclusive.*

When he composed his recollections in the early 1820s he was in his fifties, but it seemed to him that he must have lived at least a hundred years to have witnessed the remarkable changes recorded in his *Notes*. Like many other pioneers, he felt that the "rising generation" had already forgotten the hardships and sacrifices of their fathers and grandfathers and that it was his task to revive those memories. Doddridge wrote: "The task of making new establishments in a remote wilderness in a time of profound peace is sufficiently difficult; but when, in addition to all the unavoidable hardships attendant on this business, those resulting from an extensive and furious warfare with savages are superadded, toil, privations and suffering are then carried to the full extent of the capacity of men to endure them."

After Doddridge's father brought his family over the mountains to the western borders of Pennsylvania, their supply of the Indian meal from which corn bread was made was used up six weeks before their crop of corn was ready to be harvested. Wild turkey and bear meat had to take its place, but they were poor substitutes and the children were "tormented with a sense of hunger." Doddridge remembered how eagerly he and his brothers and sisters "watched the growth of the potato tops, pumpkin and squash vines, hoping from day to day to get something to answer in place of bread. How delicious was the taste of young potatoes when we got them. What a jubilee when we were permitted to pull the young corn for roasting ears. . . . We then became wealthy, vigorous and contented with our situation, poor as it was."

Doddridge enumerated the "indigenous fruits" of the Pennsylvania and Ohio frontier that were such an important part of the food supply of the earliest settlers. The first fruit in the spring was the wild strawberry. The "service trees" were next. They filled the woods with their delicate blooms in April, and the berries were ripe in June, sweet, "with a very slight mixture of acidity." On Sundays, with the men well-armed against marauding Indians, the settlers collected the berries, sometimes chopping down the trees to get them, since ladders were too awkward to carry. Blackberries grew abundantly where there were wind-felled trees. The children gathered these in the fall, again accompanied by armed and watchful adults. Wild raspberries and gooseberries were less plentiful but a welcome treat when they were found. Wild plums were excellent and numerous in bottomlands along streams. In the fall wild grapes made delicious wine. Black, red, and sugar haws grew on large bushes along watercourses. Their big berries were a special favorite of the children. Wild cherries were also abundant, along with small sour crab apples that made delicious jelly. Pawpaws were to be found along the banks of most streams. Thick-shelled hickory nuts, with their sweet meat well protected, were scattered through the forests, along with white and black walnuts, hazelnuts, and chestnuts.

Most frontiersmen dressed in a kind of modified Indian garb. The hunting shirt was universal, a "kind of loose frock" usually made of linsey (a coarse linen), "reaching halfway down the thighs, with large sleeves, open before and so wide as to lap over a foot or more when belted." A jacket or poncho-like cape covered the shirt and was sometimes fringed or embroidered with colored thread. The bosom of the belted shirt served as a pouch "to hold a chunk of bread, cakes, jerk [dried beef], tow for wiping the barrel of the rifle." The belt was tied behind and hung with further necessaries; mittens, a bullet bag, a tomahawk, and a scalping knife in a leather sheath. Breeches or leggings covered the legs. Sometimes they ran only to the upper thighs, just above the bottom of the shirt or frock, and many of the younger men affected the Indian breechclout, a width of cloth run through the front and back of the belt and around the loins.

The shoes were moccasins that reached up to, and were tied around, the ankles. In cold weather they were stuffed with deer's hair or dry leaves to keep the feet warm, but the leather was so per-meable by water that the common remark when the ground was wet was that moccasins were simply "a decent way of going bare footed." As a consequence of traveling much of the time in wet moccasins, the commonest complaint of frontiersmen was rheumatism. The women dressed in linsey petticoats and bed gowns, went barefoot in dry weather, and in winter they wore moccasins or shoepacks, shapeless creations of cloth and leather. Cabins were without closets or wardrobes, and the clothes of the occupants hung on pegs along the walls.

Domestic utensils were simple and few. Bowls, cups and plates and spoons were usually made of wood. Sometimes gourds and hard-shell squashes served. Iron pots, knives, and forks were among the few precious possessions that could be carried on a packhorse or ox over the mountains. Salt and sugar were scarce and expensive. A bushel of salt was worth a good cow and a calf. Fractions of a bushel were commonly measured by the handful. Sugar could be made from the sap of maple trees in the early spring, but salt had to be bought from a trader. "Hog and hominy," or various portions of the pig and bleached corn, were culinary staples, along with johnnycake (cornmeal and milk, baked in the ashes of the fire) and corn pone. Supper was commonly milk and corn mush, supplemented when possible with venison, squirrel, or bear. Indian corn was the essen-tial ingredient in all frontier diets—ground, leavened, bleached, in a half-dozen forms and combinations. Doddridge was eight years old before he tasted a cup of tea or coffee; and it was a wonder to him to have it in a porcelain cup with a saucer.

In the economy of the family there was a crude division of labor—a skilled mason might work in exchange for woven cloth—but most families did their own weaving; tanned their own leather; and made their own moccasins, belts, and so forth. Doddridge's father built a loom and wove cloth on it for the family's garments and made the thread for the moccasins and shoepacks. Of necessity, the men of the family were blacksmiths, carpenters, tanners, coopers, masons, and inventors.

Most families lived within hailing or running distance of a crude fort, to which they could repair, if lucky, at the first sign of an Indian raid. When any sign of hostile Indians was noted, the swiftest young men were sent from cabin to cabin in the dark to summon the families to the fort. As Doddridge recalled such a scene from his childhood, the messenger

> came softly to the door, or back window, and by a gentle tapping
> waked the family. . . . The whole family were instantly in motion.
> My father seized his gun and other implements of war. My step-
> mother waked up and dressed the children as well as she could. . . .
> Besides the little children, we caught up what articles of cloth-
> ing and provisions we could get hold of in the dark, for we durst
> not light a candle or even stir the fire. All this was done with
> the utmost dispatch and the silence of death. To the rest it was
> enough to say *Indian* and not a whimper was heard afterwards.

Collected in the fort, the settlers next had to decide how long to wait there. The Indians would seldom attack such a fort, but after filling the adjacent woods with howls of fury and frustration would depart—or at least pretend to. Often they would burn the abandoned cabins and destroy what crops they could. There were times when some of the more foolhardy families, concerned about their gardens, possessions, and domestic animals, would return to their cabins before it was certain that the coast was clear (a situation usually determined by scouting parties). These posed a hazard to everyone, because if they were trapped by Indians still lurking in the vicinity a general effort must be made to save them and a number of lives thereby imperiled.

As Doddridge put it:

> The early settlers on the frontiers of this country were like the
> Arabs of the deserts of Africa, in at least two respects: every man
> was a soldier, and from early in the spring, till late in the fall,
> was almost continually in arms. Their work was often carried on

by parties, each one of whom had his rifle and everything else belonging to his war dress. They were deposited in some central place in the field. A sentinel was stationed on the outside of the fence, so that on the least alarm the whole company repaired to their arms, and were ready for combat in a moment.

In addition to the Indians, there were a thousand natural hazards. A falling tree might smash a rail fence and horses and cattle would then get into a field and destroy a crop. Raccoons would kill the chickens. An early frost might burn the corn, a flood destroy, or a drought parch it. Bugs and rodents, birds, deer, squirrels, and every creature that crawled or flew competed with the farmer for his meager crops.

Disease, accident, and illness were the constant companions of the settlers. Without doctors, everyone must be his or her own physician, so there were numerous practical treatments, many of them traditional folk remedies, and others borrowed from the Indians. A burn or a cut could easily become infected in an environment never characterized by cleanliness and often by squalor. For burns a poultice of the inevitable Indian meal was often applied, or roasted turnips. Many children died of croup, whose cure was taken to be the juice of roasted onions. Sweating was the remedy for fevers, and there were numerous antidotes for rattlesnake and copperhead bites. Those who suffered from rheumatism used the oil of rattlesnakes, wolves, geese, bears, and skunks and warmed their aching joints in front of the fire. Coughs, consumption, pleurisy, hepatitis, and diarrhea were common and often fatal. Doddridge's mother died in her thirties from an abrasion made by a horse stepping on her foot; a poultice was applied but the wound became infected. His father died at forty-six from hepatitis.

If we except drinking, dancing was the principal diversion on the frontier. Every settlement had a fiddler or two, and no opportunity was missed to hold a dance. Singing was another entertainment. Doddridge recalled that many songs were about Robin Hood, and most of the others were "tragical . . . love songs about murder."

Young men hunted, shot at targets, and held contests with bows and arrows and tomahawks. But weddings were the greatest occasions for festivities, which usually lasted for days.

Without the normal apparatus of crime enforcements—courts, lawyers, judges, and jails—the people of the frontier "were a law unto themselves." The qualities most valued were "industry in working and hunting, bravery in war, candor, honesty, hospitality and steadiness of deportment. . . . The punishment for idleness, dishonesty, and ill fame generally, was that of 'hating the offender,'" a kind of ostracism that in small communities usually had the effect of reforming the culprit or driving him or her away. The person who did not do a proper share of the common work at house-raisings, log-rollings, and "harvest parties" was described as a "Lawrence," and when the idler needed help it was refused. A special anathema was pronounced against the man who shirked his duties in defending the settlement. He was "hated out as a coward."

So community sanctions and pressures took the place of the law, and took it, on the whole, very effectively, if often cruelly. Punishment for conventional crimes as opposed to social dereliction were harsh in the extreme, brutal whippings being the most common form. The theft of "some small article" was punished by thirteen stripes on the back (for the thirteen stripes on the flag of the United States) and then exile. A "convict-servant," that is, someone who had been sentenced to a period of servitude for a prior offense, or a slave in those frontier regions where slavery was permitted, was subjected to whippings so severe that he was often days recovering. Some were whipped each day for a series of days. Doddridge saw more than one man whipped so brutally that "in a little time the whole of his shoulders had the appearance of a mass of blood, streams of which soon began to flow down his back and sides. . . His trousers were then unbuttoned and suffered to fall down about his feet, two new hickories were selected from the bundle, and so applied that in a short time his posteriors, like his shoulders, exhibited nothing but lacerations and blood."

Doddridge was sent by his father to lodge with a relative in Baltimore so that he might have an education, but he returned gratefully to the frontier when his stint was up, revolted by what he had seen of slavery. "From this afflicting state of society," he wrote, "I returned to the backwoods, a republican, without knowing the meaning of the term, that is an utter detestation of an arbitrary power of one man over another."

The frontier to Doddridge was preeminently the region where the true meaning of freedom and independence was understood.

> The patriot of the western region finds his love of country and national pride augmented to the highest grade when he compares the political, moral and religious character of his people, with that of inhabitants of many large divisions of the old world. . . . [In the United States] instead of a blind or superstitious imitation of the manners and customs of our forefathers, we have thought and acted for ourselves, and we have changed ourselves and everything around us.

As critical as he was of luxury and the accumulation of material things, Doddridge was quick to acknowledge that "the early introduction of commerce was among the first means of changing, in some degree, the exterior aspect of the population of the country, and giving a new current to public feeling and individual pursuit." Without the remarkable growth of commerce, Doddridge declared, "our progress towards science and civilization would have been much slower."

Doddridge, like Rush and Dwight, depicted the frontiersman as someone who wanted "*elbow room*," and therefore as soon as he felt himself crowded,

> fled to the forest of frontier settlements, choosing rather to encounter the toil of turning the wilderness into fruitful fields, a second time, and even risk an Indian war, rather than endure the inconveniences of a crowded settlement. Kentucky first offered a resting place for these pioneers, then Indiana and now the Missouri and it cannot be long before the Pacific Ocean will put a final stop to the westward march of those lovers of the wilderness.

It is clear that Doddridge's own feelings about the frontier were mixed ones. While he hailed the progress of "science and civilization," he regretted the disappearance of the solidarity and sharing of hardship that characterized the frontier he had known, and he understood very well that life on the frontier was often "nasty, brutish and short." Trying to sum up his feelings, he wrote, "The truth is, the western country is the region of adventure. If we have derived some advantage from the importation of science, arts and wealth, we have on the other hand been much annoyed and endangered, as to our moral and political state, by an immense importation of vice, associated with a high grade of science and the most consummate art, in the pursuit of wealth by every description of unlawful means." It was only a strict adherence to the law, in Doddridge's opinion, that had saved "our infant country . . . from destruction by the pestilential influence of so great an amount of moral depravity." Here is the agonizing question once more: how to use "greed," or the commercial spirit, for the useful progress of society without suffering from the "moral depravity" that wealth and luxury bring with them. All the ambivalence and ambiguity was there. The central schizophrenia: the hope for, and fear of, progress; the faith that law could control the unjust, the exploiter; the dream of innocence and the desire to be thought "civilized" by the world. We could hardly find a passage more expressive of the ambiguity of our consciousness. One way to look at the mystery of frontier settlement is to reflect upon the fact that those men and women who ventured out to the frontier, wherever that frontier was at the moment, deliberately subjected themselves to the physical and psychological hardships that characterized the most depressed peasant societies of Europe. Far from seeking wealth or ease, *they sought hardship*. Did we not know they were there by their own free will we might have thought them exiled to suffering more cruel than Devil's Island or Siberia.

If the towns and cities of the Eastern seacoast represented American "culture," the frontier was the "counterculture." To the rural frontier, Easterners were tenderfoots, or later, dudes or city folk or city "slickers" whose ways and manners seemed excessively refined or effeminate. To the Easterners, the frontier settlers were picturesque and colorful but part of a crude and violent world that was infinitely remote and somewhat of an embarrassment. Frontiersmen's language was rude and rough, their clothes hardly distinguishable from the garb of Indians, their houses, huts and hovels. Easterners were, at best, patronizing toward the frontier, at worst hostile or indifferent. The closest we could come today to the atmosphere of many early-nineteenth-century frontier settlements would be a present-day agricultural commune made up of urban and suburban young men and women, barefoot, wearing tattered and dirty clothes, living in abandoned shacks or crude if colorful habitations of their own construction, proudly reproducing the conditions of hardship, dirt, and discomfort that characterized our original frontier counterculture.

If it had not been for Easterners' speculations in Western lands and their desire to find settlers for them, it is doubtful that the West would ever have been granted political parity with the East. So it might be said that the history of the country took place on two levels. One was the level of conscious political actions; of negotiations with foreign countries, of commercial regulations, laws, and statutes designed to effect particular purposes. The other was simply what ordinary people did, usually with little attention to what was transpiring in the seats of government—most of all, those people who went west. They not uncommonly felt suspicion and hostility toward the politicians in New York, Philadelphia, and later Washington, D.C., who professed to be acting in their interest. Their attachment to the Republic was often less strong than their attachment to the piece of stony or stumped-cursed land they had carved out of the forest. The most remarkable thing of all about their infatuation with the intractable forest—and something that neither Rush nor Dwight commented on—was that it existed in the face, not simply of hardships that would make a strong man blanch, but of the constant danger to life itself. As Doddridge reminds us, *worse* than disease or crippling accident, hunger, or cold, was the constant presence of the Indians. Any isolated frontier cabin or small settlement lived with the nightmare of an Indian raid hanging over it like the proverbial sword. And death itself was, of course, not the worst that could happen. There was excruciating torture for men captured alive or merely wounded and rape of the women and young girls or living in captivity in an Indian tribe. On occasion whole villages were wiped out, and there was hardly a frontier settler who had not had a relative or friend fall victim to Indians on the warpath. The Indian combination of stealth, ferocity, and shattering sound made him as frightening a figure as could well be conceived. And yet, in the face of that constant and for us today almost inconceivable terror, the settlers pushed inexorably westward onto Indian lands. Meanwhile the federal government did its best to create a buffer between the advancing settlers and the beleaguered Indians by carrying on virtually continuous treaty negotiations to buy Indian lands—or perhaps more accurately, since the Indians had no notion of landownership—to bribe them to move farther west and thus avoid confrontation with the migrating whites.

The alternative to treaty agreements with the Indians was open warfare, in which—however reluctantly—the federal government must support the settlers, fight and drive off the Indians against whose hunting grounds the settlers pressed so relentlessly, and establish forts to keep some kind of order in the frontier territories. The conclusion of a new treaty opening up Indian lands for settlement did not necessarily mean security from Indian raids. There were often dissident factions within tribes that refused to honor the treaty or tribes that claimed hunting rights on lands that had been bargained away by rivals. Moreover, it seemed as though vast new regions had hardly been ceded by tribes of Indians before word came of settlers pressing on into territory into which the Indians had been driven and which they were determined to defend against further white intrusions. And so the process must begin again, interrupted, when friction between settlers and Indians becomes severe, by Indian "wars." The federal government has often been depicted as the oppressor of the Indians. The fact is that it was, with certain notable exceptions, the Indians' best friend, in the sense that it had a vested interest in dealing fairly with the aborigines, restraining white advances into their territories, setting aside adequate "reservations," and generally attempting to impose some degree of order on a situation that was inherently chaotic.

Perhaps the strongest influence on the Indian tribes of the East was trade with whites. The whole story of white–Indian relations from the time of the earliest settlements in New England and Virginia was dominated by trading, and much of what was most negative in its effect on Indian culture was the consequence of the fact that for many tribes their principal contact with white civilization was through a human type hardly representative of the more positive aspects of that culture. Furs were the Indian commodity most desired by whites, and in the fierce competition among both whites and Indians to control the fur trade much blood was shed and the way of life of many tribes radically altered. For one thing, the fur trade disposed tribes to move away from the seacoast to river and forest areas where fur-bearing animals, particularly the beaver, were to be found in abundance. It also engendered warfare between tribes anxious to make good their claims to areas rich in beaver. As beaver were "mined out" of one river watershed, a tribe was forced, or felt itself forced, to seek new hunting grounds. In the words of one historian, "In its most destructive form, the trading activity of the white caused starvation. In its least destructive it reshaped the social organization of the tribes and altered their economic subsistence patterns." Put another way, the white man exploited the Indian desire for the trinkets and artifacts of a more sophisticated culture. The corruption of the Indian began with beads and mirrors, gold-laced jackets, knives, guns, and plumed hats.

More devastating even than European-American artifacts were the diseases the white men brought with them. Anthropologists have estimated that in a ten-year period the Huron and Iroquois confederacies lost over half their numbers to epidemics, particularly smallpox epidemics, to which the Indians were especially vulnerable.

The white–Indian conflict could not have been avoided unless Americans had been content to remain strung along a thin stretch of the Atlantic coast (indeed, strictly speaking, unless the whole of continental North America had been preserved as an Indian reservation). Paradoxically, the westward movement was a demonstration of the vices and virtues of "democracy." American enterprise, sometimes rather confusingly called "free" enterprise (as though there were also non-free enterprise), was nowhere more dramatically revealed than in that movement. The American brand of individualism with its unshakable confidence in its ability to overcome any obstacle, human or natural, was the basic ingredient. To neutral observers, it often appeared as a kind of disease, the congenital madness of a whole people. Rush and Dwight were right; it was without precedent in the long history of the race. Each lonely settler in his remote cabin, and each band of settlers, obviously felt capable of subduing a whole wild continent. The Indians, fierce and terrifying as they might be in their particular materializations, were primarily an impediment to be swept aside. The Indian culture, Indian art and lore, the Indians' close and reciprocal relationship with nature, which in the present age of "loving the land" we so admire, meant nothing to a frontiersman or settler in danger of having his brains bashed out by an artistically decorated tomahawk or his horses driven off by a magnificently accoutered band of young braves.

Frontier attitudes toward the Indian covered a wide range, to be sure. As Rush indicated, the frontiersmen and settlers were most closely associated with Indians and Indian culture. They dressed similarly, adopted Indian tactics and practices, ate Indian food, smoked Indian tobacco, took Indian women for their wives or mistresses. Their lives depended on their achieving a minimum of rapport with the Indians. Initially, they were a handful against thousands. Their successors, the more settled and stable types, by and large feared and hated the Indians. To them the Indians were savages to be rooted up and exterminated. It must be said in their defense that they saw the Indians at their worst, as simple destroyers, wild creatures, hardly human, who set their painstakingly built cabins and barns to the torch, killed their stock, and raped their wives.

HAVING DISCUSSED THE FRONTIER SETTLERS in some detail, it may be appropriate to add further reflections on their Indian adversaries. The most irresolvable conflict in the relationship between the white man and the Indian was that the Indian lived in a world before the Fall—a world of primal innocence before, in Christian terms, man acquired the knowledge of good and evil. There was about everything the Indian did, therefore, this innocence, this "good conscience." When he killed and mutilated his enemies, stole their horses, killed or carried off their women, he had no concept by which such action could be judged bad nor could he be easily made to feel guilt concerning it. His shamans and many of his talismanic animals were "tricksters." What the white man called deceit, the Indians admired as splendid cunning. The Indian tribes lived in a vast and beautiful and terrible Garden of Eden. It was only the white Christian's notion that killing and violence had been absent from the original Garden. Killing and violence were there, but they were not understood to be "sinful," since there was no notion of sin. (I might note, parenthetically, that I use the notion of sin or self-consciousness—consciousness of the nature of good and evil—as much in an anthropological as in a theological sense.) Anthropologists now understand that primitive tribal consciousness is compatible with the Christian notion of a state of innocence before the Fall. The story of Adam and Eve, seen in these terms, is simply a parable about the burden of taking on a new kind of self-consciousness, the abstract knowledge that certain acts were good and others bad. Adam's shame at perceiving himself to be naked is the story of the beginning of the modern consciousness of self as separated from, or as over against, nature. There is an unfathomable poignance about a letter from Narcissa Whitman, the missionary wife of the missionary Marcus Whitman, who wrote to her sister,

"Some among the Indians feel almost to blame us for telling them about eternal realities. One said it was good when they knew nothing but to hunt, eat, drink and sleep; now it is bad." That she herself felt the ambiguity of her mission is evident. She wrote, "Of late my heart yearns over them more than usual. They feel so bad, disappointed, and some of them angry because my husband tells them that none of them are Christians; that they are all of them in the broad road to destruction. . . . They try to persuade him not to talk such bad talk to them, as they say, but talk good talk, or tell some story, or history. . . ."

Self-consciousness, with its attendant shame and guilt, began the process out of which the modern consciousness emerged. Post-primitive consciousness produced abstract thought, science, the great "world religions," and all of the appurtenances of "civilization." But civilized man has never ceased to yearn for his lost tribal innocence when *everything* was done with a good conscience. If "shame" was known and used as a method of social control in the tribe, "guilt" was as yet to be discovered. To argue that whites who wished to see the Indian "redeemed," like the rest of the world, should have understood that to destroy the Indian consciousness was, in effect, to destroy the Indian quite misses the point. To have understood that would have been to ask the great majority of whites to reject their whole notion of civilization and, indeed, of the power of Christianity to re-form the world. A few, it turned out, were willing to do just that. They used an idealized version of Indian culture to denounce the shortcomings of an increasingly alienating urbanized industrial world.

The secular apostles of reason did no better than the evangelical Christians. While the latter wished to force the Indians to eat the fruit of knowledge of good and evil, the rational were equally ruthless in their determination to make Indians "reasonable" members of white society; they had, if anything, less patience than the Christians with the richly imaginative symbolic life of the Indian. To them it was little better than the collection of superstitions by means of which orthodox Christianity enslaved the minds of its adherents.

The Anglo-Indian philosopher Raimundo Panikkar speaks of the nature of the tribal consciousness or, as he calls it, the "Ecstatic moment" in the development of human consciousness when "Man knows Nature. Knows also his God and the Gods. He stumbles and he errs, but he allows himself to be corrected by the things themselves. Man learns above all by obedience, i.e. by listening . . . to the rest of reality which speaks to him." That was, in essence, the state of the consciousness of the American Indians. In the earthly Paradise, "Man's approach is straightforward. He does not desire something 'else' or something 'more' than what is; indeed, there is no room for anything else. . . . When man sees in the apple something 'other' than the apple, he is on the verge of losing his innocence." The universal, cosmic tragedy of man, incorporated by Christians and Jews in the story of Adam's fall, was that lost innocence and, in place of it, what Gerald Heard, the English philosopher, called "wrong appetency," imagining and wanting "something 'else' or something 'more' than what is." The initial corruption of the Indian by the white man was just this introduction of something else and something more—of beads and mirrors, blankets and plumed hats. Innocence was destroyed. The white man was the serpent in the Garden, and his trading junk was the apple. But there was no stopping this process, then or in retrospect; there was no conceivable way of avoiding the corruption of innocence, the terrible Fall into self-consciousness, into guilt, into "feeling bad," as the Cayuse Indians complained Marcus Whitman made them feel and for which they finally killed him, his wife, and child. The tragedy was that what had been for civilized man from the times of ancient Sumer and Egypt a millennia-long process was forced instantly on the American aborigine *from outside*. It was as though all the complex tragedies and remarkable achievement of civilization had to be experienced by the original American instantly.

The sense in which the aborigine saw the apple as an integral part of the whole web of nature on which he depended for the perpetuation of his life can be substantiated a hundred different ways. To the Western mind, one of the most striking ways is to be found in the numerous Indian legends where men and women have intercourse with animals and produce alternately human or animal offspring. The point that must be kept in mind is that charming as such tales may appear to the romantic modern secular imagination, the separation of man—or one might better say, the *escape* of man—from nature was a great emancipation. As enmeshed in nature as he was, the attitude of the American aborigine toward the natural world was light-years away from that of the modern nature lover or conservationist who so idealizes him. The Indian hunter killed a hundred or a thousand buffalo to butcher fifty. The rest were left for the wolves and vultures. He was completely prodigal, a stranger to deferred gratification. His appetites had to be sated instantly. That was, indeed, the clue to his vulnerability to liquor as well as to the lure of trading goods. That was not "good" or "bad" in any way that the Indian could possibly grasp, and thus the white man's world and values seemed to him hopelessly rigid and arbitrary. By the same token, it was inconceivable that the white man should ever accept (except in the most superficial way) the world of the Indian. He could hardly begin to penetrate it. He could observe and describe it, find features in it that were profoundly appealing to him, romanticize and sentimentalize it, but he was as incapable of understanding it, except in glimmering little bits or pieces, as the Indian was of understanding his world.

The final, inescapable reality of the world of the so-called Indian was that there were tribes, almost beyond numbering or recording, roaming the wilderness and, less often, farming the cleared fields of the North American continent, most of them in a constant state of transformation. They spoke over a thousand languages or variations of languages, so that it is small wonder that the white settlers were constantly tempted to believe that they were the remnants of the lost tribes of Israel whose tongues God had "confused" at the Tower of Babel. In the long development of man, transcending tribalism had meant the opening up of vast new kinds of human energy and imagination. It was one of the great liberations that the human spirit has experienced. It postulated "one world," a common human race, an abstract idea that could be imagined only when man was separated from nature and from his primitive tribal consciousness. In the New World, civilized man confronted the tribal consciousness from which he had escaped thousands of years earlier. So the white man's encounter with the Indians was, in essence, an encounter with his own primitive self; and it was, of course, dimly perceived as such.

A special irony of the white–Indian confrontation lay in the fact that the ideal type of the new age—the inner-directed, Reformed Protestant democrat on the frontier—was the classic adversary of the Indian. For every enlightened upper-class Bostonian or New Yorker who loved the Indians as brothers and sought to do good for them, there were nine, or perhaps ninety-nine, frontier settlers for whom the only good Indian was a dead Indian. John Holmes, who grew up in the staunchly abolitionist town of Mastersville, Ohio, where copies of William Lloyd Garrison's *Liberator* were treasured keepsakes, recalled that the Mastersville Literary and Debating Society seriously debated the question: "Should the uncivilized Indians be exterminated." Many less liberal towns would have considered it subversive even to take the negative side of such a topic.

IF MANY DEVOUT AMERICANS IN the early decades of the nineteenth century were convinced that the United States could be redeemed by foreswearing liquor or giving women their rights or freeing the slaves, it is not surprising that large numbers were equally convinced that the path to salvation for the nation, and indeed the world, lay through the country of the heathen. Missions to the Indians went back, of course, to the days of John Eliot. There had never been a time, since the early days of the colonies, when there had not been missionaries laboring to convert the aborigines to the Christian faith. It could not have been otherwise. If the teachings of one branch or another of Christianity were the truth, it was the obligation of every Christian to spread the good news of salvation and eternal life. So God's work was carried on by his indefatigable servants generation after generation, in the face of hardships sufficient to daunt the most saintly. To live among the aboriginal tribes was often dangerous in the extreme, as the deaths of numerous missionaries at the hands of those they tried to convert proved. In addition to the unpredictability of their savage and often reluctant hosts, missionaries usually lived under conditions of extreme austerity, sustained by the uncertain largesse of the mission boards that dispatched them and by their own ingenuity and resourcefulness. If the tribes they lived among were subject to devastating white men's diseases, the missionaries were vulnerable to maladies that their charges were relatively immune to, such as rheumatism, pneumonia, consumption, and malaria.

An English traveler, Captain Frederick Marryat, touring the Indian country, visited a missionary school for girls of the Dakota Sioux. There the children read and wrote English, French, and Sioux. "They are modest and well behaved, as the Indian women generally are. They had prayers every evening. . . . The warriors sat on the floor around the room; the missionary . . . his family in the center; and they all sang remarkably well. This system with these Indians is, in my opinion, very good," Marryat added.

In 1826 among fourteen eastern and southern tribes there were thirty-eight schools, maintained by the American Board of Foreign Missions, the Baptist General Convention, the United Foreign Mission Society, the Western Mission Society, the Methodist Episcopal Church, and the Protestant Episcopal Church. As with all benevolent enterprises carried on by Christians, there was a sharp division of opinion over whether each Protestant denomination should support its own missionary activity or whether all should contribute to a common missionary effort. For the year 1825, the various missionary agencies mentioned here contributed $176,700 out of a total expenditure of $202,070, the rest being contributed by the federal government, usually in compliance with some treaty agreement.

Year after year, labors of the faithful bore fruit, although usually in very modest quantities. The report for 1828 noted,

Among the Cherokee, Chickasaws, Choctaws . . . the preaching
of the Gospel was attended with unusual success. At Brainerd,
six natives were admitted to the church in May. In July, there
were ten more who had hope of their own piety, most of whom
appeared to be truly penitent. . . . On the 15th of November, 29
Choctaws were admitted to the church. . . . It was supposed there
are 3,000 anxious inquirers in the nation. More than 2,000 had
begun to pray.

Missionary work among the Indians continued and indeed
increased with each decade. Missionaries accompanied the Five
Nations on the Indian Removal and settled with them in Oklahoma
Territory. Marcus Whitman, who went to the Cayuse Indians as a
medical missionary with his beautiful blonde wife, Narcissa, turned
his attention particularly to improving the health of the tribe and
teaching its members improved agricultural techniques. The secretary of the American Board of Missions, which supported the
Whitmans' work in Oregon Territory, wrote, "I fear from your
account of what you have to do for the whites and the Indians, in
respect to mills, fields and herds, that you will almost lose sight of
the great spiritual object of your mission, and be too nearly satisfied with seeing the Indians advancing in industry, the arts of civilized life, and the means of comfortable living. Why should they
not grow covetous and selfish, if their thoughts are mostly turned
toward these things . . .?"

The complaint was a common one from the spokesmen of the
missionary boards that provided the money to sustain the work of the
missions. They wanted results in the form of a harvest of Christian
souls. The workers in "the field" were often far more conscious of
what needed to be done to improve the physical condition of their
charges before attention could be given to their souls. Whitman
was, indeed, a remarkable figure. He was quite ready to admit that
he was as much concerned with promoting emigration into the
Oregon country as with converting the aborigines of the region. He
took credit, in fact, for having directly assisted in the emigration of

over a thousand settlers in the territory as well as having explored the most convenient overland route to the area. He excused himself for such worldly preoccupations by stating that without such efforts "Jesuit Papists" would have come to dominate the territory. To a friend who had been seduced by Millerism, Whitman wrote, "Come, then to Oregon, resume your former motto!, which seemed to be onward and upward . . . in principle, action, duty and attainments, and in holiness . . . and then you will be cooperative and happy in Oregon. . . ." The country was a rich and fertile one. "Nor should men of piety and principle leave it all to be taken by worldlings and worldly men." If his brother-in-law came with a party of friends they could take up 640 acres of land "as a bounty," and "by mutual consent, set apart a portion for the maintenance of the gospel and for schools and learning. . . ."

The missionaries certainly did not solve the "Indian problem," which strictly speaking had no solution, but they did contribute far more than is generally realized to the amelioration of the condition of reservation Indians by establishing schools, missions, churches, and medical clinics. In the process they converted a number of Indians to Christianity, a substantial portion of whom passed over into the world of the white man. If this was not an ideal solution to those persons, Indian and white, who were anxious to preserve at least the major elements of tribal culture, it was often a form of worldly salvation for the converted and provided important links between the worlds of the white man and the Indian.

CHAPTER VIII

LEWIS AND CLARK

From his days as minister to France, Thomas Jefferson had dreamed of sending an expedition up the Mississippi to the Missouri, and then west to the "Stony" (Rocky) Mountains, and down some westward-flowing river to the Pacific. He had first tried to enlist John Ledyard, the indefatigable adventurer and explorer, to attempt such a journey from the West Coast eastward, but that venture required the permission of Catherine the Great of Russia, who claimed most of present-day Alaska as far south as California. Catherine gave her assent but then withdrew it and hustled Ledyard back to Poland. An effort in 1792, supported by the American Philosophical Society, had also proved abortive when the French minister denied passage through the Louisiana Territory to Meriwether Lewis and the French naturalist André Michaux.

In 1803, when Congress was debating the renewal of an act governing the establishment and supervision of trading houses dealing with Indian tribes of the Northwest, Jefferson saw another opportunity to further his pet project and persuaded Congress to authorize an expedition to contact other tribes that might become involved in trade. The real purpose—to explore a route to the Pacific—was concealed.

Jefferson's personal secretary, Meriwether Lewis, was afire to go, and Jefferson considered him an ideal leader, "intimate with the Indian character, customs and principles; habituated to the hunting life . . . honest, disinterested, liberal, of sound understanding, and a fidelity to the truth so scrupulous, that whatever he should report would be as certain as if seen by ourselves." Lewis chose his friend, William Clark, to accompany him, and Jefferson had both men commissioned as captains of infantry. They were issued detailed instructions and ample supplies: "Instruments for ascertaining, by celestial observations, the geography of the country through which you will pass, have been already provided. Light articles for barter and presents among the Indians [including handsome silver 'peace medals' designed by John Trumbull for distribution to important Indian chiefs], arms for your attendants, say for ten to twelve men, boats, tents, and other travelling apparatus, with ammunition, medicine, surgical instruments and provisions."

"The object of your mission," Jefferson wrote, "is to explore the Missouri River, and such principal streams of it, as . . . may offer the most direct and practicable water-communication across the continent, for the purposes of commerce." It was to the Indian tribes that Jefferson wished the explorers to give particular attention: "The extent and limits of their possessions; Their relations with other tribes or nations; Their language, traditions, monuments; Their ordinary occupations in agriculture, fishing, hunting, war, arts, and the implements for these; Their food, clothing, and domestic accommodations; The diseases prevalent among them, and the remedies they use; Moral and physical circumstances which distinguish them from the tribes we know; Peculiarities in their laws, customs, and dispositions; And articles of commerce they may need or furnish, and to what extent."

Finally, since every nation had an interest "in extending and strengthening the authority of reason and justice among the people around them, it will be useful to acquire what knowledge you can of the state of morality, religion, and information among them; as it may better enable those who may endeavor to civilize and instruct them, to adapt their measures to the existing notions and practices of those on whom they are to operate."

In their dealings with the Indians they were to "treat them in the most friendly and conciliatory manner . . . allay all jealousies as to the object of your journey; satisfy them of its innocence; make them acquainted with the position, extent, character, peaceable and commercial dispositions of the United States; of our wish to be neighbourly, friendly, and useful to them." The most prominent chiefs should be invited to visit Jefferson in Washington at the expense of the government. By the same token, if any chiefs wished to have their sons "brought up with us, and taught such arts as may be useful to them," the expedition should care for them and bring them back with them. They were also to teach the Indians how to inoculate themselves against smallpox.

Lewis and Clark were also instructed to pay close attention to "the soil and face of the country," to the plants, trees, animals, evidences of volcanic action, minerals, climate. Their observations were to be written on "paper-birch, as less liable to injury from damp than common paper." Lewis and Clark were to be Jefferson's eyes and ears. He was their brain and nervous system. The passing references to commerce are vastly outweighed by the "scientific" instructions, especially in regard to the Indians. It was the Indians who obsessed Jefferson. He was greedy for every detail of their lives, and, typically, he wished to bring to them as rapidly as possible the benefits of civilization, of "science" and "reason" and "justice," not to mention inoculation against smallpox, the most terrible killer of the aborigines. No doubt clouded his mind that all this must be beneficent. The Indians must be as susceptible to progress as the whites. Like Doddridge, and the vast majority of his countrymen, Jefferson simply could not imagine that the Indians might resist the advantages of white civilization, including eventual amalgamation with whites.

The expedition of Lewis and Clark was, of course, no secret to the American people. "Never," Jefferson wrote, "did a similar event excite more joy through the United States. The humblest of its citizens had taken a lively interest in the issue of this journey, and looked forward with impatience to the information it would furnish."

Lewis left Washington on July 5, 1803. At Pittsburgh, he picked up supplies for his journey and selected the soldiers to accompany him. Where the Cumberland joined the Ohio, the group was joined by William Clark. Various delays forced them to spend the winter months in a camp on the eastern bank of the Mississippi not far from St. Louis. On May 14, 1804, after the ice on the Missouri had broken up, they began their ascent of the river.

The group consisted of nine young Kentuckians recruited by Clark, fourteen soldiers from the Pittsburgh military post who had volunteered for the expedition, two Frenchmen—a hunter, the other an interpreter—and York, a slave belonging to Clark. A corporal, six privates, and nine experienced rivermen were also engaged to help get the expedition over the first leg of its journey. A large part of the baggage contained bales of presents for the Indians—handsome silver- and gold-laced coats and plumed hats for principal chiefs plus the usual glasses, beads, paints, and knives valued by all the tribes.

Three boats carried the party and its equipment. The main boat was fifty-five feet long, drawing three feet of water with a forecastle and cabin and locks for twenty-two oars. Two other open boats of six and seven oars completed the little fleet. Two horses were led along the banks of the Missouri "for the purpose of bringing home game, or hunting in case of scarcity."

It was hard going from the first. The party had to fight its way upstream against the current, its way impeded by innumerable sawyers lying just below the surface. The river, swollen by spring freshets, was icy cold, and a chilly May rain frequently soaked the members of the expedition to the skin. Headwinds further slowed their progress to sometimes no more than three or four miles a day.

Forty miles up the river they encountered their first Indians, a band of Kickapoo who traded four deer for two quarts of whiskey.

The home territory of the Kickapoo was the headwaters of the Kaskaskia and Illinois rivers, east of the Mississippi, but they occasionally hunted along the Missouri. The Kickapoo were a minor Algonquian tribe, consisting of no more than a hundred warriors and perhaps five times that number of women, children, and old people. They had joined forces with George Rogers Clark in his attack on Vincennes and after the war fought alongside their traditional allies, the Miami, against the incursions of white settlers into the Ohio country. After Wayne's victory at Fallen Timbers, they had ceded a substantial part of their land in return for a yearly annuity from the government.

Making their way west and increasingly northward, the expedition passed the last white settlement on the Missouri, and the next day two canoes loaded with furs were encountered coming downriver from the region of the Omaha Nation, and a large Pawnee raft from the Platte as well as three others from the Grand Osage Nation; like the Omaha, the Osage were part of the Siouan family apparently located originally in the region of Virginia and the Carolinas and pushed westward by the more numerous and powerful Iroquois. The Osage divided their time between hunting and agriculture, living in semipermanent villages of oven-shaped houses fashioned of saplings and mud. They raised corn, pumpkins, and beans. The nearby village of the Great Osage numbered some five hundred warriors. An additional thousand warriors inhabited two other villages. The warriors were large, handsome men, "said to possess fine military capacities," but because their neighbors had secured rifles from white traders, the Osage found themselves at a marked disadvantage in their encounters with the Dakota.

The Osage myth of creation held that the founder of the nation was a snail who lived a simple life on the banks of the river until a flood swept him away and left him high and dry on the shore where the sun "ripened him into a man." Tired and hungry, he was rescued by the Great Spirit, who gave him a bow and arrow and taught him how to kill and skin deer. Returning to his home as a snail, he found a beaver ready to challenge him for control of the river, but the beaver's daughter prevented bloodshed by offering to marry him and share the river. The Osage had, therefore, always abstained from killing their brother, the beaver, until the high prices offered by white traders for beaver pelts had made them less considerate of their relatives.

Now the travelers were well into Indian country where only fur traders ventured. From here on they were at the mercy of the numerous tribes, many of them warlike, who roamed the Plains and for whom the Missouri and its tributaries served both as rough dividing lines between tribal ranges and as a means of transportation for furs carried to St. Louis. The success of their mission depended on the skill and tact of the two leaders in dealing with the tribes they must encounter and on their own hardihood and perseverance in persisting in the face of increasingly difficult conditions.

Two French traders, their canoes bound together and loaded with the skins of beavers they had trapped at the headwaters of the Kansas River, informed them that the Kansas Nation was hunting buffalo on the Plains. Soon there were frequent signs of Indians, although they were seldom seen. Empty campsites, the hoofprints of Indian ponies, and the impressions of moccasins revealed their proximity. The riverbanks were a constantly changing panorama of open plain and cliffs. The party passed a series of salt licks and crumbling sandy banks and then limestone rocks inlaid with multicolored flints depicting various animals. While the main party took turns laboring at the oars, the hunters fanned out on horseback looking for game—deer and then bear.

As they approached the territory of the Sioux, the party felt considerable uneasiness. The Sioux were one of the dominant tribes of the Plains. They controlled much of the fur trade in the region and had the reputation of being warlike and unpredictable. On June 12, a French trapper named Durion was intercepted on his way to St. Louis with a raft of furs and buffalo tallow. Durion had lived as a trader with the Sioux for twenty years and Lewis persuaded him to travel upriver with them to act as their intermediary and interpreter.

The next day the expedition came to the site of the ancient village of the Missouri Indians, members of the Siouan family, who had been virtually wiped out years before by the Sac and Fox Indians, Algonquian tribes who were traditional enemies of the Sioux. From that point on, the river was full of shifting sandbars that impeded the progress of the boats. Oars and sails did little to help. Ropes were attached to the boats, and they were towed from the banks or from the shallows along the shore.

At the juncture with the Kansas, the Missouri was five hundred yards wide, slow and turbid. Three hundred braves of the Kansas tribe lived in several villages near the river. Like the Missouri, they had been greatly reduced in numbers by the Iowa, who, though they belonged also to the Siouan family, had thrown in their lot with the Algonquian Sac. The Sac and Iowa, armed with rifles, had inflicted heavy casualties on the Kansas villages.

The river Platte was one of the principal reference points for the expedition. When they reached it on July 22 they had come some two hundred arduous miles. Wide and shallow, the Platte was the region of the Oto and the Pawnee. The Pawnee, the principal tribe of the Caddoan family, had originally occupied the region directly east of the Mississippi and south of the Ohio into Louisiana. By the seventeenth century, perhaps under pressure from the Iroquois, they had moved west to the area of present-day Nebraska. A more northerly group came to be known as the Arikara, or Ree, Indians. The Pawnee were the astronomers of the North American Indians. They believed certain stars such as the Morning Star and the Evening Star were gods, and the rituals celebrating them are among the most poetic of all those of the Indian peoples. The Arikara also referred to the stars for the best time to plant and to hold their religious celebrations. They believed corn had come into the world as a maiden, and to them its germination represented the life force. They worshiped a single, remote, all-powerful deity and the Mother Earth. It was to be their boast that they had never fought the white man; they were also hospitable to the remnants of other tribes who sought their protection, among them the Oto and the Missouri.

The Pawnee, split into four small bands, were basically an agricultural people who supplemented their supplies of corn by hunting buffalo. In recent years the Osage, pushed westward by the Sac, had substantially reduced their numbers by constant warfare.

On July 31 scouts encountered and brought back to the river fourteen Oto and Missouri Indians—six of them chiefs—accompanied by a French trader who acted as interpreter. This was the first formal contact with Indians of the interior country, and Clark and Lewis rode out to meet them and give them presents of roasted meat, pork, and flour and meal. In return the Indians sent them watermelons.

Next morning a canopy made of a sail was raised for the visiting Indians to assemble under, and the members of the expedition formed up and paraded for their guests. Meriwether Lewis then addressed them, telling them that the territory was no longer under the jurisdiction of France but had been bought by the United States. The six chiefs replied in turn, expressing "their joy at the change in government; their hopes that we would recommend them to their great father (the president), that they might obtain trade and necessaries." They wished, above all, for arms and ammunition, since they were at war with the Omaha. As the "grand chief" was not present, a flag, a peace medal, and some silver ornaments were sent to him. The lesser chiefs received smaller medals, along with paint, garters, a canister of powder, and a bottle of whiskey, "which appeared to make them perfectly satisfied."

The absent grand chief had the impressive name of Weahrushhah which, as Clark noted, when translated into English, "degenerates into Little Thief." The spot was named Council Bluffs by the two leaders. They considered it an ideal place for "a fort and a trading factory," being a day's ride to the Oto, one and a half to "the great Pawnees," two days from the Omaha, two and a half from the Wolfe Pawnee, and not far from the hunting grounds of the Sioux.

Something must be said here about the Indian and the horse. Until the Spanish conquest of Mexico and the explorations of Ponce de Léon in Florida, no American Indian had ever seen a horse. In less than two hundred years, the ancient cultures of the Plains Indians had adapted to the horse in spectacular fashion. The horse was now the center of their tribal life. A warrior's or chief's standing with his fellows rested in large part on his skill as a horseman and on the number of ponies he owned or, more important, the number he could steal. The stealing of ponies thus became, next to hunting, the principal preoccupation of many tribes. Cunning, stealth, daring, and hardihood, the most admired qualities among the Indians, all were required to carry out a successful raid. The stealing of ponies had the advantage of being less hazardous than outright warfare while at the same time increasing the wealth and prestige of the successful raiders. Of course if the raiders were discovered by those they robbed from, they would be killed and scalped; in any event, as soon as their depredations were discovered, they were sure to be relentlessly pursued and if overtaken either killed on the spot or tortured to death.

The main Indian method of killing buffalo, by which, as William Clark said, "vast herds are destroyed in a moment," was to drive the herd off a precipice above the Missouri River. A young brave, disguised under a buffalo skin with the head and horns over his own head, would station himself near the herd. Other hunters on horseback would then raise a cry to start a stampede. The Indian in buffalo garb would then try to decoy the herd toward the cliffs, running ahead of them, passing over the rim, and concealing himself on a ledge below it. As Lewis and Clark noted, among the hundreds of dead and injured buffalo, the Indians "select as much meat as they wish, and the rest is then abandoned to the wolves, and creates a most dreadful stench."

Many of the abandoned villages that Lewis and Clark passed on their laborious progress upriver were reminders of the devastating smallpox epidemics that had wiped out the great majority of their inhabitants. Some once powerful tribes had been virtually destroyed. A deserted Omaha village contained the burned ruins of over three hundred cabins where three years earlier more than four hundred men and the greater part of the women and children in the village had died of the terrible disease. In Clark's words: "They had been a powerful and military people but when these warriors saw their strength wasting before a malady which they could not resist, their frenzy was extreme, they burnt their village, and many of them put to death their wives and children, to save them from so cruel an affliction, and that all might go together to a better country."

As the party approached the country of the Mandan Indians, Clark and Lewis undertook to act as peacemakers between the remnants of the Omaha and the Oto. At the same time, in order to attract "any neighbouring tribes," they set fire to the surrounding prairies. This was "the customary signal made by traders to apprise the Indians of their arrival." Chiefs of the Oto and Omaha came in, and Lewis, through an interpreter, inquired about the reason for their hostility. It began, he was told, when two of the Missouri who had found refuge with the Oto had gone on a horse-stealing raid against the Omaha but had been detected and killed. The Missouri had then felt compelled to avenge the deaths. The assembled chiefs were given the usual gifts by Lewis and Clark and were urged to reconcile their differences without fighting.

In August there were two desertions, and one of the sergeants, Charles Lloyd, died of "bilious colic." It was the first casualty of the trip and temporarily dampened the spirits of the little party.

At the end of the month three of the men, hunting game, had their first contact with a party of Yankton Sioux, who treated them to a fat dog, "of which they partook heartily, and found it well-flavored." The Yankton Sioux were part of the great Siouan family, which, in its various branches and clans, dominated the Plains. The Sioux, or Dakota, became, indeed, the archetypal Indians. They were the buffalo-hunting "horse Indians" whose great chiefs were figures like Sitting Bull and Crazy Horse. It was they who wore the headdresses of eagle feathers and the soft-fringed and bead-decorated shirts that the average person today identifies as the traditional costume of the Indians but that in fact was characteristic of only the Dakota, or Sioux. They lived in tepees made of buffalo hides, "painted with various figure and colors."

In physique, they were tall with broad shoulders and muscular bodies, high cheekbones and aquiline, or Roman, noses. Their traditional enemies were the tribes of the Algonquian family, who pressed on them from the southwest and north through southern Canada. Clark described the Yankton Sioux as having "a certain air of dignity and boldness" and noted that they were fond of decorations of white [grizzly] bear claws three inches long." The tribe had a group of young braves who had pledged never to retreat or avoid danger and who constituted a "shock force." "These young men," Clark wrote, "sit, and encamp, and dance together, distinct from the rest of the nation." They were so fanatic that once, when crossing the Missouri on the ice and coming upon a stretch of open water, they walked straight on; a number died before the remainder could be forced to stop by the rest of the tribe.

Another council was held. After Lewis had made his speech, he and Clark smoked the pipe of peace, distributed presents, and ate a substantial feast. Clark noted: "The young people exercised their bows and arrows in shooting at marks for beads . . . and in the evening the whole party danced until a late hour. . . . Their musical instruments were the drum, and a sort of little bag made of buffalo hide . . . with small shot or pebbles in it, and a bunch of hair tied to it. This produces a sort of rattling music."

The next morning the first chief, having consulted the others, replied in this fashion: "I see before me my great father's [the president of the United States'] two sons. You see me, and the rest of our chiefs and warriors. We are very poor! We have neither powder or ball, nor knives; and our women and children at the village have no clothes. . . . I wish, brothers, you would give us something for our squaws." The other chiefs spoke to much the same effect; "all the harangues," Clark wrote, "concluded by describing the distress of the nation; they begged us to have pity on them; to send them traders; that they wanted powder and ball; and seemed anxious that we should supply them with some of their great father's milk," by which they meant whiskey.

Pushing on, the expedition came upon their first prairie dogs, called *petit chien* by the French, living in villages by the thousands, and found nearby a forty-five-foot-long dinosaur skeleton "in a perfect state of petrification." They broke off some portions to send back to the president. They also saw large herds of buffalo and the swift and beautiful antelope (which they called goats), as many as three thousand at a time, dotting the plains and shadowed by numerous coyote, which Clark termed "small wolves."

At the end of September the expedition entered the territory of the Teton Sioux, the most numerous and powerful of that family. Protected from the Algonquian by Dakotan tribes to the east, the Teton Sioux grew at the expense of their neighbors. They specialized in horse-stealing raids against the Mandan, whose numbers had been reduced by smallpox, often killing and scalping women and children while they worked in the cornfields. Taking to the horse culture with a vengeance, they had virtually given up agriculture and had stopped making the pottery for which they had been famous. They befriended the Algonquian Cheyenne, refugees from the east; but Pawnee, Mandan, Crow, and all the lesser tribes of the region lived in perpetual fear of their forays.

It was therefore crucial for the expedition to ingratiate themselves with the Tetons. Under the protection of the Teton Sioux, Lewis and Clark could proceed with relative safety as far as the foothills of the Rocky Mountains. The numerous Teton chiefs were given presents of the first class—laced uniform coats and cocked hats with plumes, medals, and tobacco. The principal chiefs were invited aboard the party's flagship and were even urged to spend the night. The most delicate diplomacy was involved, since the chiefs, fascinated by the white men and, above all, by the boats and the supplies they carried, were obviously reluctant to allow them to proceed up the river, holding on to the rope and clinging to the mast of the boat when they were asked to go ashore by Clark. They wanted whiskey and more presents, one chief announced. To this Clark replied that "we were not squaws, but warriors; that we were sent by our great father, who could in a moment exterminate them;

the chief replied that he too had warriors, and was proceeding to offer personal violence to Captain Clark, who immediately drew his sword." The Indians responded by notching their arrows and forming a circle around Clark. The swivel gun on the bow of the boat was aimed at the Indians, and twelve men formed up behind Clark. It was perhaps the most dangerous moment of an expedition that had faced and would face innumerable hazards, but it passed when the chief ordered his warriors to drop back and then, having refused to shake Clark's hand in a gesture of amity, changed his mind and climbed back in the boat to accompany them to his village up the river.

At the village, Clark and Lewis were conducted to a council room formed of saplings covered with skins. There some seventy men sat in a circle around the chief. Four hundred pounds of buffalo meat were piled in the center of the circle as a gift for the whites. Near the chief, supported by two forked sticks, was the pipe of peace, the bowl made of red clay, three-foot-long stem of ash, the whole decorated with feathers, hair, and porcupine quills. An old chief spoke of the tribe's need for the protection of the Great Father, and Lewis assured him of it. Then the old man sacrificed "the most delicate parts of the dog . . . held up the pipe of peace, first pointed it towards the heavens, then to the four quarters of the globe, then to the earth, made a short speech, lighted the pipe," and presented it in turn to Clark and Lewis. At the feast that followed, the leaders of the expedition had their first taste of dog meat and of pemmican, dried and jerked buffalo meat mixed with grease and "a kind of ground potato."

The meal was followed by a dance, the music for which was provided by ten men who played a kind of tambourine of skin stretched across a hoop and a rattle with "five or six young men for the vocal part." The women, fantastically adorned and carrying poles decorated with the scalps and tokens of war taken by their husbands, danced alone in a "shuffle." Some of the scalps were fresh ones taken in a raid on their cousins, the Omaha, during which they had destroyed forty lodges, killed seventy-five warriors, and taken twenty-five squaws and children prisoners. The latter were a dejected and miserable-looking lot, and the American captains gave them awls and needles and interceded on their behalf with the chief. The Great Father, they told him, would wish them returned to their people.

The Sioux women were handsome, and both sexes appeared "cheerful and sprightly" but proved, on further acquaintance, "cunning and vicious." The warriors had their heads shaved except for a "small tuft on the top," which they allowed to grow long and wore in plaits decorated with an eagle feather. In ceremonies and on the warpath, they smeared their bodies with a mixture of grease and coal and wore over their shoulders a loose buffalo robe adorned with porcupine quills. The enlisted men of the party were at first disconcerted by the Indian custom of pressing their wives on them as bedmates, but they soon accommodated themselves to the practice.

When the expedition was ready to push on up the river, the Tetons again appeared determined to stop them, but the two captains faced them down and cast off. Now Indians rode along the shore following the boats and providing an unwelcome escort. The whites had the distinct impression that the Sioux were simply waiting for a convenient opportunity to attack them.

The next tribe the explorers encountered were the Arikara, members of the Caddoan family and cousins of the Pawnee. The Arikara women paddled out to the boats in canoes made of skins stretched over a basketlike frame and were astonished at the sight of Clark's slave, York, "a remarkably stout strong negro." York responded to their curiosity by telling them that he had once been an animal, but had been caught and tamed by his master, and he proudly displayed his strength.

Again there was a council and gifts and speeches. The Arikara were "tall and well proportioned, the women handsome and lively," but the tribe was plainly a poor one. They had little in the way of personal adornment but were "kind and generous" and did not beg as the Sioux had. The women were "disposed to be amorous and our men found no difficulty in procuring companions for the night. . . ."

The black man York participated largely in these favours..." for instead of inspiring any prejudice, his color seemed to procure him additional advantages from the Indians, who, in Clark's words, "desired to preserve among them some memorial of this wonderful stranger." In contrast to the Teton Sioux who had abandoned agriculture for the hunt and raid, the Arikara lived in semi-permanent villages of lodges constructed of willow branches interwoven with grass, the whole coated with clay (which of course made them vulnerable to raids by more aggressive and nomadic tribes) and cultivated corn, beans, pumpkins, watermelons, squash, and their own kind of tobacco.

Beyond the Arikara lay the Mandan, who, before smallpox and the Sioux had decimated them, had occupied nine large villages along the Missouri where they pursued an agricultural and hunting life. It was with the Mandan, or near the Mandan, that Clark and Lewis decided to spend the winter. The river would soon start to freeze over, and it was essential to find a sheltered spot, hopefully adjacent to friendly Indians. Parties of Iowa and Minitari—the latter also known as the Hidatsa, Big Bellies, or Gros Ventres—who were allied with the Mandan and at war with the distant Shoshone, joined the expedition as it approached the principal Mandan villages. The ritual of the council was repeated. Lewis took the occasion to urge the Mandan to make peace with the Arikara. Presents were distributed with proper attention to the rank of the chiefs. The most popular proved to be an iron mill to grind corn, what we today would call "appropriate technology." Since the expedition wished to spend the winter with the Mandan, special pains were taken to establish cordial relations. Again York was an object of fascination for the Indians, and they were delighted when the white men danced with each other. Such dances, indeed, became the principal form of entertainment for the Indians.

The members of the expedition now began to build houses to store their supplies and huts to live in. When finished, the little complex consisted of two rows of four huts, each room fourteen feet square with a slanting roof. In addition, two large rooms were built for stores and provisions. Even before the structures were completed, Indians came in a steady stream to observe what was going on and to receive gifts. One chief returned half a dozen times, bringing large sides of buffalo and deer, which were carried by his wife, who on another occasion brought a boat on her back for her husband to use in the river. Some uneasiness was created among the Indians by agents of the Hudson's Bay Company, who, anxious to discourage competition, circulated rumors that the white men intended to join the Teton Sioux in an attack on the Mandan. Clark helped to allay suspicion by offering to help the Mandan avenge the death of a young brave at the hands of Sioux raiders.

The religion of the Mandans centered on the notion of good medicine. Each member of the tribe selected a spirit or animal that became his "medicine," his intercessor with the Great Spirit. A Mandan who Clark met boasted that he had offered up seventeen horses "to my medicine." The origin myth of the Mandan held that the nation had once resided in an underground village near a lake where a grapevine grew. Some of the bolder individuals climbed the vine and emerged above the earth, "which they found covered with buffalo and rich with every kind of fruits." They returned and told of the wonders of the world above, and the members of the tribe began climbing the grapevine to this marvelous land. When half of the tribe had ascended by this means, a fat woman broke the vine by her weight and the rest of the nation was forced to remain below, where the good Mandan would return after death.

Now the weather grew bitterly cold and much of the party's energy went into keeping warm and hunting deer and buffalo, which, thin and tough as they had become with the onset of winter, provided the group's principal food. Temperatures were often below zero, and frostbite was a constant danger. The blacksmith of the party became a major asset because he was able to fashion iron weapons for the Indians in return for corn.

Early in January, with the river frozen deep and buffalo scarce, the Indians held a dance designed to attract buffalo to the vicinity. According to Clark, it was devised by the old men of the tribe, and it is easy to understand why. When the elders had assembled around a fire, "with the image of a doll dressed as a woman before them, the young men of the village bring their wives along with food and tobacco." The women wear nothing but a robe or mantle "loosely thrown round the body." Each husband then goes to one of the old men and begs him to have intercourse with his wife. "The girl then takes the old man (who very often can scarcely walk) and leads him to a convenient place for the business. . . . If the old man (or a white man) returns to the lodge without gratifying the . . . wife, [the husband] offers her again and again. . . . We sent a man to this Medicine Dance last night," Clark added; "they gave him four girls."

The party suffered a serious setback in February when raiding Sioux intercepted hunters bringing back meat to the encampment, threatened their lives, and made off with the horses and sleds piled high with meat. At the Arikara villages the Sioux left word that "in the future they would put to death any of us they could, as we were bad medicine."

By April the ice on the river had broken up, and the expedition prepared to push on. Before leaving they packed boxes to be sent back to Jefferson with a cooperative trader. Included were a stuffed antelope with its skeleton, a weasel, three squirrels, a prairie dog, the horns of a mountain goat, elk horns, a buffalo skin, and a number of Indian articles, all sure to appeal to the president's scientific instincts.

At the Mandan village, they acquired two interpreters, George Drouillard and Toussaint Charbonneau, a French trapper, whose wife, Sacagawea, was a Snake Indian captured by the Minitari in a raid and sold to Charbonneau. Sacagawea had her infant child with her.

Pushing on up the Missouri the expedition was increasingly harassed by grizzly and brown bears who invaded their camps and stole unguarded food. Clark and Lewis took turns leading a small advance party ahead of the main body to scout the country ahead, find suitable campsites, and kill game for the evening meal. A succession of scenic wonders unrolled continually before their eyes.

As they made their way up the river, the country grew familiar to Sacagawea. She recognized White Paint Creek and informed

Lewis that they were approaching the three forks of the Missouri. A sharp lookout was kept for signs of the Snake (or Shoshone) Indians from whose tribe Sacagawea had been kidnapped. The success of the expedition depended on securing horses from them to carry the party over the Rockies to a point where the Columbia River or its tributaries would become navigable.

When the expedition came, at last, to the forks of the Missouri, the two leaders named the southwest branch the Jefferson, "in honor of . . . the projector of the enterprise, and the middle branch Madison" (a river destined to become one of the great trout streams of the United States). A third river was named the Gallatin, and Sacagawea announced that they were encamped "on the precise spot" where she had been camped when the Minitari (or Hidatsa) raiding party first came upon them. They had killed twelve men, women, and young boys and made the rest of the women prisoners, she told the two captains without any sign of emotion.

Proceeding up what they took to be the Missouri (of the three forks), they passed another substantial river, which Lewis named Philosophy, again in honor of his patron, Thomas Jefferson, the philosopher of democracy. (Unfortunately, the name was later changed to Stinking Water because of the river's strong mineral taste.) The next day Lewis named a river that the party passed Wisdom and another that, symbolically, emptied into the Jefferson, he called Philanthropy, the noblest of civic virtues. So Philosophy, Wisdom, and Philanthropy flowed into Jefferson, a conceit that must have pleased Lewis.

Sacagawea identified the Beaverhead River as a spot where her tribe often made its summer camp. Now the search for her tribe became more urgent. Lewis, taking some of the hardiest members of the party with him, ranged far ahead and south of the river, resolved "to meet some nation of Indians before they returned, however long they might be separated from the party." Finally, Lewis, searching the terrain with his field glasses, saw some two miles away a single mounted Indian whom he took to be a Shoshone. The task was to approach him without frightening him off. If he took alarm he might return to his tribe with word that Sioux were in the area, whereupon the whole band would decamp. When he came to within hailing distance, Lewis took a blanket from his pack, and placing his rifle on the ground some distance away, he waved the blanket and placed it on the ground, the traditional signal that one came in peace and wished to parley, "a universal sign of friendship among the Indians on the Missouri and the Rocky Mountains." He then took off his shirt to try to indicate that he was a white and not a Sioux or Minitari warrior, calling out "*tabba bine*," or white man. Despite all his blandishments, the Indian turned his horse and dashed off through the willow brushes when Lewis was some hundred yards away.

Two days later Lewis and his companions came upon three Indian women. One fled but the others, seeing their escape cut off, sat down and bowed their heads, a classic gesture of an Indian inviting his or her enemy to strike the death blow. Lewis induced the women to stand, assured them by signs that they had only peaceful intent; he gave them some needles, beads, and two mirrors; and he daubed some red paint on their cheeks, "a ceremony which among the Shoshonees, is emblematic of peace."

Lewis conveyed that he wished the women to lead them to the camp of their people, but they had only gone a short distance when sixty mounted braves came rushing toward them. Lewis put down his gun and walked toward the braves with the women who, when the Indians had reined in, explained that Lewis and his companions were white men and showed them the presents they had received. At this, three warriors jumped from their horses and embraced Lewis. "The whole body of warriors now came forward," Lewis noted, "and our men received the caresses, and no small share of the grease and paint of their new friends." The Indians then pulled off their moccasins as a sign of friendship and indicated to the whites that they should do the same. As he did so, Lewis could not help reflecting that Moses had likewise been admonished to remove his shoes when he stood on holy ground. The peace pipe was smoked, presents were distributed—blue beads and red paint were especially popular—and the entire party headed gaily for the Indian village.

There Lewis and the men with him were the center of fascinated attention. They were conducted to a lodge of willow and leather construction, and there was more smoking and distribution of trinkets. Food was scarce in the village, but the Shoshone were so relieved to find that their visitors were friendly white men rather than hostile Indians that the night was spent in dancing and singing.

The next day, Lewis undertook to try to persuade the Indians to accompany him to the forks of the Jefferson to meet Clark and the rest of the expedition and to enter into negotiations over the purchase of horses. The Indians, suspecting a plot to deliver them to their enemies, became instantly sullen and suspicious, and it took all of Lewis's diplomatic skill to persuade their chief, Cameahwait, to accompany him. White men, he told the chief, believed it dishonorable to "lie or entrap even an enemy by falsehood." If the Indians persisted in their suspicions, no white men would ever come to trade with them and bring them the guns by means of which they might fight their enemies on equal terms. If the Indians did not have the courage to go with him, he must go alone. Cameahwait at once replied that he was not afraid to die. Eight warriors joined them and the rest of the village set up a cry of lamentation at what they conceived to be the imminent destruction of the bold ones; but the party had gone only a short distance before twelve more warriors joined them and finally all the men of the village and most of the women were trooping happily along, their fears forgotten.

As no one had had anything to eat for almost a day, Lewis sent two of his men ahead as hunters. As soon as this movement was observed a number of the Indians became uneasy and turned back to the village. Fortunately the hunters shot a deer, and when word reached the Shoshone they dashed ahead as fast as their ponies would carry them. When they reached the spot where Drouillard was skinning and cleaning the deer, "they all dismounted in confusion and ran tumbling over each other like famished dogs; each tore away whatever part he could and instantly began to eat it; some had the liver, some the kidneys . . . one of them . . . seized about nine feet of the entrails. . . . Yet though suffering with hunger they did not attempt as they might have done to take by force the whole deer." When the deer had been dressed, Lewis kept a quarter for himself and his men and gave the rest to the Indians, who ate it raw. Two more deer were shot, and the Indians, their appetites sated, were soon in excellent spirits.

When Indians and whites arrived at the river there was another awkward period because the boats under Clark's command had not reached the rendezvous, and the Indians once more suspected treachery. But Clark, leaving the boats to come on behind, had started walking along the bank with Charbonneau and Sacagawea. They had covered only a mile or so before Sacagawea began "to dance and show every mark of the most extravagant joy . . . pointing to several Indians . . . advancing on horseback, sucking her fingers at the same time to indicate that they were of her native tribe." As Sacagawea, her husband, and Clark approached them, "a woman made her way through the crowd towards Sacagawea, and recognizing each other, they embraced with the most tender affection." They had both been captured and had shared the rigors of captivity, but Sacagawea's friend had escaped and made her way back to her tribe. A few minutes later Sacagawea saw Cameahwait, one of two brothers who had survived the Minitari raid. In Clark's words, "She instantly jumped up, and ran and embraced him, throwing over him her blanket and weeping profusely."

With the expedition reunited and contact made with the Shoshone, Clark and Lewis were impatient to be on their way. They needed a guide and a number of horses. From all accounts of the Indians, the most difficult and dangerous part of their journey lay ahead of them—from the headwaters of the Missouri, or as far as it was navigable, up the steep and flinty eastern slopes of the Rockies, across the Continental Divide to the point where the rivers flowed west to the Pacific. They were told that game was scarce and that the paths, such as they were, were so strewn with sharp stones that even the tough Indian ponies came up lame or slipped from the narrow ledges with their packs. Nonetheless, there was no thought of turning back.

It was decided that Clark should set off with eleven men to search for the Columbia River and, when he found it, begin the construction of boats to carry the party down the thousand miles or so to the ocean. Meantime, bargaining for horses went on with the Shoshone. Three excellent horses were exchanged for a uniform coat, a pair of leggings, three handkerchiefs, and three knives. Another was traded for an old checkered shirt and a pair of canvas leggings.

Clark's party made slow progress along the steep slopes and deep ravines that marked the rocky spine of the continent. On the second day out they encountered a small band of Shoshone who had built weirs to trap salmon. The Indians shared some of their catch with the white men. It was their first taste of Pacific salmon, sure evidence that their course now lay downhill. They had indeed entered into a new realm. As the life and economy of the Plains Indians revolved around the buffalo, the Indians of the western slope depended primarily on salmon—dried, smoked, pulverized, and made into a kind of paste and supplemented, in the seasons when salmon no longer ran up the rivers, by river fish, berries, and roots of various kinds.

The Indians who lived along the Snake and Columbia rivers were far less prepossessing than the horse Indians of the Plains. The "Pierced Noses," or Nez Percé, as the French had named them, were disfigured by their practice of binding boards on the faces of their infants to flatten and elongate their foreheads. They were obviously pleased with the effect, but it did not enhance their appearance in the eyes of the whites.

The Shoshone, in a manner of speaking, straddled the Rockies. They were essentially Plains Indians, but they had been pushed back to the Rockies in a process by which the Iroquois, the most powerful and warlike family, had pushed the Algonquian—originally a family that had shared the Eastern hunting lands with them—into the Old Northwest and then west of the Mississippi.

The Algonquian, pressed by the white settlers and chastised by Wayne at Fallen Timbers, pushed on the Caddoan family, the Pawnee and Arikara and the Siouan family, and they, in turn, bore on the Snake, the principal tribes of which were the Kiowa, the Comanche, and the Shoshone. As we have already noted, some of the antagonisms within families were as bitter as those between tribes of different families (the family being not a confederacy but a group of tribes related by similarities in language and culture). Thus the Teton Sioux were death to the Mandan, also members of the Siouan group; and the Sioux took under their wing the Cheyenne, an Algonquian tribe. An additional irony was that the more remote tribes suffered severely in warfare with Eastern tribes from the fact that the closer the contact Indians had with the whites, the more commonly they were armed with the feared musket or rifle. Hence, the hope of the Mandan, Arikara, and the Shoshone for trade with whites that they might procure guns and ammunition and thus have a better chance in battle against their traditional enemies.

The Shoshone, always fearful of encountering the Sioux who had inflicted dreadful casualties on them, suffered acutely each year between the end of the salmon runs and the time when they dared to venture back to the western rim of the buffalo country to hunt. The members of the expedition found the Shoshone the most appealing of the many tribes of Indians they encountered. In the words of Clark: "Such is their terror [of the Minitari or Hidatsa Sioux] that as long as they can obtain the scantiest subsistence, they do not leave the interior of the mountains; and as soon as they collect a large stock of dried [buffalo] meat, they again retreat, and thus alternately obtaining their food at the hazard of their lives, and hiding themselves to consume it." Nonetheless, they were "not only cheerful but even gay," and to Clark their character had in it "much of the dignity of misfortune." They did not beg as the Teton Sioux did or steal as did the Arikara. "With their liveliness of temper," Clark noted, "they are fond of gaudy dresses, and of all sorts of amusements, particularly to games of hazard; and like most Indians fond of boasting of their own warlike exploits, whether real or fictitious."

The Shoshone were short in stature, "with thick flat feet and crooked legs." The most popular adornment of the men was a collar or cape of otter skin decorated with several hundred little rolls of ermine skin and a fringe of black ermine tails and appliquéd with shells of the pearl oyster. The seams of their leggings were sometimes fringed with "tufts of hair taken from enemies . . . they have slain." The killing of an enemy counted for nothing without the scalp to prove it. There were few old men in evidence and those the explorers saw did not appear "to be treated with much tenderness or respect." A warrior might have two or three different names in his lifetime. Each new achievement entitled him to a new name—"the stealing of horses, the scalping of an enemy, or killing a brown bear."

Their government was "perfectly free from any restraint. Each individual is his own master, and the only control to which his conduct is subjected, is the advice of a chief supported by his influence over the opinions of the rest of the tribe." The man, as with most Indian tribes, was the complete master of his wives and daughters and could barter them away, "or dispose of them in any manner he may think proper. . . . The husband will for a trifling present lend his wife for a night to a stranger." Any sexual liaison not authorized by the husband might, however, be punished by death. Clark wrote that the women of the tribe were condemned "to the lowest and most laborious drudgery . . . they collect the roots, and cook; they build the huts, dress the skins and make clothing; collect the wood, and assist in taking care of the horses on the route. . . . The only business of the man is to fight; he therefore takes on himself the care of his horse, the companion of his warfare; but he will descend to no other labour than to hunt and fish." The shield of the Shoshone was a sacred object decorated by magic symbols that deflected arrows and bullets. In addition, many of the warriors wore suits of armor made of folds of antelope skins glued together until they were stiff and hard. Favorite horses were often painted, their ears cut in various shapes, and their manes and tails trimmed with bright feathers.

By the end of August, Clark and his party were back from reconnoitering a route through the mountains; and the whole party, provided with pack horses by the Shoshone, set forth on the last leg of the journey. Their path lay along narrow mountain trails where even the surefooted horses on several occasions slipped and fell down talus-covered slopes. When that happened the party had to halt and recover the baggage carried by the animal. It alternately rained and snowed, and game was so scarce that the men had to dip into the meager food supplies they were carrying with them. It was only the Indians they encountered along their route, fishing in the streams and river and drying their catches on the bank, who saved them from acute hunger and perhaps starvation. The aborigines sold them salmon, roots of various kinds, and, most important of all, large numbers of dogs. If the members of the expedition had felt an initial squeamishness about eating man's best friend, they soon got over it, and from the Rockies to the ocean, roots, salmon, and dogs were the staples of their daily fare.

The Indians now encountered belonged to the general language group anthropologists have termed the Penutian family, made up of "California tribes" such as the Yokuts, Klamath, Modoc, Cayuse, and Chinook. In present-day Washington, a number of so-called Shahaptin tribes were scattered along the Columbia River and its tributaries, the Nez Percé being the best known. The Klikitat, Umatilla, and Yakima were among the more prominent, but there were innumerable other smaller tribes with unpronounceable names: the Eneeshurs, "inhospitable and parsimonious, faithless to their engagements," who "in the midst of poverty and filth, retain a degree of pride and arrogance which renders our numbers our only protection," Clark noted; the Walla Walla, the most honest and dependable of all the tribes the party encountered; the Skeetsomish, Towahnnahiook, and Smackshop; the Multnomah, the dominant tribe on the middle Columbia; the Chilluckittequaw, Weocksockwillacum, Nehuh, Wahclella, Clahclellah, Neerchokioo, and others too numerous to mention. The chief of the Chilluckittequaw startled Lewis by producing a medicine bag from which he proudly drew "fourteen forefingers" that he had cut off the hands of his dead enemies, apparently Indians of the Snake tribes. Tattooing was not uncommon, especially among the women; a Chinook woman had "Jonathan Bowman" tattooed on her leg.

The Nez Percé, or Chopunnish, were, as we have noted, one of the larger tribes and the first substantial one contacted by the expedition after it left the Shoshone villages. It was with the Nez Percé that the horses that had brought the party from the Shoshone to the headwaters of the Snake (Clark named it the "Lewis" but the name failed to take) were left against the day of the white men's return, and it was the Nez Percé who provided guides and food.

The Indians of the Columbia River region were all part of what might be called a root and salmon culture. They were short and bow-legged, in the opinion of Clark, from squatting on their haunches. Most were flatheaded. They lived in long lodges—sometimes over two hundred feet long, built of cedar and bark, sunk as much as six feet underground. Fires were made in pits in the center of these dwellings, often occupied by a dozen or more families. The men and women slept on shelves or bunks built along the sides of the lodge. Their dead were commonly wrapped in skins and stacked up like firewood in special structures.

The salmon and the bear were sacred, and the tribes had various rituals to propitiate their spirits. The first run of salmon in May was eagerly awaited and celebrated with joy, since it brought an end to their winter diet of roots and "pounded" salmon.

The river and coast Indians were as dependent on the canoe as the Plains Indians were on the horse. The canoes ran in size from small one- or two-man models to forty-footers that could carry twenty people or more and were handsomely carved fore and aft. All were made of redwood, and the white men marveled at the skill with which they were maneuvered even in the heavy seas of the Pacific. The status of the coast Indian women was much higher than that of the women of the Plains Indians, which led Clark to make the shrewd observation that the condition of women rested not on the degree of "civilization" of the Indian, but upon the economic utility of the women. "Where the women aid in procuring subsistence for the tribe," he noted, "they are treated with more equality, and their importance is proportioned to the share which they take in that labour." The river and especially the coast women shared the fishing chores with the men and were the principal root gatherers. They also took their turns in paddling and steering the canoes. "They were permitted to speak freely before the men, to whom indeed they sometimes address themselves in a tone of authority," a liberty unthinkable among the horse Indians of the Plains. When a great feast was prepared, the food was cooked and served by the men. The particular province of the women was basketry—the weaving and decorating of baskets, some of which were so tightly woven they could hold water.

Like the Sioux and virtually all other Indian tribes, husbands pressed their wives on their white visitors whenever they were camped near Indian villages. At the mouth of the Columbia an old Chinook woman brought six unmarried girls to the expedition's camp. She had a regular scale of prices according to her opinion of "the beauty of each female." To decline a husband's offer of his wife or daughter "for a fish-hook or a strand of beads" was "to disparage the charms of the lady, and therefore give such offense, that although we had occasionally to treat the Indians with rigour, nothing seemed to irritate both sexes more than our refusal to accept the favours of the females."

Among the hunting tribes such as the Sioux and Assiniboine, the old were usually abandoned when they became a burden to the tribe in its constant movement and interminable warfare. In Clark's words, "As they [the Sioux] are setting out for some new excursion, where the old man is unable to follow, his children or nearest relations, place before him a piece of meat and some water, telling him that he has lived long enough, that it is now time for him to go home to his relations, who could take better care of him than his friends on earth, leave him, without remorse, to perish, when his little supply is exhausted." The more settled tribes of the West Coast seldom left their old to die but were attentive to their needs and showed deference at least to the old chiefs.

Gambling was a major preoccupation of many of the tribes, a pastime they pursued "with a strange and ruinous avidity," often gambling away their most precious possessions—their wives, canoes, and weapons.

One custom common to the tribes of the Columbia Basin was the use of the sweathouse. It was not unique to these tribes by any means, but it was especially favored by them. Such a facility was formed by damming a creek outlet, digging it out, and making a hollow square six or eight feet deep, covered over with a conical roof of woven branches and mud. "The bathers descended by [a hole in the top] taking with them a number of heated stones and jugs of water; and after being seated round the room, throw the water on the stones till the steam becomes of a temperature sufficiently high for their purposes." This was followed by a plunge in the icy waters of the river. One Indian they met varied the routine by washing himself down with his urine afterward. The steam baths were "so essentially a social amusement, that to decline going in to bathe when invited by a friend is one of the highest indignities which can be offered to him." Sometimes the baths developed into a good-natured contest to see who could endure the hottest steam without fleeing.

On their passage down the river the members of the expedition passed countless fish weirs and small groups of Indians fishing with raised spears, or gigs, and occasionally with hooks. The fish were spread on raised wooden racks to dry, and the air was pungent with the odor of burning hickory limbs. The Snake and Columbia rivers and their tributaries were the highways of the Indians who passed "in great numbers up and down the river," Clark noted.

The practical hazards of the descent of the river centered on the numerous rapids that constantly threatened to overturn the expedition's six canoes. Frequent stops had to be made for repairs and to dry clothing and supplies soaked by the turbulent waters.

By November, the expedition had reached the lower waters of the Columbia. Here the river widened out to more than a mile across. Covered with flocks of duck and geese, the water was saline, indicating that the explorers had entered a tidal area. Here the Indians Clark called Clatsop predominated, with the Chinook, Tillamook, and Klamath. These tribes considered themselves the guardians of the river mouth and largely controlled the trade with the British and American trading vessels that anchored there, usually in May, and spent the summer trading. Many of the Indians wore sailors' clothes and hats. But like all the river Indians they went barefoot, because moccasins were ill-suited to their primarily aqueous environment.

In addition to such tribes as the Clatsop and Chinook, there were the Luckton, Youitt, Cookoose (these are all Clark's improvised phonetic spellings), the Ulseah, Kickawi, Kahunkle, Shiastuckle, Chilt, Clamoitomish, Killaxthokle, Quinult, and Calasthorte, most of the latter numbering no more than a hundred or so members.

Now the party suffered a new inconvenience, the perpetual rainfall of the region. For ten days rain fell almost continuously until the travelers and all their belongings were thoroughly soaked. Many of the men were stricken with bad colds and fever. Under such conditions it was almost impossible to hunt game, and hunger added to the misery of being cold and wet. Winter was coming on, and it was imperative to find a convenient and healthy spot to establish quarters. As Clark put it, the rain had "completely wet all our merchandise, spoiled some of our fish, destroyed the robes, and rotted nearly half of our few remaining articles of clothing, particularly the leather dresses."

On December 8, after several weeks of searching, the two leaders settled on a site for a fort, on which the men immediately began to work; it was named Fort Clatsop after the nearby Indian tribe. Despite the constant rain, work went ahead on the huts and the buildings to be used to hold the dwindling supplies of the expedition. Hunters scoured the hills above the bay for deer and elk, and day after day a procession of Indians of various local tribes appeared to trade, talk, or merely look. Clark or Lewis inquired the names of each of them, their points of origin and their customs, noted their dress and weapons, and, so far as they could, their languages and dialects.

Once the huts were completed and those members of the party who were ill or in bad health were provided for, the two captains devoted much of their time to describing in detail the flora and fauna of the region. The routine of camp life was interrupted in January by news of a great event. A whale had beached on the shore near the mouth of the Columbia River, and Indians came from miles away to strip it to the bones, carrying away all the meat and blubber, fighting over every morsel with other voracious scavengers—gulls and vultures, foxes and wolves.

As the winter months passed, the Lewis and Clark company impatiently awaited the coming of spring and their homeward journey. The principal difficulty that faced them on the return trip was the scarcity of game along their route up the Columbia and Snake to the Missouri. The salmon had not yet begun to run and the expedition's supply of trading goods, by means of which they might procure roots and dogs from the Indians, was much diminished. Indeed, the Indians themselves were often so short of food they could spare nothing for the white men. Elk and deer were scarce, difficult to hunt in the forest, and almost inedible from the rigors of the winter, so the members of the party had to make heroic efforts to lay in a sufficient supply of dried elk and venison, along with roots and smoked fish, to serve as a basic ration for at least the initial stage of their return trip.

On March 23, 1806, the party loaded their canoes and left Fort Clatsop. The progress was slow once the canoes had passed the lower river basin. Water was high and the rapids were far more difficult to ascend than descend. Portages were frequently necessary with all the tedious effort of unloading, carrying, and reloading. Canoes could not be towed successfully because of a lack of ropes, the irregular nature of the riverbanks, and the force of the current. Finally, the captains decided to trade their canoes (and whatever else they could spare from their supplies) for enough horses to continue by land. Once they reached the area of the Nez Percé, they expected to reclaim their horses, proceed to the Shoshone, retrieve the canoes and barges that had brought them up the Missouri, and float downriver to St. Louis.

The negotiations for horses proved to be protracted and tiresome. Although the river Indians had little use for horses, they were symbols of wealth and status, and the Indians were reluctant to part with them for the increasingly modest articles left to the expedition. Finally, the combined efforts of Clark and Lewis managed to secure enough sore-backed horses to enable the party to push on. The fame of Lewis and Clark as doctors—men who made powerful medicine—preceded them, and when they reached Nez Percé territory they had nearly fifty patients awaiting them. Short of food, the two captains established a rough fee schedule: for a dose of sulfur and cream of tartar, a dog; for a major operation such as lancing and dressing an abscess, a plump colt.

The difficulties of communication are indicated by Clark's account of a council with Nez Percé chiefs. Captain Lewis spoke in English to one of the men in the party who knew French. He translated the captain's speech into French to Charbonneau, who translated it into Minitari for Sacagawea, who in turn translated what was said into Shoshone; finally a young Shoshone prisoner of the Nez Percé, who understood their language, translated the speech for them.

With infinite labor, the party advanced toward the Continental Divide, the hunters ranging ahead in desperate search for game. Three Indians were finally engaged for the extravagant price of two guns to lead the expedition to the headwaters of the Missouri. On the trail the explorers found the cache of supplies that they had left on the way west and gratefully loaded it onto their horses. For almost two weeks the party proceeded, their pace determined in large part by the availability of grass for their horses. Where they encountered meadows free of snow, they halted to let the animals graze. At Travelers' Rest, a luxuriant valley with grass for the horses and game for the men, the party split into two groups. Lewis, with nine men and an Indian guide, headed north for the Marias River to see if it offered better access westward than the path they had followed. He would then descend it to the point where it joined the Missouri.

Clark traveled with the rest of the company to the Jefferson River. There they retrieved a cache of supplies along the riverbank, the most welcome portion being plugs of chewing tobacco. Everything was in good order, and the canoes they had sunk and weighted with stones were repaired and refloated. Half of the party then started down the Jefferson in canoes, while Clark and a half a dozen others rode on to the Yellowstone, built two canoes, and headed for a rendezvous at the confluence of the Yellowstone and the Missouri.

Coming down the Marias, Lewis and the men with him had the first serious clash with the Indians, a party of Minitari braves who tried to steal their horses and guns. In the fighting that followed, the Indians were routed and Lewis shot one brave in the stomach. The horses were recovered, and the men hurried on to their planned meeting at the forks, aware that they would probably soon be pursued by a Minitari war party. Pushing their horses as much as they dared, Lewis and his men traveled almost seventy miles down the Marias before stopping for a brief rest. Arriving at the conjunction of the Jefferson and the Missouri, they were overjoyed to meet the men who had arrived there. Now they had five canoes and a barge. The current, swollen by freshets and creeks carrying the runoff from the hills, was swift; and aided by the oars of the men the boats made a dazzling seven or eight miles an hour, the land rushing past them as they entered the last leg of their journey. Game was plentiful and plump from the spring grasses. Hunters sent ahead to replenish the larder brought in twenty-nine deer. Eager to be home, the party was early to bed under improvised mosquito nets and was on the river again at four or five in the morning. At the mouth of Yellowstone they found a note from Clark telling them that he and his men would meet them farther down the river.

It was August 12 before the two parties—Lewis's group and the men with Clark—were reunited on the Missouri near the mouth of the Little Missouri. Here they got the unwelcome word from two trappers that the Minitari, Mandan, Arikara, and Blackfoot Indians were all at war. This seemed to preclude the possibility of any of the chiefs' returning to Washington with the expedition; but Clark finally persuaded Big White, a Mandan chief, to accompany them farther. Now, however, they parted company with Sacagawea, of whom Clark wrote: "She has borne with a patience, truly admirable, the fatigues of so long a route, encumbered with the charge of an infant, who is even now only nineteen months old."

At the Arikara village, farther down the river, Clark heard that seven hundred Sioux warriors were on the warpath against the Mandan and Minitari. There he and Lewis renewed their friendships with the chiefs and urged them not to go to war with the Sioux.

Through the waning days of September the canoes and barges sped along down the river, often making fifty miles or more a day. On September 23, the expedition reached its immediate haven, St. Louis, where, in Clark's words, "we arrived at twelve o'clock, and having fired a salute went on shore and received the heartiest and most hospitable welcome from the whole village." They had been gone two years and four months. They had traversed nearly eight thousand miles across the most beautiful and terrible landscape in the world, parted from all that was familiar, all that was "civilized."

So ended one of the most remarkable odysseys in history, all of which—the endless journey up the mighty, eternal rivers, across the fearful mountains—was a projection of the imagination of Thomas Jefferson. It was his good medicine that sent them off and his spirit that accompanied them every step of the way across the continent and back. Man has been called a "reasoning animal," a "believing animal," and the like, but surely he is equally and perhaps preeminently a searching, exploring, journeying animal with an apparently insatiable appetite for traversing new landscapes. If, in America, that ancient impulse manifested itself as a national characteristic, the Lewis and Clark Expedition was the most powerful expression of it.

If the reader wonders why I have carried him or her on such a lengthy excursion, I must answer somewhat as follows. First, it is an adventure story of inexhaustible drama. Second, it serves to carry us across the whole staggering expanse of the country as it was experienced by all Americans who traversed it prior to the coming of the railroads and thereby gives us at least a fragmentary sense of our geography on the east–west axis. Third, it has introduced us to many of the Indian tribes who inhabited the country at that time and, I trust, conveyed an idea of the remarkable variety of those tribes as well as something of their customs and manner of life.

Next to Clark and Lewis in fame was the Indian woman, Sacagawea. She became a legendary figure. There were innumerable stories of her sudden appearance like a materialized myth to help a floundering party of emigrants find their way through trackless territory, to give help and encouragement in some desperate moment. Baptiste, the infant she had carried to the Pacific and back, with the encouragement of Clark, became a well-known guide.

A more modest journey of exploration was that of Lieutenant Zebulon Pike, whose encounters with Indian tribes served to supplement the information gathered by Lewis and Clark.

Pike departed from St. Louis on August 9, 1805, with a sergeant, two corporals, and seventeen privates in a keelboat some seventy feet long, provisioned for four months, with orders, as Pike put it, "to explore the source of the Mississippi making a general survey of the river and its boundaries, and its productions, both in the animal, vegetable and mineral creation; also to include observations on the savage inhabitants of its Banks."

The story of what followed was very similar, in many ways, to the experience of Lewis and Clark; laborious progress up the river against the current and sometimes against the wind, portaging around rapids, snagged by sawyers and caught on sandbars. Rowing, towing from the banks, and the use of sails carried them up the river. Hunters moved ahead shooting game and keeping the crew supplied. There were frequent contacts with Indians, primarily the Sac and Fox tribes. Past the Illinois, the Rock River, the Wisconsin, the Black, the Chippewa, and the St. Croix to Leech Lake where the Mississippi rose, the party made its way. They encountered numerous French traders who were alternately suspicious and helpful. They met William Ewing, an "Agent appointed to reside with the Sacs to teach them the science of Agriculture," an apparently disastrous choice. Again the Indians were helpful. At the Des Moines rapids the Sac toted the heaviest loads. Tobacco, knives, whiskey, and peace medals were distributed and speeches exchanged pledging peace. At the Falls of St. Anthony, Pike enlisted a mixed-blood Frenchman, Pierre Rousseau, as an interpreter and exchanged the cumbersome keelboat for smaller barges. Relations with the Sioux were sensitive, and Pike paid particular attention to their chiefs. The principal chief of the Sioux smoked the peace pipe with Pike and spoke pointedly of his "New Father," a reference to the Louisiana Purchase. "He was happy to see one who knew the Great Spirit was the Father of all; both the White and the Red people; and if one died the other could not live long: that he had never been at War with their new father, and hoped always to preserve the same good understanding that now existed." Afterward there was a feast of wild rice and venison and a dance, "attended by many curious maneuvres—Men and Women danced indiscriminately," Pike noted. "They all were dressed in the gayest manner, and each had in their hand a small skin of some description."

At the Racine River, Pike and his men watched several hundred Sioux warriors play a game called Le Crosse (now known as lacrosse), hurling a small ball and catching it skillfully with sticks having a leather webbing at their end. When his men had built a little settlement of huts, similar to those that the Lewis and Clark expedition had wintered in on the Missouri, Pike found himself "powerfully attacked with the fantastic's of the Brain . . . I was like a person entranced, and then, could easily account why so many persons who had been confined to remote places, acquired the habit of drinking to excess; and many other vicious habits, which, have at first been adopted merely to pass time."

It was an exacting journey and Pike noted in his journal several days before Christmas: "Never did I undergo more fatigue performing the duties of Hunter, Spy, Guide, Commanding officer, etc, etc. Sometimes in front, sometimes in the Rear—frequently in advance of my party, 10 or 15 miles; that at night I was scarcely able to make my notes intelligible."

Near the headwaters of the Mississippi, north of Red Cedar Lake, was a trading post of the North West Company. This was Chippewa country, a tribe traditionally hostile to Americans. Again

Pike and his men were on the alert, but an Indian Pike encountered told his interpreter that the Chippewa had greater admiration for Americans than for the English, Spanish, or French, "alluding to Warlike Achievements . . . they [Americans] are White Indians."

Pike picked up a young Chippewa near the Savannah River and made him his special companion, though the two could converse only by hand signals. Pike became so attached to his Indian friend that when the Chippewa departed he "felt the curse of solitude," which induced him to reflect on the desolation of such a life. "The wealth of Nations would not be an inducement for me to remain secluded from the Society of Mankind, surrounded by a savage and unproductive Wilderness, without Books, or other sources of Intellectual enjoyment, or ever being blest with society of the cultivated and feeling mind of a civilized fair." It could only be the attachment that the traders felt for the Indian women, he concluded, that could reconcile them to ten, fifteen, or twenty years in the wilderness.

His legs and arms swollen with rheumatism and chilblains, Pike reached Leech Lake—which he took to be the Mississippi headwaters—on February 1 and spent the following day reading Volney's account of his travels in Syria and Egypt and perhaps reflecting on how much more arduous his own expedition had been. At Leech Lake, Pike mustered his little company of soldiers who had endured such hardships, put them through the manual of arms for the edification of the Sauk Indians, and issued them new clothes. They then went back down the river; and on April 30, eight months after they had set out, they were back in St. Louis.

Overshadowed as it was by Lewis and Clark's expedition, Pike's exploration was nonetheless worthy of comparison. His journal is a fascinating record of human ingenuity and endurance, and he added very substantially to the knowledge of a part of the Louisiana Territory about which little was known to Americans.

Pike had hardly had time to set his notes and journal in order before General James Wilkinson dispatched him on another expedition, this time to return some Osage chiefs to their tribe, to make contact with the warlike Comanche, to explore the Arkansas River to its source, and then to make his way to the headwaters of the Red River and down it to the Mississippi. Wilkinson wrote: "In the course of your tour, you are to remark particularly upon the Geographical structure; the natural History; and population . . . taking particular care to collect & preserve, specimens of every thing curious in the mineral or botanical Worlds, which can be preserved & are portable. [He was also charged with bringing back a number] of the most respectable Cammanches."

On July 15, 1806, three months after his return from the Mississippi expedition, Pike was off again, this time with two junior officers, a surgeon, sixteen privates, and two interpreters, plus chiefs of the Pawnee and Osage and their wives and children, to the number of fifty-one, who had been rescued from the Potawatomi and were being returned to their native village as a gesture of goodwill by the U.S. government. Pike's plan was to make his way up the Kansas River in boats to a point several hundred miles west of St. Louis and then strike across country to pick up the Arkansas near the middle of present-day Kansas. The Indian males walked along the banks of the Kansas with a number of the soldiers as protection, while the rest of the party pushed upriver with the boats carrying the baggage of the expedition and the Indian women. A month out from St. Louis, Pike and his company arrived at the Osage village, and the return of the chiefs and their families was an occasion for general rejoicing.

At the end of November, Pike sighted and tried to reach the peak that bears his name. He failed to climb it, but his description of what he called the "Grand Peak" resulted in its being named for him, the only substantial public reminder of his expedition. Turning south from the Grand Peak, Pike and his party made their way into present-day New Mexico. This was Spanish territory, and Pike and his men were apprehended and taken prisoner by the Spanish authorities. Pike's papers were confiscated, and the Americans were carried off to Santa Fe. When they were finally released, the party made their way down the Red River to Natchitoches, arriving there almost a year after they had set out.

CHAPTER IX

THE INDIAN
REMOVAL

Andrew Jackson was the first president since Jefferson to come into office experienced in dealing with Indians and having focused on Indian affairs. While Jefferson's interest in Indians was "philosophical" or, as we might say today, anthropological, Jackson knew Indians firsthand from having fought against (or with) various tribes. His predecessors—Madison, Monroe, and John Quincy Adams—had, to be sure, devoted considerable attention to dealings with various Indian tribes, but they lacked both Jackson's knowledge of Indian manners and mores and his sympathy for the aborigines. For their part the Indians admired Jackson as a great warrior. In his initial address to Congress, Jackson had much to say about the Indians toward whom he expressed the most benevolent intentions. He endorsed the notion of a vast Western preserve to be put aside for them, to which they should be encouraged to move voluntarily. On the other hand if they preferred to remain within the boundaries of the particular states, they must be subject to the laws of those states. The proposal to remove the Indians, primarily from the Southern states where many had achieved a degree of integration with whites, caused an outcry from the friends of the Indians in the North. The supporters of the Indians had already sounded the alarm over Jackson's urging of the Cherokee to remove beyond the Mississippi and the Cherokee themselves had made it clear that they were determined to remain on their ancestral lands.

Jackson had also pressed the Creeks to move west, declaring that otherwise the federal government could not protect them from the states. In his letter to the Creeks, Jackson wrote:

> Friends and brothers, listen. Where you now are, you and my
> white children are too near each other to live in harmony and
> peace. Your game is gone, and many of your people will not work
> and till the earth. Beyond the great river Mississippi, where a
> part of your nation has gone, your father has provided a country
> large enough for all of you, and he advises you to remove to it.
> There your white brothers will not trouble you; they will have no
> claim to the land, and you can live upon it as long as the grass
> grows or the water runs, in peace and plenty. The land beyond the
> Mississippi belongs to the President and no one else, and he will
> give it to you forever.

The president's offhand dismissal of the Indians' claim that their treaties with the United States exempted them from the laws of the states in which their reservations were located aroused a furor in New England. Charles Francis Adams noted in January: "I went to a Meeting which was called in favour of the Cherokee and Creek Indians in the question with Georgia. It was very full. I never had seen a thing of the kind before. But it was not very famous for its soundness or its deliberation." One speaker "talked of sending a thousand regulars into Georgia with as much coolness as if he was going to take a breakfast" and received warm applause for his efforts. Resolutions denouncing treaty violations were adopted unanimously with the observation that such treatment of the Indians "would probably bring upon us the reproaches of mankind, and would certainly expose us to the judgments of Heaven." Charles Francis thought the speeches and resolutions "foolishly violent." In addition they gave him a headache. He wrote the elder Adams that he thought the matter should be decided on practical grounds "without reference to the abstract and impracticable views of the moralists." He was tempted to say so publicly. He received a sharp rebuke from his father, who urged him not "to make your first Essay at public speaking on the unpopular side of a great question of national policy," especially before he had gone thoroughly into the matter as a "question of justice—of Morals—of Politics—of Natural—Conventional-Constitutional, and federal Law—Of Natural History and of Political Economy. It is this and more."

In the Senate debate on the removal of the Cherokee, Henry Clay was his most eloquent and impassioned. Word had spread in the House and throughout the city that Clay was to speak on behalf of the Cherokee, and the floor and the gallery of the Senate were crowded with foreign ambassadors, fashionable women of Washington who espoused his cause, and a solemn group of Cherokee chiefs. The audience was not disappointed. "His first sentences," Harriet Martineau wrote, "are homely, and given with a little hesitation and repetition, and with an agitation shown by frequent putting on and taking off of his spectacles, and a trembling of his hands among the documents on his desk." Then as Clay warmed to his subject, "the agitation changes its character. . . . His utterance is still deliberate, but his voice becomes deliciously winning . . . trembling with emotion, falling and swelling with the earnestness of the speaker . . . and his whole manner becomes irresistibly persuasive." Martineau saw "tears . . . falling on his papers as he vividly described the woes and injuries of the aborigines." Only Martin Van Buren, who yawned ostentatiously, and the senators from Georgia seemed unmoved by Clay's speech.

The most outspoken opponents of the policy of Indian removal were the Christian missionaries among them. At a meeting at New Echota, North Carolina, in December, 1829, a group of missionaries resolved "That we view the Indian question, at present so much agitated in the United States, as being not merely of a political, but of a moral nature—inasmuch as it involves the maintenance or violation of the faith of our country—and as demanding, therefore, the most serious consideration of all American citizens, not only as patriots but as Christians."

The Cherokee were so far from accepting Jackson's policy of removal that those Indians who tried to argue in its favor were frequently killed or banished. The complexities of the issue were suggested by a report submitted by Thomas McKenney, a longtime defender of Indian rights and head of what later became the United States Bureau of Indian Affairs. McKenney had helped establish an ambitious program for "civilizing" the Indians that rested primarily on setting up numerous schools where the Indians were instructed in both practical and academic subjects. When McKenney visited the reservations in 1830 he was distressed at the conditions he found. There were a few Indians who had profited from the instruction, but "the rest was cheerless and hopeless enough. Before this personal observation," he wrote, "I was sanguine in the hope of seeing these people relieved, and saved, where they are. But the sight of their condition, and the prospect of the collisions which have since taken place, and which have grown out of the anomalous relations which they bear to the States, produced a sudden change in my opinion and my hopes."

The debate in Congress on the removal policy had ostensibly revolved around the question of what was best for the Indians. None of the speakers, however (either for or against), ever suggested that the Indians should be allowed to or encouraged to retain—or in most instances to re-establish—their own tribal life and customs. Such a course seemed manifestly impossible. Warfare, raids, and the hunting of wild animals were the essential elements around which tribal life was organized. Except for hunting, which was increasingly unproductive, these aspects of tribal life that gave form and order to aboriginal existence could not be tolerated within the boundaries of the states. To the degree that it might prove possible to sustain tribal life, the experiment could be tried only in the vast unsettled regions of the trans-Mississippi West. Even there it must be seriously inhibited by the promise of the government to protect all the tribes in their particularity and independence, a promise impossible to fulfill since many tribes bore for other tribes inveterate hatreds more deep-seated than their hostility to whites.

Lewis Cass, Jackson's secretary of war, exhausted all of his powers of persuasion trying to prevail on delegations of Cherokee chieftains to accept removal. They were adamant. "It was hoped," Cass wrote the new governor of Georgia, Wilson Lumpkin, "that the favorable terms offered by the Government would have been accepted. But some strange infatuation seems to prevail among these Indians. That they cannot remain where they are and prosper is attested as well by their actual condition as by the whole history of our aboriginal tribes." When they remained immovable, Jackson himself tried his hand, assuring them that "I am sincerely desirous to promote your welfare." They must join their "countrymen" who had already settled in the West: "And the sooner you do this the sooner will commence your career of improvement and prosperity."

The general issue of the Indians, which John Quincy Adams had tried to deal with, was complicated by the fact that Alabama and Mississippi followed Georgia's lead in passing laws placing the Indians under state jurisdiction. Requiring Indians to obey the laws of the states in which they resided seemed on the surface reasonable enough, but a Georgia law provided that "No Indian or descendant of any Indians, residing within the Creek or Cherokee Nation of Indians shall be deemed a competent witness in any court in the State to which a white person may be a party. . . ."

From all over New England memorials and petitions flooded Congress protesting the administration's policy of, in effect, handing over the Indians to the hostile citizens of Georgia, Alabama, and Mississippi. One indignant Georgia representative charged that "these country fanatics [the New Englanders] have placed themselves behind the bulwark of religion and denounce the Georgians as atheists, deists, infidels and sabbath-breakers, laboring under the curse of slavery. . . . The Georgians are described as the worst of savages; as men who can neither read nor write, and who never hear a sermon unless preached by a New England missionary."

The three Southern states made clear their intention simply to seize the Indian lands guaranteed to the tribes by treaty with the United States. The only question was how the president and Congress would respond. Jackson's return had made it clear that he had no intention of forcing the issue with the states. Indeed, he had taken the line that the best the federal government could do was to facilitate the removal of the Indians, although he had said specifically that such removal should be only with the consent of the Indians themselves. With this clue Congress, after warm debates, voted 103 to 77 to approve a bill providing land west of the Mississippi for the Indians and funds to assist them in moving. If there had been any doubt about the outcome, the discovery of gold in Georgia on land owned by the Cherokee settled the issue once and for all. By the summer of 1830 more than three thousand white men were frantically digging for the yellow metal. The Georgia legislature promptly passed laws forbidding the meeting of any Cherokee council or court under penalty of four years in prison. William Wirt, the famous constitutional lawyer, was now retained by the Cherokee to take their case to the Supreme Court. The Indian cause was given heightened drama by an incident in which an Indian named Corn Tassel, who had killed a fellow Indian, was sentenced by a state court to be hanged for murder. The verdict was appealed to the Supreme Court, which issued a writ directing the state of Georgia to show why Corn Tassel should not be released on the grounds that the state had no jurisdiction over him. On the urging of the governor of Georgia the writ was ignored and Corn Tassel was hanged.

The date set for the hearing of the Cherokee case before the full Court was in early March, 1831. Georgia refused even to appear on the grounds that the Court had no right to call a sovereign state before it. Wirt argued that the Cherokee nation had the same status as a foreign power. John Marshall, for the Court, rejected Wirt's argument. After reviewing the history of the relations between the federal government and the Indian tribes, Marshall concluded: "If it be true that the Cherokee nation have rights, this is not the tribunal in which those rights are to be asserted. If it be true, that wrongs have been inflicted, and that still greater are to be apprehended, this is not the tribunal which can redress the past or prevent the future." It is worth noting that two of the Northern justices on the Court, Joseph Story and Smith Thompson, dissented.

But that was not the end of the Supreme Court's involvement with the Indians. An act of the Georgia legislature directed that all whites in the Cherokee country must leave after March, 1831, or get a license from the state and swear an oath of allegiance to Georgia. Directed primarily against missionaries to the Indians, the penalty for failure to comply was four years' imprisonment at hard labor. Some stubborn spirits refused to leave and six were arrested. The case was tried before the superior court of Gwinnett County, with the defendants' lawyer taking the line that the Georgia law was unconstitutional on a number of grounds. It was *ex post facto*, after the fact, forbidden by the Constitution. It was in defiance of the guarantee that the citizens of each state are entitled to the privileges and immunities of the citizens of other states, and it called for unreasonable search and seizure. The court rejected all these arguments for the defense. Two of the prisoners were missionaries who were discharged on the odd grounds that they were authorized agents of the United States and thus exempt from Georgia law.

The Jackson administration denied that the missionaries were agents of the United States and a few weeks later the Reverend Samuel A. Worcester and a colleague were ordered to depart in ten days. Worcester protested that his sick wife could not be moved, but he and ten other missionaries were arrested, "chained by the neck . . . to a wagon," and carried off to jail. All were sentenced by a Georgia jury to four years in the state penitentiary. The governor then offered to pardon the offenders if they would swear to comply with the law. Nine apparently did so and were released, but Worcester and Elizur Butler refused and were sent to jail. They appealed to the Supreme Court of the United States.

The Court thus once more took up the case of Georgia and the Indians. This time it accepted jurisdiction. Marshall reminded his audience:

> From the commencement of our government Congress has
> passed acts to regulate trade and intercourse with the Indians;
> which treat them as nations, respect their rights, and manifest
> a firm purpose to afford that protection which treaties stipulate.
> All these acts, and especially that of 1802, which is still in force,
> manifestly consider the several Indian nations as distinct polit-
> ical communities, having territorial boundaries, and within
> which their authority is exclusive, and having a right to all the
> lands within those boundaries, which is not only acknowledged
> but guaranteed by the United States. . . . The act of the State
> of Georgia under which the plaintiff . . . was prosecuted is
> consequently void, and the judgment a nullity. . . . The Acts of
> Georgia are repugnant to the Constitution, laws, and treaties of
> the United States. . . .

The opinion this time was unanimous. Hearing of it, Jackson is reported to have said, "John Marshall has made his opinion, now let him enforce it." Georgia refused to release the two missionaries and denounced the verdict of the Court in unmeasured terms.

If Jackson had promptly dispatched a contingent of federal troops to Georgia to free the missionaries, the state would doubtless have submitted without armed resistance but it is unlikely that the situation of the Indians would have been materially improved. Alabama and Mississippi were, after all, as adamant as Georgia in their deter-mination to claim the land of their unwelcome neighbors. Certainly such action on Jackson's part would have alarmed the Southern states and given added impetus to the talk of secession. It was not yet evident that Jackson was disposed to seek a second term, but the enforcement of the Supreme Court's decision in Georgia might well have alienated enough Southern voters to cost him re-election. The fact of the matter was that the case of *Worcester v. Georgia* was the wrong issue on which to assert the authority of the federal government, and Jackson was a shrewd enough politician to know it.

It did not appear in this light to the great majority of National Republicans or to the champions of the Indians' cause or indeed to those to whom the Supreme Court appeared as the only hope for the preservation of the Union. The Northern press was full of denunciations of Georgia. Faneuil Hall echoed with angry exhortations to Congress and the president to act in defense of the rights of the Cherokee and the Creek. Meetings were held in innumerable towns throughout New England and more petitions and memorials poured into Congress. In the face of manifest injustice, of open defiance of the Constitution and the government itself, nothing, it seemed, could or would be done. Marshall himself was so disheartened at the failure of Jackson to support the Court's decision that he considered resigning. It seemed to him that the Court was in the twilight of its days. The words and actions of the president indicated that he was determined to reject the Court's authority over the executive and legislative branches of the government. Associate Justice Story took what comfort he could from his conviction that the Court had acted honorably. "Thanks be to God," he wrote a friend, "the Court can wash its hands of the inequity of the Indians and disregarding their rights." But Marshall wrote his younger associate: "I yield slowly and reluctantly to the conviction that our Constitution cannot last. Our opinions are incompatible with a united government. . . . The Union has been prolonged thus far by miracles. I fear they cannot continue."

John Quincy Adams noted in his diary: "there is every prospect . . . the bullies of Georgia have succeeded in the project of extirpating the Indians, by the sacrifice of the public faith of the Union and of all our treaties with them." Yet Adams must have felt some relief that he had not had to make the decision as to whether or not to enforce, by the full weight of federal authority (whatever that might be), the decision of the Supreme Court. Indeed one can hardly escape the conjecture that had Adams been re-elected, his relentless sense of personal and public rectitude might well have precipitated the secession of the Southern states thirty years before that event finally took place and long before the rest of the country was morally or materially ready to contest the issue.

Samuel Worcester, it should be noted, was faithful to the end to his Indian friends. Pardoned by the governor of Georgia not long after the ignored decision of the Supreme Court, he accompanied the Cherokee when they finally embarked on their tragic journey west and he established the Cherokee Park Hill Mission and the first printing press in Indian territory.

WHILE THE CHEROKEE REMAINED ADAMANT, other Southern tribes yielded to pressure to remove. The Indian removal was not, of course, accomplished in a year or two. It was almost ten years between the time the most tractable Choctaw Indians began their long, arduous trek and the most obdurate Cherokees were pried out of their land by the bayonets of federal troops.

Much of the difficulty of removal lay in the extraordinarily varied nature of the Indians on the reserved lands. They were divided into two main categories—"full-bloods" and "mixed-bloods." The full-blood usually looked with contempt on the mixed-bloods, a feeling that was generally returned with interest. Many of the mixed-bloods dressed like whites and adopted white styles of living, sending their children to missionary-run schools, planting crops, owning slaves, and sometimes prospering notably. A substantial number, perhaps a majority, were Christian. The full-bloods were much more disposed to cling to their Indian dress and to their tribal life. They generally resisted the missionaries' evangelizing efforts and resented their influence over Christianized Indians.

A classic example of such a division was found among the Choctaw of Mississippi, the first tribe to sign a treaty—the Treaty of Dancing Bear Creek—under the terms of the federal legislation. The two most influential leaders of the Mississippi Choctaw were Greenwood LeFlore, a mixed-blood, and the old chief, Mushulatubbe, who had fought with Jackson in the war against the

Creek. Mushulatubbe had been deposed as head chief in 1826 by a mixed-blood named David Folsom on the grounds that he was too addicted to drink and too much under the influence of the whites to be trusted. Mushulatubbe, whose name meant Determined to Kill, was a powerful and imposing figure with a large head and strong features and was famous as an orator. He maintained two separate homes with a wife at each, owned eleven slaves, and cultivated thirty acres of land at the time of the Treaty of Dancing Bear Creek. We have an old daguerreotype of Greenwood LeFlore in the formal dress of a white man, looking very much like a successful planter or frontier lawyer. (It is one of the ironies of the Indian situation that mixed-blood Indians often enjoyed more prestige in the tribes than full-blooded Indian chiefs. Certainly the quality of their intelligence, or consciousness, was conspicuously "whiter" than their full-blooded brothers'.) When LeFlore undertook to manage the removal he soon found himself in conflict with Mushulatubbe and other chiefs, although the split was not simply along full-blood–mixed-blood lines. David Folsom, who had been educated by missionaries, had, after all, deposed Mushulatubbe.

Nonetheless, the first phase of the Choctaw removal began on an encouraging note. A group of Indian chiefs, accompanied by federal troops for protection against whites and hostile Indians, set off to look at the lands the Great White Father had reserved for them in Indian Territory. Each Indian was given a rifle, powder and ball, and winter clothing, and the party started out accompanied by George Gaines, an Indian trader liked and trusted by the Indians for his fair dealings and manifest sympathy for their cause. Every morning the hunters would spread out along the trail, Gaines wrote, "always bringing into camp in the evening plenty of game for the whole party, venison, turkeys, prairie hens and occasionally bear meat." The journey soon took on the air of an extended party: "an abundance of game, and fine weather to enjoy the chase, rendered each day and night joyous and happy." The lieutenant in command of the escort of soldiers and the surgeon sent along to care for the health of the soldiers and the Indians "were both jolly soldiers and good hunters and entered into our hunts in the day and feasts and jollification at night with great spirit and zest." Near the mouth of the Canadian River, Gaines and party were joined by a "Chickasaw delegation" on the same mission and they were invited by Gaines "to join us and travel with us to enjoy our sports; wild horses were now plentiful . . . large log fires at night . . . lengthened our social enjoyments. Our Choctaw hunting, war, love stories, and wit, were now seasoned by army stories and wit."

Reaching the designated lands, the Indians were "very much pleased" with the country, but there was an immediate awkwardness about which lands should be Choctaw and which Chickasaw, and threats of an attack by "Western" Indians forced the combined parties to prepare for hostilities. The younger braves looked forward to a fight with some anticipation so that they might judge the warlike qualities of their neighbors-to-be.

On the Red River they came upon an encampment of Shawnee who had been living there since the War of 1812. A mixed-blood woman, looking at Gaines, said, "You are a white man—I hope never to see the face of another white man." Some of the land was already occupied with Choctaw and Chickasaw settlements, bands of Indians who had come west on their own. These Indians indicated that they would welcome Indian emigrants.

The happy expedition of Gaines and the Choctaw was one of the few bright spots in a story whose tragedies accumulated month by month. The demoralizing effects of intratribal struggles over removal that often resulted in murders and outbreaks of fighting among the Indians were accentuated by the uncertainties concerning the details of the government policy, the time when the actual removal would take place for those Indians who accepted it, and the flooding of white speculators and traders onto Indian lands before the removals had even begun, debauching the Indians with bad whiskey and cheating them on the sales of their homesteads. Some Indians expressed the wish to make the journey on their own—hoping, as it turned out, to feed themselves by hunting and to pocket the ten dollars allocated by the government for their food en route.

When Gaines and his Choctaw returned from Indian Territory with glowing accounts of the country, seven or eight hundred of the Indians under LeFlore's influence departed posthaste, hoping to get the first choice of the new lands. Most of these left "the aged and infirm behind," assuming that the government would bring them on later. The Reverend Alexander Talley went ahead with a small party to build a church at the site allotted to the tribe, but many of the Indians departed without adequate winter clothing, without sufficient food or supplies, and with no way to cross the Mississippi River. The winter was unseasonably cold and several Indians froze to death on the march. Gaines's brother Edmund P. Gaines, a United States Army Officer, wrote of the Mississippi Choctaw: "The feeling which many of them evince in separating, never to return again, from their own long cherished hills, poor as they are in this section of the country, is truly painful to witness; and would be more so to me, but for the conviction that the removal is absolutely necessary for their welfare."

Confronted by any unfamiliar problem, the Indians were quite helpless, waiting patiently for the whites who accompanied them to extricate them from the difficulty. When wagons carrying their meager goods got mired in the mud, the Indians stood about, reluctant to do anything that savored of physical labor. It was only by appealing to Christian congregations in the white towns they passed that Talley was able to keep his charges from starving. He had exhausted his own funds and his credit to buy supplies before venturing westward across the Mississippi River (when Talley appealed for reimbursement, the secretary of war recommended against payment on the grounds that his disbursements had not been "previously authorized by the government").

It must be said that few emigrating Indians were allowed to proceed as improvidently as LeFlore's Choctaw. In most instances there was at least a semblance of planning and organization. The real estate and the livestock and equipment that the Indians were unable to take with them were sold to whites at far less than their real worth. The aged and infirm were loaded into wagons and cars along with personal belongings, and hogs, cattle, ponies, and sheep were gathered up and driven along by the women and children. Sometimes pack horses, mules, and oxen were preferred to wagons. There was usually an escort of soldiers and a government agent responsible for disbursing funds and exercising general supervision. Where practical, the initial stage of the trip up the Mississippi to the Red River or the Arkansas was aboard steamboats on which the Indians were crowded with their livestock.

The first removals were, by and large, the most arduous. In many places roads and bridges had to be built. The military officers and civilian agents had to learn from scratch all the complex problems involved in moving large numbers of essentially passive and sometimes resistant people over long distances "through a country little settled and literally impassable to any thing but wild beasts." Viewed in one perspective, the purely technical one, the organization of the removal was a remarkable accomplishment. In addition to the building of roads and bridges, food and supplies for the emigrants had to be deposited at "stands" along the routes marked out for the journey. Cattle were driven along to provide a daily ration of meat.

That was the way it was *supposed* to work and occasionally did. More often all that could go wrong did. The most devastating of such disasters was cholera, a terrible epidemic of which coincided with the most active period of removal. One large party of Choctaw got lost in a swamp in the middle of winter; several hundred head of their horses and cattle died and the Indians themselves, who had been six days without food, were rescued only by the combined efforts of whites recruited by missionaries accompanying the Indians. From Lake Providence, some sixty miles from Vicksburg, an indignant white settler wrote the secretary of war describing a scene he had witnessed: a party of Indians had to cross a swollen river on rafts in a sleet storm "under the pressure of hunger, by *old* women and young children, without any covering for their feet, legs or body except a cotton underdress . . . before they reached the place of getting rations here, I gave a small party leave to enter a field in which pumpkins were. They would not enter without leave, though starving. These they ate *raw* with the greatest avidity."

By March, 1832, it was estimated that there were 4,500 Choctaw west of the Mississippi, but well over 8,000 remained in the state. Ironically, the Indians for whom the removal policy might have been the hardest were those who had gone further in adapting to white ways. Such a one was the Choctaw chief Toblee Chubee, who—a convert to Christianity—had converted the members of his tribe and prevailed on them to live sober, industrious lives, to abandon the habits of Indians and live like "the better class of white people." In 1845, Toblee Chubee and his followers were finally persuaded to move; many suffered from disease and died in Indian Territory. Almost forty-five years later, when Indians remaining in Mississippi were invited to apply for lands in Indian Territory, more than 24,000, most of whom were predominantly white, did so. Of these 1,445 were accepted and added to the tribe.

The Creek in Alabama had a large list of grievances against the whites of that state, and in 1831 they sent two chiefs to Washington to appeal to the government for protection against the rapacity and exploitation of the whites. "Murders," they declared,

> have taken place, both by reds and whites. We have caused the
> red men to be brought to justice, the whites go unpunished. We
> are weak and our words and oaths go for naught; justice we don't
> expect, nor can we get. We may expect murderers to be more
> frequent. . . . They bring spirits among us for the purpose
> of practicing frauds; they daily rob us of our property; they bring
> white officers among us, and take our property from us for debts
> that we never contracted. We are made subject to laws we have no
> means of comprehending; we never know when we are doing right.

They would not move west, they declared. "Our aged fathers and mothers beseech us to remain upon the land that gave us birth, where the bones of their kindred are buried, so that when they die they mingle their ashes together." One chief, Eneah Micco, sent the

United States Indian agent a list of whites living illegally on Indian lands. They numbered 1,500, among them many horse thieves and common criminals. Some were already marking the spots they intended to take over "by blazing and cutting initials of their names on the trees" around the homes of the Indians.

In Washington, the Creek chiefs met with the secretary of war and told him, "We have made many treaties with the United States at all times with the belief that the one making was to be the last . . . we have frequently given up large tracts of our country for a mere song; and now we are called on for the remnant of our land, and for us to remove beyond the Mississippi." There were then some twenty-five thousand Creek in Alabama, owning nine hundred slaves.

Colonel John Albert, directed by Cass to superintend the removal of the Alabama Creek, wrote a prophetic letter to the secretary of war in the summer of 1833. The Creek, he noted,

> are incapable of such an effort and of the arrangements and fore-sight which it requires. Nor have they confidence in themselves to undertake it. They fear starvation on the route; and can it be otherwise, when many of them are nearly starving now. . . . A people who will sell their corn in the fall for twenty-five cents a bushel, and have to buy in the spring at a dollar or dig roots to sustain life; a people who appear never to think of tomorrow, are not a people capable of husbanding the means, and anticipating the wants of a journey, with women, and children, of eight hundred miles.

Albert warned Cass that every area of good hunting, "every trivial accident, will occasion days of delay; and join with these their listless, idle, lounging habits, their love of drink . . . and what can be expected if the emigration is left to themselves? . . . You cannot have an adequate idea of the deterioration which these Indians have undergone during the last two or three years, from a state of comparative plenty to that of unqualified wretchedness and want."

This was due primarily to the fact that the state, anticipating possession of the Indians' lands, had permitted whites to invade their nation, "made encroachments upon their lands, even upon their cultivated fields, abuses of their persons and property; hosts of traders, who, like locusts, have destroyed what little disposition to cultivation the Indians may once have had. . . . Emigration is the only hope of self-preservation left to these people. They are brow beat, cowed, and imposed upon, and depressed with the feeling that they have no adequate protection in the United States. . . . They dare not enforce their own laws to preserve order, for fear of the laws of the whites." The heartbreaking consequence was that the more lawless Indians, freed from all constraints, murdered their fellows with impunity. In another report, Albert wrote of the Creek, "Their helpless ignorance, their generally good character, (for they are a well disposed people), instead of establishing claims upon good feelings, seem rather to expose them to injuries."

Cass, appalled by the stories that reached him, wrote to the governor of Alabama protesting the treatment of the defenseless Creek. "Gross and wanton outrages have been committed" upon them. "The houses of the Indians have been forcibly taken possession of, and sometimes burnt, and the owners driven into the woods . . . their horses, cattle, hogs, and other property have been taken from them. . . . And, in addition to this, the deputy marshal reports that there are four hundred persons selling whiskey to the Indians on the ceded lands." When federal marshals and United States soldiers tried to arrest the most flagrant violators of Indian rights, they were arrested by state officials and tried in state courts.

In the summer of 1834, Jackson sent Francis Scott Key, composer of "The Star-Spangled Banner," to Alabama to report on conditions in the state. Key proved an able advocate of the Indian cause both before the legislature of the state and in Washington. He also reported that angry Alabamans were ready to lynch the soldiers and the officers charged with protecting the Indians. His estimate was that more than ten thousand whites were living on Creek lands; to evict them would require an army and result in widespread civil disorder.

The story that we are now familiar with from the experience of the Choctaw was repeated with the Creek, the principal differences being that the Creek were more resistant to moving and, if possible, less capable of coping with the problems involved. Despite an intense campaign of persuasion only 630 Indians enrolled for the trip under Captain John Page, a young regular army officer with strong compassion for his charges. "I have to stop the wagons to take the children out and warm them and put them back 6 or 7 times a day," he wrote. "I send ahead and have fires built for this purpose. I wrap them in anything I can get hold of to keep them from freezing. . . . Strict attention had to be paid to this or some must inevitably have perished. Five or six in each wagon constantly crying in consequence of suffering with the cold." When they reached the end of their three-month-long travail at the Creek agency at Fort Gibson, only 469 had survived the trip.

The great majority of the Creek refused to leave and every kind of pressure—including false reports that the Creek were on the warpath—was brought to bear on them until even the *Montgomery Advertiser* spoke out in protest:

> The war with the Creeks is all *a humbug*. It is a base and diabolical scheme, devised by interested men, to keep an ignorant race of people from maintaining their just rights. . . . We do trust, for the credit of those concerned, that these blood suckers may be ferreted out, and their shameful misrepresentations exposed. . . . The Red Man must soon leave. They have nothing left on which to subsist. Their property has been taken from them—their stock killed up, their farms pillages—and by whom? By white men. . . . Such villains may go unpunished in this world, but the day of retribution will most certainly arrive.

Georgia and Alabama citizens, alarmed at indications that the Creek, driven to desperation, were ready to turn on the nearest whites, sent an angry memorandum to Congress asking that body to investigate "the most revolting facts known to the annals of history, disclosing scenes of turpitude and raping. . . . Clandestinely opening the flood-gates of savage assassination upon the defenseless women and children of this late prosperous country." The memorandum was signed by seven hundred persons. The Alabama and Georgia Creek were now rounded up by federal troops, held in stockades, and then marched off, many in handcuffs, under heavy guards to the Indian Territory.

Behind the manacled braves came some two to three thousand women and children, "shedding tears and making the most bitter wailings." "It was a deplorable sight," an army officer noted, "but the wretchedness and destruction they have caused, and the diabolical cruelty which has characterized them during this warfare, demands the most ignominious punishment, and chains are worse to them than death." But the *Montgomery Advertiser* noted: "The spectacle exhibited by them was truly melancholy. To see the remnant of a once mighty people fettered and chained together forced to depart from the land of their fathers into a country unknown to them, is of itself sufficient to move the stoutest heart." All through the summer the doleful story continued. Now it was heat and dust that prostrated the Indians, and outbreaks of the dread cholera. By November eight thousand Creek had crossed the Mississippi at Memphis and another five thousand were camped awaiting supplies and boats that would carry them across.

THE CHEROKEE CLAIMED 7,200,000 ACRES east of the Mississippi, the greater part of it in Georgia. The tribe was estimated to contain some 2,700 families (or 16,542 individuals), which worked out to roughly 2,666 acres of land per family. The kind of harassment they were subject to is indicated by the story of Joseph Vann, a Cherokee who had 800 acres in cultivation and a home of brick said to have cost $10,000. Charging him with having broken the law by employing a white overseer while he was absent, a state agent seized his property as forfeit. Two whites, claiming the house, fought for possession of it, finally setting it afire while Vann and his family fled across the Tennessee line.

The Cherokee removal began with deceptive smoothness. A first contingent of some two hundred reached Little Rock in January 1830, where an observer noted that most of them were whites or mixed-bloods with Indian wives and mixed-blood children and slaves. A number of the "Indians" look more black than red, being the offspring, in many instances, of Indians and escaped or free blacks. But efforts to persuade full-bloods to emigrate met determined opposition. An Indian named Bushyhead returned from Indian Territory with dismaying tales of suffering and want. At this point word of the Supreme Court decision in the case of the Reverend Worcester caused widespread rejoicing among the Cherokee: "Councils were called in all the towns of the nation, rejoicings—night dances, etc, were had in all parts upon the occasion. . . ."

John Ross, one of the principal Cherokee chiefs (his Indian name was Cooweescoowe), led a delegation to Washington. He was a mixed-blood whose father had been a Scottish Loyalist married to a woman of one-fourth Cherokee blood. Ross had gone to a white school and served as an adjutant to the Cherokee Regiment that fought with Jackson at the Battle of the Horseshoe in the Creek War, and he had worked to develop schools and vocational training for Cherokee youth. On the return of the delegation from Washington with a treaty, various factions of the nation became involved in bitter contentions over removal. Ross was opposed to leaving but Elias Boudinot—a graduate of the Indian School founded by the Pennsylvania philanthropist Elias Boudinot, whose name he had taken—supported the removal and was murdered as a result. Ross could not bring himself to believe that the federal government, or more specifically Jackson, would allow the dispossession of his people. Such an act was too opposed to every principle of American justice, to the Constitution of the United States, and to the doctrines of the Christian religion that many Cherokee espoused.

John Howard Payne, a popular actor and playwright who was to be known to posterity as the author of "Home, Sweet Home," was present when the chieftains of the Cherokee met at Red Clay,

Tennessee, to consider the treaty negotiated by their leaders with the secretary of war. He wrote a vivid account of the gathering:

> Every thing was noiseless. The party, entering, loosened the blankets which were loosely rolled and flung over their backs and hung them, with their tin cups and other paraphernalia attached, upon the fence. The chief approached them. They formed diagonally in two lines, and each in silence drew near to give his hand. Their dress was neat and picturesque; all wore turbans, except four or five with hats; many of them tunics, with sashes; many long robes, and nearly all some drapery; so that they had the oriental air of old scripture pictures of patriarchal processions.

The treaty was rejected and Ross instructed to return to Washington to continue the negotiations. To prevent him from leaving, twenty-five members of the Georgia guard arrested him and Payne on Tennessee soil and carried the two men to Georgia, where they were held twelve days. The *Cherokee Phoenix*, the Indian newspaper, was suppressed and the nation forbidden to hold councils at their capital, New Echota. When Payne was released, his widely reprinted story of the persecution of the Cherokee roused a storm of criticism in the North and indeed brought protests from many Southerners as well.

What distinguished the Cherokee from the other Southern tribes was their determined resistance to removal. Among the Choctaw, Creek, and Chickasaw many had been prevailed upon to remove voluntarily, or at least had eventually yielded to white pressures; but with the Cherokee bribes, threats, confiscation of property, the cutting off of desperately needed supplies of food, and other harassments failed to budge the great majority. They preserved their solidarity and General John Ellis Wool, given the thankless task of managing their removal, wrote to the War Department that "however poor or destitute," most of them would not receive "either rations or clothing from the United States lest they might compromise themselves in regard to the treaty. . . . Many have said they will die before they will leave the country."

Wool, whose sympathies were entirely with the Indians, found their plight "heartrending." He, like all other observers of the Indians' situation, favored removing them "beyond the reach of the white men, who, like vultures, are watching, ready to pounce upon their prey and strip them of everything. . . . Yes, sir, nineteen-twentieths, if not ninety-nine out of every hundred, will go penniless to the West." One Indian chief wrote to Jackson that the "lowest class of the white people are flogging Cherokees with cowhides, hickories, and clubs. We are not safe in our houses—our people are assailed day and night by the rabble. Even justices of the peace and constables are concerned in this business. This barbarous treatment is not confined to the men, but women are stripped also and whipped without law or mercy. . . . Send regular troops to protect us from these lawless assaults." The commanding officer of the Tennessee militia called out to suppress a rumored uprising of the Cherokee, declared he would never dishonor Tennessee arms by assisting in enforcing a treaty so clearly opposed by a great majority of the Indians.

Finally, early in 1837, after almost eight years of resistance, some 466 Indians out of more than eighteen thousand, "the most wealthy and intelligent," those who had the most to lose to the depredations of the whites—were prevailed upon to start west. Half of the party were children. The hardships they suffered were not as severe as those of many other migrants, but there was an inevitable accompaniment of short rations, illness, disease and death in addition to the trauma of the move itself.

Other parties left for the West during 1837, but the mass of the Indians stood firm under the leadership of John Ross, suffering endless trials and humiliations in the process. In the spring of 1838 a petition signed by more than fifteen thousand Cherokee was presented to President Martin Van Buren asking that the charges of fraud and misrepresentation in regard to the treaty be investigated. When Van Buren tried to extend the time allowed to the Indians for their departure, the governor of Georgia threatened to take matters into his own hands. May, 1838, had been set as the final date for their removal and huge flatboats had been built to carry the emigrants down the Tennessee River. The boats were 130 feet long and two stories high. They carried stoves to keep the red-skinned passengers warm and hearths on the top of the deck for cooking. Some two thousand Indians had already made the trip west. Plans were now made to force the remainder to leave and the task was assigned to General Winfield Scott, who took command of a mixed force of militia, volunteers, and army regulars totaling some seven thousand men.

One of the most unnerving features of the removal was that wherever possible, crude churches and altars were erected and Cherokee preachers conducted services, often touching on the theme of the Children of Israel in Egyptian bondage. The ministers were tireless. "They never relaxed their evangelical labors," William Coodey, a Cherokee chieftain, wrote to Payne. "They held church meetings, received ten members . . . and went down to the river and baptized them. . . . Some whites present affirm it to have been the most solemn and impressive religious service they ever witnessed."

The line of march was led by "Going Snake, an aged and respected chief whose head eighty summers had whitened, mounted on his favorite pony. . . ." Coodey watched "my poor and unhappy countrymen, driven by brutal power from all they loved and cherished in the land of their fathers to gratify the cravings of avarice."

The nearly fifteen thousand Cherokee, concentrated in seven or eight camps guarded by soldiers, constituted by far the largest number of Indians ever moved west in a limited time. By steamboat, flatboat, train, wagons, on horseback, and on foot they made their way along the "Trail of Tears," as the route came to be called in the Indian memory of their removal. Nine parties left in October 1838 and four the next month. Again various illnesses struck down many Indians, bearing especially hard on young children. Skimpy rations, lack of proper sanitation, smuggled whiskey, bad water, the heat and dust and simple misery killed hundreds of Indians in each company of emigrants and thousands in the total. Those parties led by native Indian missionaries like Jesse Bushyhead and Evan Jones got permission not to travel on Sundays so that they could hold religious services. One company of more prosperous Indians included 645 wagons and some five thousand horses, besides many oxen. "It was like the march of an army," one observer wrote, "regiment after regiment, the wagons in the center, the officers along the line and the horsemen on the flanks and at the rear."

A Maine traveler, headed for Nashville, passed a unit of some two thousand Cherokee in western Kentucky and gave a detailed account of the procession: "The Indians carry a downcast dejected look bordering upon the appearance of despair; others a wild frantic appearance as if about to burst the chains of nature and pounce like a tiger upon their enemies. . . . One lady passed on her hack in company with her husband, apparently with as much refinement and equipage as any of the mothers of New England; and she was a mother of two and her youngest child about three years old was sick in her arms. . . . " When the last stragglers had passed, the anonymous Maine traveler "wept like childhood" at the thought that "my native countrymen had thus expelled . . . those suffering exiles. . . . I wished the President could have been there that very day in Kentucky with myself . . . full well I know that many prayers have gone up to the King of Heaven from Maine in behalf of the poor Cherokees."

One of the parties that came through with the least loss of life was one whose Indian leader was the Reverend Stephen Foreman, a graduate of both Union and Princeton theological seminaries. Foreman's party began its journey with 983 men, women, and children, the great majority Christians. They lost 57 by death on the trip and had 19 births, thus numbering 921 on their arrival in their new home. The Christian Indians, having acquired with their faith that part of the white consciousness that was predominantly Christian, displayed the white's capacity for planning and organizing. Having in many instances prospered materially, they often started out with prudent provisions for the journey that helped to mitigate the inevitable suffering and hardship. Such individuals were Indians only in the most specific racial sense. Culturally, they were white. They had no more in common with Comanche or Kiowa than did a pious New England farmer.

Overall the loss of life was enormous. Of the roughly fifteen thousand Cherokee removed, it is estimated that approximately four thousand died in the course of being captured, held in camps prior to their removal, or on the journey itself.

While in many ways the Cherokee removal was less terrible than that of the more southerly tribes, the fact that, under the leadership of John Ross, the great majority of the Nation resisted removal to the bitter end drew particular attention to their plight; that is why Indian removal has been associated in the popular mind with the Cherokee, though they were considerably outnumbered by the other tribes.

The soldiers "were sent to search out with rifle and bayonet every small cabin hidden away in the coves or by the sides of mountain streams. . . . Men were seized in their fields or going along the road, women were taken from their wheels and children from their play." A Georgia volunteer, who later served as a colonel in the Confederate army, wrote many years after the event: "I fought through the civil war and have seen men shot to pieces and slaughtered by the thousands, but the Cherokee removal was the cruelest work I ever knew."

One old Indian, his house surrounded by a squad of soldiers, called his family together and all knelt and prayed together while the discomforted soldiers looked on. William Coodey, the Cherokee chief, wrote to John Howard Payne,

> Multitudes were allowed no time to take anything with them, except the clothes they had on. Well-furnished houses were left a prey to plunderers . . . The property of many has been taken, and sold before their eyes for almost nothing—the sellers and buyers, in many cases having combined to cheat the poor Indians. . . . Many of the Cherokees, who, a few days ago, were in comfortable circumstances, are now victims of abject poverty . . . this is not a description of extreme cases. It is altogether a

faint representation of the work which has been perpetuated on the unoffending, unarmed and unresisting Cherokees.

THE MOST INTRACTABLE INDIAN PROBLEM, so far as the "Eastern" and "Southern" Indians were concerned, was that of the Seminole of Florida—against whom Jackson had waged war almost twenty years earlier. Thoroughly at home in the labyrinthine recesses of the Florida swamps, they provided a hospitable refuge for runaway slaves. The Seminole, large, stout Indians, had a complex and sophisticated culture centering around sun worship. Like the other civilized tribes, they were excellent farmers, growing millet, sunflowers, pumpkins, melons, and tobacco. They made corn bread and hominy. From the whites they took over poultry and domestic animals as well as the cultivation of fruit trees.

When they found themselves included in the policy of removal, their leaders counseled them to accept the inevitable rather than engage in a futile war with the United States. A removal treaty had already been signed when the Seminole learned that no one of black blood would be allowed to accompany them. Such individuals would be sold into slavery. Since some Indian women were married to blacks, the edict meant tearing families apart and this the Seminole refused to do. In addition, some of the chiefs who had visited the lands reserved for their tribe reported that the neighboring Indians were "bad." A number of the Seminole yielded to the government's pressure, but a group led by a chief who, although he was the son of an English trader named William Powell, went by the Indian name of Osceola, refused to go. There were further negotiations. Jackson had, to be sure, declared on numerous occasions that no Indians would be removed against their will, but now he sent orders that they must go willingly or be transported in chains. An extension until the spring of 1836 was allowed, and Osceola and his fellow chiefs made good use of the time to prepare for resistance. The general in charge of the removal operation was startled to hear that five chiefs and five hundred Seminole who were willing to leave had had to flee for their lives to a federal fort on Tampa Bay.

Osceola's wife was the daughter of an escaped slave and an Indian. As such she was, under Florida law, a black and a slave, and when she accompanied her husband to Fort King she was seized as a slave. When the furious Osceola challenged the commander of the fort, General Wiley Thompson, Thompson had him put in irons for insubordination. To secure his freedom Osceola pretended contrition, signed a document promising to remove, and once released began to raid plantations in the area.

When he received word that the main body of troops would be absent from Fort King, Osceola and some of his braves concealed themselves near the fort and when Thompson came out they riddled him with fourteen bullets. A sutler and his clerks were killed and scalped, the store robbed and set on fire. The Indians then ambushed a detachment of 110 soldiers in the Wahoo Swamp and killed and scalped the whole party with the exception of three who escaped. Two days later, with two hundred Seminole warriors and fugitive slaves, Osceola intercepted General Duncan Lamont Clinch as the head of six hundred soldiers moving from Fort Drane to the Withlacoochee River. Osceola was wounded in the engagement and the Seminole withdrew after several hours of bitter fighting.

Indians and blacks now roved the northeast region of Florida, adjacent to Georgia, killing whites and burning plantations and crops in the fields. Soon the whole region was depopulated as terrified whites fled to the larger towns and the government forts for protection. A thousand volunteers were raised from Georgia, South Carolina, and Alabama and placed under the command of General Winfield Scott. Ill-equipped and commanding untrained and undisciplined volunteers, Scott was no match for Osceola. Indeed, three generals—Gaines, Clinch, and Scott—were unable to bring the rebellious Indian to a decisive engagement. Scott was recalled and his command devolved on Richard Call, an officer in the Florida militia. Osceola attacked American forces at Micanopy in June and, while he did not succeed in capturing the stockade there, he forced General Clinch out of Fort Drane. Scott's successor, General Thomas Jesup, was no more successful.

For more than a year Osceola baffled, harassed, and occasionally defeated the troops dispatched against him. Finally, in the spring of 1837, Jesup persuaded the Indians to meet in a peace conference at Fort Dade. A treaty which provided that the Seminole would "remove" and which guaranteed them "their negroes, their *bona fide* property," was signed and boats were assigned to carry them to New Orleans on the first leg of their journey to Indian Territory. Before the Indians could be loaded aboard, however, whites appeared to reclaim certain blacks as their former slaves. At this the blacks scattered, although Jesup was able to seize some ninety at Tampa Bay. The Indians, convinced that the terms of the treaty had been abrogated, took to the swamps and forests once again and the war resumed. In the fall Osceola and a band of his followers came to Jesup's command post to try to negotiate the release of two captured Indian chiefs. While talks were going on under a flag of truce, Jesup ordered the Indian camp surrounded and Osceola and other Indians seized. This act of bad faith raised a storm of protest in the North, but Jesup defended himself on the grounds that Osceola could not be relied on to observe the terms of any treaty. The Seminole chief was sent to Fort Moultrie off Charleston and died there a few months later.

There was widespread sympathy with Osceola and the stubborn Seminole. At the news of his death, New York Mayor Philip Hone, who had no toleration of that city's Irish, the free blacks, or the tailors or carpenters, noted in his diary: "This noble Indian . . . had been brought a prisoner after being kidnapped by one of those breaches of good faith which we white civilized men do not hesitate to put in practice against unenlightened heathens, as we vaingloriously call them."

After Osceola's death Colonel Zachary Taylor (with a force of eleven hundred regulars, volunteers, and Indian auxiliaries) attacked a Seminole stronghold in the Okeechobee Swamp and after bitter fighting drove the Indians out. The American loss was twenty-six killed and over a hundred wounded, however, and Taylor was forced to withdraw. At last the federal troops abandoned the fray. Some Seminole were persuaded to emigrate, but most remained in their Everglade refuges, free from white harassment.

THE POLICY OF INDIAN REMOVAL was fashioned with a particular group of Indians in mind. These were the aborigines who had proved least assimilable, who doggedly maintained their tribal customs, whose young braves persisted in stealing ponies and cattle and periodically murdering stray whites, who were most readily debauched by unscrupulous white traders, and who often lived in conditions of desperate poverty and degradation, depending increasingly on government subventions for survival. These Indians were a particular offense to the whites who wished them out of the way. The fact that the policy included, willy-nilly, thousands of other Indians in various stages of assimilation was its harshest and most unjust feature. As President Jackson had said in his first annual message to Congress, the fifty-year-long policy of helping the Indians to accommodate themselves to white culture, to become "civilized," had plainly failed. But that was only part of the story. Much racial assimilation had certainly gone on. Many "Indians" were indistinguishable in their lifestyles from whites—or, indeed, in their appearance. But for none of these variations in acculturation was there any provision in the policy of removal. Anyone living on Indian lands and having some degree of Indian blood had to leave.

Even with the benefit of hindsight it is hard to understand what policy could have succeeded in making the life of the Southern Indians endurable. The state courts denied them justice; they were cruelly used and exploited by rapacious and unscrupulous whites. Even if the then-current interpretations of the Constitution had allowed the federal government to intervene on behalf of the Indians, such intervention would undoubtedly have accelerated the talk of secession and in any event would have been impractical. Despite all that, the fact remains that the Indians were constantly cheated and exploited, robbed and sometimes killed by their white neighbors in those states in which they were found in substantial numbers. Part of the problem was that white men believed that they had as much right to cheat and swindle Indians as to cheat and swindle each other.

The whole issue of removal was complicated by the fact that the Five Civilized Nations of the South—the Choctaw, Chickasaw, Creek, Cherokee, and the Seminole—were in many ways more advanced than the Western tribes, being settled in villages and employing relatively sophisticated agricultural techniques. Tribes like the Kickapoo and Shawnee, more nomadic in character, had responded to white pressure or simply to the search for furs and game by moving westward of their own volition. To white Americans land was primarily real estate, something to be bought and sold, ideally for a profit. Such individuals simply could not conceive of the place-bound character of the Civilized Indians. The land had a particular power and significance for all Indians, settled and nomadic; it was filled with animated spirits and made sacred by the graves of ancestors. For the settled Indians it contained the essence of meaning of their existence. Whites gave their ultimate allegiances to abstractions—the Union, their states, Georgia or Virginia, God or Progress. Such abstractions had no power for Indians. They worshiped the spirit in the concrete and particular, in trees and rivers, rocks and animals.

James Mooney, a pioneer ethnologist who was himself involved in the removal, wrote: "The Cherokee removal of 1838 . . . may well exceed in weight of grief and pathos any other passage in American history." Certainly, if we take it with the removal of the other Southern tribes, it clearly constitutes the most tragic episode of our past, the Civil War excepted. The question is, Who was to blame? Clearly it was "the democracy," "the people" of Alabama, Mississippi, and Georgia. The people whose voice was said to be the voice of God. Or the Constitution, which allowed each state control over its own internal affairs and more particularly over police powers. What about the state officials? Certainly they were no help, rather the contrary; but they were, after all, only the servants of the people. Who were the people who robbed the Indians of their lands? They ranged from wealthy plantation owners and avaricious politicians to the most humble participants in the "free enterprise system." Americans have always shown a strong inclination toward criminality when the acquisition of wealth is involved. But there is still the feeling that even if the rights of the Indians had been scrupulously protected, their situation was an impossible one. It was, after all, the virtually unanimous judgment of those whites friendly to the Indians that removal was the only possible conclusion to "the Indian problem." The democracy was insatiable in its appetite for Indian lands and undoubtedly could not have been denied for long without tearing up the republic.

Americans are disposed to believe that all problems have solutions. If there is a higher order in the universe, if man is a rational animal, then there must be reasonable solutions to the most terrible dilemmas. But of course that is not necessarily so. There are "problems" that disintegrate into unmitigated tragedies. The entire Indian–white confrontation was a tragedy, but the Indian removal— perhaps because it was, on the part of the great majority of the people who fashioned it over almost a decade, well intentioned—was the most appalling chapter in a tragedy with so many acts.

Some modern historians have compared the removal to the Nazi Holocaust against the Jews, but the analogy is superficial and misleading. Official governmental policy was just the reverse of that of the Nazis toward the Jews. The purpose was not to exterminate the Indians but to *save them from extermination.*

On the credit side of the moral ledger must be placed the names of those individuals like the two Gaineses, John Page, William Armstrong, Alexander Talley, and many other named and unnamed soldiers, missionaries, and plain citizens who did their best to mitigate the sufferings of the Indians and some of whom devoted their lives to trying to improve the miserable conditions under which the great majority of the Indians lived.

Contemplating the horrors of the Indian removal, we can understand why D. H. Lawrence and others have seen America as a haunted land. The story of the whites and Indians is the story of the relationship of democracy to original sin. The Supreme Court's skirts were clean even if its injunctions were impotent. It had upheld the Constitution against popular clamor, against the democracy, the people of Georgia, Mississippi, and Alabama. When the Founding Fathers, in the name of equality, had invited the participation of *all* Americans (women and blacks and of course Indians excepted) in the political process, subject to only those rather modest constraints made necessary by the effort to apply Divine law to human affairs, they had released hitherto inconceivable amounts of human energy and, inevitably, in the process a considerable amount of original sin. That was certainly unexceptional enough; no more than might have been expected, and the Founders themselves had been well aware of the risk. But since a primary article of the democratic faith, held by its exemplars such as Jefferson and Jackson, was that "the people" were "good," we were forced into a kind of double-entry moral bookkeeping where the credit side of the ledger was constantly displayed and the debit side hidden. Moreover, God was commonly believed to be incapable of sin; thus if the United States was to take on itself the attributes of the Divine, it too must be without sin.

The Indian issue was the issue of the democracy. The reformers of New England and the aristocrats of New York were, for the most part, impeccable on the Indian issue. It was their anti-bank opponents, the supporters of Andrew Jackson, the sturdy, honest, hardworking farmers who flunked. "The frontiers," wrote Gustaf Unonius, a Swedish immigrant,

> are often settled by a peculiar kind of people who nourish inwardly a mortal hatred of the red man. They have been characterized, strikingly enough, by the statement that they have two kinds of conscience, one for whites, another for Indians. They are people whose behavior in their relations with their own race, whose kindliness—yes, whose often meticulous obedience to the commandments of religion—would entitle them to respect and esteem in any ordered community. For them, however, the red man's rights and privileges, his possessions, and his life weigh little on the scales, and they consider any injustice toward the

Indians justifiable and permissible. Brave, seasoned, and enterprising, faithful, honest, benevolent, and hospitable toward a white stranger, they lack in their hearts all kindly feeling, all compassion for nature's wild children. . . .

The obsession of Americans with the red man was subliminal, so to speak. Even when short-memoried newspapers carried no accounts of Indian wars or raids, of cruelty to or by the Indians, the Indian was there: in the novels of Cooper, in the paintings of Catlin or Bingham, in the poems of Whittier and Longfellow.

Philip Hone noted in his diary: "Indian stories are now all the rage in the United States and Canada. Col. McKenney's 'Indian Portraits' is a stupendous work, by which I am told, the publishers will realize a profit of $100,000. . . . Washington Irving's 'Tour of the Prairies' and subsequently his 'Astoria' have aided in directing public attention to the annals of the red men. Latrobe also wrote an excellent book on the same subject, all of which are seen, heard, and read by learned men and fashionable ladies . . ." McKenney had joined forces with James Hall, a capable artist, to publish the handsomely illustrated *History of the Indian Tribes of North America* which, as Hone indicated, became an immediate best-seller despite its very considerable cost.

Those Americans who sentimentalized or romanticized the Indians were usually deeply and desperately aware of the dehumanizing aspects of much of American life. They yearned for the noble and gracious and found it in the aborigine. The Indian recalled Plato's "the unreflective striving toward what is noble." In the white psyche reason/mind must dominate—the *Nous*—but in the savage, the center of life and vital energy was the *thymos*—the organ of courage and high life.

In perpetual contrast to the disintegrative effects of white society there was the tribe. The Indian could not comprehend that strange, isolate being, "the individual," so prized by the whites. He only knew a Delaware, a Shawnee, a Caddo, or an Iowa. The almost chronic loneliness that many Americans experienced, even in the midst of crowded cities, was unknown to the Indian, who was secure in his tribe. He could not have understood the perpetually asked American question, "Who am I?" He was a Sioux, a Kiowa, an Arapaho, a Comanche. Against the incomprehensible velocity of change in white America, the Indian, with his fixed tribal culture, seemed as enduring as the earth.

In the troubled area of sexuality, the white man had again to confront the Indian way. Abstract sexuality, like abstract thought, was unknown to the Indian. He did not fantasize about sex, he simply engaged in it naturally and spontaneously. He offered his wife to the white man as casually as he offered his hand—a gesture of friendship or a present that seemed depraved to the white man. Thousands of white men took Indian wives. Did they value the Indian women over their white sisters for their uninhibited sexuality?

The problem of the white American's relationship to the Indian was complicated by the fact that America was supposed to be the land of innocence. Europe represented old, worldly, corrupt, "artificial" civilization. America represented innocence and goodness, "natural man" close to nature, simple and democratic. But what was the Indian? Supernatural? Already there were numerous Americans comparing American "civilization" unfavorably with the "natural" spontaneous life of the American aborigine.

Although the removal of the Southern or civilized tribes was the most dramatic and tragic episode in the Indian–white relations because of the Indian resistance and because they had in so many instances accommodated themselves to white society, the same inexorable pressures drove the Indians out of the states of the Northwest.

CHAPTER X

PUSHING
WESTWARD

Even as the Indian Removal was beginning, fighting broke out between settlers and the Sac and Fox Indians in Illinois Territory. The Indians were led by Black Hawk, a Potawatomi whose father, a famous warrior, had become head chief of the Sauk (or Sac). Young Black Hawk had won glory in wars against the Osage and the Cherokee, and when his father was killed in a campaign against the Cherokee, he succeeded him. In 1830, the Sauk and Foxes had signed a treaty giving up all claim to their lands along the Mississippi, some seven hundred miles in extent.

A number of the Sauk and Foxes under the leadership of Black Hawk's rival, Keokuk, crossed the Mississippi to the area designated as their reservation. Black Hawk and a group of his followers refused to join them, but the land their villages were on was declared property of the United States by the territorial governor and sold by lot to white settlers. While Black Hawk and his band were on a hunting and raiding expedition, the white claimants appeared, tore down the Indians' huts, and plowed up their fields.

Black Hawk returned to the villages in the spring and ordered the settlers off what he claimed were still Indian lands. While the frightened whites watched, his warriors destroyed fences, pulled down houses, and drove off or killed the cattle. Then six companies of United States troops, augmented by fifteen hundred volunteers and several bands of Oneida Indians, went in pursuit of Black Hawk.

The disorderly and undisciplined militia could not be controlled by their officers. There was no march discipline; making haphazard camps, they drank homemade whiskey and failed to observe the commonest precautions. When a party of Indians was sighted, the volunteers set out after them, shouting and hallooing. They were led into an ambush, and when the Indians charged they took to their heels—or rather their horses took to their hooves, their frightened riders clinging to their saddles. Eleven whites were killed in the rout and a number wounded. When word of the defeat spread through the frontier, the alarmed settlers began to build a series of small forts, most of them little more than houses reinforced by logs and palisades. The Indian tactics were to avoid direct engagements with the whites and direct their attention to any undefended farms or villages. Each day brought a fresh toll of murdered settlers.

Sioux and Menominee Indians, traditional enemies of the Sauk and Foxes, were recruited along with some Winnebago—often allies of the Sauk and Foxes; these Indian auxiliaries were especially useful in such warfare as Black Hawk was waging, with small bands attacking isolated farms. On one occasion, Colonel Henry Dodge, one of the original settlers engaged in lead mining and commander of militia by virtue of his prominence in the area, led a platoon of volunteers in pursuit of a party of Sauk who had killed four men working in a cornfield. The thirteen Indian raiders were overtaken at a riverbank and killed. Drawn by the sound of firing, a band of Sioux arrived in time to take the Sauks' scalps and mutilate their bodies.

The fighting was mostly encounters between small parties of whites and Indians, often fiercely fought with mixed results. In a battle at the Rock River between a company of whites led by Major

John Dement and some two hundred Indians led by Black Hawk, the Indians killed five white men and forty horses at a cost to themselves of "two young chiefs and seven warriors." Through May and June the Indians, usually taking the initiative, killed some thirty whites, the majority of them caught outside their hastily built fortifications. But the final outcome was foreordained. As larger companies of whites closed in on the area along the Rock River that served as Black Hawk's base of operations, the Indians were forced to drop back. When Black Hawk prepared to cross the Wisconsin River with his band of several hundred warriors, accompanied by a number of women and children, the pursuing whites led by twelve Winnebago scouts attacked. Vastly outnumbered, Black Hawk saw twenty or thirty of his braves fall while the American loss was one killed and eight wounded. Darkness saved the Indians, and under cover of night they made their way across the Wisconsin. Again the whites pressed their pursuit and finally overtook the Sauk, encumbered by their women and children, at the mouth of the Bad Axe River, forty miles from the post at Prairie du Chien. A steamboat carrying a six-pound cannon blocked Black Hawk's flight across the Mississippi. Brought to bay at last, Black Hawk tried to surrender, but the Wisconsin and Illinois volunteers had come to kill Indians and were not to be deterred. The Indian leader insisted to his dying day that the whites had deliberately ignored his display of a white flag, and an American officer gave credence to the claim by writing later: "As we neared them they raised a white flag and endeavored to decoy us, but we were a little too old for them." The Indians were cut down mercilessly, and the handful who escaped across the river, including women and children, were hunted down and killed by the Sioux. Black Hawk sought refuge with the Winnebago but two of their braves seized him, brought him to Prairie du Chien, and turned him over to Joseph Street, the Indian agent.

General Winfield Scott, who had been ordered to Rock River to join in the campaign against Black Hawk with nine companies of regular army artillery, arrived too late to share in the triumph. Cholera overtook his men on their way back to Chicago and more than four hundred died of the dread disease. The Americans lost some fifty volunteers in the scattered fighting of the "war," and half again as many settlers were killed in Indian raids. The Sauk and Foxes were estimated to have lost 230 in battle, with perhaps several hundred more dying of their wounds, disease, and starvation. If there was a hero on the American side it was Henry Dodge, who proved a determined and resourceful leader.

Black Hawk carried himself with a fierce pride and dignity that impressed his captors. Before he was carried off in chains he gave a defiant speech:

> Black Hawk is an Indian. He has done nothing for which an
> Indian ought to be ashamed. He has fought for his countrymen,
> the squaws and papooses, against white men who came, year after
> year, to cheat them and take away their land. You know the cause
> of our making war. It is known to all white men. They ought to
> be ashamed of it. The white men despise the Indians and drive
> them from their homes. . . . An Indian who is as bad as a white
> man could not live in our nation; he would be put to death, and
> eat up by the wolves. The white men are bad schoolmasters; they
> carry false books and deal in false actions. . . . We were becoming
> like them, hypocrites and liars, adulterers, lazy drones, all talkers,
> no workers. We went to our great father [the president]. . . . His
> council gave us fair words and big promises, but we got no satis-
> faction. . . . There were no deer in the forest. The opossum and the
> beaver were fled. . . . The spirit of our fathers arose and spoke to us
> to avenge our wrongs or die. . . . The Heart of Black Hawk swelled
> high in his bosom when he led his warriors to battle. . . . He has
> done his duty. . . . Black Hawk tried to save you, and avenge your
> wrongs. He drank the blood of some whites. He has been taken
> prisoner, and his plans are stopped. He can do no more. . . . His sun
> is setting. . . . Farewell to Black Hawk.

Black Hawk was sent as a prisoner under the charge of a young Southerner, Lieutenant Jefferson Davis, to the army prison at Jefferson Barracks. The "war" that bore his name was the first Indian War in almost a quarter of a century. As such it had been reported in extensive detail in the newspapers of the day, and Black Hawk and his warriors had many sympathizers—especially in Boston, with its tradition of championing the underdog. Numerous petitions were dispatched to Jackson protesting the continued confinement of Black Hawk and urging the president to pardon him. When Black Hawk reached Washington the president received him courteously, gave him a little lecture on the hopelessness of opposing the whites, and soon after pardoned him. Black Hawk was conveyed through a number of Eastern cities on a kind of triumphal tour. When he reached New York, the crowd that gathered to see him was so immense that his party, made up of his wives and children, was unable to land. The farther white Americans were from the Indians, the more they romanticized them. To many of those who lined the street to watch Black Hawk pass, the fierce old warrior was a hero. Artists painted his picture, journalists interviewed him, politicians and socialites wished to meet him. Numerous individuals expressed their indignation at the treatment of his people and sought to dissociate themselves from the actions of their Western compatriots. Black Hawk dictated his autobiography, including his speech, and it became an immediate bestseller.

Keokuk, Black Hawk's rival for the leadership of the Sauk and Foxes, had kept that part of the combined tribes subject to his influence from going on the warpath. Now, to his indignation, he saw his defeated rival acclaimed and featured and, most annoying of all, loaded with presents. Keokuk was not slow to point out to the director of Indian affairs the lessons that other Indians might draw from this spectacle—the surest way to fame and honor with the whites was to kill a number of them, be finally defeated, make a moving and eloquent speech denouncing the white man, immediately become a celebrity, and go on a tour. Keokuk wanted a tour too, and the government was eager to oblige. Having negotiated a treaty in Washington surrendering a million and a quarter acres of land, he set off with a retinue of squaws, papooses, and lesser braves "making a tour of the principal cities, receiving presents and being stared at for the benefit of theatre, fairs and lectures." Black Hawk joined the party, remaining sullen and aloof.

The Sioux, traditional enemies of the Sauk and Foxes, who had assisted in massacring the fleeing remnants of Black Hawk's people, had no intention of being left out. They were certainly as deserving of presents and attention as their enemies. So they made up another Indian road company and joined the tour, staying at different hotels in recognition of their ancient hostility. When Philip Hone went with thousands of other New Yorkers to see the Indians, they were seated on the ground distributing presents of colored cord that had been given to them. Hone was especially impressed with the son of Black Hawk, "a majestic man . . . one of the noblest figures I ever saw—perfect Ajax Telamon." The hands of the Indians were small and "feminine," almost delicate, Hone noted, while their thighs and calves were heavily muscled. The pathos of absurdity hung over the whole scene, a perfect enactment of the ambivalent relationship of the two races.

Black Hawk returned to the reservation, where he lived four more years, enjoying his status as a celebrity. The white friends and admirers of the Indian who sought him out became as much a tribulation to the old man as the greedy settlers had been. Even after he was buried by the Mississippi River near present-day Des Moines, he had no peace. His bones were dug up some years later, it was said, and exhibited in the museum of the Historical Society at Burlington, Iowa.

The last of the Sauk and Fox Indians were driven from Illinois by the Black Hawk War and then forced to surrender in eastern Iowa. A series of Indian treaties was submitted to Congress in the waning months of Jackson's administration—treaties with the Caddo, who lived in the region of what was to become Nebraska and constituted a network of powerful tribes—the most prominent of which were the Pawnee; the Comanche, a warlike tribe that ranged across the Great Plains as far west as the Rockies and south to the Mexican border; the Ottawa and Chippewa, both related to the Algonquin and traditionally located in the Great Lakes region; the Wyandot, or Huron, who had been driven westward to present-day Wisconsin by the Iroquois generations earlier; and the Potawatomi, allies of the Chippewa—also members of the Algonquin family, centered in that part of Indian Territory that was to break off as Michigan. In every instance the effect of the treaties was to force the Indians off their hunting ranges.

After the Lewis and Clark Expedition, western exploration was put on the back burner, so to speak. The "Western issue," connected as it was with slavery, was an extremely delicate one, and without Jefferson's almost obsessive interest in the West, governmental initiative waned. It was 1818 before President Monroe, doubtless prompted by Jefferson, took up the issue once more.

Stephen Harriman Long, a farmer's son, was born in Hopkinton, New Hampshire, in 1784. Bright and ambitious, he entered Dartmouth at twenty-one and graduated in 1809. Like most young men of similar background, he tried his hand at teaching for five years and then, bored with his young charges, enlisted in the United States army as a lieutenant in the Corps of Engineers. After two years of teaching mathematics at West Point he was transferred to the topographical engineers with the rank of major. His absorbing interest was in exploration and he prevailed on his superiors to appoint him to the command of what was originally conceived of as a military and exploring expedition to the Rocky Mountains. A thousand soldiers were to proceed up the Missouri to the Yellowstone and establish a fort there, the intention being to intimidate the Indians of the region and doubtless to lay a base for the extension of the fur trade into the region by American traders in rivalry with the Hudson's Bay Company. The ability of the British to attach the Indians to their cause had had serious consequences for the American frontier in the Revolution and in the war of 1812. Many tribes, besides being involved in the fur trade, primarily with Anglo-Canadian fur companies, came yearly to British posts in Canada to get gifts and supplies. The British were already well established at Fort Vancouver in one person of Dr. John McLoughlin, the formidable head of the Hudson's Bay Company post there, and they were expected to attempt to extend their influence eastward, through the French-Canadian trappers, to encompass the Oregon Territory as far as the Snake River and the headwaters of the Missouri. If American traders and trappers were to compete successfully with them, the Indians of the Great Plains and the Rocky Mountain region had to be placated or over-awed. Although this motive was nowhere stated explicitly, it must have been in the minds of Monroe and his secretary of war, Calhoun, when they prevailed upon an inattentive Congress to authorize the expedition.

The military units of the Yellowstone Expedition were the first to depart. They were to be joined at Council Bluffs by the scientific detachment, led by Long and composed of a promising young ornithologist, Thomas Nuttall; Thomas Say, a young entomologist, conchologist, and herpetologist who had already been on an important expedition to Georgia and Florida; and Titian Ramsay Peale—son of Charles Willson Peale and brother to Raphaelle and Rubens and Rembrandt—as artist for the expedition. The combined party spent the winter at Council Bluffs, by which time Congress had had second thoughts about the enterprise. Dispatching such a large military force was bound to have both domestic and international repercussions. The Mexican Revolution was in its initial stages, introducing a further element of uncertainty into the Western picture. The military objectives were thus abandoned.

Long and the scientific detachment left Council Bluffs in the spring of 1820. In addition to Say, Nuttall, Peale, and Long, the dangerously small party consisted of Edwin James—"Botanist, Geologist, and Surgeon," as well as diarist—a lieutenant of artillery with the responsibility for keeping the official journal of the expedition, a French interpreter, a Spanish interpreter, two hunters and packers, a corporal, and six army privates. Edwin James made a detailed inventory of the trading goods desired by the Indian tribes:

> strounding for breech clouts and petticoats, blankets, wampum,
> guns, powder and ball, kettles, vermillion, verdigris, mackasin

awls, fire steels, looking glasses, knives, chief's coats, calico, ornamented brass finger rings, armbands of silver, wristbands of the same metal, ear-wheels, and bobs, small cylinders for the hair, breast broaches, and other silver ornaments for the head; black and blue handkerchiefs, buttons, tin cups, pan and dishes, scarlet cloth, etc.

Long's instructions directed him to

first explore the Missouri and its principal rivers, and then, in succession, Red River, Arkansas and Mississippi, above the mouth of the Missouri. The object of the Expedition, is to acquire as thorough and accurate knowledge as may be practicable, of a portion of our country, which is daily becoming more interesting, but which is as yet imperfectly known. With this view you will permit nothing worthy of notice to escape your attention. You will ascertain the latitude and longitude of remarkable points with all possible precision. You will, if practicable, ascertain some point in the 49th parallel of latitude, which separates our possessions from those of Great Britain. A knowledge of the extent of our limits will tend to prevent collision between our traders and theirs. . . . You will conciliate the Indians by kindness and presents, and will ascertain, as far as practicable, the number and character of the various tribes with the extent of country claimed by each. . . . The Instructions of Mr. Jefferson to Capt. Lewis, which are printed in his travels, will afford you many valuable suggestions, of which as far as applicable, you will avail yourself.

The reference to the United States–Canada border and the respective trading spheres of those nations gives substantial support to the argument that the expedition was conceived of as a preliminary to the aggressive extension of the American fur trade into the Yellowstone region and perhaps beyond. The mention, at the end of the instructions to Long, of Jefferson's instructions to

Meriwether Lewis makes clear the line of descent from the Lewis and Clark Expedition to Long's and the direct or indirect influence of Jefferson in the plan for the expedition.

The winter months were utilized to visit Indian tribes in the vicinity of Council Bluffs and to make extensive observations on their cultures. The Kansa, who were close at hand, were already much corrupted by their contact with the whites and showed few traces of the "nobility" for which their most westerly cousins were noted. Charbonneau, the husband of the famous Sacagawea, was of great assistance in smoothing the paths of the white explorers. The Oto, Missouri, Iowa, and Pawnee were likewise scrutinized. The party watched the Iowa do the "beggars' dance" for presents—tobacco or whiskey—a dance devised for whites. A chief rose to relate his martial exploits: "He had stolen horses seven or eight times from the Konzas; he had first struck the bodies of three of that nation slain in battle. He had stolen horses from the Icetan nation, and had struck the body of one Pawnee Loup. He had stolen horses several times from the Omahaws, and once from the Puncas. He had struck the body of two Sious." He was followed by Little Soldier, "a war-worn veteran," who "strained his voice in its utmost pitch whilst he portrayed some of the scenes of blood in which he had acted. He had struck dead bodies of all the red nations around, Osages, Konzas, Pawnee Loups, Republicans, Grand Pawnees, Puncas, Omahaws, and Sioux, Padoucas, La Plais or Bald Heads, Ietans, Sauks, Foxes and Ioways. . . ." Finally, he was interrupted by another warrior who placed his hand over his mouth and led him to his seat, an act of respect that signified that he had more exploits to his credit than the tribe had time to hear.

Among the Omaha, raids on tribes were initiated by an individual warrior who first painted himself with white clay and then went through the village, calling out to other warriors to join him and enumerating the grievances against the tribe whose horses were to be the object of the raid. Then he gave a feast for all who were willing to accompany him and "made medicine," hanging out his medicine bag and haranguing his fellow warriors to seek fame and honor by warlike deeds. When such a party came within striking distance of the enemy, the warriors painted themselves and smoked tobacco from the medicine bag, which the leader suspended from his neck. Capturing a prisoner in such a raid was the supreme achievement. "Striking an enemy, whilst active," Edwin James reported, "appears to be the second in rank, of their great martial achievements. Striking his dead, or disabled body, confers the third honour. Capturing a horse may be regarded as the fourth; presenting a horse to any person, the fifth, and the shooting, or otherwise killing an enemy, by a missile, is the sixth in point of rank of military deeds. . . . The taking of a scalp is merely an evidence of what has been done, and, of itself, seems to confer no honour."

The wounded were killed and hacked to pieces by the victors. If squaws were present the bodies were turned over to them for dismemberment. "They sever the limbs from the bodies, and attaching them to strings, drag them about with vociferous exultation." The genitals were tied to the necks of the dogs and the dogs "driven before them, with much shouting, laughter, noise and obscene expressions."

Because of the great variety of languages among the tribes, the Indians had developed a universal sign language by means of which they could convey a substantial amount of information. The members of Stephen Long's expedition prepared a descriptive glossary of Indian sign language that ran to 104 remarkably expressive "signs" or gestures. Fear, for example, was suggested by "the two hands with the fingers turned inward opposite to the lower ribs, then brought upwards with a tremulous movement, as if to represent the common idea of the heart rising up to the throat."

James also commented on the strange optical illusions that appeared on the plains—mirages that looked like lakes or rivers and the distortion of forms by the light so that "an animal seen for the first time . . . usually appears much enlarged." What appeared to be a mastodon turned out to be an elk; an apparent bison, a hen turkey.

While they were visiting the Grand Pawnee, the scientists in Long's party tried to prevail upon their hosts to allow themselves to be inoculated against smallpox. Long himself offered his arm for a demonstration of the vaccination procedure but the Indians were unimpressed. The whites watched a game employing a hoop and pole, impressed by "that ease and celerity of motion in which the savages to far surpass their civilized neighbours . . . displaying a symmetry of proportion and beauty of form."

The "horse Indians" were as much the creatures of horses as their masters. Edwin James tells us that the Grand Pawnee, numbering not more than 1,500 warriors, had between six and eight thousand horses and the need to find fodder for them kept the Pawnee constantly on the move. Their agricultural efforts were especially hampered and James noted that at harvest time the Grand Pawnee burned their crops and moved on to new grazing ranges. In the winter they were restricted in their movements to creeks and rivers where cottonwood trees grew so that the ponies could eat the twigs and bark of the trees. If people or horses had to go hungry, it was better the people than the horses, although it was true that in extremity the poorer horses were often eaten.

The plains were covered with great herds of buffalo and James noted that they commonly mated beginning in late July and continuing until early September. The cows then separated from the bulls and calved in April; the calves stayed with their mothers for at least a year, sometimes as long as three. The cows were much prized over the bulls both for meat and for their hides, but the bulls were killed in large numbers—primarily for sport. As James wrote of the great animals, "In whatever direction they move, their parasites and dependents fail not to follow. Large herds are invariably attended by gangs of meagre, famine-pinched wolves, and flights of obscene and ravenous birds." Here James indulged himself in a reflection upon human odor. It was said that buffalo panicked at the scent of white men, and various theories had been advanced as to the reason. It seemed simple enough to James. Rather than the "frightful scent of the white man" it was more likely that it was "the impolitic, exterminating war, which he wages against all unsubdued animals within his reach. . . . It would be highly desirable," James added, that some law for the preservation of game, might be extended to, and rigidly enforced in the country, where the bison is still met with: that the wanton destruction of these valuable animals, by the white hunters, might be checked or prevented. It is common for hunters to attack large herds of these animals, and having slaughtered as many as they are able, from mere wantonness and love of this barbarous sport, to leave the carcasses to be devoured by the wolves and birds of prey; thousands are slaughtered yearly, of which no part is saved except the tongues.

The odor of the Indians, James added, "though very strong and peculiar, is by no means unpleasant . . . the Indians find the odour of a white man extremely offensive."

Long's party also passed large herds of wild horses "of various colours, and of all sizes . . . Their playfulness seemed to be excited, rather than their fears, by our appearance, and we often saw them, more than a mile distant, leaping and curvetting, involved by a cloud of dust, which they seemed to delight in raising."

From the headwaters of the Missouri, Long's party turned south in a great loop to the Platte, the Arkansas, and the Red, past the Comanche and Kiowa, Arapaho, Osage, Cheyenne, and the settlements of those Cherokee and Choctaw who had moved west. They found Fort Smith garrisoned by a company of rifle-men "to prevent the encroachments of white settlers upon the lands still held by the Indians." Unauthorized white settlements had been made in the area of Skin Bayou and Six Bulls, but the officer in charge at Fort Smith had recently forced their abandon-ment. On their way down the Arkansas, the expedition came to Rocky Bayou, a Cherokee settlement, where they were received hospitably by the chief, Tom Graves. "His house," James noted, "as well as many we passed before we arrived at it, is constructed like those of the white settlers, and like them, surrounded with enclosed fields of corn, cotton, sweet potatoes, etc. with cribs, sheds, droves of swine, flocks of geese, and all the usual accom-paniments of a prosperous settlement." Graves had named his son Andrew Jackson Graves and while he spoke no English, he offered the officers in the party an abundant meal served by two black slaves. There were other Cherokee settlements in the area, and the Cherokee were at war with the Osage over whose land they hunted. They had invaded Osage territory several years earlier, accompanied by a party of whites, and had burned a village and its crops and killed or taken captive between fifty and sixty old men, women, and children.

Perhaps most ironic of all, "the introduction of a considerable degree of civilization among the Cherokees," James wrote, "has been attended by the usual consequences of inequality in the distribution of property, and a large share of the evils resulting from that inequality." The poorer Cherokees, indignant at the notion of "exclusive possession"—private property—had made themselves free with the property of their more prosperous fellows; made themselves, in James's words, "troublesome neighbours—both to the wealthy of their own nation, and to those of the white settlers in their vicinity who have any thing to lose." The result was that the more prosperous Cherokee had formed a mounted troop of Regulators or vigilantes, "invested with almost unlimited authority," to catch and punish the thieves.

All through the region of the lower Arkansas, the Long party encountered single farms and settlements, some of them adjacent to Cherokee villages. Farther downriver was a settlement of Delaware and Shawnee thoroughly intimidated by the more numerous whites. "It is painful to witness the degradation of a people once powerful and independent," James wrote, "still more so to see them submitting to the wanton and needless cruelties of their oppressors." This "miserable remnant" would soon, James suspected, be forced into the territory of the Cherokee and "their speedy and entire extinction . . . ensured."

There was much truth in Stephen Long's statement that "the condition of the savages is a state of constant alarm and apprehension. Their security from their enemies, and their means of subsistence, are precarious and uncertain, the former requiring the utmost vigilance to prevent its infraction and the latter being attended with no regular supplies for the necessaries of life."

The consequences of Long's expedition have sometimes been described as "disappointing" by modern commentators, but its accomplishments were substantial. It greatly increased the general knowledge of the regions covered. The publication of a lively *Account of an Expedition from Pittsburgh to the Rocky Mountains*, compiled by Edwin James, gave widespread publicity to the expedition and the two volumes became the bible of subsequent geographers, geologists, and topographers. The *Account* contained a vast amount of interesting and generally accurate information about the various tribes encountered on the way. The expedition's "collections," deposited in the Philadelphia Museum, comprised "sixty prepared skins of new or rare animals . . . several thousand insects, seven or eight hundred of which are probably new . . . between four and five hundred species of plants, new to the Flora of the United States, and many of them supposed to be undescribed." Peale's sketches amounted to 122, of which only 21 were finished, plus 150 landscape views by Peale's fellow artist, Samuel Seymour. Considering the physical difficulties under which the party labored, much credit is due Long and his companions. A vast miscellany, James's work remains well worth reading. Long was to go on to a distinguished career as an engineer and railroad builder. Say is honored as the father of American entomology.

The most disappointing aspect of the expedition, from the point of view of those among its sponsors who wished to promote Western settlement, was Long's opinion that the region was too barren and arid ever to support settlement by whites. Long's opinion was echoed ten years later by Josiah Gregg, the author of *Gregg's Commerce of the Prairies*, who wrote that the Great Plains, from the Red River to the headwaters of the Missouri, were "uninhabitable— not so much for want of wood (though the plains are altogether naked) as of soil and of water; for though some of the plains appear of sufficiently fertile soil, they are mostly of a sterile character, and all too dry to be cultivated. These great steppes seem only fitted for the haunts of the mustang, the buffalo, the antelope, and their migratory lord, the prairie Indian."

Another kind of westward movement, to what might be called the Fur West, was also taking place in the same period. Stretching hundreds of miles west of the Mississippi Valley were the vast and uncharted regions of the Great Plains and, beyond them, the Great Basin area of the Rocky Mountains. Over this unsurveyed, unmapped, and largely unknown region a few fur traders of the Hudson's Bay Company and John Jacob Astor's rival enterprise, the American Fur Company, made their way to trade for furs with the various tribes of Indians who controlled the fur trade. Since Lewis and Clark's expedition only a handful of Americans had penetrated the region, and none had traversed it to Oregon or California. John Colter, a member of the Lewis and Clark party, had been hired on the way home by two Illinois trappers, Joseph Dickson and Forrest Hancock, to guide them for "sheers" (shares) of their fur profits. The three men went off to trap beaver in the Yellowstone Valley, the preserve of the Blackfoot and the Crow Indians, about as hazardous an undertaking as they could have embarked on. The Blackfeet were already involved in trade with the Hudson's Bay Company. The Indians did the trapping and carried the lustrous beaver pelts to rendezvous points, where they were collected by agents of the fur company, usually Frenchmen. Colter and his companions built a cabin and prepared to winter somewhere near the mouth of the Clark River but the restless Colter made a dugout canoe and headed down the Yellowstone, trapping as he went. Where the Platte flows into the Missouri, he encountered a party of keelboats that included three other veterans of the Lewis and Clark Expedition— George Drouillard, Peter Wiser, and John Potts. In the spring of 1807, under the leadership of Manuel Lisa, they were on their way to the Yellowstone to trade for furs. Lisa persuaded Colter to join the party. Among the other members of Lisa's group was a young Baltimore lawyer, Hugh Marie Brackenridge, the son of Hugh Henry Brackenridge, who inherited his father's writing gift and described Lisa's keelboat in considerable detail. It was manned with twenty stout oars-men . . . Our equipage is chiefly composed of young men, though several have already made a voyage to the upper Missouri, of which they are exceedingly proud [these were certainly the veterans of the Lewis and Clark Expedition]. . . . We are . . . completely prepared for defence. There is, besides, a swivel on the bow of the boat which, in case of attack, would make a formidable appearance . . . These precautions are absolutely necessary from the hostility of the Sioux bands, who, of late had committed several murders and robberies on the whites, and manifested such a disposition that it was believed impossible for us to pass through their country. The greater part of the merchandise, which consists of strouding, blankets, lead, tobacco, knifes, guns, beads, etc. was concealed in a false cabin . . . in this way presenting as little as possible to tempt the savages.

Despite the fact that the Sioux had waited on the river to prevent the passage of any trading boats, Lisa's party slipped by.

The principal tribes that inhabited the headwaters of the Missouri and the Yellowstone basin were the Blackfeet, the largest and most warlike tribe in the region; the Crow, reputed to be terrible in the attack but quickly discouraged if things did not go well; and the Shoshone or Snake Indians, who lived along that river and who had been so helpful to Lewis and Clark years earlier.

The Blackfoot Indians were remarkable in the fact that they were beset on all sides of their extensive range by tribes hostile to them and in many instances armed with the white man's musket. Thus pressed upon, they responded by developing the most efficient war-making capacity of any of the Plains Indians with the possible exception of the Sioux. The Arikara harassed them from the north, the Cheyenne, Arapaho, and Comanche from the south. Discipline, cleanliness, good order, and unusual intelligence among their leaders characterized the Blackfeet when the first fur traders arrived in their domain. Initially in danger of being overwhelmed by the tribes adjacent to their vaguely defined "territory," which extended deep into Canada, the Blackfeet had encouraged the Hudson's Bay Company to set up trading posts within the area claimed by them to help thwart their enemies. Their real trouble began with the intrusion, after 1822, of Americans into the trade. Egged on by Canadian traders who wished to preserve their virtual monopoly, the Blackfeet continually attacked the American trappers, seizing their furs and selling them to Canadian traders. For a time this system seemed to the Blackfeet almost too good to be true. They were saved the very considerable labor of trapping the beaver themselves and had, in addition, the glory of killing white men and taking their scalps.

In a remarkable display of skill and determination, the Blackfeet, estimated between ten and eighteen thousand, held off the American trappers and fur traders or at least made them pay a very heavy price in lives and goods for their persistence in hunting the beaver. The downfall of the Blackfeet came with the terrible smallpox epidemic of 1836, which reduced some camps by two-thirds of their numbers and, overall, cost them more than half their population. The final blow was the penetration of the Blackfoot nation by "whiskey traders." These dealers in illicit merchandise found the Blackfeet, especially the younger braves, hopelessly vulnerable to the white man's liquor. A desperate struggle took place within the two various bands as the older chiefs, who foresaw the destruction of the tribe in the growing addiction of the younger warriors and braves to the deadly liquor, tried to prohibit its consumption.

The Snake Indians were large, noble-looking aborigines who were perpetually fighting for their lives against the more warlike Blackfeet and Sioux. At the time of the Lewis and Clark Expedition, they spent much of each year on the Pacific side of the Rockies to avoid the Sioux, coming onto the plains for hasty buffalo hunting forays and then slipping back over the mountains before the Sioux or Blackfeet could intercept them. They welcomed the coming of the white trappers as allies against their traditional enemies. Osborne Russell, a young trapper, described them as "kind and hospitable to whites thankful for favors indignant at injuries and but little addicted to theft in their large villages . . . I have found it to be a general feature of their character to divide the last morsel of food with the hungry stranger let their means be what it might for obtaining the next meal . . ."

The Crow Indians roamed over a region that they had originally wrested from the Snake, bounded on the east and south by the Black Hills, on the west by the Wind River Mountains, and on the north by the Yellowstone River. The smallpox, which virtually destroyed the Mandan, had reduced the Crow from some eight thousand to two thousand, of whom almost two-thirds were women. Russell described them as "proud treacherous thievish insolent and brave when they are possessed with a superior advantage but when placed in the opposite situation they are equally humble submissive and cowardly."

As with the Snake Indians, the chief was the one "who can innumerate the greatest number of valiant exploits. . . . All the greatest warriors below him . . . are Councillors and take their seats in the council according to their respective rank." The Crow kept a "standing company of soldiers . . . for the purpose of maintaining order in the Village. The military leader, appointed by the Chief and the Counselors, had complete control over the internal police of the tribe subject only to the check of the body that appointed him." The Crow, "both male and female," Russell wrote, "are tall well proportioned handsomely featured with very light copper coloured skins."

A stranger who stopped with the Crow, Russell reported, "can always be accommodated with a wife while he stops with the Village but cannot take her from it when he leaves." As with the Snake, children were cared for tenderly and it was "a high crime for a father or mother to inflict corporeal punishment on their male child." The Crow were notable for particular love of gaudy dress and display. A fur trader named Edwin Denig described the tribe on the march:

> When a camp is on the move in the summer, this tribe presents
> a gay and lively appearance, more so perhaps than any other. On
> these occasions both men and women dress in their best clothes.

214

Their numerous horses are decked out with highly ornamented saddles and bridles of their own making, scarlet collars and housing with feathers on their horse's heads and tails. The warriors wear their richly garnished shirts, fringed with human hair and ermine, leggins of the same, and headdresses of various kinds, strange, gay and costly. Any and all kinds of bright colored blankets, loaded with beads worked curiously and elegantly across them, with scarlet leggins. . . . The bucks are fancifully painted on their face, their hair arranged . . . with heavy and costly appendages of shells, beads, and wampum, to the ears and around the neck. The women have scarlet or blue dresses, others white cotillions made of the dressed skins of the bighorn sheep . . . covered across the breast and back with rows of elk teeth and sea shells . . . the fringes . . . wrought with porcupine quills and feathers of many colors. . . . The young men take this occasion to show off their persons and horsemanship to the women. A good deal of courting is also done while traveling.

The Crow had a more varied cuisine than any of their neighboring tribes and paid greater attention to cleanliness. Among them the old retired warriors struck Russell as being remarkably healthy. They enjoyed great prestige and loved to sit smoking in a circle "conversing upon the good old times of their forefathers and condemning the fashions of the present age." One of the most notable things about the Crow was their determined resistance to whiskey. They called it "White man's fool water." If a Crow became drunk, he was considered not to be a Crow during the period of his inebriation.

The Crow had suffered much earlier in the century when one tribe was reduced from two thousand lodges to three hundred by smallpox. In 1832 another band contracted the terrible disease. In the words of the trader LaRocque,

As soon as possible . . . the camp broke up into small bands each taking different directions. They scattered through the mountains in hope of running away from the pestilence. All order was lost. No one pretended to lead or advise. The sick and dead alike were left for the wolves and each family tried to save itself. . . . More than a thousand fingers are said to have been cut off by the relatives of the dead [as a sign of mourning]. Out of 800 lodges counted the previous summer but 360 remained, even these but thinly peopled.

Smallpox, as we noted earlier, had virtually destroyed the once powerful and warlike Mandan. An epidemic in 1837 reduced one village from 1,600 to "13 young and 19 old men." One writer who observed the effects of a smallpox epidemic on the Arikara wrote, "Many . . . formerly handsome and stately in appearance, upon recovering their health committed suicide when they saw how they had been disfigured by the smallpox. Some of them leaped from high cliffs, others stabbed or shot themselves to death. The whole wide prairie had become an immense graveyard. . . . Women and children wander about in hordes, starving and moaning among the dead bodies."

Like many other tribes of "Rocky Mountain Indians" the Snake believed in "a Supreme Deity who resided in the Sun and in infernal Dieties residing in the Moon and Stars but subject to the Supreme control of the one residing in the Sun. . . ." Snake warriors commonly had several wives with a system of divorce. Sexual promiscuity among the women was rare. They did all the labor of the tribe except caring for the horses and, in Osborne Russell's words, were "cheerful and affectionate to their husbands and remarkably fond and careful of their children." Their government, according to Russell, was "a Democracy deeds of valor promotes the Chief to the highest points attainable from which he is at any time likely to fall for misdemeanor in office." Of a population of some six thousand, about half lived in villages and the rest in small detached bands of from two to ten families. These latter groups seem to have been composed of Indians who, in some degree, were failures in terms of the tribe's dominant values. They lacked skill in hunting or fighting and depended for their subsistence on gathering roots, seeds, and berries and catching fish. They had few horses—the Indian status symbol—and were more addicted to stealing and preying upon small parties of trappers. They were usually without muskets and depended on arrows pointed with quartz or obsidian which they dipped in poison from the fangs of rattlesnakes. The large villages of Snake seldom stayed more than a week or two in the same spot. In the period of the eight or nine years that Russell was in contact with the Snake, their principal chiefs died and the tribe began to break up into smaller bands "in consequence," Russell concluded, "of having no chief who could control and keep them together." He added, "Their ancient warlike spirit seemed to be buried with their leaders and they are fast falling into degradation."

Other tribes in the region were the Bannock, the Piegan, the Blood Indians, the Flatheads, the Nez Percés, and the Gros Ventres, a dependency of the Blackfeet closely related to the Arapaho. In addition, a number of Eastern Indians, most prominently the Iroquois and Delaware, worked as individuals or in small groups for trading companies and these, of necessity, identified themselves with the whites.

It might be well at this point to say something about the fur-bearing mammal that was the object of so much avarice. Of all the animals on the American continent, the beaver was the creature whose fate was most intertwined with the American settlers. The buffalo had its relatively brief dominance in what we might call the era of the Great Plains, but the beaver was there at the beginning. When the first white settlers landed in New England they discovered the beaver and valued its pelt as an article of trade. The beaver pelt was the principal medium of exchange in all dealings with the aborigines. Many Indian tribes believed they were descended from an archetypal beaver and the beaver was thus sacred to them. The white man persuaded the Indian, in return for beads and cloth, dyes, knives, mirrors, and all the classic trading junk, to kill the sacred creature. A central issue in warfare among Indian tribes after the coming of the white man was which tribes were to control the lucrative trade in beaver skins. Many tribes moved from one watershed to another, exhausting the supply of beaver in a particular network of rivers and creeks and then pushing to another, often ousting a weaker tribe in the process.

The beaver itself was a marvelous creature, certainly worthy of the Indian's infatuation. It was a gifted engineer with an almost human facility for creating dams and houses. Beavers cut trees along the banks of streams and rivers and placed them in the water pointing diagonally upstream, interlacing the tree trunks with twigs and branches until a solid dam was created, forming a pond. Then on the dam, or sometimes along the shore when the water was too swift to dam, they built their houses, again brilliantly engineered structures approached through underwater tunnels. The inside of the house was lined with clean dry grasses and stocked in winter with a supply of green sticks and branches whose bark provided food for the often icebound beavers.

The female beaver produced each spring from two to six young, but she killed all except a single male and female in order to prevent overcrowding of the beaver range. The beavers' lodge was generally from four to seven feet in height, standing four to five feet above the water level.

The beavers' undoing was a potent yellow oil called *castoreum*, a "gummy" yellow substance secreted in glands under their forearms. Whenever a beaver passed up or down a stream it took some mud or clay from the river bottom in its paws, placed it on the riverbank, and supplemented it with castoreum. In the words of a trapper, "should a hundred Beaver pass within the scent of the place they would each throw up mud covering the old castorum and emit new upon that castorum which they throw up." The Indians had learned to extract the castoreum and carry it in a small vial or container. The Indian trapper would place some mud freshly mixed with castoreum on the bank and anchor a trap below it, under the water, so that a beaver coming up to add its castoreum, would step on the trap and spring it. The trap itself, essentially the steel trap we are familiar with today, was the critical tool in the process. Attached to the trap was a dry piece of log some six feet long known as the float, designed to keep the beaver from sinking to the bottom of the river. The trap was set five or six inches below the surface of the water and staked down so that the beaver could not get to land, where he could gnaw a leg off and escape. Trapping beaver was arduous work. The traps themselves were heavy—a trapper would carry six or eight—and the trapper must immerse himself in the chilling waters of a creek or river to set his traps and enter the water again to clear and reset them. Rheumatism was, in consequence, one of the occupational diseases of trappers.

As white trappers gradually encroached on the preserve of the Indians by taking beaver themselves rather than simply trading with the Indians for the pelts, a bitter and remorseless struggle took place between them and the Indian tribes determined to preserve their monopoly of the trapping.

The standard equipment of a trapper consisted of a riding horse and pack horse. The riding horse carried an *epishemore* (a square piece of buffalo robe much prized as a saddle blanket); a saddle and bridle; a gunnysack containing six beaver traps; a blanket; an extra pair of moccasins; powder horn and bullet pouch; a belt holding a butcher knife and a small wooden box with castoreum in it to bait the traps; and a pipe and sack of tobacco and implements for making a fire. The trapper's dress was a flannel or cotton shirt (both much preferred to buckskin shirts because they were far warmer and more comfortable and dried out more quickly), a pair of leather breeches and a blanket of buffalo skin, leggings, a coat made of a buffalo skin or a woolen blanket, and a hat or cap of wool or buffalo or otter skin. Besides the strictly utilitarian aspects of his costume, the white trapper was almost as colorful and bizarre in his dress as a Crow Indian. Indeed, it was often not easy to tell a white trapper from his Indian counterpart.

Emboldened by the success of his first venture, Manuel Lisa formed the Missouri Fur Company with Jean-Pierre and Auguste Chouteau and William Clark among his partners. Forty thousand dollars was raised and a party of 150 men set out in 1809, establishing trading stations among Arikara, Mandan, Minitari, and

Crow. Lisa defied the Blackfeet by building a substantial fort at Three Forks, the headwaters of the Missouri. But the Blackfeet were determined to protect their control of the fur trade and Andrew Henry, in command of the post, was driven back to the Snake River, where he and his men built a log fort and barely survived the winter. Thereafter the company pulled back to Council Bluffs below the Mandan villages there and established its main base of operations.

Lisa, the most enterprising and successful of the "first Generation" of fur trappers and traders, was known as Uncle Manuel in St. Louis, where he brought his rich haul of furs every summer. He had married into the Omaha tribe and ascribed his success as a trader to the fact that

> I put into my operations great activity; I go a great distance, while
> some are considering whether they will start today or tomorrow.
> I impose upon myself great privations; ten months in a year I am
> buried in the forest, at a great distance from my own house. I
> appear as the benefactor, and not as the pillager, of the Indians. I
> carried among them the seed of the large pompion, from which
> I have seen in their possession the fruit weighing one hundred
> and sixty pounds. Also the large bean, the potato, the turnip; and
> those vegetables now make a comfortable part of their subsistence,
> and this year I have promised to carry the plow . . . I lend them
> my traps. . . . My establishments are the refuge of the weak and of
> the old men no longer able to follow their lodges . . .

The principal rival to the Missouri Fur Company was John Jacob Astor's American Fur Company. It was Astor's ambition to establish trading posts along the whole route of Lewis and Clark to the Pacific Ocean and Astoria. Astor's agent in this project was a young man named Wilson Price Hunt, who headed up the Missouri in 1811 with Lisa in hot pursuit. Rather than contest the region with Lisa, Hunt decided to take off on his own to try to find a passage to Astoria, almost fifteen hundred miles away. Lisa helped him buy horses from the Arikara Indians and Hunt set off with a party of sixty-four. The party arrived in Astoria after incredible hardships. Forced to abandon their trading supplies, they had been reduced to eating their moccasins. The expedition, desperate as its fortunes were, established the basis for Astor's challenge to the North West Company and the Hudson's Bay Company.

The Hudson's Bay Company, for its part, felt secure in its hold on the Columbia River basin. McLoughlin, the famous factor at Fort Vancouver, was reported to have said, "For all coming time we and our children will have uninterrupted possession of this country, as it can never be reached by families but by water around Cape Horn." The Yankees, he declared, "As well might . . . undertake to go to the moon."

At the mouth of the Bighorn, Lisa built a trading post, some halfway between the headwaters of the Yellowstone River and its confluence with the Missouri. This was the entrance to the beaver country. Lisa sent members of his party out to contact nearby Crow Indians, and Colter was given the assignment of bringing Indians to the post to trade. With this vague commission Colter set out on a journey of some five hundred miles to the Crow in the region of the headwaters of the Missouri. From Stinking Water River Colter turned south and east into what was later to be called Jackson Hole, rimmed by the Teton Range. From here he apparently found his way to Yellowstone Lake and from it followed an Indian trail along the river, doubling back to Stinking Water and then to Pryor Creek and back to the Yellowstone and Lisa's camp. Colter's journey, which far exceeded his instructions, added substantially to the information that Lewis and Clark had gathered a few years earlier. Carefully recorded in the map that Clark kept at his headquarters in St. Louis, it encouraged other bold spirits to try to penetrate the beaver country of the Yellowstone Basin.

The next year when Colter set out to contact the Blackfeet and try to enlist them in Manuel Lisa's trading scheme, he fell in with a hunting party of Flatheads and Crow, both inveterate enemies of the Blackfeet. By casually joining the party, Colter made himself the enemy of the Blackfeet, who attacked the little band near the Gallatin River. Colter, badly wounded in the leg, managed to take refuge in a thicket and help fight off the Blackfeet. The next year trapping with a companion, John Potts, near the Jefferson, Colter and his friend were again ambushed by the Blackfeet. Potts, deciding that there was no hope of escape, fired his rifle and killed an Indian, whereupon he was filled with arrows. Colter was then turned loose, like a hare pursued by hounds. The Indian who could capture him first would get his scalp. Despite the fact that he had not fully recovered from the wounds of the previous year, Colter outdistanced all his pursuers except one. The brave tried to stab Colter with his spear. The white man evaded it and grasped the shaft, which broke, leaving the head of the spear in Colter's hand. He used it to dispatch the Blackfoot and then, with his enemies close behind him, headed for the Madison River, where he hid under a pile of driftwood until the Indians tired of searching for him. Then, clad only in a blanket he had taken from his pursuer, he made his way to Fort Lisa on the Yellowstone, a journey that took him nearly a week, "arriving there nearly exhausted by hunger, fatigue and excitement. . . . His beard was long, his face and whole body were thin and emaciated by hunger, and his limbs and feet swollen and sore. The company at the fort did not recognize him in this dismal plight," a friend wrote.

The War of 1812 led to the breakup of the Astoria enterprise since most of those involved were either Canadian or British and saw nothing to be gained in defending Astor's interests. The war also brought a virtual halt to the activities of the Missouri Fur Company. The loss of the foreign market for furs and the growing hostility of the Indians, egged on by agents of the British-Canadian fur companies, made trading unremunerative and exceedingly dangerous.

After the war, the United States government through the superintendent of Indian trade undertook to regulate and control the traffic in furs. Determined to open the fur trade to free enterprise, Thomas Hart Benton and John Jacob Astor formed an alliance to replace the government agents or factors by private entrepreneurs. Benton charged that the government factors were inefficient and corrupt, furnishing the Indians with inferior goods at inflated prices. Thomas McKenney, the able and enlightened superintendent of the Indian trade, argued that it was the private traders who debauched and exploited the Indians. Private enterprise won out. The government posts were abolished in 1822 and the trade thrown open to anyone energetic enough to seize it. The consequence was a decade or more of desperate competition, primarily between the Missouri Fur Company and Astor's reformed American Fur Company.

Manuel Lisa had died in 1820. With the opening up of the fur trade, William Ashley, lieutenant governor of Missouri, head of that state's militia and a leader in lead-mining ventures in Illinois territory, joined with Major Andrew Henry to revive the Missouri Fur Company. In March 1822, Henry ran an ad in the *Missouri Republican* that read: "TO ENTERPRISING YOUNG MEN the subscriber wishes to engage one hundred men to ascend the Missouri River to its source, there to be employed for one, two or three years. For particulars enquire of Major Andrew Henry, near the lead mines in the County of Washington . . ." A few weeks later more than a hundred trappers and "campers," "many of whom" as a local paper noted, "had relinquished the most respectable employments and circles of society," reported to Henry.

Ashley also recruited a party (in the words of one member) from "the grog shops and other sinks of degradation," adding, "A description I cannot give but Falstafs Batallion was genteel in comparison." The truth about the types who signed on as trappers was certainly somewhere in between the description of Henry's men and those recruited by Ashley. What is most striking about the young men who became trappers besides their extraordinarily varied backgrounds—French, Spanish, Scottish, English, German, Southern, New England, mixed-blood Indian, a few black—was their relatively high degree of literacy and their lust for adventure. Though some doubtless hoped to make their fortunes, the great majority were drawn by the lure of the wild.

Andrew Henry's party suffered a severe setback a few hundred miles up the Missouri when one of the keelboats capsized and sank with $10,000 worth of trading goods. Above the Mandan villages a party of Assiniboine caught the trappers crossing the river and drove off fifty horses that had just been purchased from the Arikara. But Henry and his men pushed on and established a fort they named Fort Benton.

Two lieutenants of the Missouri Fur Company, Michael Immel and Robert Jones, headed up the Missouri in the spring of 1823 with 180 men, bound for Fort Benton. They trapped beaver in the area adjacent to the fort and then headed for the juncture of the Gallatin, Madison, and Jefferson—Three Forks—with twenty-seven men. After several weeks of trapping, they encountered a band of Blackfeet. The Indians made professions of friendship and received gifts from the trappers but twelve days later some four hundred Blackfeet ambushed the whites and killed Jones and Immel in the first onslaught. William Gordon, a clerk who had gone on ahead of the party, in his words, "escaped by a run of about seven miles across a plain, pursued only by footmen. . . ." Five other trappers were killed and four wounded. The remaining trappers held off the Indians long enough to improvise a raft and got off down the Yellowstone, abandoning all their furs, traps, horses and equipment. The Blackfeet promptly sold the stolen furs to agents of the Hudson's Bay Company, who were well aware of their origin.

The agents of the American Fur Company and the Missouri Fur Company were ruthless in their fight for what was called "brown gold"—the prized beaver pelts. If the discovery of gold in California some twenty years later resulted in a Gold Rush, the abandonment by the government of the regulation of the Western fur trade resulted in a Beaver Rush. Many trappers and their auxiliaries—campkeepers, boatmen, and traders—lost their lives at the hands, primarily, of the warlike Blackfeet. A number died of disease, improperly treated wounds, of scurvy and camp fever.

Astor, in order to compete with the Missouri Fur Company, combined several of the old fur companies, among them that of the Chouteaus, originally partners of Lisa's, and Bernard Pratte and Company. In addition, Astor signed on a number of former employees of the Northwest Fur Company, many of them Scotsmen with considerable experience in the trade and good relations with the Assiniboine. The Missouri Fur Company established a post at Fort Piegan to control the Blackfoot territory, and Fort Cass, near Fort Benton, to serve as the center of trade with the Crow.

As more and more "forts" were established in connection with the beaver trade (they were, in fact, trading posts typically containing a few crude structures surrounded by palisades), they became a standard feature of the plains and Rocky Mountain area. Each collected its own characters and accumulated its own often brief but colorful history.

Edwin Denig, who had been in charge of Fort Union, wrote eloquently of the dangers at the posts and forts themselves (which appeared to the trappers as havens of refuge). Fort Union was under almost constant siege by the Blackfeet. When there were no Crow about to help defend the fort,

> those who cut wood, guard horses, or go in quest of meat by hunting feel the murderous strokes of these ruthless warriors. Each and every year from 5 to 15 persons attached to the trading establishment have been killed since commerce has been carried on with the Crows in their own district. . . . Whoever went forth to procure wood or meat placed their lives in extreme jeopardy. Every hunter there has been killed and the fort often reduced to a famished condition when buffalo were in great numbers within sight. The few horses kept for hunting were always stolen, and those who guarded them shot down. . . .

Robert Meldrum, who had started out as trapper and lived for three years with the Crow Indians, was an intelligent and literate man. Promoted in Astor's American Fur Company to a position in charge of Fort Alexander near the mouth of the Rosebud River, he was later charged with building Fort Sarpy. Meldrum told of a typical incident—a Piegan squaw going to the river to get some water was surprised, killed and scalped by a party of Blackfeet before anyone could come to her assistance. During a dance at Fort Sarpy some Blood Indians slipped into one of the houses where an old Assiniboine Indian was sleeping, "cut his throat then dragged him out about forty yards in front of the Bastion & commenced mutilating his body in a most horrible manner. . . ."

A clerk at Fort Sarpy charged that it had been turned into a "whore house," providing Indians and trappers alike with female companions. Squaws were often sold to trappers as "wives," but the price was usually high. The clerk at Fort Sarpy was offered "a dirty lousy slut" for "One horse one Gun one chief's coat one NW Blkt . . . two shirts one pr. leggins, six & half yards of Bed ticking one hundred loads ammunition twenty Bunches of beads ten large Plugs Tobacco & some sugar Coffe Flour etc. . . ."

Archibald Palmer, the bookkeeper for a time at Fort Union under the Scotsman James McKenzie and married to the daughter of a Blood chief, was reputed to be an English nobleman who "always dressed in the latest London fashions" and took a bath every day. Attired in "ruffled shift fronts and . . . a great gold chain around his neck," he was "polished, scented, and oiled to the highest degree." McKenzie himself lived in considerable elegance with a well-stocked wine cellar. A visitor dining with him was astonished to see "a splendidly set table with a white tablecloth, and two waiters, one a negro. . . ." No one was allowed at table without a coat.

CHAPTER XI

GEORGE CATLIN

In the years following the Lewis and Clark and the Zebulon Pike expeditions, which promised so much by their peaceful conclusions, innumerable contacts took place between whites and Indians—some in bitter conflict, many in amity. Traders and trappers had, as we have seen, preceded settlers and even explorers. In the period between 1800 and the Civil War the classic forms of encounter were between fur trappers and Indians; and between emigrants moving westward in a ceaseless tide and Indians who attempted to intercept them, preying upon the wagon trains as they moved across the Great Plains and the Rockies to California.

With the increase in contacts came a new literature and a new art, recording tribal life verbally and visually in fascinating detail. The greatest visual record was that of a man who devoted his life to championing the cause of the Indian. George Catlin was born in Wilkes-Barre, Pennsylvania, in 1796. His father, Putnam Catlin, had enlisted as a fifer in the Second Connecticut Regiment at the age of thirteen and had fought through the Revolution. His mother had been captured by the Indians as a child of seven in the Wyoming Valley Massacre. Putnam Catlin was an unsuccessful lawyer who abandoned law for farming and who lived more in the world of books than of torts and replevins. His son inherited his father's impractical and visionary temperament. When George was twenty-one, his father sent him off to Tapping Reeve's law school at Litchfield, Connecticut. Graduated from Reeve's institution, he tried practicing law in western Pennsylvania but, as he put it later,

> another and stronger passion was getting the advantage of me, that of painting, to which all my pleading soon gave way; and after having covered nearly every inch of the lawyer's table (and even encroached upon the judge's bench) with penknife, pen and ink, and pencil sketches of judges, jurors, and culprits, I very deliberately resolved to convert my law library into paint pots and brushes, and to pursue painting as my future, and apparently more agreeable profession.

His father gave him his blessing along with an impressive catalogue of Renaissance artists with whose work he was enjoined to become familiar, and Catlin, after painting portraits of local worthies, set out for Philadelphia. Strikingly handsome and engaging in his enthusiasm, Catlin enlisted the interest of Charles Willson Peale, and his son, Rembrandt, and of Thomas Sully. He was soon elected to the Pennsylvania Academy of Fine Arts and began to get commissions for portraits, but as he put it, he "was continually reaching for some branch or enterprise of the arts, on which to devote a whole life-time of enthusiasm. . . . The search ended when a delegation of ten or fifteen noble and dignified-looking Indians from the wilds of the 'Far West' suddenly arrived in the city, arrayed in all their classic beauty. . . . In silent and stoic dignity, these lords of the forest strutted about the city for a few days . . . "

After they left Catlin brooded about the dramatic visitation until he came to the following deductions and conclusions. Man, in the simplicity and loftiness of his nature, unrestrained and unfettered by the disguises of art, is surely the most beautiful model for the painter. . . . And the history and customs of such a people, preserved by pictorial illustrations, are themes worthy of the life-time of one man, and nothing short of the loss of my life shall prevent me from visiting their country and becoming their historian. . . . I set out on my arduous and perilous undertaking with the determination of reaching, ultimately, every tribe of Indians on the Continent of North America, and of bringing home faithful portraits of their principal personages, and full notes of their character and history. I desired, also, to procure their costumes, and a complete collection of their manufacturers and weapons, and to perpetuate them in a *gallery unique*, for the use and instruction of future ages.

The question was how. Such a splendid obsession must be costly. Catlin continued to paint miniatures, hoping to be able to save enough money to launch his venture. In New York he painted three miniatures of Governer DeWitt Clinton, the great patron of the arts and sciences and the promoter of the Erie Canal. Clinton gave Catlin a commission to paint a series of pictures of the building of the canal. Through Clinton, Catlin also met William Leete Stone, the editor of the *New York Commercial Advertiser*, who shared Catlin's infatuation with Indians. Successful and sought after as a portraitist, Catlin, in 1828, married a handsome and socially prominent New Jersey girl named Clara Bartlett Gregory. A year later, tormented by the conflict between his career as a miniaturist and the desire to begin what he conceived to be his lifework, Catlin had a kind of breakdown. When he recovered he set out for St. Louis where he found a patron in William Clark. Clark invited Catlin to paint some Indians who had come to engage in treaty negotiations and, apparently pleased with his work and his manner of dealing with the Indians, undertook to help him carry out his ambitious plan. Starting with the nearby Iowa, Missouri, Omaha, Sauk, and

Foxes, Catlin added paintings of the principal chiefs of the Delaware, Potawatomi, Kickapoo, and Shawnee. After a winter spent with his wife in Albany, Catlin was back in St. Louis in the spring ready to start up the Platte to paint the Pawnee, Oto, and Sioux. He was increasingly impatient to penetrate those regions inhabited by tribes that had suffered least from contact with the whites. These were the tribes scattered along the Missouri to the Yellowstone country, the Minitari, Mandan, Arikara, Snake, Crows, Blackfeet, and Yankton Sioux. In 1832 Catlin boarded the brand new steamboat, the *Yellow Stone*, built expressly to carry supplies to Fort Union. At every stopping point along the river, he made sketches. When the *Yellow Stone* ran aground, Catlin set out with the fur traders. "I packed on the backs and in the hands of several men such articles for painting as I might want . . . with my sketchbook slung on my own back, and my rifle in my hands. . . ."

The Mandan village on the Missouri was the first village of aborigines whose contact with whites had been limited to the occasional trader or trapper who made his way up the river. In this tribe, so little contaminated by civilization, Catlin was in his element. Always intensely curious, the men, women, and children of the village swarmed around the lodge where Catlin was painting his first portraits of chiefs. Even before they were finished the excitement had reached such a pitch that two of the paintings were brought out and held up over the doorway so that the crowd had an opportunity to see and recognize their chiefs. "The effect upon so mixed a multitude . . . was novel and really laughable," Catlin wrote. "The likenesses were instantly recognized, and many of the gaping multitude commenced yelping; others were stamping off in the jarring dance—others were singing, and others again were crying—hundreds covered their mouths with their hands and were mute; others, indignant, drove their spears frightfully into the ground, and some threw a reddened arrow at the sun, and went home to their wigwams."

When Catlin emerged from the lodge the excitement was almost as great. "Women were gaping and gazing—and warriors and braves offering me their hands . . . and whilst I was engaged, from the waist upwards, in fending off the throng and shaking hands, my legs were assailed (not unlike the nibbling of little fish, when I have been standing in deep water) by children, who were creeping between the legs of the bystanders for the curiosity or honour of touching me with the ends of their fingers."

The astonished Indians pronounced Catlin the greatest *medicine-man* in the world; "for they said I had made *living beings*—they said they could see their chiefs alive, in two places—those that I had made were a *little* alive—they could see their eyes move—could see them smile and laugh, and if they could laugh they could certainly speak, if they should try, and they must therefore have *some life* in them." After a time the squaws of the village set up a loud lamentation, denouncing Catlin as a "dangerous man; one who could make living persons by looking at them; and at the same time, could, as a matter of course, destroy life in the same way . . . That bad luck would happen to those whom I painted—that I was to take a part of the existence of those whom I painted, and carry it home with me amongst the white people, and that when they died they would never sleep quiet in their graves."

A kind of panic seized the village and it took all of Catlin's considerable powers of persuasion, filtered through an interpreter, to convince the Mandan that there was no danger in his magic. Soon the chiefs were competing to have their portraits painted, spending half a day donning their most splendid regalia. "The vanity of these men, after they had agreed to be painted," Catlin wrote, "was beyond description." An Indian often lies down from morning till night in front of his portrait, admiring his beautiful face, and faithfully guarding it from day to day to protect it from accident or harm . . . owing to their superstitious notion that there may be life to a certain extent in the picture, and that if harm or violence be done to it, it may in some mysterious way affect their health or do them other injury.

Catlin spent the summer adding to his pictorial and verbal inventory of the wild tribes, soon, he realized, to be swept aside by the irresistible tide of white migration. When a party of Indian hunters returned from a buffalo hunt with "about *fourteen hundred buffalo tongues*" to be exchanged for a few gallons of whiskey, Catlin noted that "Not a skin or a pound of the meat, except the tongues, was brought in . . ." In such waste Catlin read the extinction of the seemingly limitless herds of buffalo. He wrote,

> The Indian and the buffalo are joint and original tenants of the soil, and fugitives from the approach of civilized man. . . . It is not enough in this polished and extravagant age, that we get from the Indian his land, and the very clothes from his back, but the food for his mouth must be stopped, to add a new article to the fashionable world's luxuries . . . that white men may figure a few years longer, enveloped in buffalo robes—spread them over the backs of their sleighs and trail them ostensibly amid the busy throng, as a thing of elegance that had been made for them! . . . It may be that *power* is *right*, and *voracity* a virtue; and that these people, and these noble animals, are righteously doomed to an issue that *will* not be averted.

But it was clear that Catlin could not well reconcile himself to such a thought.

He longed both to establish a museum and a gallery for the display of their varied and remarkable artifacts and his portraits of their chiefs and principal braves, and also to persuade Congress to set aside a vast domain where they might be forever free and uncontaminated. "What a splendid contemplation it would be," he wrote, "by some great protecting policy of our government, to preserve their pristine beauty and wildness, in a *magnificent park*, where the world could see them for ages to come. What a beautiful specimen for America to preserve and hold up to the view of her refined citizens and the world, in future ages! A *National Park*, containing man and beast, in all the wild freshness of their native beauty! I would ask no other monument to my memory, than to be the founder of such an institution." But Catlin must have known in his heart that it was a vain and foolish vision. You could not treat human beings—beautiful, powerful, wild creatures—like animals in a cage, however vast and splendid that cage might be. Heartrending as the thought was, it must all go and the painstakingly collected artifacts, the brilliant pictures, would, in the end, be hardly more suggestive of the unimaginable reality than paper flowers are of real flowers.

Finally, Catlin had completed his remarkable visual record of more than forty tribes. He had succumbed. Like so many, who ventured into that fearful and enchanted world, noble and terrible, he was never to escape its thrall:

> I love a people who have always made me welcome to the best
> they had . . . who are honest without laws, who have no jails and
> no poor houses . . . who never take the name of God in vain . . .
> who worship God without a Bible, and I believe that God loves
> them also . . . who are free from religious animosities . . . who
> have never raised a hand against me, or stolen my property, where
> there was no law to punish either . . . and oh! how I love a people
> who don't live for the love of money.

It was not, of course, really the aborigines that Catlin was speaking of. He knew firsthand the terrible hardships and cruelties that were integral to their lives, of the constancy of violent death and torture; of raids and merciless warfare. In the passage quoted, George Catlin was writing far more as the unrequited lover of a faithless white America that had betrayed his ideals than as what he so often was—a scrupulously accurate portrayer of aboriginal Americans. The ideal and the reality could not be encompassed in the same frame. They constantly threatened to tear Catlin himself apart. He had seen the Indian in "the innocent simplicity of nature" abandon his ancestral ground

> and turn his face in sadness to the setting sun . . . and I have
> seen as often the approach of the bustling, busy, talking, elated,
> exultant white man, with the first dip of the plough share, making
> sacrilegious trespass on the bones of the dead. . . . I have seen the

grand and irresistible march of civilization . . . this splendid jug-
gernaut rolling on and beheld its sweeping desolation. And I have
held converse with the happy thousands, living as yet beyond its
influence, who have not been crushed, nor have yet dreamed of its
approach. I have stood amidst these unsophisticated people, and
contemplated with feelings of deepest regret the certain approach
of this over-whelming system which will inevitably march on and
prosper; reluctant tears shall have watered every rod of this fair
land. . . . All this is certain.

When he had completed his plan, so far as it was practical to
do so, he opened his "Indian Gallery" in New York City, showing
a considerable degree of shrewdness in soliciting the support of the
powerful and fashionable. He gave Daniel Webster, Philip Hone,
and other New York notables an advance showing. Hone wrote that
the Indian Gallery contained Catlin's "great collection of paintings,
consisting of portraits of Indian chiefs, landscapes, ceremonies, etc.,
of the Indian tribes, and implements of husbandry, and the chase,
weapons of war, costumes, etc., which he collected during his travels
of five or six years in the great West. . . . I have seldom witnessed so
interesting an exhibition. We had a collation of buffaloes' tongues,
and venison and the waters of the great spring, and smoked a calumet of peace under an Indian tent formed of buffalo skins."

From New York Catlin took his gallery to Boston, Washington,
and Philadelphia. It was a great initial success everywhere, but
once the novelty had worn off there was a disheartening decline in
admissions. Busy at a narrative of his adventures among the aborigines, finding it difficult to raise money for its publication in the
United States and disappointed in the unwillingness of Congress to
appropriate money for a permanent museum, Catlin decided to take
his exhibition to England—"eight tons of freight, consisting of 600
portraits and other paintings . . . and several thousands of Indian
costumes, weapons, etc."

In England, Catlin rented three large rooms in Egyptian Hall
and his exhibition was an enormous success. Queen Victoria came

to a private showing and Catlin found sponsors among the lords of the realm. He made plans to publish his account of his adventures in two large, profusely illustrated volumes, *Letters and Notes on the Manners, Customs, and Condition of the North American Indians... In Two Volumes with Several Hundred Illustrations.* The work was highly praised by English reviewers, one of whom called Catlin "one of the most remarkable men of the age."

Catlin, who had in him a good deal of the showman and promoter, hired English actors to perform in costume the songs and war dances of the Indians. Just at the point when dwindling admissions had forced him to consider taking his exhibition on a tour of British and Continental cities, a party of nine Ojibwa Indians arrived in London in the charge of an enterprising promoter named Rankin. Catlin at once incorporated them in his exhibition, and the genuine article gave the gallery new life; but when one of the Indians had a highly publicized affair with an English woman, Rankin and Catlin fell out and Catlin and the Ojibwa set up their own show. Moreover, the unhappy Ojibwa, dejected and homesick, were a far cry from the noble savages depicted in Catlin's paintings and, indeed, considerably less impressive than the actors who had preceded them. Charles Dickens reported that they were "mere animals and wretched creatures . . . squatting and spitting" and "their dances no better than the chorus of an Italian opera in England."

With the Ojibwa out of the way, several of them dead of white men's diseases and British climate, Catlin was about to pack up and head for home to try once more to prevail on Congress to provide an appropriate home for his artifacts when fourteen Iowa Indians arrived in a party organized by an old acquaintance of Catlin's named Meolody. Once more Catlin refurbished his exhibit. This time he hired horses for the Iowa to ride, whooping and yelling. Londoners, it turned out, were growing weary of imported Indians. Desperately, Catlin took them on tour. Expenses outran admissions, several of the Iowa died, and Catlin decided to break new ground by taking his gallery, with its human additions, to Paris. There he and his "savage" companions were received with considerable fanfare by the king and queen. "Tell these good fellows I am glad to see them," the king told the Indian interpreter, "that I have been in many of the wigwams of the Indians in America, when I was a young man, and they everywhere treated me kindly. . . ." In Paris, Catlin repeated his London triumph, but the Iowa languished in the alien surroundings; a number of them contracted pneumonia, several died, and the rest fled back to America. A few weeks after their departure, Catlin's wife, Clara, died of pneumonia, leaving him a widower with four young children to care for.

Another party of Ojibwa, who had been performing in London, hearing that the Iowa had departed, came to Paris to join Catlin. Then it was Belgium, where three of the Ojibwa died of smallpox and the others had to be placed in hospitals. Meanwhile, the collection and painting found a temporary home in the Louvre. Catlin tried to sell it all to Louis Philippe and then to the British Museum "or some English Nobleman or Gentleman" for $35,000, but he had no takers and he eked out a bare living through commissions to copy paintings from his gallery of Indian portraits. His son, George, died of pneumonia and his wife's parents reclaimed the three young girls. A committee of Congress proposed the establishment of the Smithsonian Institution as a national gallery of art and recommended that Catlin's collection be purchased for it, but the onset of the Mexican War left the plan in limbo. In the revolutionary upheavals of 1848, a Paris mob broke into Catlin's studio and destroyed several of his paintings and he barely escaped to London with his collection. From there, hounded by creditors, he returned to Paris in 1853 after the restoration of the monarchy.

In the 1852–53 session of Congress, the proposal to purchase Catlin's collection was revived. Webster, in his last days in the Senate, praised Catlin's work as did Jefferson Davis, senator from Kentucky, who had taken Black Hawk to Washington after the end of the Black Hawk War. But Davis ended his speech by saying that the feeling against Indians was so strong in his home state that he was obliged to vote against the bill, which as it turned out was defeated by a single vote.

Impoverished and deaf, Catlin set out at the age of fifty-six for the jungles of Brazil to paint the natives of South America. Accompanied by a giant black man, an escaped slave named Caesar Bolla, who carried the artist's paints and canvases, Catlin made three trips into the interior of Brazil, over the Andes to Peru, and then across the pampas of Argentina. It was one of the most extraordinary expeditions of the century, the aging artist back once more in that world most congenial to him—the world of primitive peoples, enduring hardships, and dangers that would make a saint blanch, protected among warlike and suspicious tribes, many of which had never seen a white person, by his "magic" as a man of "great medicine." He came back to Brussels to a studio on "an obscure street near the Antwerp railroad station." The American consul who sought him out found the deaf old man living on a few francs a day. "He talked to me often about his collections of paintings and sketches," the consul wrote, "and expressed a hope that all his works might be brought together and placed in the hands of the Government of the United States. . . . He evidently felt more anxiety for the future of his lifelong work than to execute orders . . . and always took pride in calling himself the 'friend of the Indian.' . . . His life in Brussels was almost that of a recluse . . ."

In his years in Brussels Catlin wrote two more books, *Life Among the Indians* and *Last Rambles Among the Indians*. In 1870 at the age of seventy-four, after thirty-one years abroad, Catlin came home to New York City. He opened an exhibition of his works in a gallery at Fifth Avenue and 14th Street. Joseph Henry, a friend from days long ago and now director of the Smithsonian, invited him to give an exhibition of his work there. A room in the Smithsonian was given to him as a makeshift studio and efforts were renewed to prevail on Congress to buy his collection of paintings and drawings, now numbering over twelve hundred. Too weak and ill to continue painting, Catlin moved to Jersey City to be near his daughters. He died on December 23, 1872, in his seventy-seventh year, and his last words were reported to be "What will happen to my gallery?"

George Catlin's life, tragic and disordered, paralleled, in some respects, the lives of those aborigines whom he celebrated. Its crowning irony was that he had to convert his Indians into a marketable product. He had to "sell" them, live off them. In London and in Paris he exploited the unfortunate Ojibwa and Iowa. His imagination always exceeded his means and he was as prodigal of money as he was of his talent. He spent more than half of his mature life outside of the United States, joining that company of literary and artistic figures who, it seemed, could not endure their native land or wholly escape it. He did an enormous amount of hack work merely to survive, innumerable copies of original paintings and hasty and poorly executed scenes, far inferior to his best work. He was a romantic, a visionary, an obsessive, a showman, something even of a confidence man, a hustler for the Indians. But out of the torment and disorder emerged those splendidly caparisoned immortal figures, images that will always speak to us of what was most compelling in the life, customs, and manners of the Indians of North America. It was not primarily as an artist that George Catlin thought of himself but as the recorder of a vanishing breed and way of life. Yet in his direct and intense observation of the human and artifactual reality before him, he was assuredly an artist with a fine sense of color, a powerful and convincing mastery of the body and its proportions; a deft draftsman, able, with an economy of strokes, to capture the essence of his subject. While the artists of the Hudson River school ventured out each summer into the domesticated landscape of the Catskills, George Catlin ranged over the vast expanses of two great continents.

CHAPTER XII

THE INDIANS OF THE SOUTHWEST

In 1821, just before the beginning of the brown gold rush, traders' caravans, loaded with goods to trade in Santa Fe, started out from Fort Smith on the Arkansas River. Mexico had won its independence from Spain six months earlier and, in the resultant euphoria, trade with the United States was encouraged by the revolutionary and the Mexican government.

One of the first traders to take advantage of the new opportunity was Major Jacob Fowler who, with a party of twenty men, among them five Frenchmen and a black slave of Fowler's, departed for Santa Fe on September 6, 1821. The group, officially under the command of Colonel Hugh Glenn, included "thirty Horses and mules seventeen of which carried traps and goods for the Indian trade. . . ." They traveled along the Arkansas through the range of the Osage Indians, from whom, as Fowler, the recorder of the trip noted, they "got Some dryed meet Corn Beens and dryed Pumpkins. . . ." The next contact with the Osage was not encouraging, "These last Indians," Fowler wrote, "appear more unfriendly and talk Sassy and bad to us but this is to be Expected as the[y] . . . are Said to be a Collection of the Raskals from the other villages."

Fowler's party followed the Arkansas to present-day Colorado but they found hard going. Buffalo were scarce and grass for the pack animals difficult to find. Soon they were in Pawnee country and they had to be ceaselessly vigilant lest their horses be stolen or their camps attacked. "We Have all Readey lost 13 Horses and two mules," Fowler noted on the sixth of November, "and the Remainder Hardly fit for use. . . . 11 treaks of Indians Barfooded" were observed in the sand along the river. At the Purgatory River Lewis Dawson, who had left the party to pick grapes, was surprised by a "White Bare" or grizzly, which seized and shook him like a terrier with a rat. Fowler and the others were alerted by the "dredfull Screems" of the victim and the bear was finally driven off and killed. Dawson's head was terribly lacerated, but the wounds "Ware Sewed up as Well as Cold be don by men in our Situation Haveing no Surgen or Surgical Instruments. . . ." Dawson was conscious but convinced that his hours were numbered, declaring "I am killed . . . I heard my skull break." Three days later he died.

Near the juncture of the North Platte and the Niobrara rivers Fowler's band encountered a party of Kiowa, allies of the Comanche, who "Came Riding at full Speed With all their Weapons . . . in a florish as tho the Ware Chargeing upon an Enemey but on their aproch the most friendly disposition appereed in all their actions as Well [as] gusters." It was a typically dramatic Indian encounter. As soon as the Kiowa discovered that the party was a trading expedition, they took it under their collective wing. They made it clear, through signs and gestures, that they would act as guardians and sponsors, expecting, of course, handsome presents in return for their services. The more enterprising tribes were always anxious to establish a close and profitable relationship with white traders. If that turned out to be impractical, their next intention was usually to steal what they could without excessive risk. As a last resort they robbed and killed the whites if the opportunity presented itself.

The Kiowa chief indicated that his tribe wished to trade. He prevailed on the uneasy traders to interrupt their journey. He then "took possession and Charge of all our Horses," Fowler noted, while his band gathered and placed the trading goods in the chief's lodge for their "protection." Through the rest of the day Kiowa continued to arrive and set up their lodges so that by nightfall there was, in Fowler's words, "a large town Containing up Wards of two Hondrerd Houses Well filled with men Wemon and Children— With a great nombr of dogs and Horses So that the Hole Cuntry to a great distance Was Coverd. . . ."

On November 22 Fowler noted in his journal: "Remained in Camp al day Holding Counsels Eating and Smokeing and traiding a little with Indians. . . ." It snowed and turned bitterly cold and Fowler watched with astonishment several hundred naked Indian children "running and playin on the Ice—Without the least appeerence of Suffering from the Cold."

As more and more Indians collected, including bands from several tribes friendly to the Kiowa, the traders grew understandably apprehensive. Next day came the shocker. A Comanche chief, who had recently arrived on the scene and assumed command, announced that the Indians were ready to receive the gifts in the traders' possession that "His father the President Had Sent them." Colonel Glenn replied that there were no such gifts. They were private traders on their way to Santa Fe. At this the chief flew in "a great Pashion" and told the colonel that he was a liar and thief and had stolen the goods from the President. He, the chief, would take charge of the goods and protect them and "He Wold kill the Conl and His men too upon Which the Conl and His Inturpreter With drew," leaving the Indians to confer about their fate. The issue boiled down to a conflict between the Kiowa and the Comanche, the Kiowa defending the traders, the Comanche denouncing them. So many Comanche had pitched their lodges along the river that they outnumbered the Kiowa. As Fowler put it with some understatement, "[O]ur Setuation Was not of the most plesent nature." At sundown a tall handsome Indian came running into the white camp, shaking hands all around and declaring, "Me Arapaho." The Arapaho, a third tribe included in the large Indian gathering, had declared for the traders. The Indian assured Colonel Glenn that the whites had nothing further to fear from the Comanche. Indeed, he was soon followed by the Comanche chief who had been so adamant about seizing the trading goods. Overborne by the other chiefs, he became all charm and compliance and "offered Conl glann and Mr. Roy Each one of His Wifes—the greatest token of friendship those Indeans Can offer."

Fowler estimated that there were from five to seven thousand Indians encamped on the plain stretching back from the river, among them Cheyenne, Paducah (a branch of the Comanche), and some Indians that Fowler called Snake but who could hardly have been members of the Shoshone tribe that most commonly bore that name. The white traders were, meanwhile, visited by "Spanish Indeans" from Taos in New Mexico and assured that they were on the right path and only six days easy travel from that Mexican post. Preparing to continue their journey, the white traders made camp a few miles down the river. There they learned from friendly Arapaho that the mercurial Comanche chief was preparing to attack them. As the traders erected hasty log palisades, a band of Arapaho set up camp around them, ostensibly for their protection against the Comanche. It soon appeared possible that the rumored Comanche attack was a ruse to give the Arapaho the opportunity to take charge of the expedition under the guise of defending it.

Amid indications that the gathering would soon disperse and the traders at last be free to proceed to Santa Fe, Fowler experienced a typical bit of Indian horseplay. He had lost one lens from his glasses and was startled when an Indian snatched the glasses from his head and ran off. "In a Short time," he wrote, "I heard great Shouting and laffing." The Indian who had absconded with the glasses was returning, leading another Indian wearing them. When he came up to Fowler, the latter saw that the Indian had only one eye—one eye, one eyepiece. The Indians were delighted with the joke. The glasses were returned and everyone was very merry.

But before they could extricate themselves the traders needed to purchase some horses and, additionally, were confronted by another delicate bit of Indian diplomacy. Both the Arapaho and the Kiowa now claimed sponsorship of the traders. Both insisted that the whites must stay with them and for a time it looked as though the dispute might result in "a Ware With them and destruction to our Selves." The crisis was at least temporarily resolved by splitting the party into two groups, one for each tribe, but the Indians, anxious to delay their departure, refused to sell the needed horses. Finally enough horses were traded to allow the party to resume its journey, although both Kiowa and Arapaho showed every disposition to accompany them. When Colonel Glenn took leave of the Arapaho chief and presented him with some small presents, that stoical warrior "threw himself on his bed in tears." And at the traders' camp that evening he appeared to spend one more night with his friend the white chief.

On December 6, Fowler and his companions broke camp. The month that they had lived so precariously surrounded by the unpredictable aborigines had been instructive but nerve-wracking, and they were glad to be on the move again. "It is but Justice," Fowler wrote, "to Say We find the Kiawa the best Indeans possessing more firmness and manly deportment than the arapoho and less arrogance and Hatey Pride than the letan [Comanche]. . . ." It should be noted that whites, almost invariably, found greater virtues in the tribes that were friendly to them than in those that were hostile.

A week later Fowler's group, still accompanied by some Arapaho warriors, encountered a party of Comancheros—Spaniards, or Mexicans, of mixed Spanish and Indian blood. When the two groups met there was a moment of uncertainty on the part of the Americans. For years the Spanish had been hostile and suspicious toward explorers and traders from the United States. Zebulon Pike had been arrested and held for several months when his expedition penetrated Spanish territory. But there had been a revolution. The Mexicans, like the Americans, had claimed their independence. Erstwhile enemies were now friends, both fighters in the cause of

freedom. But had this new spirit of amity reached the frontier out-
posts of the newly proclaimed Republic of Mexico? It was soon evident that it had. The Comancheros, a miserable, ragged-looking lot,
painted like Indians, "dismounted and embraced us with affection
and friendship," Colonel Glenn noted, adding, "they are all creoles
[mixed bloods]. . . . The rather more literate seem well disposed—
possess far less sence than the Indeans we are with, seem happy
and possess a greater degree of Joy at seeing us then could be
Imagined. . . ." Glenn was surprised to discover that the Arapaho
treated the Mexicans "much as we command our negroes." One of
the Arapaho ordered the Comancheros to kneel and pray "so that
we may see their fashion which they readily agreed to and went
through with the Catholic prayers, and afterwards prayed fervently
for us. . . ."

Glenn went on with the Comancheros to Santa Fe, leaving
"mager" Fowler in charge of the pack train, with instructions to
make camp and keep a vigilant eye out for Indians. Fowler sent
three of the party out to hunt for buffalo and they fell in with a
war party of Crows, herding along some two hundred horses they
had stolen from the Arapaho. The Crows took the hunters prisoner
and relieved them of their ammunition and blankets, "giving them
nine fine Horses in payment. . . ." While this negotiation was going
on, the Crows were overtaken by a party of Arapaho seeking to
recover their horses. In the fight that followed the hunters made
their escape, leaving their horses, blankets, and ammunition behind.

The next day Fowler had to contend with "a mutney." When he
ordered the hunters out of their beds to search for deer and buffalo,
they refused to stir. Fowler's response was to yank the ringleader
out of bed by his hair; the result was a "scoffel" in which Fowler tri-
umphed. The men, it turned out, were convinced that Glenn would
be arrested by the Mexican officials, in which case they were determined to divide up the trading goods among themselves as their pay
for the expedition. Fowler told them that if they persisted in their
plan he would send for the Arapaho chief, who would be glad to
help him protect the goods. This threat brought capitulation. Peace

was made and Fowler promised that if Glenn failed to return, the hunters would be dealt with fairly.

Settling down to wait for word from the colonel, the party grew more restless and impatient with each passing day. Some thirty Crows, on their way to war with the Arapaho, moved in and "Recogniseing the three men the maid Prisnors . . . Exspressed much Joh to See them." After they had "don Eating Smokeing the Sung a long Song and all lay down and Slept tell morning." But before they departed, they stole everything they could carry. One Indian came into Fowler's tent "threw down His old Roab and took a new one." He then picked up Fowler's saddle bag as well. After a brief scuffle, Fowler retrieved his belongings and ejected the Indian from the tent. Similar scenes were being enacted in various parts of the camp. An appeal was made to the chief, who ordered the warriors to return whatever they had appropriated and "moved them of[f] before Him," but when they had departed an inventory showed that the whites were missing a roll of brass wire, three blankets, five knives, and a smelting ladle. A few days later the Crows were back from their raid empty-handed. This time they tried to drive off the traders' horses and when they failed, they boldly "came to us as friends." Fowler gave them some tobacco and trinkets but he and his men remained on the alert. The chief professed to be hurt by the obvious wariness of the whites. He was their friend, he assured them. His only desire was to protect them from hostile Indians. While he orated "one of His Cheefs Stole a bridle and put it in His bosem." Fowler saw the theft and took back the bridle. There was another tense moment as the traders looked to the priming of their guns and the Crows drew off as though they were preparing to fight, but the moment passed and the head chief expressed his regrets at the actions of his war-riors. The incident is a revealing one. The Indians generally had no notion of stealing from each other, although they sometimes did so—usually with fatal results for the thief. But other Indians, and especially whites, who always appeared to have such an abundance of things that they could well spare some, were fair game. Stealing horses was accounted part of a continuing game, demanding great

stealth, skill, and daring. Stealing inanimate objects was not reprehensible, only less daring. What was, in effect, a cultural difference appeared to the white man simply another instance of Indian
depravity and wickedness. In this instance it is easy to sympathize
with the white man who heard the Indian profess devoted friendship while purloining his most essential possessions.

By the end of January word came from Colonel Glenn that
the Mexican government was anxious to encourage trade with the
United States and that he had secured permission to trap and trade
"in the Spanish provences." Fowler and his men were at once on the
move to join Glenn. The colonel met them near the village of San
Cristobal and accompanied them to Taos, where they received a
warm welcome and participated in a fandango, which the author
Josiah Gregg later described as an assembly "where dancing and
frolocking are carried on. . . . Nothing is more general, throughout
the country, and with all classes than dancing. From the gravest
priest to the buffoon—from the richest nabob to the beggar—from
the governor to the ranchero—from the soberest matron to the flip-
pant belle—all partake of this exhilerating amusement." The fiddle,
the guitar, and the tombe or Indian drum were the standard musical instruments and they were so constantly played, fandango or no,
"that," Gregg wrote, "one would suppose that a perpetual carnival
prevailed everywhere."

At Taos, Paul, Fowler's black slave, enjoyed a great vogue. One
of the older women of the town took a special fancy to him and
"takeing Hold of Him and drawing Him to the beed Side Sot Him
down with Hir arms Round His Sholders. and gave Him a Kis . . .
Sliped Hir Hand down Into his Britches. . . . It Wold take a much
abeler Hand than mine," Fowler added, "to discribe palls feelings at
this time being naturly a little Relegous modest and Bashfull."

The trading goods were sold for hard Spanish dollars at Taos
and Santa Fe, and for four months the party trapped beaver in the
mountains and rivers of western Colorado and eastern New Mexico.
They were constantly involved in close encounters with various
Indian tribes, striving always to maintain a neutrality, often in as

much danger from their Indian friends as their enemies. The Ute, whose range covered the Salt Lake and the Utah valleys as well as parts of present-day Colorado, and the Pawnee, roving over a region south and west of the Platte, were added to their inventory of tribes. By June they were on their way back to the Arkansas with a rich haul of beaver and specie. At Fort Osage on the Missouri, Colonel Glenn bought two canoes and the weary band floated down the river to St. Louis, spreading the word in the river settlements along the way that Mexico was independent and that trade had been opened with the United States.

Other expeditions were already on the way and soon the numbers increased dramatically. Although the risks and hardships were great, there were high profits to be made. It was not unusual for an investment of $20,000 in trading goods to bring a return in the $200,000 range. For the next fifteen or sixteen years what Josiah Gregg called "the Commerce of the Prairies" flourished as an alternative to the rush for beaver in the Yellowstone. Gregg, who in 1831 took much the same route that Fowler had followed, wrote the classic account of the Santa Fe trade before the growing difficulties with Mexico led to its termination. Gregg was another American original, largely self-educated, who had tried school-teaching, medicine, and law before becoming a trader on the Santa Fe route. He had been born in Tennessee, a farmer's son, but when he was three his father had moved to the St. Louis area. From there he moved soon again to the Missouri Territory, settling near Fort Cooper on the frontier and, finally, to Independence, the jumping-off point for everything and everybody going west. Gregg, an omnivorous reader, had taught himself French and Italian, learned to survey, and became a skillful cartographer. But it is also clear that he was highly eccentric and suffered a series of "identity crises" severe enough to leave him physically ill, or, in his words, "reduced and debilitated." His doctor, unable to find anything wrong with him, prescribed what was already a classic remedy—a trip west. So Gregg, more dead than alive, signed on as a kind of supercargo with a trading caravan headed for Santa Fe.

Since Jacob Fowler's journey in 1821, wagons had largely replaced pack horses for the transporting of merchandise, and in the year of Gregg's departure 130 wagons carrying $250,000 in trading goods departed from Independence, Missouri, along a well-traveled wagon road.

At Independence, the leaders of the caravans recruited teamsters, hunters, trappers, cooks, and assorted hands. Wagons, generally made in Pittsburgh and floated down the Ohio, were purchased, as were mules to draw them. Cattle for butchering were part of most trains, as buffalo and deer became scarce along the much-traveled route, and horses for those who preferred not to walk or could afford to ride. The typical wagon carried some five thousand pounds of merchandise and was pulled by ten or twelve mules. It was calculated that each man would consume during a six-week journey some fifty pounds of flour, a hundred pounds of bacon, "ten of coffee and twenty of sugar, and a little salt." Mules, once bought, often had to be trained to draw in tandem and respond to commands and to the teamster's whip. The wagons had to be expertly packed to avoid damage to goods on the long, jolting ride. The beginning of the trip, according to Gregg's account, was accompanied by a general mood of euphoria: "Harmony and good feeling prevail everywhere. The hilarious song, the *bon mot* and the witty repartee, go round in quick succession."

Gregg's caravan had hardly left Council Grove behind when his health revived astonishingly. His own reflections on the reasons for his remarkable recovery (it had been necessary to lift him onto his wagon a few days earlier) are worth noting: "The Prairies have," he wrote, "become very celebrated for their sanative effects. . . . Most chronic diseases, particularly liver complaints, dyspepsias, and similar afflictions, are often radically cured; owing, no doubt, to the peculiarities of diet, and the regular exercise incident to prairie life, as well as to the purity of the atmosphere of those elevated unembarrassed regions." Soon Gregg threw away the large supply of pills and medicines he had carried with him and dined voluptuously on buffalo meat.

Assuming Gregg's explanation of the curative consequences of prairie life to have some modest medical basis, one may be forgiven for doubting that a cure could be effected in *three days*! It seems far likelier that Gregg and the legion of valetudinarians who preceded and followed him found relief from the strains and stresses of American life, of what was rather loosely denominated "civilization," to be the greatest remedy for what ailed them—neurasthenia or bad nerves, typically manifested by a bad stomach or "dyspepsia," as it was commonly called.

At Council Grove, the various traders with their wagons or merchandise waited for a caravan to be formed. The purpose was to provide mutual protection against the Indians and to make formal arrangements for the organization of the train under the leadership of a captain, chosen democratically by a "grand council" of traders. "Even in our little community," Gregg wrote, "we had our 'office-seekers' and their 'political adherents,' as earnest and devoted as any of the modern school of politicians in the midst of civilization." The caravan was then divided into four divisions, each in the charge of a lieutenant. The lieutenants selected, or "formed," each day's encampment, assigned night watches, and distributed the major chores among the able-bodied members of the caravan. (Every caravan seems to have had its quota of invalids seeking to recapture their health who, along with the "tourists" and "genteel idlers," were exempt from the more arduous chores.) Gregg's caravan, when the roll was called, numbered some two hundred men. On May 27, 1831, the captain gave the cry "Catch up!" which was echoed through the camp and replied to by "All's set!" When the mules were harnessed and the wagons ready to move, "Stretch out" would be the captain's call, followed by the "heps!" of "drivers—the cracking of whips—the trampling of feet—the occasional creaks of wheels—the rumbling of wagons. . . ."

The job of the captain was a thankless one. He had no real authority over his contentious and often quarrelsome charges. If an individual disobeyed him, he had to bring the offender before a kind of informal court or council that, in turn, if it upheld the captain, could do little more than exercise moral suasion unless the offense was a heinous one such as stealing or murder; in such cases summary justice was commonly, though by no means invariably, inflicted. Captains and lieutenants who were too officious or demanding were often deposed. What was required in a captain, ideally, was considerable practical knowledge and experience, plus great tact and firmness in dealing with a polyglot and highly independent constituency.

Three elements governed all such caravans, whether traders in merchandise headed for Santa Fe, fur traders on the way to the Yellowstone, or emigrants headed for Oregon Territory: wood for the campfires; water for cooking and for the stock—the mules, horses and such cattle as accompanied the train; and grass as fodder for the animals. Without those three essentials no wagon train or caravan could go more than two or three days at the most and that at the cost of great hardship and suffering. This fact dictated the practical routes westward. They all had to travel along one of the great eastward-flowing rivers rising on the east side of the Rockies—the Continental Divide—and flowing to the Mississippi or the Missouri: the Missouri itself, the Arkansas, the Red, and the Platte. Where the route of the caravan departed from a major river system it had to cover the ground in increments determined by smaller creeks, streams, or water holes.

The nature of the terrain and the winding course of the rivers necessitated frequent fordings and these were, generally speaking, the most hazardous obstacles of the journey. Major rivers, especially in times of high water, in early spring or after heavy rains, were deep and swift. They could in an instant sweep away horse, rider, wagon, and mules. So there was first a search up and down the river for a fording place where, hopefully, the wagons could be driven across. If no such spot could be found, the industry and ingenuity of the train was tested to the utmost. Sometimes crude rafts were built, the wagons loaded on them, and the rafts winched across by long ropes. This was a laborious and dangerous process. Ropes might break or the raft be overturned midstream and everything lost. The Platte and the Arkansas were broad and shallow and ford-able at many places, but rivers like the Red, the Missouri, and the Yellowstone were formidable obstacles.

Traveling west from Independence, Gregg's train went along the Arkansas toward the Cimarron Desert, passing over the Great Plains, a grass-covered region often referred to as "the grand prairie ocean," flat as the proverbial pancake and seemingly limitless in its expanse. At the end of each day, when the lieutenants and their captain had formed an encampment, the wagons were drawn into a square or circle, famous from a thousand movie Westerns. When there was danger of imminent Indian attack, the mules, oxen, horses, and cattle were corralled in the center and the wagons attached to each other by heavy ropes or chains. This meant that grass had to be collected for the animals, which was an onerous chore for men already travel-weary and anxious to prepare their evening meal. The preference, of course, was to turn the animals loose to graze on the grass and brush that grew along the riverbed.

The attire of most members of the train was simple and utilitar-ian. In Gregg's words, most common was "the fustian frock of the city-bred merchant furnished with a multitude of pockets capable of accommodating a variety of 'extra tacking.' Then there is . . . the farmer with his blue jean coat, the wagoner with his flannel-sleeve vest," and of course the hunter with his hunting shirt and leather leggings. The hunter's indispensable arm was his rifle, but for other members of the party a shotgun or scatter gun was often preferred, a double-barreled fowling piece. By the time of Gregg's trip—1831— the repeating rifle had appeared and, as Gregg noted, "they are cer-tainly very formidable weapons, particularly when used against an ignorant savage foe." In addition most travelers were "furnished . . . with a bountiful supply of pistols and knives of every description, so that [our] party made altogether a very brand-like appearance."

The "kitchen and table ware" of a wagon consisted, typically, of a skillet, frying pan, sheet-iron camp kettle, a coffeepot, and, for each man, a tin cup and butcher's knife. Blankets of buffalo robes were spread beside the respective wagons on the outside of the perimeter. Tents were seldom used. If rain threatened, people slept under the wagons, or, space permitting, inside the canvas tops. Gregg judged the quantities of coffee drunk "incredible," adding, "It is an unfailing and apparently indispensable beverage, served at every meal—even under the boiling noon-day sun, the wagoner will rarely fail to replenish a second time, his huge tin cup."

The initial sighting of buffalo, especially for those who had never seen the famous animals, was always a sensation. In Gregg's description,

> Every horseman was off in a scamper; and some of the wagoners, leaving their teams to take care of themselves, seized their guns and joined the race afoot. Here went one with his rifle or yager— there another with double-barrelled shot-gun—a third with holster-pistols—a Mexican perhaps with his lance—another with his bow and arrows—and numbers joined without any arms whatever, merely for "the pleasures of the chase"—all helter-skelter—a regular John Gilpin race, truly "neck or naught." The fleetest of the pursuers were soon in the midst of the game which scattered in all directions, like a flock of birds upon the descent of a hawk.

Gregg observed that the buffalo were fast diminishing through "the continual and wanton slaughter of them by travellers and hunters, and the still greater havoc made among them by the Indians, not only for the meat, but often for the skins and tongue alone (for which they find a ready market among the traders), are fast reducing their numbers, and must ultimately effect their total annihilation from the continent." Gregg added that the annual export of "*buffalo rugs*" (also called robes) from the prairies was a hundred thousand a year, and many more of the beasts were killed for meat.

Like the first sighting of buffalo, the initial encounter with Plains Indians was the occasion of great stir and excitement. To the Indians, the pack and wagon trains that made their way across the Great Plains to the Great Basin—whether they went southerly to Santa Fe and Taos or northerly to the Yellowstone and then north again to the Oregon country; whether they were fur trad-ers, merchants, or, later, emigrants headed for the Pacific slopes—were, like the herds of buffalo, a form of game. They brought with them many attractive articles that the Indians coveted, and, most important, food in the form of cattle and wealth in the form of horses and mules. The uniform intention of the various tribes was to acquire, at the least possible cost to themselves, as much of the white man's bounty as they could, including, ideally, his scalp. The strategy to accomplish this goal was, unless the tribe was notori-ous for its hostility to all whites, to approach the train with elabo-rate manifestations of peace and goodwill. This was generally done as Jacob Fowler described it in his earlier journey—attempting to achieve maximum dramatic effect by riding up to the train en route or, preferably, when making camp for the night, at full tilt in battle attire, bristling with arms and giving the impression of an all-out attack. As the alarm of "Indians!" was raised and whites dashed for their weapons and tried to round up their stock, the Indians would pull up at a safe distance and several of their chiefs come forward professing friendship and the desire to trade. The train captain and his lieutenants would confer with the Indian chiefs. A brief pow-wow might then follow, with the ritual smoking of the peace pipe. The chiefs not uncommonly spoke of the hardships of their tribe, the scarcity of game, their admiration for the white men, their need for tobacco and beads. The Sioux, especially since the days of Lewis and Clark, were shameless beggars. Behind the begging was always an unspoken threat. Part of the ritual was to give the chiefs presents, the best presents to the most important chiefs and so on down the line. Then the members of the train might barter with the warriors for Indian garments, bows and arrows, for pieces of finery, even scalps. The Indians would use every stratagem to insinuate them-selves into the camp area and, as we have seen, while the trading was going on, help themselves to every object that was not nailed down or closely guarded by its owner.

Stealing horses and livestock from white trains was to the Indians an irresistible opportunity to minimize losses and maximize profits.

It was far easier and less perilous to steal horses from white travelers than from other Indians. First off, the trains or caravans always contained a substantial portion of travelers inexperienced in the ways of the frontier, and this portion of course grew larger each year as more and more emigrants—as opposed to hunters and trappers—headed west. Most important, if fifty horses or mules were stolen out of a train's hastily erected and often inadequately guarded corral, the leaders of the train, while dispatching a party to try to overtake the Indians and recapture their animals, could not spend more than a few hours in the task. Above everything they had to push on, for time was their greatest enemy. If they dallied, winter might catch them on the trail. So the Indians were safe from protracted pursuit.

One variation of the stealing of horses and cattle came into play when the animals were too closely guarded to be gotten at, or when they were corralled inside the wagons. Then the Indians would often content themselves with shooting arrows at the dim forms in the hope of killing a few that, abandoned the next day by the train, would provide a hearty meal.

Every Indian tribe had its own range or territory along the main-traveled routes. A tribe usually confined its pillage of the wagon trains to its territory. Thus trains headed for the Yellowstone would pass successively through the territory of the Mandan, the Arikara, the Sioux, the Blackfeet, and the Crows as well as lesser and subsidiary tribes and each would take its proper turn. The all-out, large-scale attacks on trains so vividly depicted in many Western movies were relatively rare. For the most part these came only when a state of open war existed between a particular tribe and the whites—that is to say, when the Indians were on the "war path." What we might properly call the hunting of the white trains by the Indians, rather as they hunted the buffalo, was a peacetime activity. Relatively few travelers across Indian territory died in armed clashes. They were far more frequently killed when out hunting for meat for the train in small parties of two or three or when straying, for whatever reason, from the main body. Gregg did not think there had been more than a dozen deaths on the Santa Fe route from Indians and disease combined.

Often the chiefs of a tribe might genuinely deplore such iso-lated killings of whites—and even the raids themselves—and try to prevent them, but outside the immediate limits of the village their authority was often tenuous and even within the village it rested on moral force rather than legal sanction. Young braves anxious to qualify as warriors and warriors who coveted the rank of chief had constantly to find ways to prove themselves, to make "coup," to take the scalps by which an Indian's status was ultimately measured, to capture ponies, and to have dramatic stories to tell of their prowess. They were as swift and skillful as prestidigitators—their hands were often faster than the white man's eye.

When the gifts had been given and the possibilities of trade exhausted, the Indians would withdraw with additional assurances of friendship and ostensibly ride off to steal some horses from a rival tribe. Generally they shadowed the wagons or pack train for days, slipping in each night to try to drive off horses or mules or oxen. A tribe might double its collective wealth as measured in ponies by a single successful raid, or, conversely, be impoverished by a raid against it. Josiah Gregg tells of his caravan suddenly being virtu-ally swallowed up by several thousand Blackfeet and Gros Ventres who pitched a treat tent city around the camp of the wagon train in the valley of the Cimarron River at the eastern edge of the des-ert; despite all efforts to keep them at arm's length, they swarmed through the camp. By nightfall, Gregg wrote, "we had perhaps a thousand of these pertinacious creatures, males and females, of all ages and descriptions, about us . . . every means without resorting to absolute violence, was employed to drive them away, but without entire success." Soon it was discovered that they had made off with a "pig of lead" for bullets weighing almost a hundred pounds, as well as a number of smaller articles. Next day the Indians went their way only, it was learned later, to encounter the Sioux and lose almost half their company in a desperate battle.

One of the most picturesque figures of the Southwestern fron-tier was the Mexican *cibolero*. Typically these buffalo hunters wore "leather trousers and jackets, and flat straw hats; while, swung upon the shoulder of each hangs his *carcage* or quiver of bows and arrows. The long handle of his lance being set in a case, and suspended by the side with a strap from the pommel of the saddle leave[s] the point waving high over the head, with a tassel of gay parti-colored stuffs dangling at the tip of the scabbard." Even the hunter's musket had a "fantastically tasselled" stopper in its barrel.

A few days away from Santa Fe a party of customs officials met Gregg's caravan, ostensibly to escort them to Santa Fe. From a distance that town looked to Josiah Gregg like a cluster of brick kilns painted white. As he drew closer it was apparent that these were the adobe houses of the town and soon the travelers could hear the cries *"Los Americanos!"*—*"Los Carros!"*—*"La entrada de la caravana!"*

In New Mexico the ranchos and haciendas had, of necessity, grown into villages "for protection against the marauding savages of the surrounding wilderness," as Josiah Gregg put it. The land was mountainous, arid, and barren, with grass in the high hills that made excellent grazing for large herds of cattle. But it was the air and climate that most impressed such visitors as Gregg. He rhapsodized about it: "Nowhere—not even under the much boasted Sicilian skies—can a purer or more wholesome atmosphere be found." A strange enchantment hung over the land that makes up the southern end of the Great Basin, a unique geological region of the world, created only yesterday in terms of the earth's age by volcanic upheavals too immense to imagine. Rock and earth had been thrust up thousands of feet above sea level, tilted like a great plate; then the rivers had begun their carving and cutting of the land like fabulous masons, shaping battlements and towers, red and yellow and purple escarpments and minarets, plateaus as large as countries and chasms that seemed to have no bottom—a formidable and beautiful universe. The traveler, the hunter, the trader, could hardly escape the feeling that he had stumbled into a frozen panorama of the creation of the world. For the moment it existed primarily as a formidable barrier stretching across the land, dividing the golden shores of California and the rain forest of the Northwest from the rest of the continent. Nowhere could one find a better demonstration of the overwhelming power of geography—of landscape in ceaseless interplay with ideas.

There was in those who first saw this world a kind of astonished muteness in the face of such hitherto unimagined immensities. It was not evident whether it was beautiful or merely terrifying; it was all on a scale too vast to be comprehended under any existing aesthetic rubric. It seemed to call for an enlarged perception, a new way of looking at the world and at man himself, who appeared so dwarfed and impotent by comparison. So the first comers said little about the landscape as though they hardly knew quite what to say, conscious of the unbridgeable gap between what they saw and their power to render it in words. That muteness could not last, of course, and soon there were words enough, however inadequate, for Americans were loath to concede that there was any realm of human experience, any natural phenomenon, any artifact, however fantastical, that could not be summed up or summoned up or nailed down with words. To be sure, one needed new scales, new dimensions, new conceptions. The Indians, mysterious and protean and ultimately inexplicable, were hard enough to pin down, and now there was an additional and inescapable demonstration of the incomprehensible powers and forces of the natural world—the landscape and the Indians.

Everything was further complicated by the fact that in the "go-ahead age" human perspectives changed with bewildering speed. Experiences must be swallowed in great indigestible gulps. Perhaps that was what was wrong with the American stomach—perhaps gulping down too much undigested experience had given Americans a kind of collective stomachache. The fact that this fearful and awesome and—one could hardly call it beautiful; beautiful was for a very different scale—astonishing barrier *intervened* between the bustling East Coast and the benevolent waters of the Pacific was as profound a fact as any that entered into the composition of the American character, or psyche, or sense of the self in relation to the universe or however we may put it when we try to say what America was and is.

The West entered the American consciousness in another way. The contours of the Great Basin made dramatically apparent what geologists had already been more than hinting at—that the earth was very much older than the Scriptures suggested. Hundreds of thousands of years had clearly been necessary for the Colorado River, for instance, to carve out the Grand Canyon and, indeed, for all the remarkable features of that terrain to be defined. For the orthodox, the findings of geology posed another problem for their faith. Even such a mild skeptic as Sidney George Fisher was troubled by the implications of "the truths revealed by geology. . . . The story of the creation taught in Genesis is much more ennobling to our race," he wrote. "It is a much more dignified idea that we were a special creation, made in God's own image, than that we are one link in a progressive series of development, from plants to worms, to fish, to birds, to beasts until finally a poet & a philosopher is produced of a species that began with a monkey, produced too by gradual changes of the earth's crust & temperature, by laws that are eternal & unvaried in their operation, chemical laws & laws of animal life." But while he mourned that passing of the wolf and buffalo Fisher derived comfort from the thought that higher forms of life were evolving. "The Indians . . . ere long will belong wholly to the past, as the aborigines of the West Indies do," he reflected. "Man destroys the animals, the strong races of man destroy the weak. This process is always going on and at the same time the superior races are advancing in knowledge & power." It seemed to Fisher that "in the vast spaces of time" climate and geography might well produce

changes as wonderful as those which geology teaches, and a million years hence, the ruling nations of the world may be as superior to those of today as these are to the Indians. The idea is vast and overpowering, whether we look to the past or to the future, but it is desolating to think that in this stream of humanity, our part is only the present moment, that the future is to us as the past and that we are mere bubbles upon a rushing current, coming whence we know not, going whither we know not, but not taking us with it. Nay, that man himself is to disappear like the mammoth and the buffalo and neither this earth nor any place to know him or have a habitation for him.

Josiah Gregg estimated in 1831 that no more than 70,000 "souls" inhabited the vast reaches of New Mexico and that of these only some thousand were what he called "white creoles," native-born Mexicans of pure Spanish descent. Mestizos, or "mixed creoles," he calculated to number some 59,000, while Indians of the pueblos he estimated at 10,000. Twenty United States citizens lived in the province and "not over double as many alien residents. . . . Agriculture," he wrote, "like almost everything else in New Mexico, is in a very primitive and unimproved state." Most peasant farmers used only a hoe, but Gregg took thoughtful note of a fact that would, in another day, determine the economy of the entire Great Basin. Since there was virtually no rainfall, all land planted in vegetables had to be artificially irrigated by water drawn from a stream or river by a system of crude canals and thus could grow much of the year without regard to rainfall. As Gregg put it, the Mexican farmer, primitive as his tools and practices, "is therefore more sure of his crop than if it were subject to the caprices of the weather in more favored agricultural regions."

The staple productions of the country were Indian corn and wheat. The corn was used principally to make tortillas, paper-thin cakes or crepes filled with meat or vegetables or cheese or simply with butter or salt. Indeed the ubiquitous tortilla, rolled up or dried, often served as both fork and spoon. The nut of the scrub pine, or piñon, was another prized delicacy. *El cafe de los Mexicanos* was a brew more potent than American coffee and more addictive among the "lower classes of Mexicans." With *frijoles* and *chile*, coffee or *atole* made up their principal fare. Red peppers entered into virtually every dish and every meal. Green peppers, *chile verde*, served both as a condiment and as a salad.

Goods were transported in New Mexico by mules, and Josiah Gregg was much impressed by the skill of the *arrieros*, or muleteers, in packing merchandise on the animals. In five minutes they could pack a mule so expertly that the load would hold tight over the roughest country. Like the *arrieros*, the *vaqueros* or cattle herders were excellent horsemen, usually mounted on handsome steeds, capable of performing "many surprising feats, which would grace an equestrian circus in any country, such, for instance, as picking up a dollar from the ground at every pass with the horse at full gallop." Even more impressive were the tricks they could perform with a *lazo* commonly made of horsehair or twisted sea grass "with a convenient noose at one end." As soon as the noose had been cast over the neck of a running horse, "the lazador fetches the end of his saddle, and by a quick manoeuvre the wildest horse is brought up to a stand." The same technique was employed with a runaway cow or ox, though a grown bull required the attentions of two *lazadores* to subdue it. While the *arrieros* and *vaqueros* were most skilled with the *lazo* all Mexicans were proficient in its use. As Gregg put it, "They acquire [the skill] from infancy; for it forms one of the principal rural sports of the children, who may daily be seen with their *lazitos*, noosing the dogs and chickens about the yards, in every direction." The *lazo* could also be used as a weapon and in skirmishes with the Indians a *vaquero* would often "throw this formidable object around the neck or body of the enemy," jerk him from his pony, and drag him along the ground until he was insensible or dead.

A Mexican marked his horse or mule "with a huge hieroglyphic brand," called his *fierro* or iron. When the animal was sold, it was marked with a venta or sale brand, and Gregg noted that some frequently sold animals were covered with such a network of brands as to be undecipherable except by an expert.

The Mexican women especially caught the eye of American traders. Gregg described them as often possessing "striking traits of beauty" and "remarkable for small feet and handsome figures." They used a homemade suntan lotion to protect their complexions and gazed alluringly out from under large straw bonnets. The New Mexicans in general had, in Gregg's view, "inherited much of the cruelty and intolerance of their ancestors, and no small portion of their bigotry and fanaticism." They had "a highly imaginative temperament" (by no means a compliment) and "rather accommodating moral principles—cunning, loquacious, quick of perception and sycophantic." On the other hand, Gregg found them remarkably generous to those in need and unfailingly courteous to visitors. "In their salutations," he added, "the ancient custom of close embrace, not only between individuals of the same sex, but between those of different sexes, is almost universal. It is quite a luxury to meet a pretty señorita after some absence."

The "marauding savages" were a very prominent part of the life of New Mexico. The Apache were famous for their horsemanship, for their daring raids and their cruelty. They had come to live, for the most part, on the cattle and sheep they stole from the ranchos and haciendas. Mules were reputed to be their favorite food and Gregg reported that the chiefs settled quarrels among warriors over possession of mules by killing all those in question. The Apache were the inveterate enemies, first of the Spanish, then, subsequently, of the Mexican government. In Gregg's words: "To such a pitch has the temerity of those savages reached, that small bands of three or four warriors have been known to make their appearance within a mile of the city of Chihuahua in open day, killing the laborers and driving off whole herds of mules and horses without the slightest opposition." By 1837 their raiding had become so daring and destructive that Mexican control over the entire province of New Mexico was threatened. The government reacted by putting a bounty on Apache scalps and dispatching government troops to try to exterminate the tribe. All such efforts merely made the Apache more vengeful and sanguinary, and it was not until after the Civil War, when the region was in American hands, that any serious check was put to their destructive raids. And that restraint was imposed only after a prolonged and bitter struggle.

The warlike Comanche augmented their ranks with young Mexicans captured in raids. "Strange as it may appear," Josiah Gregg wrote, "their captives frequently become attached to their masters and in the savage life, and with difficulty are induced to leave them after a few years' captivity. In fact these prisoners, it is said, in time often turn out to be the most formidable savages. Combining the subtlety of the Mexican with the barbarity of the Indian, they sometimes pilot into their native frontier and instigate horrid outrages." The Comanche, despite such periodic incursions, were on generally friendly terms with the New Mexicans. Famous horsemen in their own right, Josiah Gregg thought only the Mexican *vaqueros* and the Arabs could rival them. When they returned from a successful raid, the warriors and their chiefs would halt some distance from their village and send word ahead of their triumph. One of the "most respectable and aged matrons" of the tribe then came forward holding aloft a very long-handled lance to which the warriors fastened the scalps they had taken, "so arranged that each shall be conspicuous." The squaw then approached the wigwams "her scalp-garnish lance high in the air . . . chanting some favorite war-legend. She is soon joined by other squaws and Indian lasses, who dance around as the procession moves through the entire circuit of the village," to announce a celebration that might last for several days.

The Christianized Indians of New Mexico were known as Pueblos. Of the "wild tribes," the Navajo were the most numerous and the most "civilized." The Eutaws ranged as far north as the Yellowstone region. It was a Eutaw chief who had inspired Osborne Russell with such romantic reflections on Indian life.

Josiah Gregg estimated the number of Navajo in 1831 to be some 10,000. They were concentrated in the cordillera some hundred and fifty miles west of Santa Fe and they excelled in "original manufactures" in the making of silver jewelry and "a singular species of blanket, known as the *Sarape Navajo*, which is of so close and dense a texture that it will frequently hold water almost equal to gum-elastic cloth. It is therefore highly prized for protection against the rains." The Navajo cultivated all the grains and vegetable native to New Mexico and had large herds of sheep and goats to provide wool for their weaving; their horses and cattle were "celebrated as being much superior to those of the Mexicans; owing, no doubt, to greater attention to the improvement of their stocks."

When Josiah Gregg left Santa Fe for Independence sixteen days later, his party consisted of twenty-three Americans and twelve Mexicans with seven wagons and two small fieldpieces. "The principal proprietors," Gregg wrote, "carried between them about $150,000 in specie and bullion, being for the most part the proceeds of the previous year's adventure."

Josiah Gregg took his last trading trip to Santa Fe in 1840. The next year he traded for mules in Texas and then traveled to Philadelphia to work on his book. There the ills and aches of civilization overtook him. He suffered severe headaches and lost his hair. A brief visit to New York increased his miseries and he was forced to take a "little jaunt" on the prairies to strengthen "the tone" of his stomach. At the University of Louisville he studied medicine and received an honorary degree.

At the end of *Commerce of the Prairies* Gregg had written a kind of epitaph for himself: "I have striven in vain to reconcile myself to the even tenor of civilized life in the United States; and have sought in its amusements and its society a substitute for those high excitements which have attached me so strongly to Prairie life." Yet not a day passed that he did not feel "a pang of regret that I am not now roving at large upon those western plains." As soon as New Mexico was in American hands, Gregg returned to his beloved Santa Fe. He spent much of his time botanizing, collecting more than seven hundred specimens of the Southwestern flora. Finally, attracted by news from the California goldfields, he headed for San Francisco. There, commissioned to search out a route between the Trinity River and San Francisco, the "old gentleman"—he was forty-three—fell from his horse and suffered a fatal injury.

CHAPTER XIII

JEDEDIAH
SMITH

In the spring of 1823, when General Ashley started up the river from St. Louis, young Jedediah Strong Smith was a member of the party. Smith's father was a native of New Hampshire who had immigrated to the New York frontier after the Revolution. After the birth of the young Smith he had moved, successively to Erie, Pennsylvania, and then to Ashtabula, Ohio, producing a dozen children in the process. A doctor in Ashtabula had taken an interest in Jedediah and taught him the "rudiments of an English education and smattering of Latin." At the age of thirteen he got a job as a clerk on a Great Lakes freighter. In that rough and blasphemous world, Smith was distinguished for his industry, thrift, and, perhaps above all, his piety. At the age of twenty-three, with the poise and experience of a man many years older, he set out for St. Louis, not so much to make his fortune as to penetrate the heart of the continent. At St. Louis he signed on with Ashley for the Yellowstone expedition.

When Ashley and his men reached the Arikara villages that straddled the Missouri, they found the Arikara, or Ree, in a warlike mood, apparently intent on blocking the passage of the whites up the river. To add to Ashley's difficulties, the progress of the keelboats had become so slow as the river fell that the only practical way to continue the journey was by horseback. This meant buying horses from the hostile Rees. Word now reached Ashley from Fort Benton that Andrew Henry had been forced to abandon the Three Forks area and was in dire need of horses and further trading goods. The Ree towns contained 141 solid earth and log lodges, each of which held from five to ten Indians. The men on the keelboats could see that their appearance on the river had turned the villages into hives of activity. Ashley went ashore to parley with two Ree chieftains who were accompanied by a mixed-blood named Edward Rose, who had started life as a pirate in Louisiana, had lived with the Crows for years and was now a kind of subchief of the Rees.

A characteristically long and intricate exchange followed. Ashley had many men and guns; he also had many presents. He wished peace with the Rees and he wished to purchase horses from them to continue his trip. Everything seemed to go well. The horses were purchased, assembled along the riverbank, and hobbled preparatory to continuing the trip. That night there was a severe storm and, under the cover of it, the Rees launched an attack on Ashley's men, some of whom were guarding the horses on the shore with others asleep on the keelboats or along the shore. The Rees concentrated their fire on the horses, perhaps assuming that with the animals dead or scattered, the whites would be severely hampered in any attempt to escape. Jedediah Smith, one of the horse guards, tried to cut their hobbles and drive them into the river, but so many of the men on the riverbank were killed or wounded by the fire of the Indians that the effort failed. Thilless, a black man with bullet holes in both legs, loaded and fired from a sitting position, calling out in the dark, "They aint killed this niggah yet." The men on the keelboats, diminished as their numbers were, refused to go to the aid of their companions on the shore, some of whom wished to assault the Indian palisades. When Ashley sent skiffs ashore to pick up the wounded and the survivors, the men refused to enter the boats, declaring their determination to stay and fight it out; but when the keelboats began dropping down the river out of range, the men on shore swam after them and were taken aboard. Of the forty men in the party, eleven were either killed outright, drowned trying to regain the keelboats, or died of their wounds. The next day, when Ashley announced his determination to make another effort to pass the Ree towns, his men, to his "surprise and mortification," flatly refused. Ashley's next move was to try to contact Henry at Fort Benton more than two hundred miles away. He asked for volunteers to make the hazardous ride through Indian country to the mouth of the Yellowstone, but only Jedediah Smith came forward. A French-Canadian trapper named Baptiste was prevailed upon to accompany Smith. Two horses were captured and the men set off, traveling mostly at night and several times barely eluding capture by roving bands of Indians. Riding one night, their horses exhausted and pursuing Indians on their trail, they came on three Ree warriors asleep by a campfire with their horses tethered nearby. They killed the Indians while they slept and took their best horses; Smith was dismayed when Baptiste took their scalps as well. When Smith and his companion reached Henry, they brought him the unwelcome news that far from having horses and supplies for the men at the fort, Ashley himself was in dire straits.

Henry had no choice but to make out as best he could. He decided to spend the summer trapping. His party was augmented by a famous frontier character named Hugh Glass. A member of the party wrote, "Mr. Hugh Glass . . . could not be restrained and kept under Subordination he went off the line of march one afternoon and met with a large grissley Bear which he shot and wounded the bear as is usual attracted Glass he attempted to climb a tree but the bear caught him and hauled him to the ground tearing and lacerating his body in a fearful rate." Glass's companions killed the bear but Glass was so badly mauled that it seemed impossible that he could recover and Henry, anxious to not delay the party in Indian country, persuaded two of Glass's friends to stay with him until he died. A trapper named Fitzgerald and a young man named Jim Bridger remained behind to care for Glass. After five days, Glass, in a coma much of the time, still hung on, and his guardians, aware that the rest of the party was daily putting distance between them and anxious for their own safety, decided to leave the "old man" (Glass was in his forties) to his certain fate. They took his pack, rifle, and saddle and hurried after Henry. At the fort they reported that Glass had died. But Glass in fact was miraculously recovering. He got water from a nearby spring and found a few berries. For ten days he mended and then began to make his way to Fort Kiowa at the mouth of the White River nearly a hundred miles away. Much of the distance he crawled, too weak and severely wounded to walk. He reached Fort Kiowa, got food and essential supplies from the trader there, and then started for Fort Benton to settle his score with the men who had deserted him. He arrived at the fort on New Year's Eve when festivities were in full swing, looking very much like a ghost. Bridger he forgave because of his youth, and this was fortunate for Western lore, because Bridger was to become more famous than Glass. Fitzgerald had wisely moved downriver, allegedly to Fort Atkinson near Council Bluffs. Glass and four companions set out after that unhappy man. They were waylaid by the Rees, who killed Glass's friends and stripped him of everything but "my knife and steel in my shot pouch." At Fort Atkinson, Glass found Fitzgerald, who had enlisted in the army. Fitzgerald was forced to return the rifle he had taken and Glass was prevailed upon to spare his life. Retrieving the gun was more important to Glass than killing Fitzgerald, for his gun was as legendary a weapon as ever existed in the West. It had been responsible for the deaths of countless Indians and was as personal to Glass as a brother.

Glass had nine more exceedingly active years of life left to him. In the winter of 1833, he and two friends, Edward Rose, the ex-pirate, and a veteran trapper, Pierre Menard, were staying at Fort Cass in Crow country. Since the Crows were on peaceful terms with the trappers, Glass and his companions felt safe enough to venture down on the frozen Yellowstone to hunt beaver.

There they were ambushed by a party of Arikara "who shot scalped and plundered" the three trappers. Glass's phenomenal luck had at last run out, but he was already a legend, one of a dozen or so "mountain men" whose names are forever intertwined with the Rocky Mountain fur trade. The apotheosis would begin at once as innumerable "Western" writers and travelers repeated, often with embellishments, his heroic adventures. Soon it was said that Glass and his companions, surrounded by the Rees and despairing of their lives, had set fire to a powder keg and blown themselves to Kingdom Come—though what they were doing hunting beaver with a powder keg was not explained.

The relationship between the trappers and Indians is suggested by a story told by Jim Beckwourth, a mixed-blood trapper. When General William Ashley and his party were on their way from the Green River, hundreds of Crow warriors came down on his camp like a whirlwind, brandishing their weapons and hallooing. Not knowing whether they were friendly Crows or hostile Blackfeet, the whites prepared to defend themselves, but the general ordered his men to hold their fire until he fired. As the Indians swept to within pistol shot of the camp, Ashley pulled the trigger of his rifle but the gun misfired and the Indians dashed into the camp. They were Crows. Jim Beckwourth, who told the story, was convinced that if Ashley's rifle had fired, followed by those of his men, killing and wounding some of the Indians, the trappers would all have been wiped out on the spot.

Recognizing some of his stolen horses among the Crow ponies, Ashley said to their chief, Sparrow-Hawk, "I believe I see some of my horses among yours."

"Yes. We stole them from you."

"What did you steal my horses for?"

"I was tired with walking. I had been to fight the Blackfeet, and, coming back, would have called at your camp. You would have given me tobacco but that would not carry me. When we stole them they were very poor. They are now fat. We have plenty of horses; you can take all that belong to you."

The winter and spring of 1824 saw a significant change in the procedures followed by Ashley and Henry. They decided to abandon the tortuous spring trip up the Missouri and depend, instead, on pack trains of mules and horses loaded with trading goods. The caravans would rendezvous at predetermined spots with the trappers who had been collecting beaver pelts. Pelts would be exchanged for goods needed by the trappers and further trade would be carried on with friendly Indian tribes. The cost and danger of trying to maintain trading posts in Indian country would thus be avoided, as would the risk and uncertainty of navigating the Missouri by keelboat. A further refinement was that of taking a substantial portion of the furs down the Yellowstone and the Missouri to St. Louis in bullboats. One consequence of the new procedure was that the trappers operated much more on their own. The risks were, if possible, even greater, since they now were more widely dispersed. A party of fifteen or twenty trappers would travel together to a major river basin—the Wind, the Green, or the Gallatin—and then split up into parties of two or three to work the creeks and tributaries. Thus isolated, they were in constant danger from hostile Indians, especially the Arikara, Blackfeet, and Pawnee. When the fall trapping season was terminated by the freezing of the creeks and rivers, the trappers would gather together, build a fortified camp, and hole up for the winter. The breaking up of the ice in the spring marked the beginning of a new trapping cycle in anticipation of the rendezvous. Another consequence of abandoning the dependence on "forts" was that the trappers ranged far more widely than before, opening up large new areas beyond the Yellowstone.

In this development Jedediah Smith took the lead. From the time of the Arikara attack on Ashley's party, Smith displayed more and more conspicuously his quality of leadership.

Trapping on the Bighorn in the winter of 1823, Smith, like Glass before him, was badly mauled by a grizzly. While he recovered, two of his trapping companions, who had been nursing him, were surprised and killed by a band of marauding Indians. Smith, hiding in the underbrush, barely escaped detection. The Indians made off with everything in sight—the horses, traps, saddles and blankets, and even the pans and kettles used for cooking. All that was left was Smith's rifle, knife, flint, and a Bible he always carried with him. He opened it and read: "He is chastened also with pain upon his bed, and the multitude of his bones with strong pain. . . . Yes, his soul draweth near to the grave, and his life to the destroyers. His flesh shall be fresher than a child's; he shall return to the days of his youth. He shall pray unto God and He will be favorable unto him. . . ." The next morning, Smith, unable to walk and in severe pain, dragged himself from one beaver trap to another until he found a beaver, laboriously retrieved it, made a small fire, and cooked the flesh. The next two days he went without food, finding consolation in his Bible. The third day Smith shot a fat buck that came to drink at the creek, and until the meat turned bad, he was well fed. Again he was without food and without dressing for his wounds. Again he read, "Yea, though I walk through the valley of the shadow of death, I will fear no evil; for Thou art with me." Three days later when Smith was nearly dead, a party of trappers, led by friends of Smith's who had gone for help after his encounter with the bear, arrived.

A litter was improvised, Smith was fed and his wounds dressed, and the party headed down the Bighorn to the Yellowstone to join Henry's company. They were intercepted by Thomas Fitzpatrick, a partner of Henry's, who told Smith that a Crow Indian had given him directions to a trail along the Sweetwater River that would carry a traveler to a break in the Wind River Mountains, through which they could reach the Green. There, Fitzpatrick had been told, the land abounded with beaver.

At the mouth of the Bighorn, Henry's men had built winter quarters. The Crow Indians pitched their lodges nearby and the trappers settled in for a typical winter, trapping when the weather was warm and the ice had melted, finding other diversions when the creeks froze up. When the spring thaws came, Smith and Fitzpatrick got Henry's permission to work as "free trappers"—that is, to search for beaver on their own account, to be supplied by Henry and to pay him back with beaver pelts. Eighteen other trappers and camp keepers signed on with Smith and Fitzpatrick, and the party set out for the Wind River Valley. Some of the horses gave out on the difficult terrain leading from the Big Horn over "Bad Pass" into the Wind River area. It was thus decided that Smith would remain at the juncture of the Wind River and the Popo Agie, trapping in the region with a half-dozen men, while Fitzpatrick and the balance of the party pushed on to the pass that Fitzpatrick's Crow friend had told him led into the Green River Valley. After crossing through an arid region of red sandstone peaks and precipices, Fitzpatrick's men came to the Sweetwater, running along the base of the Wind River Mountains and then turning southwest.

At first the going was deceptively easy. Then, as they advanced, the snow grew deeper and the weather sharp and cold. Finally the valley of the Sweetwater debouched on a high rolling plain. There the weather was warmer and the snow melting. They soon found themselves at what came to be called the Little Sandy, a river that flowed into the Colorado, which, in turn, ran to the Gulf of California. They had traversed the South Pass, probably the first white men through the pass that was to become the gateway to Oregon and California for hundreds of thousands of overland emigrants.

The valley of the Green River was all that the Crow chief had promised, and Fitzpatrick and his men took advantage of the virgin beaver streams and ponds to collect a rich bounty of furs; but before they could start back, a party of Snake Indians stole all their horses, some twenty in number, leaving them without the means to bring their packs of beaver skins back to the winter rendezvous. With the horses gone, the most prudent course would have been to cache the furs and return to the Popo Agie, where they could get horses from Jedediah Smith's party and return to retrieve the fruits of their summer labors, but Fitzpatrick's men wanted the sport of following the Snake and recapturing their horses. They therefore cached their furs and set out in pursuit on foot—fourteen of them against many times that number of

Snake. For eight days they followed the trail left by the band of horses, traveling the last part of their journey at night and lying concealed during the daytime, the scouts out a mile or more ahead. Finally they came on the Snake village of some twenty lodges. More than a hundred horses were loosely corralled nearby. The trappers' strategy was for each to seize a horse at a given signal, leap on its back, and drive the rest of the herd through the village and back down the trail in the direction of their own camp on the Big Sandy. Changing horses frequently and stopping only briefly to rest and eat, they got back to their cache in three days. For the twenty horses that had been stolen they now had forty, and what was as important, they had had a splendid adventure to yarn about in winter camp.

When Fitzpatrick and his men rejoined Jedediah Smith and his party at the Popo Agie and told them of the fabulous beaver trapping in the Siskadee country, Smith and William Sublette, another "captain" working as a free trapper under the general aegis of Ashley, decided to have a try themselves. While Fitzpatrick took their combined beaver packs in bullboats down the Sweetwater to the Platte, and the spot designated for the fall rendezvous, Smith and Sublette went through the South Pass to try their luck on the tributaries of the Green.

Meanwhile, General Ashley had returned from St. Louis, determined to follow up Fitzpatrick's expedition through the South Pass. He recruited twenty-five men including Fitzpatrick himself, Jim Beckwourth, and Moses or "Black" Harris. Ashley made poor progress initially. It was bitterly cold and there was little grass to be found for his horses or game for his men. By the time they reached the village of the Loup Pawnee half their horses had died of starvation and exhaustion, and their thin, tough meat had been eaten by the party. The Pawnee sold them horses and a quantity of corn, dried meat, dried pumpkin, and beans.

Leaving the Pawnee village, Ashley and his men encountered a terrible blizzard in which a number of their newly acquired horses died. For three weeks the party remained in camp on the South

Platte while small detachments of trappers scouted for a passage through to the Green River Valley. At the end of February, Ashley and his men struck out through the snow and three days later penetrated the watershed of the North Platte. Now there was plenty of deer and buffalo and Ashley later wrote, "I was delighted with the many small streams issuing from the mountains, bordered by a thin growth of small willows and richly stocked with beaver." Trapping beaver as they went, Ashley and his men turned west from the river and crossed, on the twenty-sixth of March, the Continental Divide at a spot that was later named Bridger's Pass. The next night a band of Crow Indians stole seventeen of their horses and mules. Finally they reached the Big Sandy and started down the river, turning west for six days and coming at last to the Green after a journey of a hundred and sixty-six days in the dead of winter over country that no white men had traversed. It was one of the most remarkable journeys of that era of remarkable journeys, and it is worth remarking that while it could not have been accomplished without the assistance of the Pawnee, it was almost wrecked by the raid of the Crows. Ashley had covered a substantial part of present-day southern Wyoming on his peregrinations, penetrated into northern Colorado, and entered the Great Divide Basin. At the end of April he began a perilous journey down the Green in bullboats to a point some fifty miles south of its juncture with the Uinta.

Crossing the Uinta Mountains, Ashley and his party reached what was later named the Weber River. Along its banks they encountered some of the trappers who had set out with Smith and Sublette the previous summer to retrace Fitzpatrick's course through the South Pass into the valley of the Green. With the Smith–Sublette party were twenty-nine deserters from the Hudson's Bay Company who had been persuaded by Smith to bring their furs to the Wind River rendezvous.

By the first of July, 1825, a hundred and twenty trappers had gathered at Henry's Fork on the Green. There they were joined by the train from St. Louis carrying its cargo of supplies—"flour, sugar, coffee, blankets, tobacco, whisky, and all other articles necessary for that region," as Jim Beckwourth put it. The free trappers constituted a kind of mountain aristocracy. As Joseph Meek, himself a free trapper, tells it,

> They prided themselves on their hardihood and courage; even on their recklessness and profligacy. Each claimed to own the best horses; to have had the wildest adventures; to have killed the greatest numbers of bears and Indians; to be the favorite with the Indian belles, the greatest consumer of alcohol, and to have the most money to spend—that is, the largest credit on the books of the company. If his hearers did not believe him, he was ready to run a race with them, to beat them at "cold sledge," or to fight, if fighting were preferred—ready to prove what he affirmed in any way the company pleased.

It might be said parenthetically, that long after the heyday of the beaver trappers, enterprising journalists and ghostwriters wrote the "autobiographies" of many of the more famous mountain men, some of whom, like Beckwourth, were fond of drawing a long bow and became in fact professional storytellers. While there is no reason to doubt the practical details of daily life in their narratives, the rather formal and sometimes flowery language they are couched in is that of their amanuenses and not their own.

While Ashley and his men made their extraordinary circuit from Fort Atkinson to the Green River, Smith and Sublette had followed the Green to Horse Creek and from there to the Hoback River, which emptied into the Snake. Sublette made camp not far from the headwaters of the Yellowstone, while Smith went on some hundred miles down the Snake, trapping its tributaries. Thereafter he turned north with the hope of reaching Clark's Fork of the Columbia. He was now in the territory claimed by the Hudson's Bay Company and there he encountered a party of Iroquois who had been hired by the Company as trappers. They were starving and destitute and begged Smith to help them. They were operating out of Spokane House, a trading post on the river of that name, and they had a rich haul of furs from trapping in the Three Forks region at the headwaters of the Missouri and as far east as the Yellowstone. There the Snake Indians had made off with their guns, horses, and most of their furs. They still had nine hundred furs, worth some $5,000. Smith agreed to help them get back to their base of operations on the condition that they would give him their remaining furs. Smith then took advantage of the opportunity to scout out the lay of the land in the Hudson's Bay Company's backyard.

Smith and his men were at the Flathead Trading House on the upper waters of Clark's Fork of the Columbia for almost a month before they started back with a party of Hudson's Bay trappers under the leadership of Alexander Ross. Separating from Ross near the Snake, Smith came upon the Great Salt Lake on his way to the Green. In Cache Valley on the Bear River, Smith was reunited with Sublette, who had made his winter camp there. During the winter, Jim Bridger had undertaken to follow the Bear River to its mouth. When he reached the Great Salt Lake, he was convinced that he had discovered an inlet of the Pacific.

At the 1825 rendezvous Ashley's trappers and the free trappers contracted to him brought in a hundred and thirty packs of beaver furs to the value of nearly $200,000—enough for Ashley to retire from the fur business. He took a dozen of his trappers down the Missouri with him to St. Louis for a farewell spree. When Ashley retired he sold his business to Smith and Sublette. They thereby advanced to the status called bourgeois by the French and "booshways" by the Americans.

It was soon clear that Jedediah Smith was less interested in collecting large sums of beaver skins than in exploring a passage through the Rockies to California. He thus set out in August, 1826, from the Great Salt Lake with eighteen men and fifty horses, leaving Sublette to carry on with trapping in the Green River Valley. The two parties were to meet at Bear Lake the next summer. Among those accompanying Smith was James Read, a hotheaded blacksmith; Harrison Rogers, a pious young man, much like Smith in temperament, who kept a careful journal of the party's progress;

Peter Ranne, a free black; a mixed-blood Nipisang Indian, called, conveniently, Nipisang; Marion, an Umpqua Indian slave from the Pacific coast; Manuel, a "native Mexican"; two Kentuckians; two Scotchmen; John, a black slave; an Irishman; a German Jew named Emmanuel Lazarus; and three men from Indiana, Ohio, and New York, respectively.

As Smith wrote in the introduction to his journal,

> In taking the charge of our western Expedition, I followed the bent of my strong inclination to visit this unexplored country and unfold those hidden resources of wealth and bring to light those wonders which I readily imagined a country so extensive might contain. I must confess that I had at that time a full share of that ambition (and perhaps foolish ambition) which is common in a greater or less degree to all the active world. I wanted to be the first to view a country on which the eyes of a white man had never gazed and to follow the course of rivers that run through a new land.

Smith followed the Portneuf River from the southeastern end of the Great Salt Lake to Utah Lake, stopping to lay in a supply of dried buffalo meat. Near Utah Lake, Smith encountered the Ute Indians and negotiated a "treaty" with them "by which Americans are allowed to hunt & trap in and pass through their country unmolested." Smith found the Ute "cleanly quiet and active." They were, in his view, "nearer . . . to civilized life than any Indians I have seen in the Interior." The Ute had captured two young Snake girls who, after having been forced to act as servants for Ute masters, were turned over to the women of the tribe to be tortured to death. Smith bought them from the Ute and they accompanied his party for a time, apparently as the companions of Manuel, the Mexican. When he deserted the expedition a week or so later, they went with him, as did the mixed-blood Nipisang.

Smith crossed over the Wasatch Range to the Price River, then turned west to the Sevier River (which he named the Ashley), following it south, crossing the Escalante desert, and picking up the Virgin River in what is now southwest Utah. Along the way he encountered the Paiute, a degenerated branch of the northern Ute who lived primarily on roots and a kind of cake made out of grasshoppers and berries. The shy Paiute spread a warning of the white men's coming by setting small fires of grass and brush, so that Smith and his party got only occasional glimpses of them. They had no horses, were commonly naked, and were remarkably enduring and fleet of foot. Some days later, when the men had exhausted their supply of dried buffalo meat and found no game to appease their hunger, they met a tribe of Southern Paiute who traded with them for a very welcome supply of corn and pumpkins. Several times subsequently, when the party had run out of food, they encountered Indians (apparently Mohaves) who replenished their food supplies with squash and pumpkins. Here the Indians had horses and showed signs of a more advanced civilization. Smith's horses were now breaking down from the hard travel and poor grazing. For a time two Mohave Indians acted as guides, but they abandoned Smith and his men as they pushed down the Colorado.

The going was arduous in the extreme, the party often moving along narrow ledges far above the river where one misstep meant disaster. Finally Smith and his men came out in Cottonwood Valley, where there was grass for the horses. There Smith killed a mountain sheep. There also he encountered the first large settlement of Mohave Indians, who had obviously had contacts with the Spanish. The Indians greeted Smith hospitably. "Melons and roasted pumpkins," he wrote, "were presented in great abundance." The Mohaves were tall and well-built with light complexions. The men were commonly naked or wore a "Spanish blanket" thrown over their left shoulder. They wore "no head dress moccasins or leggings. The dress of the women," Smith noted, "is a petticoat made of material like flax. . . . The men appear to work as much in the fields as the women which is quite an unusual sight among the Indians." They collected locust pods and raised wheat, squash, corn, beans, and melons. The Mohaves told Smith that he was some ten days travel from the Spanish settlements in California. Smith, who had not informed his men that he had any intention of pushing on to California and later insisted to suspicious Spanish officials that such a notion had been far from his mind, now told his men they must go farther west on the not unreasonable grounds that the region that they had passed through was too barren to hazard a return trip.

After a day's travel without sighting water, Smith began to suspect that the Indians had deliberately given him instructions intended to draw him into a desert region where he and his men must perish from lack of food and water, the Indians thereby falling heir to all their belongings. His suspicion was strengthened when, retracing his steps, he found that Indians were following him. But peace was made and Smith prevailed on two Indians, who had escaped from the Mission at San Gabriel, to accompany him as guides across the Mojave Desert.

The passage across the desert was from one small brackish stream or spring to another until the party hit the mouth of the Mojave River a few miles beyond Soda Springs. The next day they encountered Vanyume Indians, poor cousins of the Serranos who shared with the travelers small cakes of acorns and pine nuts and rabbits they caught in a long net. Two days later they saw signs of cattle and horses, which, Smith wrote, "awakened many emotions in my mind and some of them not the most pleasant. . . . I was approaching a country inhabited by the Spaniards, a people of different religion from mine and possessing a full share of bigotry and disregard of the right of a Protestant that has at times stained the Catholic Religion. . . . They might perhaps consider me a spy imprison me persecute me for the sake of religion or detain me in prison to the ruin of my business."

Soon they were through the San Bernardino Mountains into the valley of the San Gabriel, dominated by the great mission there. The Indians working in the fields gazed at the strange, ragged band with astonishment. At a farm or hacienda, an elderly Indian greeted them in Spanish and asked the famished men if they would like to have a bullock killed. After a fine feast, Smith wrote a letter to the head of the Mission San Gabriel, Father José Bernardo Sánchez—a Franciscan—which was at once carried off to that dignitary, who replied in Latin. The father wished Smith to visit him and the trapper set off with his interpreter, arriving at "a Building of ancient and Castle-like appearance. . . . I was left quite embarrassed," Smith wrote, "hardly knowing how to introduce myself." The father took Smith by the hand and "quite familiarly asked me to walk in. . . . Soon bread and cheese were brought in and some rum. . . ." which the teetotaler Smith drank to be polite.

Their efforts to understand each other coming to naught, despite the interpreter, Father Sánchez sent for a young American, Joseph Chapman, who had been the first citizen of the United States to settle in Los Angeles. (He had been sent there as a prisoner after participating in a raid on Monterey.) Chapman was another "American original." He claimed to have been shanghaied in the Sandwich Islands, or Hawaiian Islands as they were later called. He had made himself indispensable to the friars of the Mission of Los Angeles by his array of practical skills. He could construct a grist mill or a sailing ship, splint broken bones, pull teeth, fashion improved farm implements, and do a hundred other ingenious things.

While they waited for the arrival of Chapman, Smith was seated beside the father at dinner. "As soon as we were seated," Smith wrote, "the Father said Benediction and each one in the most hurried manner asked the blessing of heaven—and even while the last words were pronouncing the fathers were reaching for the different dishes." Smith described the meal in some detail, the good food, the wine and the cigars, adding, "I may be excused for being this particular in this table scene when it is recollected that it was a long time since I had had the pleasure of sitting at a table and never before in such company."

When Joseph Chapman finally appeared with a translator of his own, Smith learned that he and his men were, in effect, under detention until instructions were received from the governor of California at San Diego, which, it was predicted, might be a long time coming since that gentleman was notoriously indecisive.

While Smith waited for word from the governor, he and Harrison Rogers took note of mission life. The number of Indians attached to each mission varied from four hundred to two thousand and made up "with their dependencies" roughly three-fourths of the population of the province. The Mission San Gabriel, where Smith and his party landed, had some two thousand acres under cultivation in wheat, beans, peas, and corn, along with orchards of apples, peaches, pears, olives, "and a beautiful grove of 400 Orange trees." Within the walls of the mission compound, besides the quarters of the friars, there were apartments for visitors and a guardhouse for the soldiers who were assigned to protect the mission and keep order among the Indians. There were, in addition, store houses, a granary, a "soap factory," distillery, blacksmith, carpenters' and coopers' shops, and rooms given over to weavers. Rogers saw in a side room of the church "molten Images, they have our Saviour on the cross, his mother and Mary the Mother of James, and 4 of the apostles, all as large as life." He was presumably comforted to discover that the room was being used as a "sugar Factory."

The friars' meals were preceded by a glass of gin and some bread and cheese and Smith noted that "wine in abundance made our reverend fathers appear to me quite merry." Smith's two Indian guides were arrested and put in the mission's prison, to be punished as runaways, Smith noted regretfully, adding, "I thought them fine honest and well disposed boys."

The mission was a strange mixture of the authoritarian and benign. Most of the Indians had been forced to attach themselves to a mission and they were, for all practical purposes, confined to it and punished by flogging when they stole or fought or shirked their work or tried to run away. Rogers described the Indians as "compleat slaves in every sense of the word." He saw five "old men, say from fifty to sixty," whipped for not going to work when ordered, and a priest asked Jim Reed, the party's blacksmith, to "make a large trap for him to set in his orange garden to catch the Indians when they come up at night to rob his orchard." Rogers also noted that the soldiers at the mission "appear at times some what alarmed for fear the Inds—will rise and destroy the mission." Rogers also noted that while "friendship and peace prevail with us and the spanyards—our own men are continuous and quarrelsome amongst ourselves and have been since we started the Expedition." Rogers thought the Indian women "very unchaste." One came to his room, he wrote, "asked me to make her a Blanco Pickaninia, which being interpreted, is to get her a white child—and I must say for the first time I was ashamed, and did not gratify her."

Rogers noted that the mission "ships to Europe annually from 20 to 25 thousand dollars worth of skins and Tallow and about 20 thousand dollars worth of soap." "The Missions," Jedediah Smith wrote, "setting aside their religious professions are in fact large farming and grazing establishments and conducted at the will of the father who is in a certain degree responsible to the President of his order." It was certainly an exploitative system, yet its harshness was softened by the kindness of many of the friars and the work required of the Indians did not appear to Smith "unreasonably hard." After Mexican independence, the Indians had, of course, been formally emancipated but in most of the missions the fathers had used their authority and their powers of persuasion to prevail upon their charges to remain at their labors. Many of them had, indeed, no place to go to and faced starvation if they left the missions.

Harrison Rogers, who had told Father Sánchez quite candidly that he was a Calvinist who "did not believe that it was in the power of man to forgive sins. God only had that power," had not suffered in the esteem of the urbane and tolerant padre. In January, 1827, in the absence of Jedediah Smith, who had gone to San Diego, Father Sánchez invited Rogers to deliver "a New Years Address" and Rogers cheerfully obliged, reviewing the life and teaching of Christ. "Reverend Father, remember," Rogers admonished him, "the whole world was missionary ground. Before the day of Christ Jesus our Saviour we never heard of missionaries to the Heathen," with the exception of Jonah. Paul aside, the missionaries of the early church, he reminded the father, "were not learned in the arts and sciences; were ignorant of books and of men; yet they went forth unsupported by human aid—friendless—opposed by prejudices, laws, learning, reasonings of Philosophy, passions and persecutions. . . . On the whole," he concluded, "we have no reason to doubt, on the Testimony, of history and tradition, that the last command of Christ was so obeyed, that in the Apostolic age, the Gospel was preached in every part of the Globe which was then known." How much of this remarkable discourse survived translation we cannot guess, but Father Sánchez, who had become much attached to this young American fur hunter, could hardly have failed to be astonished. Appearing with his companions out of the wilderness, looking as wild as an Indian, he seemed entirely at home in a thoroughly alien society and had delivered a sermon as learned and literate as any priest or preacher.

Early in December, Smith had been summoned to San Diego to be interrogated by Governor José María de Echeandía. On the way to San Diego he was the guest of a large landowner, Don Yorba, who was described by another visitor a few years later as "a tall, lean personage, dressed in all the extravagance of his country's costume. . . . Upon his head he wore a black silk handkerchief, the four corners of which hung down his neck behind. An embroidered shirt, a cravat of white jaconet tastefully tied, a blue damask vest, short clothes of crimson velvet, a bright green cloth jacket with large silver buttons, and shoes of embroidered deerskin."

San Diego was a thoroughly unimpressive presidio, perhaps testifying to the qualities of the governor. Everything was rundown and in disrepair. For days the governor, obviously much embarrassed by his unwanted guest, vacillated. The governor must wait until he had received orders from Mexico; then Smith himself must go to the capital. Finally, after more than two weeks of waffling, Governor Echeandía at last proposed a solution. If the captains of the various American ships in the San Diego harbor would sign a paper saying they believed Smith's presence in California to be due to the circumstances he claimed he would be allowed to trade for necessary provisions and depart. But he must go the way he had come, a very severe constraint for Smith, who, the difficulties of the route aside, was determined to find a more convenient way back to the meeting with Sublette at Bear Lake.

Rogers parted from his friend Father Sánchez (he writes his name Sancus, Sannes, and Sanchius in his journal) most reluctantly. "Old Father Sanchius has been the greatest friend that I ever meet with, with all my Travels," he noted in his journal, "he is worthy of being called a Christian as he possesses charity in the highest degree—and a friend to the poor and distressed, I shall ever hold him as a man of God . . . and may god prosper him and all such men. . . ."

The governor's requirement met, the party started back to Bear Lake. Two more men now deserted, although it was far from clear that the Mexican authorities would permit them to remain behind. Smith headed dutifully for the Mojave Desert as though to retrace his steps, but once out of the range of Mexican officialdom, he turned north along the Tehachapis to Kern Lake at the southern end of the present San Joaquin Valley. At Tulare Lake the party encountered a band of Yokut Indians who lived on an island in the lake and used rafts made of the tule that grew along the riverbanks bound together by grass thongs.

There Smith discharged one of his men, John Wilson, for "seditious disposition" and then continued his northward journey, passing a large Indian village of the Wukchumni Indians on Cottonwood Creek and trapping for beaver as he went. The Wimilchi Indians were camped in a beautiful oak grove on the banks of the Peticutry, later the San Joaquin.

The San Joaquin River flowed up the valley that bears the same name and emptied into the San Francisco Bay; into it flowed the Merced, the Tuolumne, and the Stanislaus. Smith and his party made their way up the course of the San Joaquin, trapping beaver and shooting elk and antelope for food. Wild horses were everywhere in great abundance, as well as geese, brant, heron, cormorant, and many species of duck. Smith saw a California condor, one of the most majestic birds in the world. There were scattered bands of Indians—the remnants, Smith was told by an Indian guide, of those tribes that had been absorbed by the missions.

Smith was now in the region of the Penutian-speaking Indians of central California, estimated at some two to three hundred tribes or bands, whose main divisions were the Miwok, Costanoan, Yokuts, Maidu, and Wintun. Their food staple was the acorn from the great oaks that lined the foothills of the Sierras. The acorns were gathered and stored in bins until they dried, then they were pounded into a fine yellow meal that was placed in a sandy pit; water was poured over it to remove the poisonous tannic acid. When the meal was sufficiently leached out by this process, it was allowed to dry and bread was made from it. The Indians also hunted deer, rabbits, and squirrels and were provident in putting by food for the winter months. Their weapons were simple and since the weather was mild they seldom wore any kind of garment. They had developed their arts to a relatively modest extent, and, as contrasted with the dramatic and "noble" Indians of the eastern forests and Great Plains, they were mild and nonmilitant. Their culture had taken form around gathering rather than fighting. Thus, they seem to present a classic example of Arnold Toynbee's concept of "challenge and response." In a salubrious climate, with a plentiful supply of food and protected by the Sierra Nevada from their more warlike eastern neighbors, they lived a happy existence, never really challenged to develop and extend their primitive cultures. They had, in consequence, been integrated into the missions with relative ease by threats and blandishments. Their experiences with the Spanish had made those who remained free of the missions understandably wary of white men, as Jedediah Smith's experiences were to prove, and increasingly militant, stealing horses and cattle from the missions and ranchos and killing stray whites when the opportunity presented itself.

Smith began to turn his thoughts toward the spring meeting with Sublette and Jackson near Bear Lake. He had some two hundred beaver skins that he had collected on the way and his men were anxious to get back to what for them passed for home—Bear Lake and then Fort Atkinson for the fall rendezvous. The Sierra Nevada presented an apparently impassable barrier. Smith nevertheless turned eastward, searching for a pass. Following the foothills of the Sierra, he crossed the Mokelumne River and encountered an Indian village of several hundred mud lodges of the Mokelumne Indians, a branch of the Northern Miwok. There Smith found a Spanish-speaking Indian, a refugee from one of the missions. After a good deal of wandering about in the course of which his Indian guide absconded with two of his horses and he lost twelve traps in the Mokelumne, Smith found himself still stymied. Now the Indians were more numerous and bolder, and Smith and his men had several narrow escapes. On the American River, Smith pursued an Indian girl, intending to give her presents and through her to reassure the elusive Maidu Indians, but the girl died of fright and Indians soon pressed dangerously close on the party. Smith tried to convince them of his friendly disposition but to no effect. As the Indians continued to menace them, Smith ordered two of his best shots to fire at two of the most distant Indians. At the report of the rifles the two Indians fell. "For a moment," Smith wrote, "the Indians stood still and silent as if a thunder bolt had fallen among them then a few words passed from party to party and in a moment they ran like Deer." The experiment was repeated once more and the Maidu thereafter kept their distance.

Going in advance of his men to try to discover some passage through the mountains, Smith was moved to reflect on the vanity of human pretensions. "I thought of home," he wrote, "and all its neglected enjoyments of the cheerful fireside of my father's house of the Plenteous harvest of my native land and . . . the green and wide spread Prairies of joyous bustle and of busy life thronged in my mind to make me feel more strongly the utter desolateness of my situation. And it is possible thought I that we are creatures of choice and that we follow fortune through such paths as these. Home with contented industry could give us all that is attainable and fortune could do no more."

Blocked by the formidable range of snowcapped mountains before him, Smith decided to turn back and try the Stanislaus River once more. He planned to leave most of his men in a secure camp on the river and then try to find a way through the mountains with two of his hardiest and most reliable trappers. He would send back for the rest of the party once he had reached Bear Lake and made contact with his partners. Crossing the swift Cosumnes River, the horse carrying the party's ammunition was swept down the river. "This was a terrible blow," Smith wrote, "for if our ammunition was lost with it went our means of subsistence and we were at once deprived of what enabled us to travel among hostile bands feared and respected. But my thoughts I kept to myself knowing that a few words from me would discourage my men." The drowned horse and his load were fortunately recovered and the men continued to the Stanislaus. There friendly relations were established with a local village of Mokelumne Indians through the generous distributions of gifts to the old chief, Time; meat was dried, horses shod, and grass collected for fodder. Harrison Rogers was left in charge of the camp on the Stanislaus. If he received no word from Smith by September 20, he was instructed to go to the Russian post on Bodega Bay, buy what supplies he needed, and try for Bear Lake himself. Alternately he and his companions might sign on for the Hawaiian Islands and then try to get a ship back to the United States from there.

On May 20, Smith, accompanied by Silas Gobel and Robert Evans, left behind a rather glum little party that hardly knew whether they were better off to stay or go, and headed up the river with six horses and two mules, sixty pounds of dried meat and a quantity of hay. For almost a hundred miles the three men made their way toward the summit of the Sierras before they were overtaken by a violent sleet storm that lasted two days and in the course of which they had to watch two of their horses and one mule freeze to death before their eyes. "It seemed," Smith wrote, "that we were marked out for destruction and that the sun of another day might never rise to us. But He that rules the Storms willed it otherwise. . . ."

The next day, the men passed through what came to be known as Ebbetts Pass and began the rapid descent of the east side of the Sierra Nevada. They had another nerve-wracking encounter with a party of Southern Paiute who surrounded their camp one evening with their bows and arrows in their hands and then carried on, in "loud and harsh" voices what was clearly a debate about whether to kill the white men. "After about two hours," Smith wrote, "they became peaceable and made a fire. I then offered them some tobacco they took it and smoked and remained all night. . . . I do not know how to account for the singular conduct of the Indians. They did not appear unanimous for the massacre and perhaps saw our intention of making our scalps bear a good price."

The last leg of the journey to what Smith called the "Depo" was an endurance contest. Every few days another horse gave out and what little flesh was left on its bones was eaten by the travelers. Their progress was from creek to water hole in the burning sun across the present-day state of Nevada. Smith described the land as "extremely Barren" and a "desolate waste." The men were reduced to four ounces of dried meat a day. A rare rain gave them an opportunity to collect enough precious water to water the horses and fill their own canteens. Smith killed a hare and saw an antelope and a black-tailed deer, "solitary and wild as the wind."

Through the Grant Range and the Horse Range, through dry valleys and cruel mountains, finally to the tributaries of the White River they made their slow and painful way. For twelve days they were without fresh meat. On June 16 they ate their last portion of food. The hooves of the remaining horses were worn almost to the quick. They killed the most depleted horse and ate him, and the next day they covered thirty miles without water. The following day, when Evans had collapsed of thirst and been left behind, Smith and Gobel fell in with a party of fourteen Paiute. The Indians helped them find a small spring and bring water back to Evans, who revived enough to join his companions. The Paiute then gave the white men two small ground squirrels, which they eagerly consumed, and showed them a water plant that the Indians ate and which the famished white men "found . . . pleasant."

The next day some wild onions helped to make the remaining horse meat go down and again they met Indians who, once their fears had been assuaged, were endlessly curious. "All the Indians I had seen since leaving the Lake [Bear Lake]," Smith wrote, "have been the same unintelligent kind of beings, nearly naked having at most a scanty robe formed from the skin of the hare peculiar to this plain which is cut into narrow strips and interwoven with a kind of twine. . . . They form a connecting link between the animal and intellectual creation and quite in keeping with the country in which they are located." If the California tribes could be taken to represent human beings insufficiently challenged to develop greater creative resources, the Indians of the desert country were clearly examples of human social groups living in an environment so demanding that the mere problem of existence allowed no margin for the development of higher culture.

At the Salt Marsh Lake near present Gandy, Utah, Smith and his companions encountered the Goshute Indians, perhaps the least prepossessing of all the tribes belonging to the general family of Shoshonean Indians since they inhabited a region most uncongenial to human life. As described by a later traveler, "They wear no clothing of any description—build no shelter. They eat roots, lizards and snails . . . and when the lizard and snail and wild roots are buried in the snows of winter, they . . . dig holes . . . and sleep and fast until the weather permits them to go abroad again for food. . . . These poor creatures are hunted in the spring of the year when weak and helpless . . . and when taken, are fattened, carried to Santa Fe and sold as slaves."

By June 24, Smith and his men were without food or water and their few remaining horses were so weak and lame that they could hardly walk. The men had to dismount and assist their exhausted animals. The soft sand underfoot made walking difficult in the extreme. "Worn down with fatigue and burning with thirst," they dug holes in the sand and "lay down in them for the purpose of cooling our heated bodies." Rising, they plodded on until ten o'clock at night hoping to find water, and then, lying down to sleep, dreamed "of things we had not and for want of which it then seemed . . . probable we might perish in the desert unheard of and unpitied. In such moments," Smith added, "how trifling were all those things that hold such a sway over the busy and prosperous world." After a few hours of fitful sleep the three men started on to take advantage of the cool of the night, conscious that they were very near the end of their resources and would soon die of thirst and exhaustion if they did not find water. By ten the next morning, Evans could go no farther. Smith and Gobel made him as comfortable as possible and hurried on to try to find water to save their companion's life. In three miles they came, to their "inexpressible joy," to a spring at the foot of Little Granite Mountain. Gobel "plunged into it at once" and Smith poured it over his head and then drank it down in great gulps. Smith then took a small kettle of water and some meat and returned to the prostrate Evans, who was "indeed far gone being scarcely able to speak." When Smith had revived him Evans drank four quarts of water and asked for more. "I have at different times," Smith wrote, "suffered all the extremes of hunger and thirst. Hard as it is to bear for successive days the gnawings of hunger it is light in comparison to the agony of burning thirst . . . . Hunger can be endured almost twice as long as thirst."

For several days the men rested and tried to regain sufficient strength to continue: They were now near the Great Salt Lake and had reached a lone lodge of Goshute Indians who "cheerfully divided with us some antelope meat." For many years the Goshute told the story that the first white men they had ever seen were tattered, starving men who appeared out of the Salt Desert.

On June 27, Smith, with his telescope, got the first glimpse of the Great Salt Lake. "Is it possible," he asked, "that we are so near the end of our troubles. For myself I hardly durst believe that it was really the Big Salt Lake that I saw." They were almost "home." The next night they ate the last of their horse meat. They now had a horse and a mule left, the mule carrying the pack of beaver skins and the horse the rest of the party's equipment. The three men "talked a little of the probability of our suffering being soon at an end. I say we talked a little," Smith wrote, "for men suffering from hunger never talk much but rather bear their sorrows in moody silence which is much preferable to fruitless complaint."

The next day Smith shot a fine buck and, he noted, "[W]e employed ourselves most pleasantly for about two hours and for the time being forgot that we were not the happiest people in the world. . . . So much do we make our estimation of happiness by a contrast with our situation that we were as much pleased and as well satisfied with our fat venison on the bank of the Salt Lake as we would have been in possession of all the Luxuries and enjoyments of civilized life in other circumstances."

From a village of friendly Snake Indians, Smith learned that his partners and their trappers were only some twenty-five miles away, and two days later Smith and his companions arrived at the rendezvous point where they had been given up for lost.

Smith's remarkable journey, arduous as it was, like the Lewis and Clark Expedition, could not have been carried through without the assistance of numerous tribes of Indians encountered along the way. It was thus, like so many other white ventures in the West—of the trappers, hunters, explorers, traders—a kind of cooperative venture, albeit unwittingly. Certainly, the lives of Smith and his companions were often in danger from hostile or suspicious Indians, but without the Indian guides, the food so often provided from the Indians' own meager supplies, and the information about the terrain, unreliable as it sometimes was, Smith and his men could never have reached California or, once there, gotten back to the "Depo" at Bear Lake.

Smith had little time to enjoy the pleasures of "home." Rogers and the men left on the Stanislaus were much on his mind. He was afraid they might try to follow in his footsteps and he knew they would perish in the attempt. Summer was getting on, and September 20 was the deadline he had given Rogers. He had only eight weeks to assemble a party and set out for California once more. Evans, understandably, had had enough, but Silas Gobel was ready to dare the now-familiar hazards of the journey once more. Smith enlisted eighteen trappers, accompanied by two Indian women, and set out to retrace his steps down the Sevier to the Virgin River, thence to the Colorado and west across the Mojave Desert. With the experience gained in the first expedition, the party made good time and suffered relatively little hardship until they reached the Mojave Indians. Smith had spent fifteen days with them in amity on his original trip and he looked forward to replenishing his party's larder at the Mojave village. But in the intervening months Governor Echeandía had sent out orders to the free Indians to intercept any Americans who might pass through their territory. This time Smith traded with the Mojaves for three days in apparent friendliness and then, as he and his men were crossing the Colorado the Indians surprised them and massacred the ten men of the party who had not crossed the river. Smith and the rest had to watch in horror as their companions, Silas Gobel among them, were killed and scalped. The eight survivors made a dash for the haven of the San Gabriel mission. This time Smith, knowing that any delay would make it impossible to catch Rogers's group on the Stanislaus, simply wrote a report to Governor Echeandía and started north up the San Joaquin Valley. He found the men he had left there hungry and demoralized. Competent as Rogers was, he was not a natural leader and the men had suffered in health and, more important, in morale. Smith's party was little better off and he decided to appeal once more for help from a mission, this time the Mission of San Jose, a three-day journey. Governor Echeandía had by now established himself at Monterey, a far more congenial spot than San Diego. He must have thought he was having a recurring nightmare when the presumptuous American who had caused him so much vexation the year before made his unwelcome reappearance. It was now evident that Smith had failed to obey the governor's order to return the way he had come—back through the Mojave Desert—but had, instead, gone north, spreading, in the governor's view, trouble and unrest among the non-mission Indians. Once again Echeandía vacillated until four American ships' captains whose vessels were tied up in the Monterey harbor came to his rescue, persuading the governor to accept a bond of $30,000 to guarantee that Smith and his men would leave California as soon as they were adequately supplied. The men in Smith's party had been sent to the village of

San Francisco to await the outcome of their leader's negotiations with Echeandía. Smith, having posted his bond and bought horses, guns and ammunition at Monterey, joined them there. From San Francisco, Smith and his men worked their way north along the Sacramento River, searching its tributaries for beaver. Smith also probed the lower reaches of the Sierras looking for a pass north of the one he had taken the previous winter. As the months passed, he decided to push north to the Columbia River and return to the region of the Green along the well-established route used each fall by the Hudson's Bay Company trappers. From the Sacramento to the coast proved an unexpectedly difficult and hazardous passage. One horse fell to its death and several others were injured. Harrison Rogers records the obstacles that the party had to surmount. Rogers and Thomas Virgin, who had recovered from serious wounds suffered in the Mohave attack months earlier, set out to reconnoiter a way to the ocean, but Indians ambushed them and shot a number of arrows at Virgin before he killed one and drove the rest off. Rogers, who had endured so much and been such a faithful scribe, felt his spirits sink under the conviction that Smith had led them into a hopeless impasse where they would fall victims to hostile Indians. "Oh, God, may it please Thee," he wrote in his journal, "in Thy divine providence to still guide and protect us through this wilderness of doubt and fear, as Thou has done heretofore, and be with us in the hour of danger and difficulty. . . ." For two weeks the weary and demoralized men tried to find a trail to the ocean. Finally, defeated, they had to turn south "entirely out of provisions with the exception of a few pounds of flour and rice."

On June 8 they finally reached the mouth of the Klamath River and made their camp on the beach. From the river north they rode along the beaches, making rafts to cross the intersecting rivers. There were berries and clams and occasional fish bought from generally sullen and unfriendly Indians. Now they were in the region of the Klamath and Modoc tribes of lower Oregon. At the Umpqua River they encountered the Indians from which the river took its name.

The Umpqua were members of the great and extensive Athapaskan family whose tribes were to be found in western Canada, Alaska, and the Pacific Northwest. They belonged to the subfamily of Chastacosta and lived by fishing and gathering wild fruits and berries. More advanced in some ways than the California tribes, they were a far cry in their manner and appearance from the Crows, Sioux, Snake, and Blackfeet of the Great Plains and Great Basin regions. Perhaps their inferiority misled Smith in his dealings with them. Some of the Umpqua joined Smith's party to trade and one stole an ax. To force him to return it, Smith tied him up hand and foot, put a rope around his neck, and threatened to hang him. The other Indians watched the episode in silence. The ax was recovered and trading for otter and beaver skins resumed. Next day the Umpqua brought wild raspberries and blackberries and the trading resumed. The Indians gave the explorers the welcome information that the famous Multnomah (Willamette) River was not many miles distant.

Cheered by this word, Smith and another man pushed ahead of the rest of his party next morning, looking for the easiest passage north. Smith left orders that, despite the apparent friendliness of the Indians, none should be allowed in the camp during his absence. The orders were disregarded. The Indians crowded in and at a signal from their chief, who was the Indian that Smith had chastised for stealing the ax, they turned on the trappers and killed fifteen of them before they could reach their guns. Turner, the cook, seized a burning log from the fire, scattered his attackers, and ran in the direction that Smith had taken earlier. Another white man named Black, who had his gun in his hand, fired it at a group of Indians and then fled in the confusion that his shot created. Turner met Smith and his companion on his way back to camp and the three men set out to try to reach the Hudson's Bay Company post on the Willamette. While they struggled on to reach Fort Vancouver, Black followed the shoreline until he could go no farther and then, "broken down by hunger and misery," threw himself on the mercy of the Killimour Indians, who "treated him with great humanity," and brought him to the fort at Vancouver. John McLoughlin, the factor at the fort, who had declared so confidently that there was as much chance of Americans reaching Oregon territory by a northwest route as there was of their going to the moon, was, in his own words, "One night in August, 1828 . . . surprised by the Indians making a great noise at the gate of the fort saying that they had brought an American. The gate was opened, the man [Black] came in, but was so affected he could not speak. After sitting down some minutes to recover himself, he told us he was the only survivor of eighteen men conducted by Jedediah Smith. All the rest, he thought, had been massacred."

McLoughlin, having heard from an Indian that other whites had escaped, immediately dispatched "Indian runners with tobacco to Willamette chiefs to tell them to send their people in search of Smith and his two men, and, if they found them, to bring them to the fort and I would pay them, and telling them that if any Indians hurt these men we would punish them. . . ." Before a search party of forty men could depart, Smith and his two men reached the fort. McLoughlin then sent a party of men from the fort to try to recover all they could of Smith's property from the Umpqua. "The plan was," McLoughlin wrote, "that the officer [in charge of the party] was, as usual, to invite the Indians to bring their furs to trade, just as if nothing had happened. Count the furs, but as the American trappers mark all their skins, keep those all separate, give them to Mr. Smith and not pay the Indians for them, telling them that they belonged to him, that they got them by murdering Smith's people."

Everything went as planned. The furs were recovered, along with several of Smith's horses and some personal belongings, among them Harrison Rogers's journal. McLoughlin paid Smith $20,000 for the furs in the form of a draft on a London bank and Smith procured horses, supplies, and ammunition from McLoughlin.

Since the fur company of Smith and Sublette was a serious rival of the Hudson's Bay Company and, indeed, had prevailed on a number of their trappers to desert to their company, McLoughlin's kindness is a great tribute to him. A friend described the Vancouver factor as "over six feet in height, powerfully made, with a grand head on massive shoulders, and long snow-white locks covering them . . . a splendid figure of a man." The Indians of the region called him White Eagle and he exercised a remarkable influence over them. "He was a convert to Catholicism, and in no sense was he a bigot or lacking in Christian charity. . . . His policy to effect peace with the Indians was potent for good. . . . With his grand manner and majestic port, he was the embodiment of power and justice. . . . He was indeed, as he was styled, 'the Czar of the West.' His rule was imperial for a thousand miles, and his mere word was law." McLoughlin believed in living well in the wilderness. His house had something of the air of a Scottish castle with handsome paintings, a large library, fine wines, silver, and china, a band of bagpipers, and two Sandwich Islanders as servants. There was more than a little irony in the fact that devout Protestant Jedediah Smith's two principal benefactors at the southern and northern ends of the Pacific coast should have been Roman Catholics.

Smith and his three companions spent the winter at Fort Vancouver as guests of McLoughlin. In the spring the four men set out up the Columbia to the trading post on Clark's Fork and then south to the Snake. It was at Pierre's (later Jackson) Hole near the juncture of the Hoback and the Snake that a small party of Sublette's men found Smith and his companions trapping in the streams of the valley. Joined by his partner, Smith and the trappers worked the area thoroughly and then spent the fall trapping in the country between the Missouri and the Yellowstone. The combined parties wintered on the Wind River while Sublette returned to St. Louis with the packs of beaver furs.

In the winter camp, Jedediah Smith wrote a revealing letter to his brother, Ralph.

It is that I may be able to help those who stand in need that I face every danger. It is for this that I pass over the sandy plains, in the heat of summer, thirsting for water where I may cool my over-heated body. It is for this that I go for days without eating, and am pretty well satisfied if I can gather a few roots, a few snails, or better satisfied if we can afford ourselves a piece of horse-flesh, or a fine roasted dog; and most of all it is for this that I deprive myself of the privilege of society and the satisfaction of the converse of my friends.

The letter he had written to his brother is one of the most remarkable and revealing of the considerable number of documents that survive from the era of the fur trade. It makes clear the manner in which the Protestant passion for personal rectitude invaded even such an improbable venture as the fur trade. It reminds us of Meriwether Lewis's on his thirtieth birthday, halfway across the continent of North America. Smith was thirty-one when he wrote his letter not far from where Lewis had written these words: "I reflected that I had as yet done but little, very little, indeed, to further the happiness of the human race or to advance the information of the succeeding generation . . . I resolved . . . in the future to live for *mankind*, as I have heretofore lived *for myself*."

Exactly how Jedediah Smith thought the sacrifices occasioned by his remarkable journeys were "to help those who stand in need of help" is far from clear. Was he amassing money from the fur trade to use in future philanthropic ventures? Surely the men and women who might follow the trails he had blazed to California were not the poor and downtrodden, those "in need of help." Perhaps "thirst" was a clue. He had written eloquently of "thirst" in his journal. Thirst was far worse than hunger. If he had not consciously sought "thirst" on the Cimarron Desert, had he perhaps subconsciously invited it by not taking the precautions his experience told him he should take? To a devout Christian, "thirst" must be associated with Christ's death on the Cross and his most poignant human cry, "I thirst!" This may seem too bold a speculation by half, but it will serve its purpose if it does no more than remind us of the power of the idea of sacrifice for a pious American Protestant in the nineteenth century. Whether Jedediah Smith associated his own terrible thirst—first on the Salt Desert and then on the Cimarron—with his Savior's thirst on the Cross we can never know, but we know beyond any doubt that he felt compelled to justify his restless passion for exploration and adventure, a passion that cost the lives of twenty-five of his fellows, by insisting that it was all done "to help those who stand in need."

The next summer saw the arrival of the first wagons to make their way up the increasingly well-marked trail from St. Louis to the headwaters of the Missouri. Smith and William Sublette were ready for new ventures. They had heard glowing reports of the trade between Independence and Santa Fe and they were determined to sample it. The fur trading firm of Smith and Sublette thus sold its assets to the Rocky Mountain Fur Company headed by Sublette's brother, Milton; Jedediah Smith's old friend, Thomas Fitzpatrick; Jean-Baptiste Gervais; and Jim Bridger; and left to them the thankless job of battling John Jacob Astor for the control of the fur trade.

Smith and Sublette headed down the Missouri to St. Louis with 190 packs of beaver to the value of some $80,000 and began to make plans to enter the Santa Fe trade. Smith's brothers, Peter and Austin, joined them and on April 10, 1831, a party of eighty-five men with twenty-two heavily loaded wagons headed up the Missouri to Independence. There they turned southwest to the poorly defined trail that led to Santa Fe.

In three weeks the train reached the ford of the Arkansas, a distance of 392 miles from Independence. One man, who had wandered away from the train, had been captured and killed by the Pawnee, but the company was otherwise in good condition and spirits. Entering the Cimarron Desert, they neglected to lay in a sufficient supply of water. The summer was a dry one and the water holes they had counted on using had dried up. Some of the mules began to die of thirst and suddenly the train was faced with disaster. Josiah Gregg was told by a Mexican buffalo hunter what followed. Smith, desperate to find water, broke a cardinal rule of travel in Indian country and rode off alone to search for a creek or spring. After riding for some miles he finally sighted a stream that was, in fact, the Cimarron River. When he reached the riverbed he found that it was dry but, taking a stick, he dug down several feet and water slowly filled the hole. Intent only on quenching his thirst, he was unaware that a party of Comanche had come up behind him. His first intimation may have been when arrows struck him. According to the Comanche themselves, he killed two or three of their party before he died. Scalped and stripped, his body was never found and the details of his death were only subsequently pieced together by Gregg.

Was Jedediah Smith's recklessly invited death a propitiation for those deaths of which he had been the unwitting agent, by failures in the extraordinary leadership he normally exercised? On the surface his life seems the simple, unreflective existence of the classic man of action. But we know it to be otherwise. Jedediah Smith was an addict, an inebriate of the wild geography of western America. He prayed to God to sanctify his addiction so that, in the end, it might serve Him.

CHAPTER XIV

OSBORNE RUSSELL

Our best source for the life and feelings of a trapper is the account of Osborne Russell of the nine years between 1834 and 1843 that he spent trapping beaver in the Yellowstone basin area. By 1834 the fierce rivalry between the Missouri Fur Company and John Jacob Astor's American Fur Company—and later between the Rocky Mountain Fur Company and the Astor enterprise—was coming to a climax; shortly before the end of the era of the beaver hat, the struggle would end in the triumph of Astor's ruthless and irresistible endeavor. Russell, twenty years old at the beginning of his career as a trapper, was born in Bowdoinham, Maine, one of nine children. He ran away to sea at the age of sixteen but soon tired of the disciplined life of a sailor and headed west. He spent three years in the region of Wisconsin and Minnesota, working for the Northwest Fur Trapping and Trading Company and then joined a party led by Nathaniel Wyeth, who was determined to take a group to the Oregon country under the banner of the Oregon Colonization Society.

The Oregon venture failed but Wyeth obtained a contract to deliver $3,000 worth of trading goods to Milton Sublette and Thomas Fitzpatrick, partners in the Rocky Mountain Fur Company, at the rendezvous of 1834. Russell signed on with Wyeth and his newly formed Columbia River Fishing and Trading Company for eighteen months at a wage of $250. When the Rocky Mountain Fur Company, pressed to the wall by the far better capitalized American Fur Company, defaulted on its contract to Wyeth, the latter decided to build a fort and establish his own fur trading operation. Fort Hall at the juncture of the Snake and the Blackfoot rivers was a stockade some eighty feet square built of cottonwood tree trunks sunk three feet in the ground and reaching a height of fifteen feet. Russell was left with nine other men to keep the fort while Wyeth pushed on for the Columbia.

Russell's first trapping expedition included ten trappers and seven camp keepers. They set out from Fort Hall on March 15 for the Bear River but the snow was so deep and the game so scarce that the party had to live for ten days on roots. A grizzly bear was shot and the camp keepers, who cooked the meals and guarded the camp while the trappers ventured off to set their traps, soon filled the kettles with delicious "fat bear meat cut in very small pieces."

In the "fall hunt," Russell was a member of a party of fourteen trappers and ten camp keepers dispatched in the direction of Yellowstone Lake. At the Salt River, the party, unable to ford the river, built a bullboat of buffalo hides to carry themselves and their equipment across, but young Abram Patterson, a Pennsylvanian, determined to try to swim his horse across, was swept away and drowned. Camped near Henry's Fork of the Snake, the party found itself surrounded by some sixty Blackfeet—a third of whom were mounted. There was a wild rush to round up the horses before the Indians drove them off but six escaped and were caught by the Blackfeet. Russell was then treated to a classic Indian deployment. While the unmounted Indians took refuge behind rocks and trees, their mounted companions rode back and forth just out of rifle range, shouting and hallooing "brandishing their weapons and yelling at the top of their voices." It was like seeing a painting come to life. As Russell watched, enthralled, "the whistling of balls about my ears gave me to understand that these living Creatures were a little more dangerous than those I had been accustomed to see portrayed on canvas."

The experienced Indian fighters in the party directed some of the company to fire their rifles at the Indians scattered across the front of the camp while they slipped into the brush to attack the Blackfeet from the flank. Russell placed "a large German horse pistol" by his side as a precaution and then blazed away at the elusive foe. The Indians were armed with muskets, bows and arrows, spears and knives. None of these weapons was, of course, a match at long range for the rifles of the white men. The Indian strategy was to try to work their way within musket range, fire, and then try to close, shooting their arrows, five or six of which could be discharged while a rifleman was loading his piece. The arrows, though capable of being fired much more rapidly than the rifle bullets, were not nearly so lethal. A white trapper might and often did continue to fight with half a dozen arrows stuck in him unless they struck some especially vulnerable spot. Because the arrows might be poisoned, they had to be plucked out as soon as possible.

On this occasion, Russell, protected by a tree trunk, placed his hat on top of a nearby bush which he jostled from time to time with his foot, thereby drawing the fire of the Indians "and giving me a better shot at their heads." After two hours of such fighting, the Indians withdrew carrying their dead and wounded with them and setting up, typically, "a dismal lamentation."

One of the hunters had been wounded by musket balls in three places in his right leg and one in his left; another had received a superficial groin wound. Three horses had been killed and several more wounded. The next day the trappers found a spot where the Indians had stopped to bind up the wounds of their injured. They counted nine places where the crushed grass and bloodied soil indicated that bodies had been lying.

Cold, soaking rain fell for days, and while Russell's party was trying to cross the swollen Lewis River with a raft, all their equipment was swept away, including their rifles and ammunition. The next day, July 4, huddled at a sputtering fire in the drenching rain, Russell

> thought of those who were perhaps at this moment Celebrating the anniversary of our Independence in my Native Land or seated around tables loaded with the richest dainties that a rich independent and enlightened country could afford or perhaps collected in the gay Saloon relating the heroic deeds of our ancestors or joining in the nimble dance forgetful of cares and toils whilst here . . . a group of human beings crouched round a fire which the rain was fast diminishing meditating on their deplorable condition not knowing at what moment we might be aroused by the shrill cry of the hostile savages with which the country was infested.

The next day, following the riverbank, they retrieved most of their goods and pressed on with the trapping. From a band of Snake they obtained "a large number of Elk Deer and Sheep skins . . . in return for awls axes kettles tobacco ammunition etc." With the improvement of the weather and the fortunes of the party camped in the beautiful Yellowstone Valley, Russell reflected, "I almost wished I could spend the remainder of my days in a place like this where happiness and contentment seemed to reign in wild romantic splendor surrounded by majestic battlements which seemed to support the heavens and shut out all hostile intruders."

Early in September Russell and his party encountered fourteen white trappers, members of a larger party of some sixty white men and twenty Flathead Indians under the leadership of Jim Bridger. It was a happy meeting, with the two parties staying up the better part of the night around a large campfire exchanging mountain yarns and passing on "news from the States." Next morning a detachment of eight started off to set traps on the creeks leading into Henry's Fork. Soon they were back pursued by a large war party of Blackfeet.

The Indians found places behind rocks on bluffs overlooking the camp and kept up a constant musket fire on the trappers below them. Unwilling to venture within range of the trappers' rifles, they did little damage except to the horses. Finally the Indians set fire to the dry grass to try to smoke the whites out. "This," Russell wrote, "was the most horrid position I was ever placed in death seemed almost inevitable . . . but all hands began immediately to remove the rubbish around the encampment and setting fire to it to act against the flames that were hovering over our heads." A change in the wind soon carried the fire toward the Indians, who were forced to beat a hasty retreat. Since Russell's small party had lost half its number through "the desertion of men and loss of animals," it joined forces with Bridger's band. Now hostile Indians lurked all about and the trappers had to be constantly vigilant. Leaving the forks of the Madison for a sweep through the network of rivers to the north, a Frenchman went out on his own to trap, despite warnings, and was promptly killed and scalped by a party of Blackfeet. Another smaller party was ambushed and narrowly escaped, finding refuge in a Flathead village of 180 lodges near the Beaverhead River. There Russell, grateful at having eluded the Blackfeet, noted, "The Flatheads are a brave friendly generous and hospitable tribe strictly honest with a mixture of pride that exalts them far above the rude appellation of Savages when contrasted with the tribes around them. They boast of never injuring the whites. . . . Larceny, fornication and adultery are severely punished. . . ."

Russell, restless with his fellow trappers, set out on his own, trapping along the Snake in a region that the Blackfeet avoided unless on a large-scale raid. Here he was comparatively safe. He now knew enough of the Snake language to carry on a conversation. At a Snake village of 332 lodges, he was welcomed warmly by the "Old Chief" and watched the slaughter of a thousand buffalo cows to provide food for the tribes. It was a brilliant display of Indian riding and hunting prowess. The Snake had recently been fishing for salmon at the headwaters of those rivers flowing to the Pacific, and were now following the cycle Lewis and Clark had observed, killing and drying buffalo and making pemmican to see them through the winter. Pemmican—dried buffalo meat, bone marrow, and berries mixed up together into a kind of cake—was the most nutritious and essential food of white and Indian alike in the Great Plains region.

It was Russell's first sight of an Indian buffalo hunt and he was an enthralled observer. A mounted brave rode toward the herd at an angle designed to bring him up to the running buffalo at the point where it was easiest for him to cut out a bull or cow and kill it. In Russell's words, "he gives his horse the rein and darts thro the band selects his victim reins his horse up along side and shoots and if he considers the wound mortal he pulls up the rein the horse knowing his business keeps along galloping with the band, until the rider has reloaded usually the hunter carried four or five cartridges in his mouth when he darts forward upon another buffalo . . ." Cows were more desirable for their meat and there was an art to picking a cow or bull with the greatest amount of fat on it.

Buffalo were of course an essential source of food and hides of warmth and shelter for the Indian, the trapper, and plainsman. But the hunting of them was also the most exhilarating of sports for those who engaged in it. Russell wrote, "If Kings Princes Nobles and Gentlemen can derive so much sport and Pleasure as they boast of in chasing a fox or simple hare all day which when they have caught is of little or no benefit to them what pleasure can the Rocky Mountain hunter be expected to derive in running with a well trained horse such a noble and stately animal as the Bison? which when killed is of some service to him." Certainly it was true that every foreign visitor with sporting instincts yearned to participate in a buffalo hunt and many of them did.

The old chief, Want a Sheep, put Russell up in his own lodge; told him in great detail of his life, his coups, his children and relations; and amused him "with traditionary tales mixed with the grossest superstition some of which were not unlike the manners of the Ancient Israelites." To which Russell added, "There seems to be a happiness in ignorance which knowledge and Science destroys here is a nation of people contented and happy they have horses and lodges and are very partial to the rifles of the white man. If a Eutaw has 8 or 10 good horses a rifle and ammunition he is contented if he fetches a deer at night from the hunt joy beams in the faces of his wife and children." Perhaps in the last analysis it was this sense on the part of the white man that the Indian was a "happy" being that was so compelling. Time and again we hear the same theme sounded—the happiness of a simple life with few wants and those easily satisfied, the absence of striving in the Indian's life, of competition and tension. A people dedicated to "the pursuit of happiness" but often finding little enough of it, saw it or, more properly, thought they saw it in the life of the aborigines—the carefree existence of the "noble" savage.

In many white reflections on Indian life, the phrase "happy children of nature," or some variant of it, appears. What haunted Americans when they contemplated the Indians, what floated around in the buried depths of their consciousness, was the suspicion that with all their progressive, go-ahead civilization, they were missing out on happiness, that they were paying too heavy a psychic price for all these marvels. That was the question that the mere existence of the Indians perpetually posed and, it might be said, poses once again for a new generation of Americans, making a more self-conscious audit of the psychic costs of being an American.

Of course the notion that the Indian was a happy, carefree creature was only partly true. If one observed the life of an Indian village on "vacation" from warfare or hunting, with the games and play, the freedom and openness, the colorful pageantry, one might readily succumb to that charming illusion. But we have seen enough of various Indian tribes by now to know that they often suffered acutely from hunger when game was scarce, that the weaker tribes lived in terror of their more powerful enemies, that there were Indians who "failed" by the standards of their tribe just as there were whites who failed. What the white man saw that so intrigued him was that every Indian who preserved his tribal identity belonged to a close-knit group that supported him in every moment of his existence. With all the terrors of primitive tribal life there was one

terror missing—the terror of being a discrete, single, atomized creature called "an individual," who was, in a particular excruciating
sense, "on his own," at war with all other "individuals," an individual whose "tribe" was as vague and ill-defined as the state of Maine
or Pennsylvania, or that most amorphous entity, the United States
of America, and whose fate as it was to be constantly searching for
his "identity," having always to hold it precariously in his *mind* lest
he forget who he was.

Russell soon rejoined a group of trappers under Jim Bridger's
direction and began trapping on Blackfoot Creek. A few weeks
later the party gathered with other bands of trappers and Snake,
Bannock, Nez Percé, and Flathead Indians for the yearly rendezvous near the Green. They made, in Russell's words, "a mixed multitude" that included "Americans and Canadian French with some
Dutch, Scotch, Irish, English, half-breed and full blood Indians of
nearly every tribe in the Rocky Mountains." Not to mention some
Iroquois, Delaware, Shawnee, and Mohawk. "Some were gambling
at cards, some playing the Indian game of hand and others horse
racing while here and there could be seen small groups collected
under the shady trees relating the events of the past year all in good
spirits and health for Sickness is a Stranger seldom met with in
these regions." In this fashion the trappers passed the time until the
"cavalcade" appeared. When it arrived early in July, led by Nathaniel
Wyeth, it consisted of some forty men and twenty mule-drawn
carts carrying supplies for the coming winter and headed, after the
rendezvous, for Oregon. With Wyeth were Marcus Whitman and
his wife, Narcissa, as well as another couple on their way to establish a mission with the Cayuse Indians. The two women were the
first white women most of the Indians had ever seen and they never
tired of staring at them. One of the trappers shot a fat elk and juicy
ribs and pieces of meat were soon suspended over a fire. After supper, "the jovial tale goes round the circle the peals of loud laughter
break upon the stillness of the night. . . . Every tale puts an audi-
tor in mind of something similar to it but under different circumstances which being told the 'laughing part' gives rise to increasing

merriment and furnishes more subjects for good jokes and witty sayings such as Swift never dreamed of. Thus the evening passed with eating drinking and stories enlivened with witty humor until near Midnight all being wrapped in their blankets lying around the fire gradually falling to sleep one by one . . ."

Such a life was, as Russell tells it, the archetypical camping trip, the ultimate male ritual of hardihood and companionship, hunting and playing—a life indeed very much like that of the Indians. It is easy to see why it cast such a spell on those young men of various nationalities who entered it. This was the magic relationship, "deeper than love," that D.H. Lawrence writes of in *Studies in Classic American Literature*. As old as Achilles and Patroclus, it reached to the profoundest levels of the masculine psyche and made all other modes of life seem bland and innocuous by comparison.

With the arrival of the cavalcade, "joy beamed in every countenance," Russell wrote. "Some received letters from friends and relations and Some received the public papers and the news of the day others consoled themselves with the idea of getting a blanket or a Cotton Shirt or a few pints of Coffee and sugar to sweeten it just by way of a great gratis that is to say by paying 2,000 percent on the first cost." A pint of coffee thus cost $20 and tobacco $2 a pound. For several weeks after the cavalcade arrived the trappers reveled in their sense of well-being and camaraderie. They drank and ate excessively, enjoyed their new luxuries, disported themselves with Indian girls, played crude musical instruments, sang and danced together, and told their interminable mountain yarns, recounting in detail their skirmishes with the Blackfeet, their narrow escapes, or the death of a companion. Finally after several delightful weeks they divided into parties and turned back into the valleys and mountains where the beaver, in constantly diminishing numbers, awaited them.

Russell joined up with Bridger and a party of some sixty, mostly Americans. He found the group an especially congenial one. There were a number of New Englanders, including Elbridge Trask, a young New Hampshire man, who, like Russell, had started in as a camp keeper and who became Russell's closest friend. The party soon began breaking off into smaller and smaller groups and spreading out over as wide a range as possible. Russell and Trask, with five companions, found themselves working the waters in what is now Yellowstone Park; there they observed new wonders every day—geysers, blue pools of boiling water, a field covered "with a crust of Limestone of dazzling whiteness." At the forks of the Clark River, Joe Meek, a famous trapper, and Dave Crow rode in and joined them. Blood was running down the neck of Meek's pony. The two men had been setting their traps on Prior's Fork, Meek told Russell and Trask, when they found "old Benj Johnson's boys [Meek's name for the Blackfeet] . . . just walking up and down them ar' streams with their hands on their hips gathering plums, they gave me a title and turned me a somerset or two shot my horse 'Too Shebit' in the neck and sent us head over heels in a pile together but we raised arunnin . . . and the savages jist squattin and grabbin at me but I raised a fog for about half a mile . . ."

By the end of October the streams had begun to freeze over and Bridger established winter camp on the Yellowstone. This interlude was as highly ritualized as the rendezvous. From November through March, excepting those intervals when the weather was unseasonably warm, the trappers lived in their central camps, fifty or sixty to a camp, and entertained themselves by hunting (as Russell put it, "we had nothing to do but slay and eat") and in such other ways as their ingenuity might devise. The camp keepers' business in winter quarters was to guard the horses, cook, and keep fires. The trappers had "snug lodges made of dressed buffalo skins in the center of which we built a fire and generally comprised about six men to lodge. The long winter evenings were passed away by collecting in some of the most spacious lodges and entering into debates arguments or spinning long yarns until midnight in perfect good humour," Russell wrote, adding, "I for one will cheerfully confess that I have derived no little benefit from the frequent arguments and debates held in what we termed The Rocky Mountain College and I doubt not but some of my comrades who considered themselves Classical Scholars have had some little added to their wisdom in these assemblies however rude they might appear."

One of the most fascinating aspects of the society of trappers, at least of the American trappers, was that far from coming from the lower classes, the urban or rural poor, they were in the great majority—especially those from New England—the thoroughly literate sons of middle-class parents. Russell may indeed be taken as an excellent representative of the young men who made up the companies of trappers and hunters. Despite his practical disregard of commas and periods, he writes well and has obviously had a much better than average education.

Russell found the scenery a constant inducement to reflect upon the nature of the world and the proper ends of life. Looking at the incredible landscape, the flowers, "the scattered flocks of Sheep and Elk carelessly feeding or thoughtlessly reposing beneath the shade having Providence for their founder and preserver and Nature for Shepherd Gardner and Historian . . . wonder is put to the test . . ." If many of the trappers were, like Russell, delighted to "argue and debate," others "never troubled themselves about vain and frivolous notions as they called them." The Scottish and English especially were prone to denigrate the American scenery and laud the castles and gardens of their native land. Russell recounted one conversation where an Irishman yearned to "fill my body wid good ould whisky 'yes' said the backwoods hunter on my left, as he cast away his bone and smoothed down his long auburn hair with his greasy hand, 'yes you English and Irish are always talking about your fine countries but if they are so mighty fine (said with an oath) why do so many of you run off and leave them and come to America to get a living?'" which query ended the conversation.

Besides Osborne Russell with his knowledge of Shakespeare and the classics, there was the Virginian James Clyman, who wrote poetry and discussed sophisticated concepts of time and space. Edwin Denig, the son of a Pennsylvania physician, was an accurate observer of Indian life and customs. David Thompson, a Welshman, had gone to the Grey Coat School at Westminister, England. Jean

Baptiste Trudeau had been a schoolteacher. These men were primarily traders, but the boundary line between traders and trappers was a very fine one.

In January, with the weather fine and warm, Russell and six other trappers decided to treat themselves to a buffalo hunt of some five or six days. Two days out of camp,

> riding carelessly along with our rifles lying carelessly before us on our saddles . . . we came to a deep narrow gulch . . . when behold! the earth seemed teeming with naked savages. A quick volley of fusees [muskets] a shower of balls and a cloud of smoke clearly bespoke their nation tribe manners and customs and mode of warfare: A ball broke the right arm of a man and he dropped his rifle which a savage immediately caught up and shot after us as we wheeled and scampered out of reach of their guns. There was about 80 Indians who had secreted themselves until we rode within 15 feet of them. They got a rifle clear gain and we had one man wounded . . . so they had so much the advantage and we were obliged to go to Camp and study out some plan to get even as by the last two or three skirmishes we had fell in this debt.

The opportunity was presented several days later when some twenty Blackfeet were sighted. A party of trappers took after them at once and cornered them in an abandoned Indian fort. Four Indians were shot and killed by the trappers, their bodies pushed under the ice of a nearby stream by their fellows, and a half-dozen braves were wounded. The American casualties were one Delaware hit in the leg with a poisoned bullet and one trapper slightly wounded in the hip.

The next move was up to the Blackfeet. The score had now swung decisively in favor of Bridger's trappers, and they might anticipate a raid in force by several hundred Blackfoot warriors. The next day Bridger, scouting with his brass telescope, saw the plains "alive with Indians." A palisade of cottonwood logs some six feet high and 250 feet square was quickly erected around the camp. The horses were brought inside and a double guard was mounted. That night there was a remarkable display of northern lights with a "deep blood red" spreading across the sky. The next morning a force that Russell estimated to number more than a thousand Blackfoot warriors drew up in a line facing the hastily improvised fort with the manifest intention, Russell wrote, "of rubbing us from the face of the earth." But apparently the sight of the rather formidable fortification coupled with the fiery display in the heavens of the night before, which the Indians took as an evil omen, deterred them and shortly they turned and rode off as swiftly as they had come, leaving Bridger and his men to amuse themselves "with playing ball, wrestling running foot races, etc."

By early April the trappers were out again setting their traps, their tracks dogged by parties of Blackfeet. Six men trapping on the Musselshell River had a trapper killed and lost all their horses and traps. Russell himself had a close call when he and two companions were ambushed by a war party and Russell's horse was shot from under him. He jumped up behind one of his comrades and they dashed off, shots whizzing past them.

The Blackfoot Indians were not the only hazard. The Crows, while enemies of the Blackfeet and ostensibly friends of the whites, could seldom be trusted. Russell, an Englishman named William Allen, the camp keeper, and two trappers named Greenberry and Conn were trapping on the Bighorn when they were joined by a party of Crows on the way, they said, to steal Blackfoot ponies. They pushed into the camp of the white trappers and grew, as Russell put it, "very insolent and saucy saying we had no right in their country and intimated they could take everything from us if they wished." The next morning they demanded that Russell and his companions divide their tobacco and ammunition with them and when they complied the Crows made as if to take it all. The trappers made clear they were determined to fight for their possessions and their lives whereupon the Crows put down their arms "and told us with an envious Savage laugh they were only joking. . . ." But the Indians followed them, stealing horses and traps until it became evident that they were bent on robbing and then killing them, whereupon Allen, who had lived two winters in a Crow village, made clear that the trappers were determined to be rid of their unwelcome companions. He knew their intentions. "If you follow or molest us we will besmear the ground with the blood and guts of Crow Indians and do not speak to me more for I despise the odious jargon of your Nation!" At that the trappers rode off, expecting a hail of arrows or musket balls in their back but they had gone little more than a mile or so before a chief caught up with them, approached them unarmed, and declared, "You are very foolish you do know how bad my heart feels to think you have been robbed by men belonging to my village but they are not men they are Dogs who took your animals." If the trappers would return with him to the village he would see that they got their horses and belongings back. Otherwise he would have to bear the reproaches of "the Blanket Chief," Jim Bridger. The trappers, still suspecting treachery, refused and pressed on for the site of the winter camp. Stripped of much of their equipment and reduced at times to walking, the four made their way with great hardships and suffering to Fort William, where they replenished their supplies.

A few weeks later, Russell joined Bridger and a large party headed for the Madison. On their way, they came on a Blackfoot village ravaged by smallpox. The village was a large one and Bridger wished to detour to avoid a possible clash with Indians who might be healthy but his men protested, in Russell's words, "against trying to avoid a Village of Blackfeet which did not contain more than 3 times our numbers." They thus camped near the Indian village, prepared defensive works, and then set out in a party of twenty men to, in effect, challenge the Blackfeet to a battle. Approaching the unsuspecting Indians, the trappers fired three or four rounds apiece before the aroused warriors were ready to take the offensive. Then, pursued by the Blackfeet, they retreated to the camp. The Indians stationed themselves just beyond rifle range and kept up a musket fire for several hours, wounding a few horses. Finally a Blackfoot called out, saying the trappers were not men but women and should dress as such. They had challenged the Blackfeet to fight "and then crept into the rock like women." At this insult, an old Iroquois warrior who had lived long on the shores of Lake Superior, turned to the white trappers and said, "My friend you see dat Ingun talk? He not talk good he talk berry bad He say you me all same like squaw, dat no good, you go wid me I make him no more talk dat way." With which the old warrior stripped off his clothes except for his powder horn and bullet pouch and began a war dance, uttering "the shrill war cry of his Nation . . . which had been the death warrant of so many whites during the old French war," as Russell put it. Twenty whites rallied around the old man and followed him as he started up a long rocky slope of some three hundred yards to where the Blackfeet to the number of some hundred and fifty were stationed. In the face of heavy musket fire, the attackers reached the rocks without loss and without firing their rifles. Pausing to catch their breath, they jumped over the final barrier and, "muzzle to muzzle," drove the Indians ahead of them "like hunted rats among the ruins of an old building whilst we followed close at their heels loading and shooting until we drove them entirely into the plain where their horses were tied." Next morning the fighting was renewed, this time in the vicinity of the village, until the Indians were once again driven from the field.

It is clear from Russell's account of the battle that the fighting was, for the trappers, not much different from hunting buffalo: a more dangerous, but a far more exciting sport. One is inevitably reminded of the "fighting" games of children, shouting "bang-bang you're dead"—the game of children here became the deadly game of grown men. Perhaps the most mysterious and fearsome line written by an American in the nineteenth century was the exclamation of the hero of Melville's novel *Pierre* as he kills his cousin, Glen, "'Tis speechless sweet to murder thee!" The terrible secret that the trapper shared with the Indian was that it was "speechless sweet" to kill; that killing was an addiction, the most compelling game of all. Suffering from the constant raids and murders of the Indians in the California goldfields, Quaker Charles Pancoast found himself taking on his rider companions' conviction that "the only good Indian was a dead Indian." One day, hunting, he came upon three Indians intent on skinning an animal and totally unaware of Pancoast's proximity. Pancoast raised his gun to shoot them when the thought came to him "that I should be taking the life of a Human Being without necessity or adding to my own security, and should perhaps regret the Murder." He was plainly startled at his almost instinctive impulse to kill the unoffending Indians and he subsequently "rejoiced that I did not pull the trigger of my rifle that day."

IF WE OMIT THE FIRST tentative ventures of Manuel Lisa and the Missouri Fur Company in the period prior to the War of 1812, the "beaver rush" had started with the expeditions of Ashley and Henry in the spring of 1822. Sixteen years later the era was over, a substantial period of time in terms of American capitalistic enterprise and one that left a residue of stories and legends, apparently inexhaustible in their retelling, one of the great romantic episodes in all history, a saga as compelling as the tales of Homer. The trappers, like Lewis and Clark, were men of the new consciousness. Their values, as the social psychologists put it, were "internalized—that is to say, they were able to function as 'individuals.'" Indeed they were the prototype of the "rugged individual," which is one reason that American captains of industry have been so obsessed with the "frontier ethic," the lonely individual making his way against all the terrors and hazards of the wilderness. John Jacob Astor, living in opulence in New York City, fancied himself a kindred spirit to Andrew Henry and William Ashley. Even Philip Hone, the ultimate urbanite, was charmed by stories of the West. He found Washington Irving's *A Tour on the Prairies* the very best kind of light reading. Killing buffaloes, hunting wild horses, sleeping every night on the ground for a whole month, and depending from day to day for the means of subsistence upon the deer, wild turkey, and bears which the rifles of their own party can alone procure, are events of ordinary interest to the settlers in the great west, but they are matters of thrilling interest to citizens who read them in their green slippers seated before a shining grate.

The Indians lived collectively, that is to say tribally, but they fought individually. The whites, on the contrary, lived individually, but usually fought collectively—as an integrated unit with a preconceived strategy. Whites, experienced in fighting Indians, were thus always more than a match for considerably larger bands of Indians. It was not a matter of courage but of culture, specifically of organization. In order to organize people into new groups for various enterprises, from running a cotton mill or digging a canal to fighting the Indians, they had first to be broken down, so to speak, from the traditional corporate bodies to which they belonged, whether family, congregation, or community, into what we might liken to individual human molecules or atoms, and then reformed or reorganized into new corporate bodies. The disintegrative effects of American life accelerated that breaking-down process and meant that there were always innumerable free-floating "individuals," as we called them, available for every new venture. The fact that the breaking-down process was often an excruciating one for those individuals involved was the price that Americans paid for their capacity to form new human groups for new tasks with astonishing speed. The Blackfeet were to have revenge, of a kind at least, on Russell. Trapping with three companions in the creeks that ran into Yellowstone Lake, Russell had set off with a trapper named White. Walking along a stream he glanced up to see the heads of Indians. His powder horn and bullet pouch, lying on the ground some distance away, were seized by an Indian before he could reach them. But cocking their rifles and aiming them at the nearest Indians the two trappers made their way through a circle of warriors followed by a shower of arrows. White, struck in the hip, paused only long enough to pull out the arrow. Russell was also hit in the hip. Finally an arrow from the pursuing Blackfeet went through Russell's right leg above the knee. He fell across a log and the Indian who had shot him leaped forward with his tomahawk to administer the *coup de grâce*. In Russell's words,

> I made a leap and avoided the blow and kept hopping from log
> to log thro a shower of arrows, which flew around us like hail,
> lodging in the pines and logs. After we had passed them about
> 10 paces wheeled about and took aim at them. They then began
> to dodge behind the trees and shoot their guns we then ran and
> hopped about 50 yards further in the logs and bushes and made
> a stand—I was very faint from the loss of blood and we set down
> among the logs determined to kill the two foremost when they
> came up and then die like men.

The Indians, searching through the down timber for their prey, twice passed within fifteen or twenty feet of the two men and then, more interested in dividing the spoils—the traps, horses, and equipment—they turned back, giving Russell and White a reprieve. The two wounded men then set off hobbling painfully toward the lake. Russell was so weak from loss of blood that he had to rest every few hundred yards. At the lake they patched their wounds as best they could and continued their tortuous progress along the shore. In the distance they could hear the shouting of the Indians over their booty. White, a Missourian, brought up, Russell wrote scornfully, as "the pet of the family" who "had never done or learned much of anything but horseracing and gambling," was convinced that he would die wretchedly in the wilderness far from his friends and doting parents. To such lamentations Russell replied, "If you persist in thinking so you will die but I can crawl from this place upon my hands and one knee and Kill 2 or 3 Elk and make a shelter of the skins dry the meat until we get able to travel." Russell's leg was so swollen that he could walk only with the aid of a crutch that White fashioned for him. The two men then took refuge in a grove of pines and had hardly done so when some sixty Indians appeared along the shore shooting at elk swimming in the lake. Returning to their original campsite, Russell and White found a French-Canadian trapper who had been one of their small party and a sack of salt overlooked by the Indians. Russell then bathed his wounds in warm salt water and made a salve of beaver's oil and castoreum. The three men had not eaten since the Blackfoot attack. The Canadian shot several ducks and they had a meal of sorts. That night they camped at a hot springs where Russell was able to soak his swollen leg. Next day they shot a doe elk, cut the meat in thin slices, dried them over a fire to provide food for their journey back to the fort, and used the hide to make moccasins. By now Russell could limp along at a slow walk. The fall nights were growing increasingly cold and the three men, huddled around small fires and without blankets, could get little sleep. With infinite difficulty, they pressed on, sometimes going several days without food, to Fort Hall a hundred and thirty miles away, arriving there "naked hungry wounded sleepy and fatigued."

After ten days of rest and good food at the fort, Russell was out setting traps for beaver again, and by the end of October he had traveled to the region of the Jefferson River and back, finally making winter camp early in December with three companions, one from Missouri, one from Massachusetts, and one from Vermont. They felt themselves fortunate to find some books to read—Byron's works, Shakespeare, Sir Walter Scott, the Bible, and Clark's *Commentary*, as well as works on geology, chemistry, and philosophy. In May Russell was off trapping solo with "two horses six traps and some few books." After a summer and fall of trapping he joined a village of Snake Indians, and there a Frenchman with a Flathead wife invited Russell to pass the winter with him. The racial composition of the village provided an interesting insight into the process of amalgamation of various tribes with each other and with whites. In the lodge next to Russell's host was a mixed-blood Iowa with a Nez Percé wife and two children, his wife's brother, and another mixed-blood. The next lodge was that of a mixed-blood Ree, his Nez Percé wife, two children, and a Snake Indian. A third nearby lodge was occupied by a mixed-blood Snake and his Nez Percé wife and two children. The dwellers in the other fifteen lodges in the village were all Snake.

The Snake were far more casual about intermarriages than tribes like the Blackfeet and generally hospitable to Indians or whites who came to them in peace. Nez Percé women were particularly prized as wives by white men and mixed-bloods for their cleanliness and affection.

The whites and mixed-bloods living among the Snake felt a common bond at Christmas—"all who claimed kin to the white man (or to use their own expression, all that were gens d'esprit)." Russell was one of a party, only three of whom spoke English, that sat down to a Christmas feast of stewed elk meat, boiled deer meat, a boiled flour pudding prepared with dried fruit and four quarts of sauce made of the juice of sour berries and sugar, followed by cakes and six gallons of strong coffee. Large wood chips or pieces of bark served as plates and tin cups held the coffee. "The principal topic which was discussed," Russell wrote, "was the political affairs of the Rocky Mountains, the state of governments among the different tribes, the personal characters of the most distinguished warriors Chiefs, etc." It was the general opinion of the group that a certain Snake chief who was misusing his authority would soon be deposed and replaced by his brother. "In like manner were the characters of the principal Chiefs of the Bonnak, Nez Percé, Flathead and Crow Nations and the policy of their respective government commented upon . . . with as much affected dignity as if they could read their own names when written or distinguish the letter B from a Bulls foot."

In the Yellowstone region Russell noted that "the trappers often remarked to each other as they rode over these lonely plains that it was time for the White man to leave the mountains as Beaver and game had nearly disappeared." After a futile hunt for mountain sheep, Russell himself decided to head for Oregon territory. He and Elbridge Trask "took an affectionate leave of each other," Trask to return to Vermont, Russell to push west. Russell prepared for his journey to the Willamette Valley by killing elk and drying the meat. Then, climbing to a high peak in the Pont Neuf Range, he "sat down under a pine and took a last farewell view of a country over which I had travelled so often under such a variety of circumstances. The recollections of the past connection with the scenery," he noted, "now spread out before me put me somewhat into a Poetical humour and for the first time I attempted to frame my thoughts into rhyme but if Poets will forgive me for this intrusion I shall be cautious about trespassing on their grounds in the future."

The impulse was more significant than the poem, which was neither better nor worse than most of its genre, celebrating "the hoary icy mantled towers" and "cyrstal streamlets," the "smooth vale" where "skillful hands prepared a rich repast" and "hunters jokes and merry humor'd sport/Beguiled the time enlivened every face/ The hours flew past and seemed like moments short/'Til twinkling planets told of nighttimes pace." But now "those scenes of cheerful mirth are done/The horned herds are dwindling very fast . . ."

Ye rugged mounts ye vales ye streams and trees
To you a hunter bids his last farewell

I'm bound for shores of distant western seas
To view far famed Multnomahs fertile vale

I'll leave these regions once famed hunting grounds
Which I perhaps again shall see no more
And follow down led by the setting sun
Or distant sound of proud Columbia's roar

The rendezvous of 1838 brought word that the fur companies intended to discontinue all further operations. The American Fur Company had driven its less–well-capitalized rivals to the wall, but its victory, expensive in terms of men and money, was a hollow one. The halcyon days of the beaver trade were over. Fashion had created the insatiable appetite for beaver hats, and fashion ended it. Fashion now decreed that beaver hats must be replaced by silk, and beavers had a reprieve. The fur trading business would continue but in a much modified form. That branch of it based on the beaver had been a "brown gold rush," a boom-time business full of intrigue, unscrupulous maneuvers, desperate struggles for dominance among the competing fur companies, of dog-eat-dog competition and the ruthless despoiling of the Indians who were so often the eager instruments of their own undoing. It had been, in short, a classic capitalist undertaking, given a heightened color and intensity by the wildly romantic circumstances under which it took place. Individual trappers or small parties of trappers continued to carry on a greatly diminished trade. Many, like Osborne Russell, pushed on westward into Oregon territory to provide the nucleus of American settlements and strengthen American claims in that region. Most of those who were married to Indian squaws and had children by them remained in the region, living with friendly Indians and serving as army guides and scouts and, increasingly, as caravans of settlers began crossing the Great Plains for the Oregon country, as guides for emigrant trains.

The American frontier was the world's frontier, the most compelling and dramatic representation of the fact that the United States belonged to the world. The Fur West drew to it, irresistibly, representatives of a number of peoples or nations—French-Canadians, Spanish Americans, Iroquois, Shawnee, and Delaware Indians, Scotsmen, Irishmen, Germans, Dutchmen—and formed them into human groups, in this instance bands of trappers and traders, who, not even speaking the same language, ate, fought, played, and died or survived, welded together by the overwhelming power of the environment. The "language" of the frontier was a bizarre mixture of Indian signs and words, French words, Spanish words, English words, made-up words, a universal argot created out of the most practical necessities. We hear much today of the desirability for a *lingua franca*, a global language that all of the world's people might in time speak. But the experience of the American frontier reminds us that common tasks create their own forms of communication. The act gives rise to the word.

No account of the Trans-Mississippi West or indeed of the relations of white Americans to the Indians and trappers of the Old Northwest would be complete without mention of General

William Clark. It was Clark's painful lot to watch from his strategically located post at St. Louis while the Indian nations were slowly destroyed by the westward migration his expedition had done so much to stimulate. While the Indians had been "strong and hostile" it had been the policy of the United States to weaken them. "Now that they are weak and harmless, and most of their lands fallen into our hands, justice and humanity require us to cherish and befriend them," Clark wrote. "To teach them to live in houses, to raise grain and stock, to plant orchards, to set up landmarks, to divide their possessions, to establish laws for their government, to get the rudiments of common learning, such as reading, writing and ciphering." These were the first steps to improving their condition. But before any of these steps could be taken, they had to be removed from the corrupting presence of the whites to a land "where they could rest in peace, and enjoy in reality the perpetuity of the lands on which their buildings and improvements would be made."

The common practice of the United States government had been to "buy" Indian lands at treaty meetings where presents were given to those chiefs willing to enter into such negotiations and yearly "annuities" were promised to the tribes involved. Of the difficulties and complexities of such "purchases" we are well aware. Even where the Indian claims were extinguished with some shadow of fairness, the consequences of the "annuity" were demoralizing to the tribes. They came every year, war bonnets in hand, to receive their "annuity" in the form of supplies and baubles, ammunition and clothing. Or they waited impatiently for it to arrive by steamboat up the Missouri or down the Mississippi. Clark was strongly opposed to the annuity policy. The value of the annuities was small enough but in the long run they made once-proud tribes mendicants, living from handout to handout.

Clark saw the basic problem with the Indians as one of poverty. It was a strange word to enter into the language of the Indian. He had always been "poor" in the sense that he lived very close to the margin of existence. However powerful a tribe he belonged to, a bad hunt, a hard winter, destructive storms might bring him to the point of starvation. But he had never considered himself poor. And soon his speech was sprinkled with that demeaning word: "The white man is rich. He has many horses and cattle. The Indian is poor. He begs his White Father to give him food and clothing. . . ."

Nothing of any enduring value could be done for the Indian until he was no longer poor, Clark argued. "It is vain to talk to people in this condition about learning and religion," he wrote. "They want a regular supply of food, and, until that is obtained, the operations of the mind must take the instinct of mere animals, and be confined to warding off hunger and cold."

Property had "raised the character of the southern tribes. Roads and travellers through their country, large annuities, and large sums for land from the United States, and large presents to chiefs," Clark wrote, "have enabled them to acquire slaves, cattle, hogs, and horses; and these have enabled them to live independently, and to cultivate their minds and keep up their pride. . . ." But all that they had accomplished was to count for little against the avarice of their white neighbors.

Clark, with Lewis Cass as an ally, made numerous suggestions to the federal government for laws "under which those scattered & miserable remnants of the people of America" might experience the "just & benevolent views of the government." In 1825, six months before Jefferson's death, Clark wrote his old commander-in-chief expressing his determination to continue his fight on behalf of "the people of America"—the Indians of the West. It would give him pleasure to find some way to improve "the conditions of these unfortunate people placed under my charge, knowing as I do their wretchedness and their rapid decline. It is to be lamented that the deplorable Situation of the Indians do not receive more of the human feelings of the nations."

When Clark died in 1838, the last year of the Yellowstone rendezvous, things were no better for his Indian wards despite congressional legislation four years earlier that had followed his advice in part by strengthening the role of the military in protecting the Indians.

CHAPTER XV

THE
NORTHWEST

Until the establishment of the Bear Republic, California had been foreign territory that Americans entered, as we have seen, at considerable risk. The same could not be said of the Oregon territory. The majority of Americans believed that it belonged by right to the United States and a number were determined to help substantiate that claim by going and settling there.

As early as 1829 the Oregon Colonization Society had been organized in Boston. Its purpose was to dispatch both missionaries to convert the Indians and settlers to strengthen the American claim to the region. Each prospective settler was required to give proof of good character and was promised a town lot of five hundred square feet or two hundred acres in the Multnomah Valley, but few people came forward and the project languished. By the mid-1830s the Yellowstone beaver rush and Jedediah Smith's explorations had revived interest in Oregon. In 1835 Marcus and Narcissa Whitman, with several other young missionary couples, stopped at the fur trapper's rendezvous at the New Fork River on their way to Oregon. The beautiful blonde Narcissa charmed the trappers, and Whitman, a medical doctor as well as missionary, removed an old arrowhead from Jim Bridger's back. We have already taken note of the fact that the settlers who followed close on the heels of the missionaries besieged Congress with petitions to extend federal jurisdiction over the region. As president, James Polk, under the moderating influence of his Cabinet, pursued a more conciliatory course with Great Britain than that suggested by "54° 50' or Fight." Richard Pakenham, the British ambassador to the United States, was directed by Lord Aberdeen to propose the 49th parallel as the boundary between the United States and Canada, with Vancouver reserved to the British and free navigation of the Columbia River guaranteed to both powers. These terms were incorporated in a treaty that was confirmed by the Senate in July, 1846. The most important consequence of the treaty was a fresh influx of settlers to the Oregon territory. Among these was a young Virginian of New England antecedents, named Samuel Hancock. Hancock set out across the plains from Independence, Missouri, in a train of two hundred wagons, headed up the Platte to South Pass, and then on to the Oregon territory, which, Hancock wrote, "seemed to our adventurous citizens, to possess the inducements, necessary for them to go, and undertake the settlement, and there build up new homes, and if possible new everything. . . ." Hancock's party encountered all the classic hazards of the passage—rainstorms, floods, hostile Indians, cholera, hunger and thirst, exhausted stock, and internal dissension. At one point the presence of Indians caused first a mule and then a line of teams to stampede

> and the whole train of forty wagons dashed across the plains, the drivers having no control over the frantic animals, and the women and children who were inmates of the wagons, screaming with all their voices . . . and it was some time before we could again exert any control over our teams and stop them; when we finally did it was ascertained that we had sustained considerable injury, some of our wagons lying on one side and teams detached from them in some instances, others with wheels broken, and the contents

strewn promiscuously round, while some of our company were lying about with broken legs, and others seriously injured, the whole scene presenting a most disastrous appearance.

The Crow warriors, the cause of the stampede, were interested observers.

Beyond Fort Laramie, Hancock observed Indians and mixed-bloods trapping crickets, filling baskets with them, drying them in a stone kiln, and then grinding them up in a kind of meal "which seemed to be regarded as a staple and delicate article of food among them, which they eat heartily and grow fat."

Dust was a terrible plague. Hancock found it "scarcely endurable." It hung like a great choking cloud over the train, coating the faces and clothes of the emigrants and advertising the movements of the train for many miles. Everywhere they were accompanied by the Indians.

Crossing the Cascade Mountains, Hancock's party reached the Willamette Valley. "Each of us," he wrote, "felt that he had accomplished a great undertaking and been exceedingly fortunate in surviving all the perils and exposure to which we had been subjected on our long journey. . . . Everyone too seemed pleased with the country, presenting all the requisites of a rich and productive soil; money is rather scarce," Hancock added, "but with strong hands and stout hearts, what may we not accomplish." Meanwhile the emigrants were near to starvation and were forced to hire out to traders of the Hudson's Bay Company, splitting shingles for whatever wage they would pay. At Oregon City some settlers who had arrived the year before shared their wheat with the new arrivals so they managed to survive. For every family able to avail themselves of it the government of the territory offered a parcel of land a mile square in the two-hundred-mile-long valley that "being abundantly timbered and watered . . . all were soon comfortably settled, the land producing all necessary vegetables, while venison could be procured easily and in abundance, and those who had cattle were constantly increasing their stock."

But Hancock, without family responsibilities, was too restless to stay put long. He found an equally daring companion and they set out to explore the surrounding country, encountering Indians everywhere and moving as stealthily as the Indians themselves. Here and there they found settlements of a few cabins, and at one a Methodist mission. All along there were beautiful clearings with deep rich soil and giant fir trees that took "two looks to enable one to see to the tops." At the Methodist mission they met the Reverend Mr. Campbell, "a very gentlemanly person, who had been at this place . . . for four years, preaching and doing all the good in his power to the benighted savages." They remained for a service, although to Hancock's eyes the congregation seemed "a rather hard set of Christians, coming to church without any very great regard to their appearance other than being painted in a way doubtless very satisfactory to themselves, but to us they looked perfectly hideous. Some of them were entirely without clothing. . . . What a contrast between the positions of this poor divine and the pampered ministers of the fashionable churches of our Atlantic cities." The minister gave a sermon in the tribe's native tongue. "When he commenced singing, he was joined by the entire assembly old and young, then they all kneeled and offered a prayer. . . . Indeed such was the devotion which prevailed that it imparted a solemnity to the occasion which quite astonished me besides hearing them sing familiarly the old Methodist hymns we used to hear at home."

Back in the Willamette Valley Hancock found the beginnings of a village started by "a Mr. [Francis] Pettygrove," who had laid off part of his land at the confluence of the Willamette and the Columbia rivers for a town to be named Portland. As Hancock noted, by 1847, "there were built at Portland, twelve or fifteen houses, mostly of logs, which were occupied by the people variously engaged in and about the town."

In the absence of money, settlers sold their produce to storekeepers in Oregon City and Portland for "orders payable in goods" and these circulated like currency. During the summer a trading ship arrived from the Sandwich Islands and one "from the Atlantic coast of our own country around Cape Horn, with an assorted cargo of merchandise. . . ."

The following year the settlers combined their efforts to build a sawmill on the Tumwater, a nearby stream, which provided them with lumber both for their own houses and for trading to the vessels that found their way each year in increasing numbers up the Columbia River. Into this classic scene of pioneer enterprise came the horrifying news of the massacre of Marcus and Narcissa Whitman by the Cayuse Indians. Fear of a general massacre swept through Portland and the adjacent settlements, and Hancock joined those men who volunteered to chastise the Cayuse. In Hancock's words, "they went forth to avenge the wrongs perpetuated by these Indians with all the cheerfulness of a people sanguine of best results from a full consciousness of doing right."

While Hancock was making a living in the goldfields and even putting a little by, word reached him that the Oregon settlements were enjoying great prosperity because of the demand for lumber created by the gold rush in California. Hancock decided on Puget Sound as his headquarters, and the lumber business as his next venture. He sailed to San Francisco with a load of lumber, laid in a supply of merchandise, and returned to Puget Sound "with my goods, built a house and soon disposed of my supply." In San Francisco he had heard much talk of coal as the coming fuel, so he determined to go on an exploring expedition up the Columbia River looking for coal. He bought a canoe, hired seven Indians to paddle it, and started up the river. Everywhere he encountered curious and sometimes hostile Indians and constantly had to be on guard against surprise attacks. Hancock helped to negotiate a peace between the Snoqualmies and the Snohomishes, but found no coal.

Back in Puget Sound, Hancock decided to put all his remaining merchandise on board a ship bound for the Strait of Juan de Fuca, running between Vancouver Island and Cape Flattery, and establishing a trading post on the northwestern-most point of the Oregon Territory, Neah Bay. There Hancock and a friend built a house "that would answer for a trading establishment," and here he was soon visited by "large numbers of the most primitive looking creatures imaginable; some with furs covering parts of their bodies, others entirely without and some with blankets manufactured by themselves from the hair of dogs." These were members of a lesser Athapaskan tribe, and Hancock's hopes of setting up as a prosperous trader were dashed when the Indians informed him that they wished him to leave at once. When he demurred, saying, quite rightly, that he had no way to depart, he was visited by two hundred heavily armed warriors who ordered him to go. Hancock saved his hide by sitting before the chiefs and appearing to write a letter that, he informed them, would be sent to the Great Chief, the President of the United States, telling him of the treatment he had received at the hands of the Indians. This at once reduced the Indians to supplicants, pleading with him not to write the letter, offering him twenty baskets of potatoes, and promising not to molest him further. With this assurance, Hancock bought a canoe and enlisted three Makah Indians to paddle him up the strait to Port Townsend. Once again he resumed his search for coal and found a "fine looking vein" up the Snohomish River, where he was befriended by the chief of the Snohomish tribe. Back at the site of a town to be called Olympia, he sold a half-interest in the mine and started back with his partner to explore the region more thoroughly and establish their claim. They passed Snoqualmie, Duwamish, Puyallup, and Nisqually villages. At Olympia, some weeks later, Hancock took passage on a ship bound for San Francisco, hoping to get back to his trading post at Neah. But the ship's captain was an inept navigator, so that when Hancock and several others of the ship's company pushed off in a longboat to try to find the entrance to Neah Bay they found themselves hopelessly lost and surrounded by curious Indians. For days they blundered about trying to catch sight of their ship or locate Neah Bay. Each day brought some potentially danger-ous contact with one tribe of Indians or another and all Hancock's resourcefulness and, by this time, shrewd understanding of Indian psychology were required simply to preserve their lives. Again the situation was full of irony. On several occasions Indians saved them from starving and showed great kindness to the white men. In other situations the whites barely escaped being murdered. Finally they encountered a canoe manned by English-speaking Indians who told them they were only four days paddling away from Vancouver Island and the town of Victoria, where they met the ship and the captain who had abandoned them.

Convinced that he would have nothing but trouble with the Indians at Neah Bay, Hancock decided to relocate his trading post, with a sawmill added, at Clallam Bay, a hundred miles farther up the Juan de Fuca Strait. But the carpenters and millwright struck for higher pay and Hancock, unwilling to meet their demands, refused to pay, and abandoned the project, turning his attention instead to the now flourishing settlement at Olympia. There he became a lumber contractor, buying lumber, shipping it to San Francisco, and bringing back merchandise needed in the town. It was a "lucrative occupation" but Hancock, always restless, was "determined to make another effort to locate at the lower end of the Sound." In the fall of 1852, he was back at Neah Bay with two men he had hired to build a house and trading post. This time the Indians appeared "greatly pleased" at the prospect of having a handy source of trading goods where they could bring their furs, oil, and salmon in exchange for cloth, beads, rings, ammunition, and a hundred other desirable items. "My coming," Hancock wrote, "seemed to have imparted new life to them; and stimulated them to habits of industry. . . ." They were skilled whalers and now, with an outlet for their whale oil, they repaired their canoes, sharpened their harpoons, and gave an attentive Hancock a striking demonstration of their prowess in whaling.

But the Indians resented the more and more frequent visits of trading vessels to the bay. Sailors going ashore sold whiskey to the Indians, cheated them, and debauched their women. Hancock became aware of a growing atmosphere of hostility toward him on the part of the natives. "On several occasions," Hancock noted, "nearly all the Indians . . . have been drunk fighting and brandishing their knives and threatening to kill me and my two men." Such demonstrations prompted Hancock to build a fort. A ship was anchored in the harbor and Hancock warned its captain that he should not permit Indians aboard his ship since they were in a warlike mood and might attempt to seize the vessel. Hancock then called a number of the most prominent Indians together and admonished them to conduct themselves in a manner more friendly to the whites, employing those classic elements of Indian diplomacy, threats, and promises. Shortly afterwards, an old Indian chief told Hancock a story that helped to explain the attitude of the Indians in the area. Some years before, a ship had anchored in the bay to trade and after several weeks of amicable trading, natives had killed the captain and most of the crew and seized the ship, whereupon a wounded sailor had set the powder magazine afire and blown it up.

In the spring, Hancock happened to overhear two Indians, who had come in a party of forty canoes to trade, talking about plans to seize the fort and post, kill the whites, and divide up their possessions. Once again Hancock made preparations to rebuff any attack and the Indians, seeing that their plans were discovered, paddled off. A few weeks later a ship from San Francisco put into the bay; aboard were two natives of the region who had the smallpox. The two went ashore and spread the disease, with disastrous consequences. "After resorting to every means in their power to arrest its progress and fatality in vain . . . those who had escaped became almost frantic with grief and fear, and conceived the idea of crossing the Strait and going to the Nitanat tribe living on Vancouver's Island. They of course carried the disease with them. . . ."

> It was truly shocking to witness the ravages of this disease here at Neah Bay. The natives after a time became so much alarmed that when any of their friends were attacked, all of the other occupants who lived in the house would at once leave it and the sick person with a piece of dried salmon and some water . . . not intending to ever approach them again; sometimes the retreating ones would lie down anywhere on the beach till they died. I have, in walking along, encountered them lying in this situation where they would beg in the most supplicating manner for medicine or something to relieve them. . . . In a few weeks from the introduction of the disease, hundreds of the natives became victims to it, the beach

for the distance of eight miles was literally strewn with the dead
bodies of these people, presenting a most disgusting spectacle.

The Indians believed that Hancock could help them and many,
as soon as they felt the onset of smallpox, came to his house and
lay down in the yard. "They continued this until the dead were so
numerous I could scarcely walk about around my house, and was
obliged to have holes dug where I deposited fifteen or twenty bodies
in each." Still they died. Some bodies were dragged to the beach to
be carried away by the tide and the dogs "became fat on the bodies
of their deceased masters."

The survivors blamed Hancock; when he managed to persuade
them that he was innocent, they turned on one of the Indians from
the schooner who had brought the disease ashore, placed him in a
canoe, and set him adrift in the Strait without food or a paddle to
die of hunger and exposure.

Soon afterwards, Hancock set out in the *Eagle* to trade with
the Indians on Vancouver Island. The first were the Nitinats. After
collecting their oil and salmon, the ship continued along the coast
to the region of the Quachiniwhit tribe, north of Nootka Sound.
These Indians, virtually naked otherwise, wore broad-brimmed
waterproof hats of finely woven roots. While the trading was going
on a storm came up and drove the *Eagle* onto the rocks. The ship
began to break up under the pounding of the waves, a sight that
prompted the Indians, gathered to observe the scene, to "loud and
wild" laughter. Hancock and the crew struggled to salvage some of
the cargo, loading blankets into the ship's longboat and prevailing
on the Indians to bring off some supplies in their canoes. As quickly
as the Indians secured the blankets, they began tearing them into
strips and distributing them around. Hancock stopped this sport
by giving a number of blankets to the Indians to make "a favorable
impression." As soon as the captain and the crew had abandoned
the ship, it was surrounded by hundreds of Indians who swarmed
over it stripping it of everything movable. There were now ten persons, eight whites and two Indians from the Neah Bay, marooned

among the Quachiniwhit Indians. The Quachiniwhits had no intention of letting them escape. Hancock distracted those who had been left to keep watch on them, while the looting of the ship went on, by scattering irresistible beads around in the underbrush. While their guards searched for the tiny glittering objects, the crew of the *Eagle* slipped away, four in a canoe and six in the longboat, paddling for their lives. Several days later, working their way down the coast toward the British post at Nootka Sound, the entire party was captured by another tribe of Indians who clearly planned to murder them. Hancock, noticing the large cedar boards that braced the chief's lodge, promised, if the chief would provide them with a canoe and some Indian paddlers, to come back with a ship full of trading goods in exchange for a number of such boards. The chief agreed but the men of the tribe refused to be party to the bargain. The chief therefore started out himself, the canoe paddled by his slaves, Indians of other tribes captured in war. But he, too, got cold feet and turned back.

In the midst of this dilemma, friendly Clayoquot Indians from the Nootka Bay region intervened to rescue the party. At Nootka Bay, Hancock found a ship headed for Olympia and took passage to get down to Neah Bay where he "found everything in good condition." The man he had left minding the store had been very successful in trading with the natives for oil, and Hancock's post was piled with barrels. But once more the Indians, still believing Hancock responsible for the terrible smallpox epidemic, became surly and threatening, insisting that he must leave the bay. So, trading for three large canoes, Hancock bound them together with cedar timbers, laid a platform across them on which he placed his supplies, and started for Whidbey Island, a hundred miles up the strait. By considerable effort and impressive seamanship, he reached his new haven, where, he wrote, "arriving in due time without any extraordinary adventures and completing them here in a short time with the *adventure of matrimony*, I then settled on a farm on this island, leading the quiet life of a farmer."

CHAPTER XVI

THE
SAND CREEK
MASSACRE

The Mexican War, the annexation of Texas, and the acquisition, under the terms of the Treaty of Guadalupe Hidalgo in 1848, of present-day Arizona and New Mexico had presented the federal government with vastly enlarged Indian problems by adding to its jurisdiction the tribes of the Southwest, the Apache and Comanche among them. While the federal government had from the first accepted the principle that the Indians had rights in the lands that they occupied, the states had been equally insistent that the Indians within their borders were subject to *their* jurisdiction. It was this controversy that had led to the Indian Removal. The Southern states had rejected the argument of John Quincy Adams and the Supreme Court that Indians were wards of the national government. Texans likewise rejected the argument. The first Texas legislature had declared in 1846: "We recognize no title in the Indian tribes resident within the limits of the state to any portion of the soil thereof; and . . . we recognize no right of the Government of the

United States to make any treaty with the said Indian tribes without the consent of the Government of this state."

A number of the tribes, the Apache most prominently, had long been accustomed to raiding Mexican villages with impunity and saw no reason to desist simply because Americans had replaced Mexicans as intruders. But when federal commissioners concluded a treaty with the eleven principal tribes in Texas, promising trading posts, presents, and protection, Texans in Congress were furious. Congress backed away from the issue, and the tribes found themselves, as so many others had, caught between the claims of the federal government and those of the state. In the words of one Comanche chief: "For a long time a great many people have been passing through my country; they kill all the game, and burn the country, and trouble me very much. The commissioners of our Great Father promised to keep these people out of our country. I believe our white brothers do not wish to run a line between us, because they wish to settle in this country. I object to any more settlements."

State authorities were indifferent to pleas or warnings. Indian lands were freely granted to speculators. Four surveyors were killed on land claimed by the Comanche, and a familiar pattern of white intrusion and Indian response emerged. As the danger of open warfare increased, the Texas governor at last drew a line beyond which he forbade white settlers to encroach. The order was largely ignored. The Texas Emigration and Land Company, made up of some of the most powerful men in the state, began to recruit its own army to fight the Indians. When Texas Rangers, seeking retribution for the murder of a white settler, massacred twenty-five Wichita who apparently had nothing to do with the murder, war was inevitable. Wichita, Waco, and Comanche went on the warpath, destroying crops, burning buildings, and driving off horses. The Texas legislature, under strong pressure from the federal government, agreed to sell land to the United States to be used for Indian reservations. Needless to say, the Indians were not consulted. But even on reservations the Indians were not safe from the hostility of the whites. Texans invaded the reservations and hunted down Indians like deer or bear for the sport. Finally the federal government undertook to move the tribes out of Texas entirely.

With the acquisition of New Mexico, General Stephen Kearny assured the Mexicans who had been preyed on for years by bands of Apache, Comanche, and Navajo that the United States would protect them. As soon as Kearny left for California, however, the Indian raids resumed. When the news reached Kearny, he directed Colonel Alexander Doniphan to organize the Mexicans and the Pueblo Indians, also the victims of frequent raids, into "war parties, to march into the country of their enemies, the Navajos, to recover their property, to make reprisals." A series of forts was built to check Indian raids, and confine the more warlike tribes to vaguely defined reservations, where Indian agents were assigned to help them adapt to settled agricultural life.

If some tribes—especially those whose original habitat was in the Old Northwest, in the Ohio country, and the region of the Great Lakes—were prevailed upon by various blandishments, typically in the form of presents and subsidies, to try the novel experiment of a settled, primarily agricultural life, they were almost invariably the victims of raids by nomadic tribes that scorned them for adapting the white man's ways. The Missouri, Potawatomi, Ottawa, Winnebago, Delaware, and some remnants of Black Hawk's Sac and Fox were among the tribes that turned to the federal government for protection. Certainly their condition did little to encourage the less tractable Indians to accept domestication. Filthy and squalid, they suffered from a variety of white men's diseases and vices.

The plight of the Pawnee was particularly awkward. North of the Platte they were subject to constant harassment from the Sioux, who viewed them as encroaching on their own territory. When they withdrew south of the Platte, their young braves could not be restrained from preying on the emigrant wagons trains moving west and being, in turn, hunted down by U.S. cavalry.

By 1850 the notion had emerged of clearly defined reservations, where Indians could be both protected from white incursions and restrained from harassing emigrants or raiding the "civilized" tribes.

Related to the reservation plan was the agitation for a transcontinental railroad, which must, of necessity, run through land claimed by various Indian tribes. If these Indians could be persuaded to take up residence on clearly defined reservations, conflict might be avoided. The commissioner of Indian affairs, Orlando Brown, urged that reservations be established for each tribe in areas "adapted to agriculture, of limited extent and well-defined boundaries; within which all with occasional exceptions should be compelled constantly to remain until such time as their general improvement and good conduct may supersede the necessity of such restrictions." The government should give the tribes "agricultural implements, and useful materials for clothing; encourage and assist them in the erection of comfortable dwellings and secure to them the means and facilities of education, intellectual, moral and religious."

Brown's proposals indicated that there had been no essential change in American attitudes toward the "Indian problem" since the days of Thomas Jefferson. Men were rational creatures; Indians were men—therefore, Indians were rational beings. It thus followed that when given education, "intellectual, moral and religious," they would become indistinguishable from white Americans and soon assimilated into the general population. But generation after generation the American aborigines showed a stubborn determination to remain unequivocally Indian.

The Plains Indians presented a special problem. One writer has divided the tribes in the decade of the 1850s into "wild, undecided, and subdued" Indians. The wild Indians resisted every effort to prevail on them to limit their depredations or confine their hunting ranges. The "undecideds" sometimes remained aloof and sometimes, if sufficiently angered by the actions of whites, whether of the army, the Indian Bureau, or aggressive civilians, threw in their lot with the unregenerate. The "subdued," having decided that caution was the better part of valor or having had their spirits broken by a series of disastrous encounters with whites, did what they were instructed to do and avoided any actions that might bring further suffering and destruction upon them. Part of the difficulty was that there was no surefire way to distinguish between "wild" and "undecided." They dressed the same, looked the same, and often belonged to the same tribe.

The first great council called by the government to try to stabilize the situation of the Plains Indians was charged with responsibility for negotiating a treaty or series of treaties with the tribes through whose territory emigrant trains headed for the Pacific coast. The direction of the council was in the hands of the famous trapper and mountain man Thomas Fitzpatrick, onetime partner of Jedediah Smith. Known as Broken Hand to the Indians because of a crippled hand, Fitzpatrick had written one of the best-known guides for the wagon trains that wound their way across the prairie and through mountain passes he knew so well. Since 1846 he had been Indian agent for the tribes in the region of the Platte and the Arkansas. He called on all the major Plains tribes to meet on September 1, 1851, at Fort Laramie, in the Wyoming Territory. Weeks before the meeting, the tribes began to assemble—the Oglala, Teton, and Brulé bands of the Sioux; the Arapaho and the Cheyenne. When the Shoshone, traditional enemies of the Sioux, arrived, a fight almost broke out between the two tribes. Day after day tribes or portions of tribes arrived—Assiniboine, Crow, Arikara, Pawnee—until a city of tepees covered the plain around the fort. It was the greatest gathering of tribes in the history of the West, numbering by various estimates between eight and twelve thousand with as many ponies. While they waited for gifts to arrive from the federal government, the tribes entertained themselves with games and contests. Finally, the parley began in a large tent where the brilliantly caparisoned chiefs gathered each day for twenty days. In the parley the superintendent of Indian affairs, David Mitchell, insisted that the tribes must not attack or harass travelers on the Oregon Trail. To do so would mean war with the United States. Moreover they must give the government the right to establish forts for the maintenance of the trail and as places where emigrants could get supplies and assistance in case of need. Most important of all, the tribes must cease their constant warfare among themselves; as long as the repeated raids and counter raids continued the whites had great difficulty avoiding involvement. Finally, to ensure peace, the tribes must accept boundaries that would define their hunting ranges. In return the government would provide each of the tribes with the equivalent of $50,000 a year in supplies, much-needed food for the winter months, farm animals, and tools; the latter items representing the perpetually renewed hope that the Indians could, in time, be prevailed upon to take up a more settled agricultural life. When the great council broke up at the end of September and the bands of Indians drifted away, it was hoped, to their assigned ranges, the feeling that the stormy relations between whites and Indians in the Great Plains had been fairly resolved and an era of peace lay ahead lingered in the air like the smoke of their campfires.

Fitzpatrick moved on to Fort Atkinson on the Arkansas River to meet with the Comanche and Kiowa and conclude a treaty with them. The message was substantially the same. Forts, they were told, would be built to protect them from incursions by marauding whites. In turn, they must allow passage over the Santa Fe Trail and, most difficult of all, refrain from raids into Mexico. One of the purposes of the Fort Atkinson council failed. The Kiowa and Comanche had captured a number of children, the majority of them Mexican, in raids on isolated farms and ranches, raids in which, generally, the children's parents had been killed. Fitzpatrick had been instructed to secure the return of such captives, but on this point the Indians were adamant. More important, the captives themselves refused to leave the families that had adopted them. Many of the males had become warriors, and the females had grown up to become the wives of Comanche or Kiowa braves.

In 1853 at a conference at Fort Benton, Isaac Stevens, the governor of Washington Territory, met the Blackfoot and their allied tribes and declared: "Your Great Father . . . wishes you to live at peace with each other and the whites. He desires that you should be under his protection, and partake equally with the Crows and the Assiniboines of his bounty. Live in peace with all the neighboring Indians, protect all the whites passing through your country, and the Great Father will be your best friend."

Chief Low Horn of the Piegan replied that the problem was restraining their young men who "were wild and ambitious in their turn to be braves and chiefs. They wanted by some brave act to win the favor of their young women and bring scalps and horses to show their prowess." The governor professed to believe that the Blackfoot Indians could be prevailed upon to abandon their nomadic ways and adopt the life of peaceful farmers. To ask them (or any other of the hunting tribes for that matter) to do so was to ask them to abandon the very essence of their existence. The whites, of course, saw nothing degrading in being a farmer; most of them were farmers themselves. It was a matter, once again, of an inadequate anthropology. In return for giving up their way of life, the "vital root" of their existence, the Indians were to receive the classic benefits—presents—at the conclusion of the treaty, yearly subsidies to the extent of $20,000 a year among the four tribes, and $15,000 to carry on the work of Christianization.

With the conclusion of the Blackfoot treaty, the Indian problem appeared "solved." All the tribes had been assigned, if not precisely to reservations, at least to areas marked by definite features of the terrain—most commonly rivers and mountain ranges.

In 1854 the Eastern Indians who had been removed to the Indian Territory about twenty-five years earlier with the assurance that they could remain there until the end of time were told that they must move again; their lands were wanted by the white man. By that time it was already clear that the treaties so hopefully concluded three years earlier had begun to break down. When Thomas Fitzpatrick traveled through the region under his superintendence, he found the condition of the Indians had deteriorated. He wrote,

> They are in abject want of food half the year. The travel upon the
> road [the Oregon Trail] drives the buffalo off or else confines
> them to a narrow path during the period of migration, and the
> different tribes are forced to contend with hostile nations in

seeking support for their villages. The women are pinched with want and their children are constantly crying with hunger. . . . Already, under the pressure of such hardships, they are beginning to gather around a few licensed hunters . . . acting as herdsmen, runners, and interpreters, living on their bounty; while others accept most immoral methods with their families to eke out an existence.

Within the year Fitzpatrick, a great figure in the early history of the West, was dead, and the Indians were deprived of the services of one of their most sympathetic advocates.

A few months later a hungry Brulé Sioux, coming on a lame cow near Fort Laramie, killed and ate it with some fellow braves. The owner, an indignant Mormon, demanded that the Sioux brave be punished. A Sioux chief, Conquering Bear, offered to pay $10 for the cow and, when the emigrant demanded more, angrily broke off the discussion and returned to his lodge. When the lieutenant in charge of the fort was appealed to by the Mormon, he mustered up a party of thirty soldiers and two cannons, made his way to the Sioux camp, emplaced his artillery, and threatened to blow up the camp unless the cow was paid for or the brave who had killed her was surrendered to him. When Conquering Bear expostulated, the lieutenant ordered his men to open fire. Three Indians were killed, and Conquering Bear was fatally wounded. The Sioux then annihilated the soldiers.

The matter did not end there. The generally accepted principle of the army in dealing with Indians of whatever tribe was that the killing of United States soldiers could not go unpunished whatever the provocation. Colonel William Harney, therefore, set out as soon as the weather permitted with 1,300 troopers to chastise the Sioux. He soon came on a camp of Sioux who had had nothing to do with the Fort Laramie episode. Harney opened fire with his artillery, and before the fighting was over, eighty-six Sioux, many of them women and children, had been killed.

* * *

IT WOULD HAVE BEEN ODD indeed if, in an age dedicated to reform, the American aborigine had not had many devoted advocates. The Black Hawk War had called forth a substantial body of pro-Indian sentiments, as, indeed, had the infamous Indian Removal. One of the earliest and most effective advocates of the Indian cause was John Beeson, whose indignation at the treatment of the Nez Percé in Oregon aroused the ire of his neighbors to such a degree that he was shot at and his house burned down. Beeson toured the Eastern cities in the late 1850s, speaking in Faneuil Hall in Boston, among other places, and helping found the national Indian Aid Association.

Henry Benjamin Whipple, the Episcopal bishop of the diocese of Minnesota, was a coadjutor of Beeson's. He made the condition of the Chippewa and Minnesota Sioux his special concern. Two years before the bloody Sioux uprising in Minnesota he had warned President James Buchanan that, unless there was a reform of the Indian Bureau and its agency, there would be an explosion of Indian wrath; "a nation which sowed robbery would reap a harvest of blood." When, in the aftermath of the uprising in which more than a hundred white settlers were killed, Whipple, whose Indian name was Straight Tongue, drew up a proposal to reform Indian policy, he collected the signatures of thirty-eight Episcopal bishops (pretty much the whole lot) and a number of prominent citizens and went to Washington to plead with Lincoln to commute the sentences of those Indians who had been captured and sentenced to be hanged. Lincoln was horrified at Whipple's account of "the rascality of this Indian business. . . . If we get through this war, and I live," he told an aide, "this Indian system shall be reformed . . ."

Beeson also secured an audience with Lincoln to press the cause of the Sioux, and the President told him to "rest assured that as soon as the pressing matters of this war are settled the Indians shall have my first care and I will not rest until Justice is done to their and to your Satisfaction."

Beeson, a farmer of only modest literacy, made a striking contrast with the articulate, college-educated Whipple. The bishop's office gave him financial independence and enabled him to tap philanthropic funds to carry on his mission, while Beeson lived a hand-to-mouth existence, retiring to his Oregon farm when he had exhausted his funds.

With the outbreak of the Civil War, the Confederacy asserted its authority over the Indian Territory—the region, including much of present-day Oklahoma, to which the Five Civilized Nations had just been driven not many years before. The Seneca and the Shawnee were recruited for the Confederate army along with many warriors from the Civilized Nations. The North Carolina Volunteers counted in their ranks 850 Cherokee Indians, and Georgia enlisted 1,000 more. Many more Indians could be recruited, Emma Holmes, the Charleston diarist noted, if the Confederate generals would consent to a policy of no quarter asked or given. The principal obstacle to the use of Indians was that they could not be restrained from killing Union soldiers taken prisoner or wounded.

The forays by Federal and Confederate forces into the Indian Territory, the confused fighting, and the acts of retribution directed against Indians who had cast their lot with the Union or the Confederacy make too involved a story to retrace here. It is enough to say that, whichever side they adhered to (and some changed their allegiance with changes in the fortunes of the war), events worked as always to the eventual disadvantage of the Indians.

When the Minnesota Sioux, incited by Confederate agents and angry at the violation of treaty agreements, broke out in a rampage of killing, Lincoln was subjected to strong pressure to remove the inoffensive Winnebago and Chippewa as well as the Sioux. Gideon Welles, secretary of the navy, noted in his diary: "The members of Congress from Minnesota are urging the President vehemently to give his assent to the execution of three hundred Indians captured, but they will not succeed . . . it would seem the sentiments of the Representatives were but slightly removed from the barbarians whom they would execute. The Minnesotans are greatly exasperated and threaten the administration if it shows clemency." When the report on the Minnesota "Indian Wars" was received by the Cabinet, Welles wrote: "It shows that the Indian War was not war at all; that our people, not the Indians, were in fault. . . . After aggression on the part of the whites, the Indians killed a number, and our army succeeded in killing six Indians. This war will cost the country scarcely less than fifty millions."

Conflict with the Cheyenne in the Colorado Territory increased as miners encroached on Indian hunting ranges. John Chivington, a circuit-riding Methodist minister of mammoth proportions, who had dedicated his life to the Free Soil cause and had defied the efforts of the pro-slavery men in Missouri to drive him from the pulpit, had moved on to Denver. At the outbreak of hostilities Chivington had volunteered to serve in a Union force being organized by the governor of the territory. The governor offered to make him a chaplain, but Chivington reportedly replied, "I feel compelled to strike a blow in person for the destruction of human slavery and to help in some measure to make this a truly free country." He was commissioned a major and began whipping the raw recruits of the First Colorado Regiment of Volunteers into some semblance of military order. When outnumbered Union forces in New Mexico appealed to the governor of Colorado for help, he dispatched Chivington. Joining forces with Colonel John Slough, a lawyer from Denver, after a three-hundred-mile forced march, Chivington came upon a Confederate supply train of eighty-five wagons loaded with ammunition and supplies intended to support an invasion of California.

In a battle at Apache Canyon near Santa Fe, his men destroyed the train, killing five hundred horses and mules in the process. It was undoubtedly the most decisive single engagement of the war in the Rocky Mountain region and may well have saved both Colorado and California for the Union. With the Southern invaders forced to retreat to Texas, Chivington's main responsibility became the protection of the settlers of the area from the raids of the Cheyenne and the Arapaho, who operated between the Platte and the Arkansas, and to preserve peace between those tribes and the Ute and Pawnee. Disturbed by the influx of settlers, the Arapaho chief Little Raven went to Denver with some of his principal braves to urge authorities there to impose restrictions on the settlement of whites on Arapaho land. In a spirit of mutual forbearance promises were made on both sides to practice restraint.

Despite the efforts of the famous trapper and "squaw man," Jim Beckwourth, and whites friendly to the Indians, the Arapahos and Cheyenne had been prevailed upon to sign a treaty—the Treaty of Fort Wise—much like those signed earlier by the Sioux and their associated tribes, a treaty that in effect surrendered their rights to large portions of their hunting lands in return for subsidies and assistance in adopting a farming rather than a nomadic life. But the Cheyenne had continued to raid the Ute and threaten the settlers. Returning from a war party against the Ute, they flourished fresh scalps in a white settlement and frightened the whites half out of their wits with their war whoops and wild yells.

Arapaho, debauched by the white man's whiskey, stole horses and supplies and raided white ranches. An officer sent to try to find and arrest the culprits reported: "The Indians talk very bitterly about the whites—say they have stolen their ponies and abused their women, taken their hunting grounds, and they expected that they would have to fight for their rights." More cattle stealing followed; a party of soldiers, sent to retrieve the cattle, killed three Indians. Public feeling in Denver was further exacerbated when the mutilated bodies of a rancher, his wife, and their children were brought into the town. Supply trains, hearing rumors of an Indian war, refused to venture on the trail, and Denver and nearby mining towns found themselves short of supplies. The governor of the territory, hoping to avert open hostilities, ordered the various tribes to go to the nearest fort to receive food and protection from soldiers on the hunt for hostiles, but when the Kiowa chief Satanta rode up Fort Larned, he was refused admission. The enraged chief wounded a soldier, and he and his warriors drove off all the fort's horses. A number of Cheyenne and Arapaho were treated in a similarly cavalier fashion by the army. The infuriated Indians were soon on the warpath. Remote ranches were burned, their occupants tortured and killed. In a period of a few weeks more than two hundred settlers and emigrants lost their lives. One woman who was later rescued declared, "An old chief . . . forced me, by the most terrible threats and menaces, to yield my person to him." Other chiefs then raped her in turn. Some whites, like William Bent, who understood the provocations suffered by the Indians, tried to arrange a peace council, but Chivington's superior had telegraphed him: "I shall require the bad Indians delivered up; restoration of stock; also hostages to secure. I want no peace until the Indians suffer more. . . . I fear the Agent of the Indian Department will be ready to make presents too soon. . . . No peace must be made without my direction."

Governor John Evans of Colorado was more conciliatory. Black Kettle, the Cheyenne chief, took his grievances to Evans at a council. The governor reminded him that he had earlier refused to parley and had sent word that he wanted nothing to do with Evans or the Great White Father in Washington, the United States government. A state of war existed, Evans declared, and matters were out of the hands of the military. General Patrick Connor, who had won his laurels as an Indian fighter against the Bannock and Shoshone, was dispatched in pursuit of the Sioux and Cheyenne. His orders to his troops declared: "You will not receive overtures of peace or submission from Indians, but will attack and kill every male Indian over twelve years of age."

Under the threat of punishment, one of the Arapaho bands returned some of the plunder from its raids. Meanwhile, Major Edward Wynkoop at Fort Lyon had negotiated an exchange of prisoners with the Cheyenne chief Black Kettle. Chivington immediately replaced Wynkoop with Scott Anthony, who soon was confronted with the problem of 650 Arapaho under Left Hand, who had come to Fort Lyon for gifts and protection. Unable to feed them and uneasy over rumors that they intended to attack the fort, Anthony sent them off. To a request for peace from Black Kettle and his Cheyenne, Anthony replied that he had no authority to negotiate peace but that they could camp at Sand Creek, forty miles away. The Cheyenne, some seven hundred men, women, and children, established a village at Sand Creek.

Meanwhile, Chivington received a message from the army commander in the state, General Martin Curtis, ordering him "to pursue everywhere and chastise the Cheyennes and Arapahos."

In the late fall of 1864 Chivington, as the head of the Third Colorado and six companies of the First plus four twelve-pound howitzers, began a forced march through snow and bitter cold to Fort Lyon. There Anthony told him that the Cheyenne were camped at Sand Creek, and Chivington and his troopers pushed on, traveling all night and guided unwillingly by Robert Bent, son of William Bent—the first white settler in Colorado—and a Cheyenne woman. Robert Bent believed that the planned attack on the Cheyenne village where the chiefs were awaiting word of further negotiations was a classic example of white treachery. Chivington suspected that Bent was deliberately leading the cavalry astray; he tapped his revolver suggestively and told Bent, "I haven't had an Indian to eat for a long time. If you fool with me and don't lead me to that camp, I'll have you for breakfast."

At daybreak the soldiers found themselves within a mile of the Cheyenne camp. When it was evident that Chivington planned to attack the sleeping Indians, Lieutenant Joseph Cramer, who had served under Wynkoop, protested that the Indians were peaceful, that they felt confident that Wynkoop's word protected them, and that an attack would be an unjustifiable breach of faith. Chivington reportedly replied: "The Cheyenne nation has been waging bloody war against the whites all spring, summer, and fall, and Black Kettle is their principal chief. They have been guilty of robbery, arson, murder, rape, and fiendish torture, not even children. Damn any man who is in sympathy with them." Chivington was later accused of having declared: "Kill and scalp all, big and little; nits make lice." He denied having made such a statement, but two of his officers testified that he did say, "No, boys, I shan't say who you shall kill, but remember who murdered our women and children."

Thereupon Chivington's men fell upon the unsuspecting Cheyenne. A hastily formed line of Cheyenne warriors met the attack and turned it back. White Antelope, an old chief, refused to take refuge along the riverbanks. He folded his arms and began the Cheyenne death song: "Nothing lives long except the earth and the mountains." Soon he was dead by a soldier's bullet. Major Scott Anthony wrote later: "I never saw more bravery displayed by any set of people on the face of the earth than by these Indians. They would charge on the whole company singly, determined to kill someone before being killed themselves." The fighting continued throughout the day. Some women and children escaped, but the warriors suffered heavy casualties. By four in the afternoon the Colorado volunteers were in complete command. The Indians who had not escaped had been killed, among them a number of women and children. Twenty-five soldiers had been killed or wounded.

Back in Denver, Chivington and his men were acclaimed as heroes. The *Denver News* declared: "Colorado soldiers have again covered themselves with glory." Some of the volunteers were introduced between the acts of a play at a Denver theater and exhibited Indian scalps to loud applause.

Soon ugly stories began to leak out of Indians killed in cold blood. Equally troubling was the circulated story that the Cheyenne and Arapaho had been attacked when they were confident that they were at peace with the whites and indeed under the nominal protection of Fort Lyon. In rebuttal to the argument that the Indians were entirely peaceful, some weight should be given to testimony that fresh scalps of whites were found in some of the Indian lodges by Chivington's soldiers.

Two congressional investigations produced a mass of conflicting testimony. There was no agreement even on the number of Indians killed. Estimates ranged from sixty-nine to "five and six hundred Indians left dead upon the field." Since the Cheyenne carried off all the wounded and many of the dead, the true number could not be determined. The most controversial issue of all was the number of women and children who had been killed. Some said two-thirds of the dead were women and children. A corporal testified that only "twenty-five of the dead were full-grown men." Robert Bent reported seeing a dead woman "cut open with an unborn child lying by her side. I saw the body of White Antelope, with the privates cut off." An Indian agent testified, "I saw the bodies of those lying there cut all to pieces . . . children two or three months old . . . from sucking infants up to warriors."

The congressional committee that came to Denver to investigate the Sand Creek episode called Kit Carson as a witness and asked him what he thought of Chivington's actions, and Carson replied with a bitter denunciation. The Commission on Indian Affairs concluded in its report that the war that ensued "cost the government $30,000,000 and carried conflagration and death to the border settlements." During the summer of 1865 no fewer than eight thousand troops were withdrawn from the effective force engaged in suppressing the rebellion to meet this Indian war. "The result of the year's campaign . . . was useless and expensive. Fifteen or twenty Indians were killed at an expense of more than a million dollars apiece while hundreds of our soldiers had lost their lives."

By 1866 the "war" had dwindled down to sporadic raids. William Bent and Kit Carson, strong advocates of the Indian cause, could offer no better solution than the often-tried notion of persuading the tribes to take up an agricultural way of life. Charles Bent, a Cheyenne warrior and half-brother of Robert, survived the Sand Creek battle. He devoted himself to hunting down white men and women and torturing them to death. Having lured two settlers out of a station on the Smoky Hill Trail, he staked one to the ground, cut out his tongue, built a fire on his stomach, and castrated and disemboweled him. William Bent disowned him for his cruelties, and Charles set out to kill his father.

Chivington's reputation never recovered. He remained under a cloud as the instigator of the "Sand Creek Massacre."

CHAPTER XVII

POSTWAR RELATIONS

By the end of the Civil War, with the national government firmly in the hands of the radical Republicans, there was a strong disposition on the part of Congress to do justice to the Indians as well as to the ex-slaves. There were three major proposals for dealing with the aborigines. One, generally espoused by the military, was a policy of armed force combined with fairness. Its proponents argued that the Indians, in the last analysis, respected only force. To impose order on the constantly warring tribes, it was essential to demonstrate the determination of the United States government, through the agency of the army, to suppress warfare between tribes as well as raids against white settlements.

The most conspicuous alternate proposal—backed by a majority of abolitionists who enjoyed a considerable if fleeting prestige as the agents of emancipation, as well as by the pacifists (in many cases one and the same)—was called the peace policy and eschewed all use of force in dealing with the tribes. Force bred force, the argument ran. If the Indians' better natures were appealed to, if they were provided with schools and teachers and missionaries, they would welcome civilization. The army was not the solution but the problem. All matters having to do with the Plains tribes should be placed in the hands of civilians committed to civilizing the aborigines.

The third proposal, held by a considerable majority of Americans living west of the Mississippi and north of the Ohio, was to exterminate the "uncivilized" Indians on the ground that they were beyond hope of reform.

The government policy in the period from the end of the Civil War to the end of the century was a combination of the first two proposals or an alternation between them. As early as 1865 the proponents of the peace policy had mustered their forces for an all-out campaign to win over the Johnson administration. Included in their ranks were such veterans of the abolitionist movement as Wendell Phillips, Frederick Douglass, Harriet Beecher Stowe and her brother Henry Ward Beecher, Lydia Maria Child, Julia Ward Howe, and Lucretia Mott and her faithful husband, James, now in their seventies but still on fire with righteous wrath wherever injustice might reveal itself.

Wendell Phillips, always outspoken, described the treatment of the Indians as "one of the foulest blots in our history." It was the task of the coming generation, he said, to give effect to the Fifteenth Amendment. "With infinite toil, at vast expense, sealing with 500,000 graves, we have made it true of the negro. With what toil, at what cost, with what devotion, you will make it true of the Indian and the Chinese, the coming Years will tell." When peace agreements with the Sioux began to unravel a few months after they were achieved, Phillips wrote in *The New York Times* that "the Indians have begun to tear up the rails, [and] to shoot passengers and conductors on the Pacific Road. . . . We see great good in this." The work started by the Indians should be completed, Phillips declared, and the Great Plains returned to them. While few reformers were willing to go as far as Phillips, it was certainly true that many cheered on the Indians in their clashes with army troops.

In the view of the reformers, justice for the aborigines meant observing the terms of existing treaties when possible or practical and, when either not possible or not practical, negotiating in good faith with *all* the members of particular tribes, not merely with some splinter group of more compliant Indians. It meant paying the tribes a fair price for their lands and, finally, undertaking to "civilize" the aborigines through training in agriculture and, through Christian education (there was, in their view, no other), the inculcation of the virtues of thrift, hard work, piety—the so-called Protestant ethic—and perhaps, above all, individualism. This was the task in which all friends of the Indians combined their very considerable talents and resources, social and political. In their crusade they commanded a network of liberal publications, journals and newspapers, from the sometimes wavering support of Godkin's *Nation* to *Harper's Weekly*, the *Boston Daily Advertiser*, the *Boston Evening Transcript*, *The New York Times*, and, usually, the *New York Tribune*. All the anti-slavery and reform journals that survived were eager to contribute their bit, and soon there were a number of ephemeral journals concerned only with the reform of Indian affairs.

The policy of prevailing on Indians to settle on reservations was at least as old as the Indian Removal. The argument for reservations on the part of those friendly to the Indians was that it was only on reservations that Indians could be protected from predatory whites. The "assimilationists," on the other hand, attacked the reservations on the ground that they postponed assimilation.

Lyman Abbott, a Congregational clergyman, editor of the *Christian Union*, coadjutor to Henry Ward Beecher, and a champion of the Indian cause, was convinced that the long record of "dishonor which justly attaches to the history of our dealing with the North American Indians is due to a lack of prophetic vision . . . and an ignorance and indifference, not pardonable, in the nation at large, rather than to any deliberate policy of injustice adopted by the nation." To Abbott, the reservation system was the villain of the piece. "From the reservation," he wrote, "all the currents of civilization were excluded by federal law. The railroad, the telegraph, the newspaper, the open market, free competition—all halted at its walls. The reservation system had made a prisoner [of the Indian] that it might civilize him, under the illusion that it is possible to civilize a race without subjecting it to the perils of civilization. The reservation system is absolutely, hopelessly, incurably bad, 'evil and wholly evil' and that continually."

Abbott's remedy was to treat the Indians

> as we have treated the Poles, Hungarians, Italians, Scandinavians. Many of them are no better able to take care of themselves than the Indians; but we have thrown on them the responsibility of their own custody, and they have learned to live by living. Treat them as we have treated the negro. As a race the African is less competent than the Indian; but we do not shut the negroes up in reservations and put them in charge of politically appointed parents called agents. The lazy grow hungry; the criminal are punished; the industrious get on. . . . Let the Indian administer his own affairs and take his chances. . . . Turn the Indian loose on the continent and the race will disappear! Certainly. The sooner the better. There is no more reason why we should endeavor to preserve intact the Indian race than the Hungarians, the Poles, or the Italians. Americans all, from ocean to ocean, should be the aim of American statesmanship. Let us understand once for all that an inferior race must either adapt and conform itself to the highest civilization wherever the two come in conflict, or else die. This is the law of God, from which there is no appeal.

Richard Henry Pratt, perhaps the most notable "educator" of Indians in the post–Civil War period, also supported assimilation. Pratt estimated that there were some 250,000 Indians in the United States. Since there were approximately 3,000 counties in the various states, Pratt recommended dividing up the Indians

> in the proportion of about ninety Indians to a county, and [finding] them homes and work among our people; that would solve

the knotty problem in three years' time, and there would be no more an 'Indian Question.' It is folly to handle them at arms-length; we should absorb them into our national life for their own good and ours. . . . It is wicked to stand them up as targets for sharp-shooters. The Indians are just like other men, only minus their environment. . . . We can, by planting the Indians among us, make educated and industrious citizens of them.

Indians were "naturally religious." All that was necessary was "to familiarize their reverent minds with the truths of the New Testament." Captain Pratt told Frances Willard that "the history of the Indians as set forth in books is a bundle of falsehoods. They are like other people, and, unprovoked by outrage and injustice, behave far more peaceably than they get credit for."

It is important to emphasize here that, Lyman Abbott and Richard Pratt aside, among the great majority of Americans who considered themselves the friends of the Indian there was no substantial difference on the reservation issue. From reformers like Beeson and Whipple to President Grant himself, there was virtual unanimity on the reservation plan as the only fair solution to the Indian problem; the Indians must consent to go onto reservations and must be fairly compensated for the lands they surrendered. What if they refused all arguments and inducements? That, clearly, was the sticking point. No one could think of any better solution than sweetening the pie with more money and more gifts and larger annuities—bigger bribes. And then what? If all those inducements failed? Here force must obviously be used, however reluctantly. And what if, once on reservations, the Indians refused to remain, slipped away to prey on other tribes or on white settlers or emigrants within their range? Again, they must be punished by the army. But everyone was confident it would not come to that. The key was fair dealing, fair compensation, kindness and goodwill.

In addition to the Eastern philanthropists there were men like Jim Bridger, Jim Meeker, and Thomas Fitzpatrick, who knew the Indians as intimately as any white man could know them, who married or lived with Indian women and played and fought with the warriors. For the Indian life, compared with the life of the average white American, was irresistibly alluring. Some of them simply became "squaw men," white men who "went native"; others served in a variety of capacities: as guides for emigrant wagon trains, as scouts and guides for the army, even as Indian agents. One of the most engaging of such men was Thomas LaForge.

Thomas LaForge was of French Huguenot ancestry. His family had emigrated from South Carolina to Kansas in 1853. There on the Missouri river, young LaForge encountered his first Indians. Kickapoo and Potawatomi Indians lived nearby, and members of other tribes frequently visited the LaForge farm. Young Tom was enthralled. His playmates were young Potawatomi children. A few years later the LaForge family set out for Montana, attracted by reports of the discovery of gold. With the family settled at Bozeman, Tom LaForge found himself in constant contact with Crow Indians. Increasingly captivated by tribal life, he attached himself to a lodge and gradually took on the customs and manners of a Crow Indian. Adopted by the tribe, he became a classic "white Indian," marrying a Crow girl named Cherry, fighting against the always threatening Sioux, acting as a translator for the U.S. military and later becoming a Crow scout with Custer.

Recounting his experiences to an anthropologically-minded doctor, Thomas Marquis, in later life, LaForge (his Indian name was Horse Rider), declared:

> Oh, it was a sweet life. I had a good wife who made for me fine buckskin clothing, kept my hair in the best of order, kept me scented with sweetgrass, had my bed and my entire lodge always in neat condition, prepared for me the sweat-bath lodge whenever I wanted to use it, did everything a woman can do to make a man comfortable and happy. I alternated at hunting and doing duty in the military service, each a congenial employment. . . . At all times I had ample leisure for lazy loafing and dreaming and visiting. In summer I wore nothing but breechcloth and moccasins

when out in the camps . . . As I idled and smoked, my wife sat by
my side and did sewing or beadwork. . . .

Since the Crow were the traditional enemies of the Sioux,
LaForge made his living as a guide and scout for the cavalry in
their expeditions against the Sioux. LaForge recounted a meeting
with a Sioux chief who told LaForge's Crow "father," speaking of
the "white" Sioux of his tribe: "These kind of men we have with us
too. They have strong hearts. They are good because they know us
and also the white people. We like to have them, for they talk to the
[Indian] agent in our interest." The same chief denounced "Indian
white men who guided soldiers" (LaForge was of course such a man).
"Nevertheless," the Sioux said, "the soldiers have good hearts."

The connecting links between the Eastern reformers and the
Western advocates of the Indian cause were the Christian missionaries, who carried on their hazardous and often fruitless labors
wherever they could find Indians "settled" enough to listen to the
Gospel or to send their children to mission schools.

Westerners were furious at what they considered the foolishly
sentimental attitude of Eastern reformers toward the Indians. The
Kearney (Nebraska) *Herald* in July, 1866, declared: "The earnest
defenders of this barbarian monster would turn away in disgust could
they see him in all of his original desperation. The best and only way
to reconcile the blood-washed animal will be to impose upon him a
worse schooling than has ever befallen the inferior races." The editor of a Boise, Idaho, newspaper suggested that the Nez Percé, who
were protesting the invasion of their reservation by whites, be sent
a shipment of blankets infected by smallpox. In Montana, when
several Indians were killed in a fight with miners, the whites cut off
their ears and pickled them in whiskey, stripped and bleached their
skulls, and wrote on them: "I am on the Reservation at Last" and
"Let Harper's Tell of My Virtues." The *Kansas Daily Tribune* stated
in July, 1866: "There can be no permanent, lasting peace on our
frontiers till these devils are exterminated. Our eastern friends may
be slightly shocked at such a sentiment, but a few years' residence

in the West, and acquaintance with the continued history of their outrages upon settlers and travelers in the West, has dispersed the romance with which these people are regarded in the East."

That, indeed, proved to be the case with a number of reformers who went west and encountered real Indians. They promptly and sometimes publicly recanted and came to sound disconcertingly like the most unreconstructed pioneers. Mark Twain, an avowed "Indian worshipper," was dismayed at the Goshute Indians of Nevada and confessed that he had been viewing the Indian "through the mellow moonshine of romance." A.J. Grover wrote to the *National Anti-Slavery Standard* that he was convinced the editor of the journal and Wendell Phillips himself would experience a change of heart if they were to travel through the West: "My sympathies have changed sides, and are now decidedly with the settlers and against the Indians who are prowling, stealing and murdering continually. . . . How would you and Wendell Phillips denounce such a policy against the Ku-Klux of the South? And yet the Indians are ten times as savage and blood thirsty."

An even more serious defection was that of Samuel Bowles, the liberal editor of the *Springfield* (Massachusetts) *Republican*, one of the founders and leaders of the Republican Party in Massachusetts, and a staunch anti-slavery man. Bowles traveled through the West and reported to his readers that "the wild clamor of the border population for the indiscriminate extermination of the savages . . . is as unintelligent and barbarous, as the long dominant thought of the East against the use of force, and its incident policy of treating the Indians as of equal responsibility and intelligence with the whites, are unphilosophical and impracticable." Bowles was convinced that the best that could be done for the Indian would be to "make decent the pathway to his grave." He could not survive as a "wild" Indian and he could not be tamed.

In fairness to the Westerners, it must be kept in mind that customs and manners of the Indians were, for the most part, antithetical to everything that the white American valued and esteemed. Indian revenge, as we have noted, fell most commonly on the innocent. (The reverse, of course, was often true of white revenge for Indian depredations.) The practice of most tribes of mutilating the dead (so that they would enter the afterlife bereft of vital organs), of subjecting captives or the wounded to terrible tortures, and, above all, of raping captured white women placed the aborigines, in the minds of many of those whites most often in contact with them, beyond the pale of humanity. John Holmes grew up in one of the most enlightened towns of western Ohio—Mastersville. It was solidly Republican and anti-slavery in the era before the war. Many of the citizens subscribed to or shared William Lloyd Garrison's *Liberator* and the *Boston Evening Transcript*, a tireless organ of reform. There was an Indian reservation not far away, and small parties of Sac passed near the town occasionally, often on the prowl for stray Indians of rival tribes. On one occasion a resident of the town discovered the body of a young brave who had been skinned alive, the flesh torn from his body in great strips. If there had been any residual sympathy for Indians in Mastersville, that one episode dissipated it. A few years later an Indian woman, married to a white man, was shot by an Indian of a rival tribe as she sat on the porch of her house. It is not surprising that one of the topics of the Mastersville Literary and Debating Society was "Should the uncivilized Indians be exterminated?" What was surprising was not the topic but that it was considered debatable. Included in the topics listed in the society's minutes as having been debated in the same era were "Should capital punishment be abolished?" and "Is a liberal education essential to a happy life?" In a town hospitable to blacks and even willing to tolerate Democrats, there was no sympathy for Indians. Seventy years later, reading the minutes of the Literary and Debating Society that he had recorded as a boy, John Holmes shook his head in bewilderment that such a topic as the extermination of the Indians could have been seriously debated by decent and liberally disposed men, many of them his relatives.

We might try the exercise of simply listing those qualities that white Americans most commonly attributed to red Americans.

To the Eastern reformers, Indians were noble, free, wild, courageous, stoic, daring, nature-loving, worshipers of the Great Spirit, loyal, faithful, honorable (the white man on the other hand, spoke with a "forked tongue"). By contrast, the settlers and soldiers who were in most direct contact with the aborigines were inclined to describe them with such words as vile, savage, inhuman, barbarous, cunning, deceitful, treacherous, cruel, dirty, foul-smelling, and insolent—adjectives often followed by a lurid list of particulars. I think we must concede that the Indians were, in varying degrees, all these things—characteristics, of course, varied widely from tribe to tribe—in different degrees and at different times and among different people. But taken together the words were, in essence, meaningless. They were white perceptions of the Indian. They did not begin to exhaust or even to describe sufficiently the reality that was the aborigine. In the most fundamental sense the Indian was the victim of the inadequacy of the white man's categories. The categories were both real and not real. They delineated a line or a feature, described an episode or evoked an aroma, but they failed to touch the indescribable heart of the reality. The issue was much larger and more complex than Indian cruelty or white prejudice.

The reformers had another irony to contend with. At the end of the war some fifteen to twenty thousand blacks were held by the Choctaw, Cherokee, and Chickasaw Indians as slaves. Forced by the terms of the peace treaty to free their slaves, the Indians kept them in a state of subordination very similar to that imposed on Southern blacks by white Southerners, the difference being that there was no Reconstruction army in the Indian Territory to protect the rights of the ex-slaves, who complained of "many ills and outrages" at the hands of their former owners, "even to the loss of many a life." Congress did its best to prevail upon the Indians to incorporate some three thousand freed slaves into their tribes and give them each forty acres of land, offering $300,000 to facilitate matters. The Choctaw and Cherokee reluctantly complied, but the Chickasaw declared tellingly, that they could not "see any reason or just cause why they should be required to do more for their freed slaves than the white people have done in the slave-holding states for theirs."

After the Civil War, William Tecumseh Sherman's sympathies seemed, at least initially, with the Indians. He had a soldier's admiration of their bravery and skill in battle, and he looked on the white settlers, miners, and traders who crowded westward as greedy and unscrupulous civilians. At Colorado Springs, when the residents asked the general to build a fort to protect them from the Indians, Sherman suggested that they were more interested in the business that a military installation would bring than in warding off the Indians—whom they seemed to exploit. When Sherman was appealed to by importunate miners and prospective settlers for protection, he wrote to General Alfred Terry: "I agree with you perfectly that we are not in a position to permit an invasion of that region, for no sooner would a settlement be inaugurated, than an appeal would come for protection. . . . You may, therefore, forbid all white people going there at present, and warn all those who go in spite of your prohibition, that the United States will not protect them now, or until public notice is given that the Indian title is extinguished." When a party of three hundred men was recruited in Yankton by an ex-army officer for an incursion into the Black Hills reservation under the name of the Black Hills Exploring and Mining Association, the military commander of the Dakota district was ordered to stop the party by force if persuasion failed.

Many whites in the region were calling for a war of extermination against the tribes and proposing a bounty of $100 per scalp. Sherman had no patience with such talk and made it clear wherever he went that he was as concerned with protecting the rights of the Indians under existing treaty arrangements as he was with protecting the lives of the whites. He discerned readily the difficulty of using locally recruited soldiers, poorly disciplined and filled with hatred of the Indians, to preserve order on the frontier and set about to replace such volunteers with regular army officers and enlisted men.

Sherman took it as his principal responsibility to keep open the Oregon, Smoky Hill, and Santa Fe trails. He was convinced that only by ensuring access on those now well-traveled roads to the Southwest and to the Pacific coast could the clamor for intervention by the military be stopped. If emigrants could pass over those roads with safety, time might be bought to "solve" the Indian problem on a permanent basis. There was one other potentially dangerous issue on the horizon: the building of a transcontinental railroad. Ever since the end of the Mexican War there had been talk of such a line, tying together the East and West coasts of the continent. It had grown insistent by the time of Fort Sumter, and only the coming of the war had delayed it. Now half a dozen "corporations" were vying for the right to run the line across the Great Plains through the Rockies, over the deserts of the Great Basin and on to San Francisco, Los Angeles, and the Northwest. It was clear that nothing could prevent or deflect the building of such a line or, eventually, lines. They had to go through Indian hunting grounds, and there was ample reason to believe that the Plains tribes would resist that final intrusion. Indeed, the Union Pacific was moving west from Omaha at the rate of ten miles or so a day when Sherman assumed his responsibilities as military commander of the region through which the line was destined to run. The Kansas Pacific was also running a roughly parallel line from Kansas City to Denver.

To complicate matters further, the so-called Bozeman Trail had been discovered by John Bozeman and a companion who had been seeking gold in Montana. The two men found their way through a pass from Virginia City into the valley of the Yellowstone and thence to the Oregon Trail near Fort Laramie. For their pains, the Sioux stripped them of their horses, rifles, and clothes. They were back, nonetheless, the next spring with a large party of miners, determined to run the risks of Indian attack. Sherman was ordered to establish army posts along the established trail to protect those using it. He dispatched Colonel Henry Carrington with a battalion of 700 men, 226 wagons, a 26-piece band, a number of ambulances carrying the wives and children of some of the officers who were to garrison the forts along the trail, and 1,000 cattle to provide food for the expedition. Jim Bridger, a relic of the great fur trapping days in the Yellowstone, was the guide.

Just as Carrington departed, the Sioux chiefs were summoned to Fort Laramie for a parley. Chief Red Cloud of the Oglala Sioux protested: "Great Father sends us presents and wants new road but White Chief goes with soldiers to steal road before Indian says yes or no." When Red Cloud and Young Man Afraid of His Horses refused further discussions, Carrington repaired to Fort Reno (formerly Fort Connor) on the Powder River and then pushed on and established Fort Phil Kearny at Little Piney Creek—a substantial settlement of twenty or so buildings in a space 400 by 400 feet surrounded by palisades. Before the fort was completed, a party of Sioux drove off 175 horses and miles. Pursued, they killed two soldiers and wounded three. Fifty-one such attacks were made in the space of five months. A favorite tactic of the Sioux was to raid the parties bringing lumber for the construction of Fort Kearny from the nearby foothills, the slopes of which were covered with pine trees.

Emigrant trains were shadowed and attacked whenever vigilance was relaxed. Bozeman himself was killed in 1867 on the trail that bore his name by a party of Blackfoot. Despite the attacks, Carrington pushed the construction of a third fort, Fort C.F. Smith, ninety miles beyond Kearny.

The Sioux attacks continued, gradually wearing away the morale of the expedition and driving off horses and cattle. In November, Carrington was reinforced by a company of cavalry and two officers, Captains James Powell and William Fetterman. Fetterman was a fire-eater with an outstanding record as a regimental officer in the Civil War. He ridiculed Carrington for his caution in not pursuing the Sioux raiders more aggressively and volunteered to be a "scourge to the savages." When a party of Sioux were spotted headed for the "wood train," Carrington sent Fetterman with the cavalry company to reinforce the guards that accompanied the train. Fetterman and his junior officers, having driven off the Sioux, could not refrain from headlong pursuit. They promptly ran into an ambush; one of the lieutenants was found later with more than fifty arrows in his body. Encouraged by the success of the skirmish, Red Cloud and his fellow chiefs decided to employ similar tactics to try to draw a larger force out of the fort and into an ambush.

Everything went according to Red Cloud's plan. The wood train was attacked; the soldiers at the fort prepared to go to its relief. Captain Fetterman, as the next in line to Carrington, demanded to be given command of the relief party of eighty men, including a number of volunteers anxious to get in on the action. Carrington's orders to Fetterman were: "Support the wood train. Relieve it and report to me. Do not engage or pursue Indians at its expense. Under no circumstances pursue over Lodge Trail Ridge." Carrington took special pains to be sure Fetterman understood his orders. The cavalry followed Fetterman's infantry detachment, and Carrington again repeated his instructions: no pursuit of the Indians over Lodge Trail Ridge.

When the detachment from the fort appeared, the Indian raiders withdrew, as they commonly did, to avoid being cut off or outflanked. Fetterman, in open defiance of his orders, took up the pursuit. Soon he and his men found themselves surrounded by Indians and vastly outnumbered. The fighting was fierce, and Carrington, hearing the shots and suspecting what had happened, dispatched a relief force of fifty-four men with an ambulance and wagons to reinforce Fetterman. The relief party arrived just as the Indians withdrew, leaving the ground strewn with the dead and mutilated bodies of the soldiers. Fetterman and a fellow officer had apparently shot each other to prevent capture and torture. The scene that confronted the rescue party was a grim one. Two civilian employees of the army, experienced Indian fighters armed with the sixteen-shot repeating Henry rifles, had held off the Indians for some time before their ammunition ran out. Sixty-five pools of frozen blood were counted in front of the rocks where they had taken refuge. Indian fury was indicated by the fact that one body had 105 arrows in it when it was retrieved by a burial detail from the fort.

Fire Thunder, a young Sioux brave, later recalled the battle:

[T]here were many bullets, but there were more arrows—so many
that it was like a cloud of grasshoppers, all above and around the
soldiers; and our people shooting across, hit each other. The soldiers were falling all the while they were fighting back up the hill,
and their horses got loose. . . . Then the soldiers got on top, there
were not many of them left and they had no place to hide. . . . We
were told to crawl up on them, and we did. When we were close,
someone yelled: "Let us go! This is a good day to die. Think of
the helpless ones at home!" . . . I was . . . quick on my feet, and I
was one of the first to get in among the soldiers. They got up and
fought until not one of them was alive.

Only a dog was left and it ran away howling. "Dead men and horses
and wounded Indians were scattered all the way up the hill, and
their blood was frozen. . . ."

Carrington reported on the condition of the corpses. "Eyes
torn out and laid on rocks; noses cut off, ears cut off, chins hewn
off; teeth chopped out; joints of fingers, brains taken out and placed
on rocks with other members of the body; entrails taken out and
exposed; hands cut off; feet cut off, arms taken out from sock-
ets. . . ." The engagement into which the rash Fetterman had led
his command to death was one of only two battles in our history in
which there were no survivors; the other would be also at the hands
of the Sioux.

When word of the debacle, along with the news that the hills
around the fort were swarming with several thousand hostile Indians,
reached Carrington, he made hasty preparations for defense, doubtless having in mind the fate of the ten women (among them his
own wife), and eleven children under his protection. Only some 120
men remained in the fort to defend it. With the wood train were
fifty soldiers and thirty civilians, and ninety-four were in the relief
party, which had not yet returned and the fate of which was still
uncertain. Under the cover of darkness the wood train reached the

fort and was soon followed by the relief party. Everything was done to prepare for an all-out assault, but it failed to materialize. The Sioux, who themselves had suffered heavy casualties, withdrew to bury their dead, treat the wounded, and savor their victory.

General Philip St. George Cooke, in command of the Department of the Platte, relieved Carrington of his command when word reached him of Fetterman's disaster. But Cooke, who had fought in the Black Hawk War thirty-four years earlier, was in turn relieved by Sherman. Although he had taken up his duties with a determination to deal justly with the Indians, Sherman experienced a change of heart on hearing the news of the annihilation of Fetterman's party. "I do not understand how the massacre of Colonel Fetterman's party could have been so complete . . .," he wrote. "We must act with vindicative earnestness against the Sioux, even to their extermination, men, women and children. Nothing else will do." Sherman soon had second thoughts about such a draconian policy, but his words, written in the heat of his anger and dismay over the gory news, were to haunt him. They would be cited by innumerable historians of the Indian wars as evidence that the hero of Atlanta and the March to the Sea was bent on the destruction of the Indians.

It was apparent that maintaining the three forts along the Bozeman Trail—Reno, Kearny, and Smith—was going to be a major drain on the resources of the army. Red Cloud and his Sioux warriors kept up a constant pressure, attacking any party that ventured out of the forts. The parties dispatched to cut wood were especially vulnerable, and they were the frequent objects of classic attacks by yelping warriors, who circled the woodcutters' camps on their ponies, hanging over the off-sides of their mounts and firing underneath their necks at the beleaguered whites. The forts and their occupants, surrounded by thousands of hostile Indians, were actually little more than hostages to the tribes.

In the aftermath of the Fetterman episode a good deal of soul-searching was done on the subject of Indian policy. The Indian Bureau of the Department of the Interior and the War Department accused each other of various sins of omission and commission.

The War Department charged the bureau with a weak and inconsistent policy toward the tribes, with corruption among its agents, and with condoning the exploitation of the Indians by rapacious traders. The bureau replied that it was expending millions of dollars each year in subsidies to the tribes and to assist in missionary work among those settled on reservations, especially in the establishment and maintenance of schools. The army, on the other hand, had no policy other than beating the Indians into submission in campaigns that were extremely costly in money and lives and often unsuccessful to boot. The army held to the line that the Indians were warriors who understood only force. Compromise and concession were to them evidence of weakness. They respected soldiers (warriors), and the soldiers should be left to deal with them. The Fetterman fiasco undercut the military, and for at least the moment the balance shifted to the Department of the Interior and its Indian Bureau. Congress, firmly in the hands of the radical Republicans, intervened with a bill, passed in March, 1867, that established a peace commission to work out a blueprint for achieving peace with the Plains tribes.

A wave of optimism was created by the appointment of the Peace Commission, chaired by the commissioner of Indian affairs and including among its members such radical Republicans and friends of the Indian as Senator John B. Henderson of Missouri, George Julian of Indiana, William Windom of Minnesota, and Samuel Tappan, a member of the great family of reformers and an early recruit to the Indian cause. Alfred Terry and William Harney, both strong anti-slavery men with outstanding war records, were also members of the commission, as was General Sherman. While the military was thus strongly represented, it was the best and most liberal element of the army. The charge to the commissioners was to make a thorough investigation of the general state of affairs regarding the Plains Indians, to negotiate treaties with the tribes in question, and to propose a long-range plan for civilizing the aborigines.

When the commissioners' report was delivered in 1868, it was overflowing with enlightened sentiments. "We have spent 200 years in creating the present state of things," it declared. "If we can civilize [the Indians] in twenty-five years, it will be a vast improvement on the operations of the past." They recommended a "hitherto untried policy of endeavoring to conquer by kindness." At the same time the commissioners rejected the notion that a "handful of savages" could seriously impede the age of progress and enlightenment that clearly lay ahead for the American people and in which the orderly settlement of the West and the exploitation of its natural resources were clearly essential elements.

The military members of the Peace Commission who knew the Indians best, Sherman most prominent among them, suppressed their doubts and acquiesced in the report, primarily on the ground that time would demonstrate whether the hopes expressed were extravagant. Sherman took the view that even if the report were excessively optimistic, its goals might be realized in the long run after the more recalcitrant tribes had been so chastened that they would accept life on their reservations. Enlightened as the report was, in many ways, it bore unmistakable evidence of white prejudices and predilections, most notably perhaps in its ban on polygamy. It was to that aspect that Lydia Maria Child objected strongly. "Let it be discountenanced, and reasoned against, and privileges conferred on those who live with one wife . . .," she wrote. "Indians like other human beings are more easily led by the Angel Attraction, than driven by the Demon Penalty." The aborigines should be treated "simply as younger members of the great human family, who need to be protected, instructed and encouraged, till they are capable of appreciating and sharing all our advantages."

On the other side, Samuel Crawford of Kansas was unequivocal in his condemnation of the commissioners' report. "It was largely through their recommendations and misrepresentations," he declared, "that the wicked policy . . . was adopted by the government and persisted in by the Interior Department." Behind the Interior Department "was a gang of thieving Indian agents in the West, and a maudlin sentimentality in the East."

In the spring of 1868 at Fort Laramie, the commissioners signed a treaty with the Sioux and the Cheyenne that abandoned the forts on the Bozeman Trail (and, of course, the trail itself) in return for a promise on the part of the Indians to remain on their reservations, not to wage war against each other, and, most important, to permit the passage of the Union Pacific roadbed through their lands. William Dodge, chairman of the commissioners, explained to the Indians: "There are a great many people east who love the Indians and want to do them good. They wish to save the Indian from ruin. They remember that many moons ago the red man lived where the white man now lives but they are gone." Now the Indians must "begin to live like the white man. Cultivate your land, and we will send good men to teach your children to work, to read and write, and then they will grow up able to support themselves after the buffalo has gone."

The abandoned forts on the Bozeman Trail were burned by the triumphant Sioux. The last dramatic touch was added when Red Cloud, who had remained aloof from all the treaty negotiations, rode up to Fort Laramie in November after the forts on the Bozeman Trail had been abandoned and added his signature to the treaty. He must have done so with the conscious air of the victor.

Having concluded the treaty with the Sioux and Cheyenne at Laramie, the peace commissioners proceeded to Medicine Lodge Creek in Kansas to negotiate a similar treaty with the Comanche, Kiowa, Arapaho, and Southern Cheyenne. Three thousand Indians gathered in a wildly romantic scene. The purpose was similar, and the technique the same: the classic combination of gifts and threats. The Indians must accept limitations to their hunting ranges. It was clear that many were resistant. The Kiowa chief Satanta declared: "I love the land and the buffalo and will not part with it. I want the children raised as I was. I don't want to settle. I love to roam over the prairies. A long time ago this land belonged to our fathers, but when I go to the river I see camps of the soldiers on its banks. These soldiers cut down my timber; they kill my buffalo; and when I see that it feels as my heart would burst with sorrow."

Albert Barnitz, a young lieutenant in Custer's Seventh Cavalry, described how the Indians pressed into the regimental camps of the cavalry. "We are drilling daily," he wrote, "and the camp is daily thronged with Indian spectators of all ages, sexes and tribes. Last night 'White Man' an Arapaho Indian brought me a young squaw which he assured me was 'heap good' and which he desired to present to me for the evening." The officers in turn visited the camps of various tribes, among them the band of the Comanche leader Ten Bears. Ten Bears told his visitors that the Comanche called themselves "*nim*" or "a people," and his band was called "nim-nim" or "a people of people." The Indians crowded in, observing every detail of army life with fascinated curiosity, the chiefs often "inviting themselves for dinner," Lieutenant Barnitz wrote his fiancée.

Reluctantly but inevitably, as they had done many times before, the tribes assented to the treaty. The Cheyenne and Arapaho were assigned some three million acres north of the Washita River. There were the now-standard promises of yearly subsidies—food, clothing, farm implements, and teachers—and then the distribution of the presents, bribes in truth.

From Medicine Lodge Creek the commissioners proceeded farther west to conclude treaties with the friendly Crow, the Ute of Colorado and Utah, the Bannock and the Shoshone, who, like the Crow, had kept peace with the whites. The Navajo and Snake, beguiled by mounds of presents, likewise fell in line, and now the system seemed complete. Under the terms of the treaties no white might "ever" enter the reserved areas "except those . . . designated and authorized to do so, and . . . such officers, agents, and employees of the government may be authorized to enter upon Indian reservations in discharge of duties enjoined by law. . . ."

The response of the frontier was what might have been expected. The *Yankton Daily Press & Dakotan* declared indignantly:

> This abominable compact with the marauding bands that regularly
> make war on the white in the summer and live on government
> bounty all winter, is now pleaded as a barrier to the improvement
> and development of one of the richest and most fertile sections in

America. What shall be done with these Indian dogs in our manger? They will not dig the gold or let others do it. . . . They are too lazy and too much like mere animals to cultivate the fertile soil, mine the coal, develop the salt mines, bore the petroleum wells, or wash the gold. Having all these things in their hands, they prefer to live as paupers, thieves and beggars, fighting, torturing, hunting, gorging, yelling and dancing all night to the beating of old tin kettles. . . . Anyone who knows how utterly they depend on the government for subsistence will see that if they have to be supported at all, they might far better occupy small reservations and be within military reach, than to have the exclusive control of a tract of country as large as the whole State of Pennsylvania or New York, which they can neither improve or utilize.

Grant's election in 1868 spurred the friends of the Indians to renewed efforts on their behalf. The most enlightened viewpoint was expressed by the valiant elderly Lydia Maria Child. She cautioned against the heavy-handed approach to "civilizing" the aborigines. The teachers of the Indian must respect the Indian's own culture, scrupulously avoid "our haughty Anglo-Saxon ideas of force." In her eloquent *An Appeal for the Indians* (1868), she urged: "Let their books, at first, be printed in Indian, with English translation and let them contain selections from the best of their own traditional stories."

Peter Cooper, the indefatigable philanthropist, the bankroller of a hundred good causes, inspired by Child's *Appeal*, assembled a company of kindred spirits at the Cooper Union to form an association—the United States Indian Commission—"for the protection and elevation of the Indians, and to cooperate with the United States government in its efforts to prevent desolation and wars on the frontiers of our country." Like the Peace Commission, the report of which it endorsed, the new association emphasized that peace, not the sword, and justice, not expropriation, were the proper path to follow in all dealings with the aborigines. The Indian Commission, somewhat a misnomer since it suggested an official governmental tie,

called for Indian representation in Congress and a separate department of Indian affairs not under the jurisdiction of the army *or* the
Department of the Interior. John Beeson and Bishop Whipple were
active in the new organization as were a number of clergymen and
prosperous merchants along with the usual company of reformers.

Vincent Colyer, sent by the commission to report on the state
of mind of the Indians, returned with the assurance that "in less
than two years we shall have heard the last of 'Indian outrages.'"

The principal task undertaken by the Indian Commission was
to arouse the public to the wrongs suffered by the Indians and to
advance the peace policy in dealing with the Indians. All the wars
with the Indians, they insisted in a spirit that ensured the angry
opposition of the West, had been the result of injustices perpetrated by white men. In a memorandum to Congress, drafted by
Beeson, the commission declared that "when the true history of the
Indian wrongs is laid before our countrymen, their united voice will
demand that the honor and interests of the nation shall no longer
be sacrificed to the insatiable lust and avarice of unscrupulous men."

The formation of the United States Indian Commission was
followed by the founding of numerous associations dedicated to
advancing, in one way or another, the welfare of the aborigines.
Other reform and philanthropic organizations extended their
interests to include the Indians—the Boston Radical Club, the
Union League, the Friends Social Union, and the American
Equal Rights Association prominent among them. Foremost in its
eleemosynary activities was the American Peace Society under the
leadership of Alfred Love. In addition to pushing for Indian representation in Congress and for vastly extended federal assistance
to the tribes to establish schools, build houses, buy agricultural
implements and train the Indians in their proper use, the reformers proposed that Congress, after ridding itself of the horde of
corrupt Indian agents, dispatch "true friends" of the aborigines to
"mingle among the Indians, and in a few months settle the existing
troubles." One rather wishes this bizarre proposal had been put
to the test. Certainly a meeting of Alfred Love, Lucretia Mott,

Gerrit Smith, and Lydia Maria Child with Red Cloud, Two Bears, Spotted Calf, and Crazy Horse would have provided inexhaustible material for parodists.

On the eve of the worst period of Indian troubles in our history, the optimum conditions prevailed in the government for fair and just treatment for the aborigines. Never before and never again would a national administration be as deeply committed to what it conceived of as a humane and liberal policy.

Moreover, no one could doubt the sincerity of President Grant himself. He endorsed the plan to bring delegations of Indians to Washington to present and dramatize their grievances, and Congress authorized him to "organize a board of Commissioners, to consist of not more than ten persons . . . eminent for their intelligence and philanthropy," to play an active role not only in advising on Indian policy but in supervising, jointly with the Department of the Interior, the proper observation of treaties and the best use of a so-called civilization fund of $2,000,000.

Determined to protect the emigrants while dealing justly with the tribes, Grant wished to remove, so far as possible, any grounds for Indian recalcitrance. Clearly one of the reasons most tribes were reluctant to remain on reservations was that they had no confidence that they would be treated fairly by the Indian agents. Grant's solution to this classic grievance was ingenious. The various Christian churches—which, since the turn of the century and in many instances well before, had been dispatching missionaries to the various settled tribes to try to convert them to Christianity and to establish mission schools (often subsidized by the government)—had performed a thankless task, but they had also shown, with the inevitable exceptions, a genuine concern for the aborigines and a degree of honesty considerably above that of the average government agent. Grant therefore decided to seek his Indian agents among the Christian denominations. Because many of those chosen were Quakers, Grant's innovation came to be called the Quaker policy, and it did indeed substantially improve the quality of Indian agents and, in consequence, life on the reservations.

CHAPTER XVIII

WAR IN THE SOUTHWEST

In the winter of 1866, while Sherman was attempting to keep the Bozeman Trail open by dispatching Colonel Carrington to establish a line of fort, a bloody conflict was taking place in the Arizona Territory between the military forces of the United States and the Chiricahua Apache. The trouble began when Colonel Pitcairn Morrison dispatched a young lieutenant to recapture a white boy kidnapped by an Apache band. The chief of the Apache was Cochise, one of the greatest Indian leaders in the country's history. Over six feet tall and famous for his strength and agility, he had carried on a long and bitter warfare with Mexico. When the Arizona region passed into American hands at the end of the Mexican War, Cochise decided that the Americans were too numerous and too warlike to attack. His policy, therefore, became one of caution and restraint. He believed that in the long run the only hope for his tribe was to adopt some of the ways of the white settlers, specifically, to abandon a nomadic life for the more settled one of ranchers. The role that Cochise envisioned for the Apache was one that they had already undertaken—that of providing beef for emigrant trains moving west, for miners, and for new settlers. The beef initially had been stolen from Mexican rancheros, but Cochise was determined to establish the raising of cattle as a legitimate business whereby his tribe could preserve much of its culture. As the country filled up with white settlers, the relations between them and the Apache, guided by Cochise, were exemplary.

Such was the general state of things when a Lieutenant Bascom, unfamiliar with Indian ways and innocent of any knowledge of Cochise, summoned the Apache chief to his camp to answer for the kidnapping. Cochise came with his wife and son, two nephews and a brother. Bascom charged him with responsibility for the kidnapping and threatened retribution unless the boy was returned. Cochise replied mildly enough that he had no knowledge of the kidnapping and would be glad to do what he could to ensure the boy's return. Thereupon Bascom is said to have declared, "Cochise, you are a liar! You and your people are my prisoners until the child is returned." At that Cochise slashed his way out of Bascom's tent and although wounded, made his escape, calling to the members of his family to follow him. They failed to escape, however, and the enraged Cochise attacked the Butterfield stage, intent on capturing whites to exchange for the members of his family. The braves captured three whites and killed eight others in the attack. Cochise then surrounded the stage station and kept the soldiers and civilians pinned down by musket fire until they began to suffer acutely from thirst. When the manager of the station, who knew Cochise well, went with two employees to parley with the chief, the three men were added to the group of whites offered by Cochise in exchange for his family. Bascom refused to make the exchange, although the manager called out to him that the result would be the death of the six white prisoners and the beginning of a fearful war. When one of Bascom's sergeants, who knew the ways of the Apache well expostulated with Bascom, he was placed under arrest for insubordination.

At this point Bascom either hanged Cochise's wife, son, brother, and nephews and Cochise retaliated by killing his white prisoners, or vice versa. Another version has it that reinforcements arrived and took Cochise's wife and son back to Tucson, where they were set free. In any event the consequences are not in doubt: bitter and merciless warfare between the whites and the Chiricahua Apache, led by Cochise. Cochise's policy was now extirpation of the whites. His warriors spread out in deadly raids on ranchers, stagecoach stations, and unwary travelers throughout the territory. Reuben Bernard, the sergeant who had tried to prevail on Bascom to accept Cochise's terms, wrote that he "personally knew of thirteen white men whom Cochise had burned alive, five of whom he tortured to death by cutting small pieces out of their feet, and fifteen whom he dragged to death after tying their hands and putting lariats around their necks. . . . This Indian was at peace," he noted, "until betrayed and wounded by white men. He now, when spoken to about peace, points to his scars and says, 'I was at peace with the whites until they tried to kill me for what other Indians did. I now live and die at war with them.'"

In 1865 an army colonel sent out to command the U.S. troops in the territory reported: "When I arrived, every ranch had been deserted south of Gila. The town of Tucson had but two hundred souls. North of Gila, roads were completely blocked, ranches abandoned and most of the settlements threatened with annihilation."

Cochise found a ready ally in Mangas Coloradas ("Red Sleeves"), the Mimbreño Apache chief, but the two of them together could seldom muster more than a hundred or so warriors. With these slim numbers they held the United States Army at bay. Moreover, Cochise prevented the mail from moving freely from the East to Tucson. Time and again couriers riding from Fort Bowie to Tucson were intercepted—fourteen in the first sixteen months of the line. In charge of getting the mail through was a remarkable Indian scout named Tom Jeffords. Jeffords finally decided to seek out Cochise and try to prevail upon him to let the mail go through. It was a bold and extremely dangerous enterprise that would, in a later day, provide dramatic scenes for a dozen or more movie Westerns: the intrepid scout confronting one of the most feared

Indian chieftains of the age. Jeffords reached Cochise's village, gave his gun and revolver to a woman, and walked to Cochise's lodge. For seven years no white man had come near Cochise; but Indians honored courage, and Cochise was fascinated by the resolution of "Sandy Whiskers," as he called Jeffords. He promised to protect the mail and told Jeffords he was free to visit the band whenever he wished. Jeffords took advantage of Cochise's offer and in time became a blood brother and Cochise's biographer.

When peace seemed a possibility in the winter of 1870, a band of renegade whites with ninety-two Papago Indians, longtime enemies of the Apache, and forty-eight Tucson Mexicans fell on a band of unsuspecting Aravaipa Apache, most of them women and children, and slaughtered them all. The episode roused a storm of indignation in the East. President Grant initiated an investigation and ordered that the culprits be tried. All of them were acquitted. In the summer of 1871 Grant reached the conclusion that the only hope for protecting the Indians against whites as well as against other Indians was by locating them "upon suitable territories . . . under control of the proper officers of the Indian Department." A central aim was making peace with Cochise and his Chiricahua Apache. For this assignment, the President chose the secretary of the Board of Indian Commissioners, Vincent Colyer, a man known to be sympathetic to the Indians.

Cochise agreed to meet with Colyer and the army officer in charge of the military forces of the territory. The suggestion was made by Colyer that Cochise and the Chiricuhua Apache live on the Tularosa Reservation, almost two hundred miles from the country where they had lived and fought the intrusion of the white man so successfully. Cochise replied:

> I have come with my hands open to you to live in peace with
> you. I speak straight and do not wish to deceive or be deceived. I
> want a strong, lasting peace.When I was young I walked all over
> this country, east and west, and saw no other people than the
> Apaches. After many summers I walked again and found another

race of people had come to take it. How is that? Why is it that the Apache want to die . . ? They roam over the hills and plains and want the heavens to fall on them. The Apache were once a great nation; they are now but a few, and because of this they want to die. . . . Many have been killed in battle. You must speak straight so that your words may go as sunlight into our hearts. Tell me, if the Virgin Mary has walked throughout all the land why has she never entered the wigwam of the Apache? Why have we never seen or heard her? . . . When I was going around the world, all were asking for Cochise. Now he is here—you see him and hear him—are you glad? If so, say so. Speak, Americans and Mexicans. I do not wish to hide anything from you nor have you hide anything from me. I will not lie to you; do not lie to me.

As for the Tularosa, that was far away. "The flies on those mountains eat out the eyes of the horses. The bad spirits live there. I want to live in these mountains. I have drunk of these waters and they have cooled me; I do not want to leave here."

General Gordon Granger, the military commander, gave Cochise his word that he and his people could remain in their mountains. Cochise thereupon declared the war at an end and prepared to adapt the life of his tribe to the limitations of a reservation, broad though it might be. But Washington rejected the part of the treaty that allowed Cochise and his people to remain on their tribal land. They must go, with the other Apache, to Tularosa. Cochise took to the warpath once more with almost a thousand Apache, many from other tribes. Again settlers lived in fear of their lives. Horses and cattle by the hundreds were driven off, and fifty settlers killed or wounded in raids. No isolated settlement or ranch in the Southwest was safe from Apache revenge. This time Grant sent two of his favorite generals to subdue the Apaches and bring peace to the region: George Crook and Oliver Otis Howard. Crook, who had graduated from West Point, class of '52, had served for almost eight years in the West, in California, on the Rogue River expedition against the tribes of the Northwest and in command of the Pitt

River expedition, during which he was wounded by an arrow. With the outbreak of the Civil War he had advanced to the rank of brigadier, distinguished himself at the Battle of Chickamauga, and subsequently served as Sheridan's right-hand man in his famous raid on the Shenandoah Valley. By the end of the war Crook was sent to Boise, in the Idaho Territory, where he proved himself adept at Indian warfare and forced peace on the tribes in the region around Boise. Oliver Otis Howard, a year younger than Crook, was one of the genuine heroes of the Civil War. He was the pious officer whom Sherman teased by saying "damn" in his presence. He had lost an arm at Fair Oaks, won the Congressional Medal of Honor for his heroism, and distinguished himself at Gettysburg. An ardent abolitionist, Howard had served as commissioner of the Freedmen's Bureau, founded Howard University, and been its first president. Now he was given the assignment of pacifying Cochise while Crook was given the task of rounding up the rest of the Apache and forcing them to return to the reservation at Tularosa. Crook was of the threat-and-intimidation school of Indian fighters, as, it must be said, most military men were. He ordered the rebellious chiefs to return to their reservations or "be wiped from the face of the earth."

Howard, by contrast, was determined to try to put his Christian precepts to use, and Grant promised that he would support any peace plan that Howard might negotiate with Cochise. Howard knew of Tom Jeffords's friendship with Cochise, and he asked Jeffords to take him to the Apache chief without any accompanying soldiers other than the general's aide, Captain Joseph Sladen. After a long, trying trip the little party reached Cochise's mountain stronghold. Howard was introduced to Cochise. "He gave me a grasp of the hand," Howard wrote later, "and said very pleasantly, '*Buenas dias*.' His face was really pleasant to look upon, making me say to myself, 'How strange it is that such a man can be the robber and murderer so much complained of.' . . . We walked together, and sat down side by side on the blanket seat beneath a fine spreading oak." With Jeffords acting as interpreter, Howard told Cochise, "I came with the hope of making peace between you and the citizens, and thus saving life and property." Cochise replied, "I am as much in favor of peace as anyone. I have not been out to do mischief for the past year. But I am poor; my horses are poor and few in number. I could have taken more horses on the Tucson road but have not done it. I have twelve captains out in different directions who have been instructed to go and get their living." Cochise's reply suggested the real nature of the problem. Ever since the whites had come to the land of the Apache, that warlike people had lived off the horses and cattle of the invaders. It was an essential part of the Indian economy. Under the Mexican government the efforts to force the Apache, the Waco, and the Comanche especially to stop their depredations had been intermittent and, for the most part, unsuccessful. With the Americans it was different. They were determined to make good their claims to inhabit the region. The Indians must become farmers. But that was, in essence, asking them to cease being Indians and to become some indeterminate, undefined creature that was neither an Indian nor a white man. The fact was that the Apache could not live as *Apache* without taking from white Americans, as they had taken from Mexicans for generations, an essential increment of food and other white artifacts. Denied the right to raid, they faced starvation. The white answer was "Stay on the reservations, and we will take care of you. Leave the reservation, raid white ranches and white settlements, and we will destroy you."

But Cochise and Howard could not say precisely this to each other. Howard instead urged Cochise to accept life-death on a reservation. "I would like to have a common reservation on the Rio Grande," he told Cochise, "for the Mimbreño Apache and Chiricahua Apache."

"I have been there and like the country," Cochise replied. Rather than not have peace, he would go there, but he could not guarantee that all his people would follow him. He believed, rather, that the move would "break my band." If Howard would give him a reservation at Apache Pass, then he might indeed be able to control his young braves and assure the safety of emigrants and settlers.

How long would Howard stay? Cochise asked. He must consult with his twelve sub-chiefs before he could agree to any move. "I came from Washington for the purpose of making peace," Howard replied, "and I will stay as long as necessary." Cochise seemed pleased with the general's response, but suddenly he broke out with a bitter recitation of the wrongs his people had suffered at the hands of the whites. "My best friends were taken by treachery and murdered," he reminded Howard. The infamous Bascom had left their bodies hanging until the elements and the predators had stripped their bones. "The Mexicans and Americans kill an Apache whenever they see him. I have fought back with all my might. My people have killed many Mexicans and Americans and have captured much property. Their losses are greater than ours; yet I know we are all the time diminishing in numbers. Why do you shut us upon a reservation? We want to make peace, and we will faithfully keep it; but let us go wherever we please, as the Americans do." To this Howard had no answer except to repeat that the Apache must accept settlement on a reservation. That was now the government's policy. Otherwise they could not be protected from the rapacity of the white settlers who were determined to occupy their lands. The land belonged to God, Howard decided. It did not belong to the white man or to the Indian. So there must be boundaries. The second point did not seem to Cochise to follow from the first. If the land belonged to God, why was it not open to all His children without distinction and without boundaries? Cochise did not, of course, allude to the fact that the Apache had, at the height of their power, appropriated the lands claimed by weaker tribes. It was, in any event, beside the point.

When the sub-chiefs arrived, the council began, and now Cochise, speaking for the others, insisted that the land of the Chiricahua must be their reservation. Howard at last reluctantly agreed. Jeffords must be the Indian agent for the reservation, Cochise declared, but Jeffords, knowing only too well the kinds of political pressures to which Indian agents were subject, refused. No Jeffords, Cochise declared, no treaty. Jeffords gave in. He would be agent if he were given complete authority so that no person could come onto the reservation without his permission. Confident that Grant would back him up, Howard agreed to Cochise's and Jeffords's conditions. The treaty, perhaps the most remarkable negotiated with any tribe in the post–Civil War period, was concluded, dispatched to Washington, and there twelve days later accepted by the President. "Hereafter," Cochise declared upon hearing the news, "the white man and the Indian are to drink of the same water, eat of the same bread, and be at peace."

Cochise observed the terms of the treaty. The Apache, unwilling to farm, cut hay and wood for the military units in the area, but the work was uncongenial to the warriors, and the promised supplies of government food were delayed in arriving. Cochise led a raiding party into Mexico on the ground that he had no treaty agreement with the Mexicans. He was wounded in the raid. The wound became infected, and soon it was evident that Cochise was dying. Jeffords remained with him much of the time.

According to Jeffords's account, one day when he was about to leave, Cochise said, "Chickasaw [brother] do you think you will ever see me alive again?"

"No, I do not think I will. I think that by tomorrow night you will be dead."

"Yes, I think so too—about ten o'clock tomorrow morning. Do you think we will ever meet again?"

"I don't know," Jeffords replied. "What is your opinion about it?"

"I have been thinking a good deal about it while I have been sick here, and I believe we will; good friends will meet again— up there."

"Where?"

"That I do not know—somewhere; up yonder, I think," Cochise said, pointing to the sky.

Early the next morning, he asked his warriors to bear him up the mountain to watch the sun rise over the mountain peaks. After Cochise's death Jeffords, knowing the white man's passion for exhuming the bones of Indians, told several conflicting stories of where the great chief's remains were placed. Twenty years later he took Nino Cochise, the chief's grandson, to the country of the Chiricahua Apache. It was dotted with ramshackle settlements and marginal ranches. Jeffords and young Cochise stopped at a ranch run by an old friend of the former scout, Billy Fourr, and Fourr declared bluntly, "If old Chose were alive and could see what happened to his land he'd blow a gasket."

Two years after Cochise's death, the treaty he and Howard had negotiated was broken. Without Cochise's restraining influence, incidents occurred. Ranchers complained of losing horses and cattle. The Chiricahua Apache were ordered to move to a reservation in New Mexico. Many of the young braves refused and once more there was warfare in the territory.

It has been estimated that in the efforts to bring Cochise and the Chiricahua Apache to account, more than a thousand soldiers were killed or died of disease with a loss of barely a hundred Apache. Nowhere else was there such an imbalance in white–Indian casualties. Cochise and his warriors ranged over a land they knew like the palms of their hands, a land so bleak and barren that soldiers followed at their peril.

If the Chiricahua Apache were the terror of the Southwest, other Apache tribes and their allies ranged over the area from south of the Platte to the Missouri. This territory was assigned to George Crook for pacification. Crook, as we have noted, was an experienced Indian fighter. He had won the admiration of many of the Indians he had defeated in battle, particularly the Shoshone. He accepted as inevitable the reservation system. Within its narrow limits, he was determined to deal fairly with the various tribes, knowing that they respected the military virtues and felt a kind of rapport with soldiers that did not extend to the civilians who pushed their way onto their lands. Crook clearly had a flair. Tall and thin, he wore a stained canvas hunting jacket and a pith helmet, both items strictly nonissue, and rode a handsome mule named Apache. With patient attention to the smallest detail, especially to the condition of his prized mules, he created excellent morale in the officers and men under his command. Not content to remain at the headquarters of his command, Crook undertook an expedition through Indian country, seeking out the various Apache chiefs and assuring them that they must cease their warlike ways or be utterly defeated. His story was always the same. If they would consent to adapt to a settled, agricultural life, he would protect them from any whites who tried to disturb them. He also stated that he would find work for all Indians who wished work and would pay them the same wages as those given to white men. Well aware of their resistance to reservation life, Crook assured them that they would be confined to reservations only until, with the help of Indian agents and teachers, they had learned white ways well enough to hold their own in white society. Then they would be free to mix in white society, attend white schools and churches, and become full citizens of the United States rather than wards of the federal government. It was an enlightened, if perhaps excessively optimistic, picture that Crook, in good conscience, painted for the suspicious chiefs.

To modern critics it smacks of ethnocentricity. The white man's ways were better; therefore, the Indians must abandon their traditional ways and become, for all practical purposes, nineteenth-century whites. But, it must be said, with the benefit of more than a hundred years of hindsight, no one has proposed a better solution to the "Indian problem." Considering that virtually all frontier settlers and many Americans who were in all other respects kindly and charitable wished to exterminate all Indians, Crook's policies and, even more, his attitude appear exemplary.

With his headquarters temporarily at Prescott, Crook displayed an insatiable curiosity about the surrounding countryside. Not only was he an eager anthropologist, anxious to learn everything he could about the cultural life of the tribes, but he was equally curious about the flora and fauna of the region. In addition, the general formed an alliance with the Paiute and Hualapai tribes, planning to enlist them if the efforts to persuade the Apache to accept reservation life failed and it was necessary to resort to force.

Believing that there was no hope of an enduring peace until the Apache bands felt the weight of military force, Crook prepared for that type of fighting for which the Indians were least prepared— winter campaigning. Winter was at best a precarious time for the Plains Indians. Like the deer and buffalo they depended upon, they grew lean and hungry, scratching up food where they could find it, often suffering acutely in hard winters. Their mobility was severely limited. Often they were reduced to eating their ponies or raiding neighboring tribes. The women and children were a heavy responsibility as well. Hence the disposition of all tribes was to sue for peace at the approach of winter. As important as his winter strategy was Crook's systematic enlistment of Apache who were disposed to peace or simply willing to work for a white man's wages. It was a policy that aroused the resentment of soldiers and settlers alike. The notion of paying an Indian a white man's wages offended them profoundly, but it drained away Apache strength, and when fighting came it provided Crook with a substantial body of Indian scouts familiar with the locations of the various Indian refuges.

Crook's practice was to place well-equipped and well-disciplined troops under the independent leadership of officers whose resourcefulness he trusted, with instructions to give the Indians no respite, to pursue them until they were defeated or until they could flee no longer. Women and children were not to be harmed, or prisoners mistreated. The strategy soon proved its effectiveness. Some Indians surrendered, others were killed. A troop commanded by Major William Brown surprised a large band of Apache in the Salt River Canyon and killed seventy-four braves. Those who escaped intercepted a party of Englishmen, killed a number, and tortured two to death. Crook caught up with the war party at Turret Peak a week later, and soon the survivors of the winter campaign were suing for peace on behalf of some 2,300 Apaches. Crook's terms were that those who surrendered must immediately start work on an irrigation project designed to bring water to the farms they would be required to till. Crook would see that the Indians were fairly paid for the crops they grew and that order was preserved on the reservation by Apache police. Those Indians who committed crimes would be tried by Apache juries. The Apache turned to and dug a canal five miles long, three feet deep, and four feet wide, the first such physical labor most of them had ever performed. Crook had also promised schools, but the federal government proved delinquent in providing them, and the general turned to missionaries for assistance.

Crook's principal obstacle proved to be the so-called Indian Ring, made up of private traders who fattened up exploiting the Indians and providing supplies for the army units sent out to fight them. They had a vested interest in perpetuating a state of warfare and did their best to discredit Crook with those authorities in Washington to whom he was accountable. Grant, however, gave the general his full support, and Crook in turn showed remarkable tact and skill in keeping the restless Apache appeased.

It might be well at this point to consider the life of the army officers and enlisted men charged with keeping peace in Indian country and with fighting the Indians when treaty agreements broke down.

There was a strange, symbiotic relationship between the "wild" Indians and the military men sent out to "tame" them. Men like Terry, Crook, and Howard were the best representatives of the army, decent and humane men who suffered pangs of remorse and bitter frustration when the government failed to make good on the promises it had authorized them to make to persuade hostiles to stop their predatory ways and remain on or return to their reservations. Better than bureaucrats of the Department of the Interior and the higher echelons of the War Department, better even than the pro-Indian lobby, they understood and respected the "savage" ethos of the tribes they were directed to bring to account. When the Bannock or Snake Indians, who had accepted reservation life in good faith and cooperated with the army in a number of its campaigns against other tribes, failed to receive their promised supplies from the government and were, in consequence, faced with starvation, Crook wrote a bitterly critical article for the *Army and Navy*

Journal, describing the situation in the bluntest terms. When there were not enough jackrabbits or buffalo to sustain them, "What," he asked, "were they to do? Starvation is staring them in the face, and if they wait much longer, they will not be able to fight . . . I do not wonder, and you will not either that when these Indians see their wives and children starving, and their last resources of supplies cut off, they go to war. And then we are sent out to kill. It is an outrage."

The life of U.S. soldiers in the frontier army post was an arduous one. The toll from illness and disease as well as Indian arrows and bullets was heavy, and the job, in a large measure, thankless. What glory there was went to the officers. For many white Americans it was, after all, the Indians, not the U.S. Army, who were the heroes. On the more positive side, the wild beauty of the landscape itself, combined with the aura of romance that hung over everything that had to do with the Indians, gave the life a strong appeal to the young and venturesome. Even the "Indian fighter," Custer, trying to persuade a civilian friend to accompany the Black Hills expedition of 1874, wrote:

> You shall taste of greater varieties of game than a New Yorker ever dreamed of and it will not be such as you obtain in the market houses . . . but it will be of such delicious flavor and condition as will make you wonder if you ever tasted game before. . . . The appetite you will have for food and the soundness of your sleep will be so different from those usually enjoyed by professional gentlemen in all kinds of life, that you will think you have fallen into fairyland and when you return to the states you will feel like a man who has been granted a renewed lease of life.

Among the most experienced troopers were the black cavalry-men of the 9th and 10th regiments—the Indians called them buffalo soldiers because of their kinky black hair that reminded them of a buffalo's mane. They made excellent soldiers. "They fight like fiends," Frances Roe reported. "And they certainly manage to stick on their horses . . ."

If Indian chiefs and U.S. Army officers respected each other as warriors, relations between the aborigines and the soldiers assigned to "protect" or to fight them were often tense. Those aborigines who were "at peace," or, as they were referred to, "treaty Indians," often got their kicks by scaring and harassing the soldiers and civilians at the forts and Indian agencies where they came for supplies, to trade, or simply to cause mischief. Well aware that soldiers were forbidden to fire at "friendly" Indians, they did not hesitate to take advantage of that fact by assuming arrogant or threatening manners. The wives of officers and new recruits were often the special targets of the devilry. Frances Roe, the wife of a cavalry officer, was horrified by her first contact with the "savages" at her husband's post at Fort Lyon. "Well, I have seen an Indian—number of Indians—but they were not Red Jackets," she wrote a friend, "neither were they noble red men. They were simply, and only, painted, dirty, and nauseous-smelling savages!" Shopping with a friend in a store at Las Animas, a small Mexican town near the fort, Frances Roe was alarmed when ten or twelve Indians dashed up on ponies, crowded into the little store "in their imperious way," and pushed the two white women aside "with such an impatient force that we both fell over the counter." They demanded from the intimidated shopkeeper powder, balls, and percussion caps, and one of those who had remained outside rode his piebald pony into the doorway of the store, preventing the frightened women from escaping. When the Indians departed, the storekeeper told the women that the visitors were Ute, much excited at the news that their traditional enemies, the Cheyenne, were in the vicinity. "Not one penny did they pay for the things they carried off," Frances Roe reported indignantly.

> They were all hideous—with streaks of red or green paint on their faces that made them look like fiends. Their hair was roped with strips of bright-colored stuff, and hung down on each side of their shoulders in front, and on the crown of each black head was a small, tightly plaited lock, ornamented at the top with a feather, a piece of tin, or something fantastic. These were their scalp locks.

They wore blankets over dirty old shirts, and of course had on
long, trouser-like leggings of skin and moccasins. . . . The odor
of those skins, and of the Indians themselves, in that stuffy little
shop, I expect to smell the rest of my life.

At Camp Supply, Frances Roe reported, a party of forty or fifty
Comanche "came rushing down the drive in front of the officers'
quarters, frightening some of us almost out of our senses. . . . They
rode past the houses like mad creatures, and out on the company
gardens, where they made their ponies trample and destroy every
growing thing." The Indians were "young bucks out on a frolic,
but quite ready, officers say, for any kind of devilment. They rode
around the post three or four times at breakneck speed, each circle
being larger, and taking them further away. . . . I presume there
were dozens of Indians on the sand hills around the post peeking
to see how the fun went on." A few nights later Frances Roe and
her husband were awakened by rifle shots and cries of "Indians!
Indians!" Pandemonium followed. Drums beat the long roll call to
arms, and the cavalry bugles sounded boots and saddles, sounds
that "strike terror," Frances Roe wrote, "to the heart of every army
woman." With the fort thoroughly aroused, the Indians rode off
with triumphant shouts. It was all a game.

The sense that they were always under surveillance by Indian
lookouts was strengthened by the not-uncommon experience of
being out hunting or simply riding for pleasure only to discover
that one was being watched by some motionless brave. Frances Roe,
through her husband's binoculars, watched an Indian sentinel on
a distant ridge. "He sat there on his pony for hours," she noted,
"both Indian and horse apparently perfectly motionless, but his face
always turned toward the post, ready to signal to his people the
slightest movement of the troops."

White men continued, as they had since the days of the
Yellowstone rendezvous, to live with various Indian tribes. Often
the reasons were more "anthropological" than commercial, a fascination with Indian culture and Indian ways.

Thomas Henry Tibbles, a journalist, Populist, and ardent friend of the Indians, spent a winter with the Omaha and eventually married an Indian woman. Tibbles gave a delightful account of tribes at play, of the endless dancing and storytelling, the garrulousness of the older braves and the bravado of the young. The lodges of the tribe were divided into groups Tibbles called clubs, the primary purpose of which was entertainment. The clubs vied among themselves for Tibbles's company. At Prairie Chicken's club, the young men danced first, "gaily painted and covered with bells. Then came a masked dance in which the men covered their faces with the heads of animals, then the young women danced and partners were chosen by means of a guessing game." Tibbles was pressed to teach his Indian friends some white dance steps. A drum was brought, he whistled a waltz, and after a time an Indian girl came forward to join. She had learned the "Rocky Mountain Waltz" from another tribe, and as she and Tibbles sang and danced the others joined in. "The whole group," Tibbles wrote, "was wild with excitement . . . and soon the tent was filled with pairs of Indians whirling around in a half-civilized, half-barbaric style that seemed to take all our senses away." Half the tribe, attracted by the noise, joined in; "everywhere there were shouts of laughter, screams of delight, the racket of drums." Finally the older women and men of the tribe, aroused by the revels, appeared and angrily put a halt to the festivities. White men's dances were forbidden to Indians; they were a corruption, "dangerous and indecent," prohibited by the tribal council "as long as the grass grows and the waters run."

When Tibbles next visited the Omaha, they had been forced to accept life on a reservation, and they were dramatically changed in health and appearance from the Indians he had visited a few years earlier. "The reserve was the poorest soil in the state and the Indian agency was made up of a few rough structures housing a blacksmith shop, a sawmill and a government storehouse." Seeing his friends reduced to hunger and misery and jeered at by the white loafers around the agency, Tibbles "felt a wave of fury toward our government's whole Indian policy. . . . Could it be God's will," he asked himself, "that men [like those he had known] brave, generous to a fault, dignified, intelligent, faithful to every trust, loving their families, and children and every inch of their native plains, should become beggars and gradually be swept off the face of the earth? Must they make room for a race of sordid people who were subordinating every noble instinct to a ruling passion for accumulating property?" The Indian's greatest failing, Tibbles reflected, was giving; the white man's custom was taking. He took everything the Indian gave and demanded more.

CHAPTER XIX

SCATTERED CAMPAIGNS

When Grant had been elected President in 1868, he had summoned Sherman back to Washington to take overall command of the army. Philip Sheridan had replaced him as commander of the Division of the Missouri, with responsibility to preserve peace with the Indians by making every effort to meet their most serious grievances.

Sheridan found his hands full. Among the Southern tribes the Comanche and Kiowa kept New Mexico and Texas in a state of continual agitation by their daring raids. While they were nominally confined to their reservations, they used them primarily as a base of operations for their raids. A chorus of outraged cries from settlers and traders penetrated the halls of Congress, and a proposal was made to shut off the Texas border by constructing a string of military reservations along the Texas boundary with New Mexico. In May, 1869, Kiowa chief Satanta led an attack on a wagon train and killed six teamsters. Satanta freely admitted that he was responsible. He was arrested, tried in a civil court, convicted of the murders, and sentenced to be hanged. Such a storm of protest was raised by champions of the Indians that Grant brought pressure on the governor of Texas to commute Satanta's sentence to life imprisonment. When the public clamor continued, the governor pardoned the chief and another Indian, to the rage of his Texas constituents. The episode is significant for what it reveals of the strength and numbers of what today we would call the Indian lobby. Upon the news of the chief's release, Sherman wrote to the offending governor that he hoped the first scalp that Satanta took would be his.

Raids and murders increased in number in the Southwest, motivated in large part by the frustration of the tribes over the systematic slaughter of their principal source of food, clothing, and many other essential items: the buffalo. The Kansas Pacific Railroad, for example, ran excursions from Leavenworth to the areas along its line where the buffalo abounded, and hunters, armed to the teeth, shot the great beasts, often from the train windows. Many were shot only for the tongue, others for their hides; in most cases their carcasses were left to rot. The situation was exacerbated by the fact that a new method of tanning buffalo hides greatly increased their value and started a kind of "buffalo rush" of professional hunters, who often killed more than a hundred buffalo at a single stand, or shooting station. Buffalo Bill Cody was famous for shooting hundreds of the animals at a time.

Raiding and fighting began anew. This time Nelson A. Miles was given command of five columns of regulars, infantry and cavalry, and the assignment of tracking down the Cheyenne, Comanche, and Kiowa who had strayed off their reservations. Miles's Fourth Cavalry found the tribes in winter camp in the Palo Duro Canyon on a fork of the Red River, surprised them, drove them out of their villages, and then systematically destroyed tepees, food supplies, cooking utensils, and more than 1,400 horses and mules. Soon hungry and demoralized Indians began trickling into the reservations, asking for food and shelter. They were disarmed and fed. Miles's troopers continued their pursuit relentlessly, fighting fourteen battles or skirmishes and destroying seven or eight Indian villages. Finally, the word came from Sherman to "ease down on the parties hostile at present." By March the last of the Southern Cheyenne had come into the agency at Darlington near Fort Reno, but when they considered themselves abused, a party broke free and took to the hills once again. The Comanche and Kiowa came into their reservations in June. Chiefs identified as leaders in the "revolts" from the reservations were sent into exile in Florida. Some went to Hampton Institute in Virginia for an education; and a school, headed by Richard Pratt, was started at Carlisle, Pennsylvania, for others.

By the late summer of 1869 the Cheyenne and Arapaho were also on the warpath once more, raiding settlements, killing 117 men, women, and children, and taking women captive, most of them to suffer the proverbial "fate worse than death," not once but numerous times. Short of regulars, Miles rounded up an odd lot of some fifty available males with a taste for Indian fighting and sent them off as scouts under Major George Forsyth with instructions to maintain contact with the Indians. When the Indians, several thousand in number, discovered they were being pursued by only a handful of soldiers, they launched an all-out attack on Forsyth's camp. The recruits were armed with seven-shot Spencer carbines. Classic Indian tactics were to ride close enough to the soldiers to draw fire from their laboriously loaded guns and then attack before they could reload. Now the Indians found that the new repeating rifles denied them that precious interval to close with the troopers. Nonetheless, they so far outnumbered the soldiers that it seemed as though the latter must suffer the fate of Fetterman's force. Forsyth's legs were broken by bullets, and another bullet fractured his skull, at which point he cried out, "We are beyond all human aid, and if God does not help us, there is none for us." Lieutenant Frederick Henry Beecher was fatally wounded, and Roman Nose, one of the most famous of the Cheyenne warriors, was killed. At dusk the attackers drew back, disheartened at the tenacity of the scouts' defense but confident that they could finish off the survivors the next day. Three scouts were dead, and seventeen wounded. After dark two men volunteered to go for help, and the rest dug foxholes in the sand. After a siege that lasted five days, the Cheyenne withdrew in frustration. Without horses and encumbered with wounded, Forsyth, suffering acutely from his wounds, had no choice but to wait for help to arrive. Nine days after the engagement had begun, a black cavalry regiment, the Tenth, arrived. Forsyth's experience convinced Sherman that there was no alternative to forcing the Indians to remain, as the treaty provided, on the reservations assigned to them. "All who cling to their old hunting grounds are hostile," Sherman wrote, "and will remain so until they are killed off." And to his brother, John, the Senator, he wrote: "The more we can kill this year, the less will have to be killed in the next war, for the more I see of these Indians the more convinced I am that all have to be killed or maintained as a species of pauper. Their attempts at civilization are simply ridiculous."

Meantime, the spectacular career of Colonel George Custer suffered a severe setback. Custer had graduated from West Point in the class of 1861. He promptly displayed qualities of leadership, along with a flamboyant style, that won him a series of promotions until at the end of the Civil War he was one of the youngest brevet major generals in the Union army. At the close of the war he reverted to his regular army rank of lieutenant colonel and was given command of the Seventh Cavalry.

Annoyed by the evasiveness of the Cheyenne and bored by the monotonous routine of campaigning against such an elusive adversary, Custer abandoned his men and headed back to Fort Riley for a conjugal visit to his adoring wife, Elizabeth. He covered the 150 miles to Fort Riley in fifty-five hours but twenty soldiers of his troop, exhausted by their commander's relentless pace, deserted, and he ordered twelve of the deserters shot. Custer was subsequently court-martialed for leaving his command in the field, for ordering the shooting of the deserters, and on five lesser charges. Convicted, he was sentenced to be suspended from his command for a year.

In the aftermath of the breakdown of the treaties of 1868–69, on which so much time and money had been expended, even Grant's patience began to run short. Doubtless influenced by Sherman, he expressed his determination to ensure the peaceful passage of emigrants across the Plains "even if the extermination of every Indian tribe was necessary to secure such a result." Despite such privately expressed opinions, no war of extermination took place. Efforts, fumbling and ineffective as they were, continued to be made to cajole or force the tribes to observe the terms of the treaties. It was as certain as the tides that Americans were going to pour westward. That issue had been settled by the gold rush of '49, by the subsequent discovery of gold and silver in the Rockies, by the settlement of the Northwest, and by every emigrant train that ventured out of Independence or Omaha, as well as by the laborious but irresistible movement of the railroads west (and eastward from the Pacific). It was just as inevitable that the tribes would do the only thing they knew how to do: hunt and fight for their way of life. Even if the United States government had faithfully observed every provision of every treaty, the westward progress of the nation could not have been arrested. The destruction of the tribes would have continued by one means or another, and the doomed tribes fought back, ferociously, cunningly, unavailingly.

Sherman decided to use a variation of the tactics he had employed successfully, on a smaller scale, in Georgia: a winter campaign of attrition that would give the Indians no rest and no opportunity to hunt or to protect their women and children in winter camps. Accordingly, Sheridan planned a three-pronged attack on the winter camp of the Cheyenne and Arapaho. He himself would lead the campaign. "I deemed it best to go in person," he wrote, "as the campaign was an experimental one—campaigns at such a season having been deemed impractical and reckless by old and experienced frontiersmen, and I did not like to expose the troops to great hazards without being present myself to judge of their hardships and privations." The words were those of a seasoned soldier. Under him was Custer, who, having served his year of exile, now was restored to command of the Seventh Cavalry, the horses and men of which he had so cruelly abused. Custer made amends by reorganizing and drilling the regiment until it was the best disciplined in

Sheridan's expeditionary force. Sheridan knew that good soldiering began with discipline, though it did not end there. He instructed Custer, who was to lead one of the columns, to hang all Indians found off the reservation and to take women and children prisoners. No distinction was to be made; and probably none could have been made, between Indians off the reservations who had been engaged in raids on white settlers and wagon trains and those who were simply roaming about, hunting.

A band of Cheyenne under Black Kettle, who had been present at Sand Creek, was surprised in its village on the Washita River. Although the Cheyenne fought back courageously, Black Kettle and many of his warriors were killed, the village itself was destroyed, and 875 ponies were killed; but there was none of the wanton killing that had disgraced the attack of Chivington's undisciplined soldiers. Although some women and boys were killed, it was alleged that they had been engaged in the fighting and were killed in self-defense. Meanwhile, word reached Custer that another column under the command of Joel Elliott was heavily engaged by a large war party. Custer, inexplicably, made no move to go to Elliott's support, and the glory, such as it was, of Custer's victory was severely compromised by the fact that the column was destroyed, and more than a thousand horses captured. Elliott and his staff were killed and mutilated. The uncharitable conjectured that Custer's failure to go to Elliott's support may have been related to the fact that Elliott had commanded the Seventh Cavalry during Custer's period of punishment.

Sherman wrote to Sheridan:

> I am well satisfied with Custer's attack and would not have wept if he had served Satanta [the Kiowa chief] and Bull Bear's band in the same style. I want you to go ahead; kill and punish the hostile, rescue the captive white women and children, capture and destroy the ponies, lances, carbines, etc, etc, of the Cheyennes, Arapahos and Kiowas; mark out the spots where they must stay, and then systemize the whole (friendly and hostile) into camps with a view

to economical support until we can get them to be self-supporting like the Cherokees and Choctaws.

Custer and Sheridan, perhaps sobered by the destruction of Elliott's column, decided on a more conciliatory line. Custer followed a Cheyenne band, caught up with it, rode into the camp with two aides, and persuaded Dull Knife, Fat Bear, and Big Head to go to their reservation without further resistance. The incident suggested that there were better ways to prevail on the tribes to observe the terms of the treaty than killing them. Sheridan's Washita campaign against the Southern Cheyenne brought a storm of protest from the Indian advocates. Grant was implored to withdraw the army and confer citizenship upon the Cheyenne, thereby ending the conflict.

On January 23, 1870, another Sand Creek massacre was enacted when Colonel Eugene M. Baker made a surprise attack on a band of Piegan in Wyoming Territory and killed 173 Indians, the great majority women and children. Piegan had been raiding white settlements, stealing cattle and horses and whatever else was not nailed down. When news of the attack reached the East, there was once again a storm of angry protest. In Congress Daniel Voorhees, an Indiana Democrat, declared that such attacks "cannot be justified before God or man," and *The New York Times* denounced the "sickening slaughter." Correspondingly, the response in the territory was to praise Baker and call for more such actions until all the Plains tribes were disarmed and placed on reservations. Lydia Maria Child placed the blame squarely on the military. The army's "approved method of teaching red men not to commit murder is to slaughter their wives and children . . . indiscriminate slaughter of helpless women and innocent babies is not war—it is butchery; it is murder. . . ." Wendell Phillips, in his characteristic vein, declared at a meeting of the Reform League: "I only know the names of three savages upon the Plains—Colonel Baker, General Custer, and at the head of all, General Sheridan (applause). . . . Thank God for a President in the White House whose first word was for the negro, and the second for the Indian; (applause). Who saw protection for the Indian, not in the rude and blood-thirsty policy of Sheridan and Sherman, but in the ballot, in citizenship, the great panacea that has always protected the rights of Saxon individuals."

Frederick Douglass sounded the same theme, declaring that, slavery aside, the condition of the Indian was "the saddest chapter of our history. The most terrible reproach that can be hurled at the moment at the head of American Christianity and civilization is the fact that there is a general consent all over this country that the aboriginal inhabitants . . . should die out in the presence of that Christianity and civilization." Both houses of Congress joined in with a resolution declaring that the "present military policy is unwise, unjust, oppressive, extravagant, and incompatible with Christian civilization."

Lydia Maria Child, always firm in her convictions, was determined to see the matter from the settlers' side as well as that of the Indians. In the aftermath of the Piegan Massacre, which she roundly condemned, she declared that the settlers "must be protected! . . . It is more than can be expected of human nature that the white frontier settlers, living as they do in the midst of deadly peril, should think dispassionately of the Indians, or treat them fairly." It was the responsibility of the government, she said, to protect both the lives of the settlers and the rights of the Indians.

The Piegan Massacre gave fresh impetus to the move to bring certain Indian chiefs to Washington. Red Cloud, who had wiped out Captain Fetterman's company in 1866, sent word to the army office in charge of Fort Fetterman that he and some of his chiefs were ready to go to Washington to inform the Great White Father firsthand of their grievances. They were received in Washington by Peter Cooper and other members of the United States Indian Commission like visiting royalty with parties and receptions that were concluded with a reception and splendid feast at the White House. Red Cloud, unimpressed by all the pageantry, addressed the members of the Board of Indian Commissioners in direct language: "The Great Father may be good and kind but I can't see it. . . . [He] has sent his people out there and left me nothing but an island. Our nation is melting away like the snow on the sides of the hills where the sun is warm; while your people are like the blades of grass in the spring when summer is coming."

Convinced that nothing was to be gained by further parleying in Washington, Red Cloud and his fellows demanded to be sent back to the Black Hills, but numbers of enthusiastic friends of the Indians were waiting to greet them in New York City. The chiefs professed indifference; they wanted to return to their tribe. They were put on the train, presumably headed for Omaha, but they found themselves a few hours later in New York—another instance of white deceitfulness. Peter Cooper did his best to smooth their ruffled feathers. When Red Cloud mentioned that Grant had refused him a gift of seventeen horses, Cooper promised to provide them. But before the chieftains could be presented to their sponsors, wicked James Fisk, the Wall Street speculator, spirited them away to his Grand Opera House, where reporters noted, "they appeared to take special delight in the fantastic gambols of the semi-nude coryphees and the gorgeous display of parti-colored fustian, glittering tinsel and red fire." It seems safe to assume that the chiefs felt far more at home with Jim Fisk than with serious, sober Peter Cooper.

The next night Red Cloud and his chiefs were introduced to a packed house by Peter Cooper himself. Red Cloud, wearing a high beaver hat, spoke through an interpreter. The Sioux were being punished, he declared, for the actions of a few maverick warriors who had been debauched by the whiskey given them by whites. "You have children," he said. "So have we. We want to rear our children well and ask you to help us in doing so. . . . We do not want riches, we want peace and love."

Red Dog, now an ancient chief but still a famous orator, followed Red Cloud.

> I have but a few words to say to you, my friends. When the Great
> Spirit raised us, he raised us with good men for counselors and
> he raised you with good men for counselors. But yours are all

the time getting bad while ours remain good. . . . I know all of
you are men of sense and men of respect, and I therefore ask you
confidently that when men are sent out to our country, they shall
be righteous men and just men, and will not do us harm.

I don't want any more men sent out there who are so poor that
they think only of filling their pockets. We want those who will
help to protect us on our reservations, and save us from those who
are viciously disposed toward us.

The success of the visit by Red Cloud, Spotted Tail, and the
other Sioux chiefs, which led to the formation of a whole new group
of organizations dedicated to helping the Indians, was followed
by another such excursion the next year, also sponsored by the
United States Indian Commission. This time there were Cheyenne,
Arapaho, and Wichita chiefs. The crucial issue, the chiefs made
clear, as their predecessors had done, was the intrusion of the railroads on Indian land. All else might be compromised or resolved,
but they would not tolerate the "iron horses" snorting their fiery
way across their hunting grounds, frightening the buffalo, and periodically setting fire to the dry grass. Columbus Delano, the new
secretary of the interior, told the delegation, "We cannot stop this
clearing of land and building of cities and railroads all over the
country. The Great Spirit has decreed it and it must go on." When
the chiefs addressed another overflow crowd at Cooper Union, they
begged their white friends to stop the building of railroads. Buffalo
Good, a Wichita, declared, "The white people have done a great
deal of wrong to our people and we want to have it stopped. If you
are going to do anything for us we want you to do it quick."

In reply, William Dodge promised that the commissioners
would continue to do their best to "manufacture public opinions"
favorable to the Indians and reiterated the commission's commitment
to "educate, elevate and Christianize them." A vast gap, which the
enthusiastic audience perforce ignored, lay between the Indian plea to
be left alone in the enjoyment of their lands and the white assurances

that they would help in every way to "civilize" them. It was plain beyond doubt or equivocation that the Indians had not the slightest disposition to be "civilized." That was the whole point; that was why they were there, pleading to be spared further infringements of their hunting ranges. Dramatic, absurd, and, above all, heartbreaking as these ritual meetings were, doomed as they were to fail in the overall hopes and expectations invested in them by Indians and reformers alike, they nonetheless served to emphasize the determination of the reformers to see justice done for the aborigines.

In Boston at the Tremont Temple, before another vast crowd, the theme was the same. This time Stone Calf was even more explicit: "Stop at once the progress of any railroads through our country, so that we may live in peace for a long time with the American people." It was like asking that the sun be arrested in its course or that the earth cease to turn. Wendell Phillips's plea that the sense of justice of the American people would ordain protection "to every atom of property and the most trifling right of the smallest Indian tribe" rang hollow.

Now chiefs of the most militant tribes came thick and fast. Red Cloud and twenty-nine members of his tribe were back again in 1872, this time under pressure to make way for the Northern Pacific Railroad, which was nearing the Powder River. Before the summer of 1872 was over, six more delegations of chiefs had visited the Eastern cities and the capital, presented their grievances to various official and unofficial bodies, drawn huge crowds at public meetings, and returned home to tell their fellow tribesmen of the great wealth and power of the United States as well as of the support of many white friends. In the end the ardent assurances of those same friends may have encouraged the more militant tribes to resist and thereby, inadvertently, made more fighting and more bloodshed inevitable. That was certainly what the furious Westerners believed with all their hearts and souls.

The year of 1872 was also the year of the presidential election, the year of the defection of the Liberal Republicans, under the leadership of Carl Schurz, Charles Francis Adams, and other dissenters, from the policies and scandals of Grant's administration. At this juncture Grant's strong support of the Indian peace policy, the so-called Quaker policy, stood him in good stead with the reformers. Many, like Wendell Phillips, who stood by him and refused to defect to Horace Greeley, cited, as their principal reason, Grant's firm and just treatment of the freedmen and the Indians. William Dodge praised the President's Indian policy, which, he declared, has "attracted the attention and sympathy of the whole Christian and philanthropic world."

Grant's victory in the election was not long past when the so-called Modoc War in California reactivated the friends of the Indians. The Modoc tribe, led by a skillful and rather devious chief named Captain Jack, had been rudely shuttled about from reservation to reservation (starting out in unhappy conjunction with their traditional enemies, the Klamath Indians). They rebelled against further shifts, and a force moved into their camp to round them up at gunpoint. They resisted, and a fight began. The Modoc withdrew to nearby lava beds, where they held the soldiers at bay. Finally, Captain Jack agreed to a meeting with General Edward R. S. Canby and two peace commissioners to discuss terms for peace. Canby and one of the commissioners were thereupon killed by Captain Jack and his chiefs, and the other commissioner, Alfred B. Meacham, was so severely wounded that he was left for dead. Californians immediately demanded severe punishment for the treacherous attack, and seventeen Modoc, Captain Jack among them, were rounded up by the army. The Eastern reformers were shaken by the episode, and the president's peace policy suffered a severe setback; but the philanthropists rallied vigorously, declaring that the murders, reprehensible as they were, were simply the inevitable fruit of decades of abuse and exploitation of the Western tribes. In the midst of a loud and bitter controversy over the murder of Canby and the peace commission, a group of whites waylaid the Modoc captives and captors and killed three of the Indians before they were driven off. Now the cry was raised in the East for equal justice under the law. The killers of the Indians had to be apprehended and brought to trial. Alfred Meacham, the surviving commissioner, added his voice to those who called for restraint and moderation in meting out punishment to the Modoc, declaring that there were "white men in California and Oregon more responsible for the blood of General Canby than Captain Jack himself." Meacham's emergence as an advocate of peace with the Indians caused joy in the ranks of the reformers. When he spoke at the Park Street Church in Boston, defending the Modoc Indians, Wendell Phillips declared, "Never before have we had such a witness upon the stand. Covered all over with wounds received at the hands of the Indians; having suffered all that man can suffer and still live—that he should yet lift up his voice in their behalf, affords a marvelous instance of fidelity to principle, against every temptation and injury." Recovered from his wounds, Meacham gave as many as five lectures a week in churches of the Northeast.

When Jack and five other Modoc were sentenced by an army court-martial to be hanged, the peace forces, led by the Universal Peace Union, turned their attention to trying to win executive clemency from the president. A party that included Lydia Maria Child was given an audience with Grant, who assured its members that "all the condemned Modocs should not be hung." After months under siege by delegations, memorials, and petitions the president commuted the sentences of two of the convicted Modoc to life imprisonment. Under the circumstances it represented at least a partial victory for the reformers and was taken as a reaffirmation of Grant's commitment to a policy of peace and reconciliation.

The reformers now began to place their principal emphasis on persuading the aborigines to accept land in severalty—i.e., individual landholdings. This campaign, undertaken with the best of intentions, had little support from the tribes themselves. The charge that it was simply another ruse to deprive them of what little was left of their reservations was answered by the provision that once each male Indian had received 160 acres, the remaining lands on the reservation would be held in trust for the tribe, with any income that might accrue from their rental to be allocated for the use of the tribe.

CHAPTER XX

THE END OF THE INDIAN WARS

The so-called Red River War of the winter of 1874–75 was, in fact, far less a war than a campaign of attrition waged to force the destitute Indians to accept life on the reservations. It did mark the end, however, of the free hunting life of the Southern Plains Indians, specifically the Southern Cheyenne, the Kiowa, and most tribes of the Comanche.

In the region set aside for the Sioux and the Northern Cheyenne, a vast area whose centerpiece was the Black Hills, Sherman and his lieutenants had demonstrated their determination to keep whiteskins out and redskins in. But pressure built up constantly from lumbermen and mining prospectors to open the area. Rumors persisted that the Black Hills were full of gold and silver. The Panic and Depression of 1873, it was argued, might be relieved by the economic stimulus provided by the discovery of great new gold mines. For the Sioux and the Cheyenne the Black Hills were objects of religious veneration, filled, the aborigines believed, by spirits and to be avoided; their concern was with the deer and buffalo of the Yellowstone Basin.

In addition to these pressures, the Cheyenne and Sioux were suspected of raiding south of their southern boundary line into the Department of the Platte, where General Edward O. C. Ord was charged with protecting the Pawnee and the Osage. General Terry, in command of the Division of the Missouri's Department of the Dakota—which included the Black Hills region—argued that the only way he could control the activities of the Sioux and Cheyenne was by establishing a strong military post on the reservation. He put his case to Sheridan, who recommended to Sherman that "In order to better control the Indians making these raids toward the south," a large post be established "so that by holding an interior point in the heart of Indian country we could threaten the villages and stock of the Indians, if they made raids on our settlements." With this in mind it was necessary to make a reconnaissance into the Indian territory. Custer was chosen to make a detailed report on the country with special attention to the Black Hills themselves.

In addition to ten companies of cavalry and a vast wagon train of supplies, the Custer expedition included five newspaper reporters, among them twenty-three-year-old William Eleroy Curtis, reporting for the *New York World*. Curtis fell immediately under Custer's spell and soon became a kind of personal flack man for the colonel. "He is a great man—a noble man," Curtis wrote, " . . . a slender, quiet gentleman, with a face as fair as a girl's, and manners as gentle and courtly as the traditional prince." The reporter found the great Indian fighter teaching two small girls to read—one was white and one black.

Prominent in the expeditionary force was Bloody Knife, an Arikara warrior, a number of whose relatives had been killed by the Sioux and who served as chief Indian scout and personal aide to Custer. Even before the expedition was under way, a national debate began over whether it should have been authorized. The friends of the redskins denounced Grant for allowing it. William Hare, Episcopal bishop and special commissioner to the Sioux, declared it a "high-handed outrage," but General Terry insisted it was merely a necessary reconnaissance, consistent with the government's policy—going back more than fifty years to the days of Stephen Long—of "sending exploring parties of a military character into unceded territory. . . . Can it be supposed," Terry wrote, "that it was the intent of the treaty [of 1868] to set apart, in the heart of the national territory, a district nearly as great as the largest State east of the Mississippi River— two-thirds as large as the combined area of the six New England States—within which the government would be forbidden to exercise the power which it everywhere else possesses, of sending its military forces where they may be required?"

When the expedition set out in early July, 1874, it was a classic Custer performance. Sixteen musicians on white horses played "The Girl I Left Behind." Custer rode at the head of the column, gay with flags and company guidons, in his buckskins with his famous broad-brimmed hat and red neckerchief; his greyhounds ranged ahead, and Frederick Grant, the president's son, rode alongside. Fred had earlier been sent on a sea voyage by his father in hopes of drying him out. Now he would try a land expedition, with, as it turned out, no more success.

At least one member of the expedition, Private Theodore Ewert, had no illusions about the expedition or its commander. One of the burdens of American officers has always been that they have had in the ranks of enlisted men well-educated and literate individuals eager to record their superiors' foibles and shortcomings. Ewert was a German immigrant who had served as a lieutenant in the Civil War. In his view, Custer was more interested in winning military acclaim than in collecting scientific data. "The unknown and unexplored Black Hills offered all the inducements for more fresh laurels, and to enable him to gather these, no matter at what cost of labor, trouble, or life, became his study by night and by day," Ewert wrote. "The honor of himself and his country weighed lightly in the scale against the 'glorious!' name of Geo. A. Custer. . . . The United States Government forgot its honor, forgot the sacred treaty in force between itself and the Dakota Sioux, forgot its integrity, and ordered the organization of an Expedition for the invasion of the Black Hills."

Ewert was by no means an uncritical champion of the Indians. He expressed indignation that chiefs like Red Cloud, "the cause, author and instigator of the Fort Phil Kearny massacre," who were guilty of murdering settlers and killing numerous Indians of other tribes, were allowed to go about unmolested. "Indian agents," he wrote, "would lose their profitable situations, were every red scamp punished according to their deeds. . . . Oh thou mighty and omnipotent, great and revered 'Almighty Dollar' thou makest men corrupt and rotten, for thy smile men commit murder, sacrifice every noble feeling, cut the throat of father, mother, brother or sister, to gain thee." The victims, in Ewert's view, were the common soldiers sent off on a perilous mission the ultimate aim of which was to provide profits for avaricious speculators.

The expedition seldom saw Indians, but it was kept under constant surveillance by lookouts, and word of its progress was sent ahead by smoke signals. "So far," Curtis wrote at the end of July, "we have seen nothing remarkable; the miners have discovered no gold; the geologists have wacked in vain for the fossil of the 'missing link'; the naturalists have emptied their saddle pockets day after day without revealing the existences of any new wonders in life; the soldiers have fought no Indians, and so far, the expedition in a positive sense, has been unsuccessful." In the Black Hills the expedition came on an Edenic valley, filled with wildflowers. The band played "How So Fair," and the troopers stuck flowers in their caps. The soldiers got up a baseball game between the Actives and the Athletes; a glee club performed, and the expedition became rather like an extended camping trip. Finally, the miners in the party began to find indications of gold-bearing quartz, and soon most of the members of the expedition were panning for gold. It was far from a gold strike or the "new El Dorado" that many advocates of the expedition had predicted, but it was enough to feed the rumors. Although Custer in his report to Sheridan warned that on such a slim basis "no opinion should be formed . . . regarding the richness of the gold," opinions *were* formed. When word of the modest finds reached Fort Laramie, the *Yankton Daily Press & Dakotan* announced: "STRUCK

IT AT LAST! Rich Mines of Gold and Silver Reported Found by Custer. PREPARE FOR LIVELY TIMES! . . . National Debt to Be Paid When Custer Returns."

A correspondent's dispatch to the *New York Tribune* was far less fervent. "Those who seek the Hills only for gold must be prepared to take their chances," he wrote. "Let the over-confident study the history of Pike's Peak. The Black Hills, too, are not without ready-made monuments for the martyrs who may perish in their parks." After eight weeks the expedition was back at Fort Lincoln, from where it had departed. It had covered more than eight hundred miles and seen only a handful of Indians. Elizabeth Custer added a final dramatic touch by fainting in her husband's arms on his return.

A prolonged and acrimonious debate on the gold question now followed. The Eastern, generally pro-Indian, press took the line that the talk of gold was all fantasy intended to draw miners to the region and nullify the Treaty of 1868. Fred Grant was widely quoted as declaring that he had seen no gold, news that enraged the citizens of such towns as Bismarck and Yankton. Army or no army, there was no stopping the gold-hungry whites. Within six months it was estimated that at least eight hundred miners were prowling about the hills, many of them anticipating a new treaty with the Sioux that would open the hills to mining for gold and silver. The treaty meeting took place in the summer of 1875. Twenty thousand Sioux gathered along the banks of the White River. They and their chiefs, now convinced that vast wealth was hidden in the Black Hills, were divided between those who were opposed to ceding the land under any terms and those determined to strike a hard bargain with the government negotiators.

When the parleying began, Red Dog announced that he and his tribe, in return for abandoning their claim to the Black Hills, wished to be taken care of by the government for "seven generations ahead." Red Cloud echoed the demand. Little Bear added: "Our Great Father has a house full of money. . . . The Black Hills are the house of gold for the Indians. We watch it to get rich. . . ." Spotted Tail, who had carefully abstained from making war against the whites, added his own note: "As long as we live on this earth we will expect pay. We want to leave the amount with the President at interest forever. . . . I want to live on the interest of my money. . . ." What would the government pay? It offered $400,000 a year for the mining rights or $6,000,000 for purchase. That was not enough, the chiefs declared, and the negotiations were broken off.

The government had a final weapon to use. Under the terms of the Treaty of 1868 the government was obliged to provide "annuities" for the tribes for four years. After the four years had expired, the government had continued the subsidies. Unless the tribes now agreed to sell or lease the Black Hills, the government would withdraw the subsidies. In a real sense the independence of the Plains Indians (and, indeed, all the rest of the tribes) had ended the day they first agreed to accept a yearly issue of food and goods. Thereafter the life of each tribe revolved, to a greater or lesser degree, around the yearly distribution of highly desired items. In addition to making the Indians hopelessly dependent, the purchase and distribution of the supplies provided, as we have noted, endless temptations for cheating and corruption on the part of those whites (and, in some instances, Indians) charged with making the distributions. Often the annuity goods arrived late while the aborigines grew increasingly impatient and hostile. Indeed, the terrible Minnesota uprising that resulted in the deaths of so many unsuspecting settlers had derived some of its impetus from the delay of the government's yearly quota and dissatisfaction over its distribution. The Indians both longed for, and often desperately needed, the foodstuffs and resented that longing, knowing that it was the mark of their dependence.

The more militant Indians from every tribe began to repair to the standards of the more intractable chiefs, Crazy Horse and Sitting Bull most prominent among them. The tales of Indian outrages mounted, along with rumors that the Sioux and Northern Cheyenne were joining forces for a campaign of extermination against all whites. Many of the chiefs were convinced that they must make a stand at all costs or lose whatever remained of the game. Others warned against provoking a showdown with the army. There were far too many white men ever to think of conquering them. These chiefs argued that the best that could be hoped for was an agreement that would protect the tribes from starvation—through yearly allotments of food—and guarantee them sufficient land on which to establish themselves as farmers or ranchers. The more warlike argued, much as the United States military men did, that the only thing the whites understood was force. Recent experience had proved that killing substantial numbers of white soldiers was the only way to make the United States government more tractable. Hadn't the destruction of Fetterman's force led directly to the Treaty of 1868, the abandonment of the forts on the Bozeman Trail, and eight years of relative peace? It was a hard argument to answer. Red Cloud's reputation was tarnished by the fact that he had settled down in good faith to try to prevail on his people to learn the white man's agricultural techniques. The more militant Indians, while rejecting Red Cloud's leadership, pointed to his victories in 1868 as evidence that the United States Army could be decisively defeated in battle.

Gall, leader of the Hunkpapa Sioux, threw his weight and that of his tribe behind Sitting Bull and Crazy Horse. The so-called non-treaty Indians withdrew to the Yellowstone Basin and, in effect, dared the U.S. Army to try to root them out. Things were brought to a head by the advance of the railroad line into territory reserved to the Sioux and Cheyenne under the Treaty of 1868. One of the purposes of that treaty had been to ensure the peaceful construction of the railroad; but the commissioners had failed to define the route carefully, and now it was evident that it would pass south of the Yellowstone, in Sioux country. Two commissioners were sent to try to negotiate a passage for the railroad, but the Indians were adamant. No railroad.

After the failure of the White River parley, the Indian Bureau ordered all the tribes in the Black Hills Reservation to report to Fort Laramie. It was the dead of winter, a time of year when traveling in the Montana–Wyoming region was exhausting and hazardous.

It is not even clear that all the tribes were notified of the order. In any event only one tribe responded to the call. Those that did not were assumed to be hostiles, and Sheridan made plans to launch a campaign against them. Again he decided on the three converging columns strategy. Terry was to command one column of some thousand soldiers. General George Crook was to advance from the region of the North Platte River toward the Yellowstone Valley. Colonel John Gibbon would proceed along the Yellowstone from Fort Ellis. The three columns would meet near the junction of the Bighorn and the Yellowstone.

The campaign of 1875–76 began in the dead of winter, and the soldiers, in consequence, suffered severely from the weather. Pushing on to the Powder River, Crook encountered the tracks of Indian ponies in the snow, followed them, and fell on a camp of sleeping Cheyenne, who were, in fact, preparing to return to their agency. The Indians fought back doggedly and finally routed the soldiers, who fled, leaving their dead and, it was said, a wounded soldier. The Cheyenne chief, Two Cloud, swore revenge on the whites for what he believed to have been a treacherous attack. It was not a promising beginning. The tribes took heart, and the numbers of hostile Indians increased dramatically. Meanwhile, Sheridan called off further campaigning until early spring.

A renewal of the campaigning was delayed by the prolonged absence of Custer from his command. When Secretary of War William Belknap's bribe-taking began to come to light, Custer had offered to testify about the secretary's misuse of his powers in various army posts on the frontier. He was called to Washington, where his testimony turned out to be primarily hearsay and conjecture. Indeed, Custer went so far as to implicate Grant's brother and hint that the president himself had been involved in dubious practices in regard to the boundaries of Indian reservations. All this delayed the beginning of the campaign against the Indians since Custer was still in command of the Seventh Cavalry and was to have led the column under Terry's overall command. Finally, orders came from Sherman that Custer was to be relieved of his command and that

Terry himself was to take personal charge of the column. Custer was to remain at St. Paul. Custer's numerous friends and admirers hastened to intercede with Grant, to whom Custer wrote a pleading letter that contained the sentence, "I appeal to you as a soldier to spare me the humiliation of seeing my regiment march to meet the enemy and I not to share its dangers." Doubtless aware of the public clamor that would be aroused by grounding Custer and conscious that his enemies would charge him with vindictiveness, Grant reluctantly gave his consent. In forwarding the president's permission, Sherman added a cautionary note to Terry: "Advise Custer to be prudent, not to take along any newspaper men, who always make mischief, and to abstain from personalities in the future." But Custer was beyond redemption or reform. He took a newspaper reporter with him, and he told a fellow officer that he intended to "cut loose from General Terry during the summer," even though it was to Terry's support that he largely owed his restoration.

With Terry in command, the column of 1,200 men left Fort Lincoln at dawn on May 17, 1876; Custer's Seventh Cavalry was the largest and most experienced unit. The column contained 45 Indian scouts, most of them Arikara, and 190 civilians. Custer's brother Thomas commanded C Company, and his brother-in-law James Calhoun was in command of L Company. A nephew, Armstrong Reed, was also a member of the expedition, as was another of Custer's brothers, Boston. Terry's column made contact with that of Colonel Gibbon near Rosebud Creek, and the two forces awaited the arrival of Crook, coming up from the Platte. Crook, with 180 Crow scouts and a force generally comparable to that of Terry, advanced along the Bozeman Trail past the sites of the three forts once intended to guard it. As Crook approached Rosebud Creek, having forded the Powder, his scouts informed him that a large party of Sioux lay ahead. On June 16, Crook prepared to do battle.

The Sioux were spoiling for a fight. Sitting Bull, after undergoing ritual torture involving the cutting of some fifty pieces of flesh from his arms and chest, had had a vision of the soldiers being defeated. The next day the Cheyenne and the Sioux, some thousand strong, led by Crazy Horse, swept down on Crook's column. Crazy Horse, the Oglala chieftain, gave his cry, "Come on, Dakotas, it is a good day to die." The fighting soon broke down into small groups of whites and Indians engaged in desperate combat, often hand to hand. Crook's efforts to form conventional lines failed, and throughout the day the battle was a standoff, with neither side able to gain a decisive advantage. What was unsettling to Crook was the fact that the Indians fought with much more than ordinary tenacity. Generally, if an attack failed, the Indians, easily discouraged and seldom under any overall discipline, would withdraw after an hour or so. Now they fought all day long, not abandoning the field until dusk. Crook claimed victory—"My troops beat these Indians on a field of their own choosing and drove them in utter rout from it. . . ."—but it was soon apparent that he had accomplished nothing in terms of routing the tribes or seriously diminishing either their capacity or their resolution to resist the intrusion of the white soldiers.

Meanwhile, finding no Indians on the Yellowstone or the lower reaches of the Rosebud, Major Marcus Reno, second-in-command of the Seventh Cavalry, had been sent with six companies on a reconnaissance toward the Powder River. Disobeying orders, Reno headed for the Tongue, crossed the valley of that river, and turned toward the Rosebud, where Crook was already engaged with Crazy Horse's warriors. When Reno returned without encountering any Indians, Terry concluded that the main body of aborigines must be in the vicinity of the Little Bighorn. His strategy was to send Gibbon up the Bighorn while Custer and the Seventh circled around by way of the Little Bighorn to take the enemy in the flank or rear. Custer resisted all suggestions for augmenting the Seventh with howitzers or additional companies of cavalry. The Seventh could take care of itself, he assured Terry. Before it departed on its mission, Custer presented a dashing review with the regimental band playing and the men smartly turned out. Terry's parting words were "God bless you." Colonel Gibbon, often a rival, called out, "Now, Custer, don't be greedy. Wait for us."

It was, of course, just the moment Custer had been waiting and hoping for: to be off on his own beyond Terry's immediate control with a golden opportunity to whip Indians and acquire more fame and glory. At the point where the trail, followed a few days earlier by Reno, dropped into the valley of the Rosebud, another trail diverged toward the Little Bighorn. This trail Terry had specifically told Custer to avoid. He was to push farther along toward the waters of the Tongue before he turned west toward the Little Bighorn, but Custer, greedy to engage the hostiles before the rest of the expedition could arrive to share the glory, devised a very different plan. He would cross over to the Little Bighorn, thereby stealing a march on Terry's main force (actually the troops were almost evenly divided between Terry and Custer), and spend the next day concealed, while his scouts located the lodges of the Sioux and Cheyenne. Custer's men moved by night. At dawn the scouts, climbing the divide between the valley of the Rosebud and that of the Little Bighorn, observed a large Indian camp along the banks of that river. The campfires of the Seventh, meanwhile, were visible for miles, and any hope of a surprise attack was lost. Custer, without waiting for support from Gibbon, decided to attack at once. Rousing his weary men, he hurried them along into the valley of the Little Bighorn, where he divided his force into combat units. One, under the command of Captain Frederick Benteen, consisting of approximately 125 troopers, was sent off in pursuit of any Indians that could be discovered. (Benteen, it should be noted, despised Custer as a self-promoter, who had callously abandoned Joel Elliott at the Washita battle, and he referred to Custer's account of his accomplishments—*My Life on the Plains*—as "My Lie on the Plains.")

Custer, meanwhile, advanced with the remaining companies toward the river. The objective he was approaching in such cavalier fashion was, it turned out, a vast encampment, as large as any recorded (except for treaty meetings) in the history of the Plains Indians. It has been estimated that there were more than 2,000 lodges and wickiups and, with the rough rule of thumb being at least two warriors to a lodge, some 4,000 warriors and perhaps 12,000

Indians, counting women, children, and old men. There were Gall of the Hunkpapa, Crow King, Sitting Bull, Hump, Spotted Eagle, Low Dog, Big Road, and, most important of all, Crazy Horse, elated by his victory over Crook a week earlier, a victory of which, incidentally, Custer knew nothing.

When Custer saw a small party of Indians fleeing, he concluded that the hostiles were already on the run. Anxious to prevent their escape, he ordered Major Reno to pursue them, promising that he would be "supported by the whole outfit." Reno took off with some 112 soldiers and 25 Indian scouts. As soon as he had crossed the river, he was disabused of the notion that the Sioux and Cheyenne were in flight. A large party of warriors—it was later estimated at 1,000 or so—rode out of the encampment to meet him.

Reno sent word at once to Custer, undoubtedly assuming that he would, as he had promised, come to his support. But Custer had other plans, and Reno was left to fight his way out of the mass of attacking Indians as best he could, taking heavy casualties in the process and abandoning the wounded to slow deaths by torture. By the time Reno had re-crossed the river half his men were dead or wounded and he deployed the survivors among the rocks to hold off the assailants as best they could. Meanwhile, Benteen, on the way back from his fruitless expedition in search of Indians, was met by a messenger, Giovanni Martino, ordering him to hurry on to support an attack on a "big village." In a few miles Benteen came on the remnants of Reno's battalion, making a desperate, last-ditch defense. Benteen took command of the combined units from the demoralized Reno.

As the warriors opposing the Reno–Benteen force drifted away, Benteen moved his command, trying to make contact with Custer. Before he could, he found himself surrounded by hundreds of mounted warriors, who forced him to take up defensive positions once again. When nightfall came, Benteen's men were still beleaguered, and they began to work with any implement at hand to strengthen their defenses. The position that Benteen had chosen on a hilltop was a natural fortification, and the following day the soldiers kept the enemy at bay, even making several charges to drive back Indians who ventured too close for comfort.

Custer had followed Reno until he received word that the latter was under attack; he then turned along the east bank of the river, apparently with the intention of attacking the Indians on their flank. The Sioux had seen Custer and anticipated this attack. To Custer it appeared that the Sioux and Cheyenne had abandoned their villages, and he prepared to gallop gloriously into the encampment and rout out whatever Indians might remain. Before he could carry out his plan, more Indians than the colonel had ever seen before in a single engagement poured over a nearby ridge, screaming their war cries. Custer hardly had time to dispose his troops in defensive positions before they were inundated by Gall's Hunkpapa, followed by successive waves of warriors, Crazy Horse's Oglala Sioux and Two Moon's Cheyenne. In almost less time than it takes to tell, the outnumbered soldiers were beaten down. Fifty-one of the survivors, many wounded, gathered around their colonel for a last desperate stand and were cut down one after another. Custer had had his famous shoulder-length golden hair, now streaked with gray, cut before the campaign began, and the Indians left his hair and his naked body intact. It was a gesture of respect for the most famous of the Indian fighters.

Meanwhile, the combined companies of Reno and Benteen held off their attackers. The Indian fire became desultory, and after noon on June 26 Benteen's scouts brought word that the Indians, having learned of the approach of Terry and Gibbon, were breaking camp and preparing to move. The next day Gibbon's column arrived to lift the siege. Reno and Benteen between them had lost some 50 killed and as many wounded out of a combined force of fewer than 250 men.

No one knew where Custer and his troopers were. Finally, they were discovered by scouts—the stripped, scalped, and mutilated bodies of 197 men, scouts, soldiers, Custer's brothers and brother-inlaw, Custer himself, and the unfortunate newspaper reporter who had accompanied him to record his brilliant deeds.

Not one man was left to tell the tale of the worst military disaster in the long series of Indian wars that stretched back to the beginning of the century.

Undoubtedly, Benteen and Reno and the men under their command who survived did so, in large part, because the Indians were drawn off by the threat that Custer posed to the village. There has been much controversy over the question of mutilation—how many bodies were mutilated, how many scalped, etc. The matter is, to a large degree, irrelevant. The Indians commonly mutilated the bodies of their enemies—white or red. Indian representations of the battle, of which there are a number, indicated mutilations. If the bodies of some of the slain soldiers were not scalped or mutilated, it was due to the fact that the victors had more pressing matters on their minds rather than to any change in traditional practices.

Grant, remorseful that he had weakened in his resolution not to allow Custer to accompany the expedition, did not hesitate to place the blame on that officer, but in all the charges and countercharges that followed the Battle of the Little Bighorn, the popular disposition to see Custer as hero proved insurmountable. Truth was powerless before the myth. Although the soldiers themselves were well aware of the series of horrendous blunders that had led to the disaster, it would be years before the full story was unraveled. Custer's image as heroic Indian fighter was so firmly established in the public mind—primarily, of course, by Custer himself—that it would prove impervious to anything as simple as the truth. Moreover, all efforts to reveal the facts were relentlessly opposed by his bereaved widow, who spent the balance of her long life protecting the reputation of her hero, going so far as to threaten lawsuits against anyone bold enough to step forward with the truth.

The fact that the news of the "massacre," as it was called, or, more commonly, "Custer's Last Stand," reached the nation just at the moment of national apotheosis, when Americans were engaged in an orgy of self-congratulation over the first glorious hundred years of the Republic, made it perhaps inevitable that the episode would be taken as proof that the remaining aborigines must be punished in such a conclusive way that they would never again pose a serious threat to the lives of American citizens. Viewed in the light of the widespread public reaction of horror and anger, Little Bighorn may have been the costliest victory ever suffered by a people fighting for survival against enormous odds. The voices of that not inconsiderable company that espoused the cause of the Indians were drowned out by those who pressed for a "final solution" to the Indian problem.

General Terry was supplied with new recruits and he and Crook, who had come off comparatively lightly at Rosebud, were heavily reinforced by Sheridan and given the assignment of bringing the culprits to account. They set off in early August with 2,100 soldiers and 225 scouts, primarily Shoshone and Ute, after the elusive Cheyenne and Sioux. In Terry's command was a white scout named Bill Cody. Their efforts proved abortive. Combing the vast area of the Black Hills Reservation, they found no Indians and engaged in no battles. At last, Crook, largely through the efforts of his Indian scouts—some of them Sioux and Cheyenne—found the village of Dull Knife and his band of Cheyenne, killed a number of Indians in a pitched battle, and destroyed their village. Colonel Miles, meanwhile, drove Gall and Sitting Bull into Canada and persuaded many of their followers to return to their Indian agency. With Gall and Sitting Bull in Canada, the military forces under Miles and Crook concentrated on hunting down Crazy Horse, the last of the great Sioux leaders still at large. Crook finally persuaded Crazy Horse and some 800 of his followers to come to the Red Cloud agency and give up their arms.

In the course of the peace conference the now powerless Sioux, Cheyenne, and Arapaho were deprived of a third of the region reserved to them in the Treaty of 1868, including the Black Hills. Crook, who had prevailed on Crazy Horse to abandon his intransigence with the promise of a reservation on the Tongue River—an area that the chief prized—found that he was unable to deliver on his promise (though to his credit, it must be said, he left no politician or bureaucrat unturned in his efforts to make good on his word). There was to be a tragic denouement. Crook was determined to try to enlist Crazy Horse in a campaign against the Nez Percé who had left their reservation and were raiding in the area of eastern Montana. A sequence of misunderstandings led Crook to order the arrest of Crazy Horse. When Crazy Horse saw that he was being taken to the guardhouse at the agency, he began to resist and was stabbed and fatally wounded by a soldier's bayonet. It seems apparent that part of the confusion that led to the death of the famous chief was caused by Indians at the agency hostile to Crazy Horse. The incident might thus serve to remind us of one of the major disadvantages that the tribes labored under in their effort to preserve their land and their way of life against white encroachments. The hostility among the various tribes was almost invariably greater than the hostility of the respective tribes for the whites. Black Elk, one of the Sioux warriors, was convinced that Crazy Horse was deliberately assassinated. "Afterwards," he declared, "the Hang-Around-the-Fort people said that he was getting ready to tie up his horse's tail again and make war on the Wasichus [the whites]. How could he do that when he had no guns and could not get any? It was a story the Wasichus told, and their tongues were forked when they told it. Our people believe they did what they did because he was a great man and they could not kill him in battle and he would not make himself over into a Wasichu, as Spotted Tail and the others did."

Inveterate tribal hatreds made common action against the whites impossible except like the Sioux and Cheyenne that had been allied with each other. In some instances, it is true that tribes traditionally hostile to each other joined in fighting the white men's soldiers, but such alliances were relatively rare. It was far more common, as we have seen, for Indians to join whites in hunting down their tribal enemies. Without the skillful assistance of Crow, Utes, Pawnee, and Shoshone scouts, the efforts of Sheridan, Terry, Crook, and Miles would have been severely handicapped. The Sioux had helped to defeat the Sac and Fox warriors fighting under Black Hawk.

As the most powerful and warlike tribe in the Great Plains the Sioux had, over decades, driven other tribes—the Pawnee, Crow, and Shoshone prominent among them—from their ancient hunting grounds. Thus, when they came at last to stand as the principal barrier to the white man's westward advance, their only substantial allies were the Northern Cheyenne and a handful of Arapaho. The hands of most other tribes were turned against them. Nonetheless, the various tribes of Sioux, along with the Cheyenne and Arapaho in the north, for forty years impeded, if they could not stop, the westward movement of emigrating white Americans, while the Apache, Comanche, and Southern Cheyenne did the same in the region of the Red River, in New Mexico, and along the borders of Texas. They exacted a heavy toll in lives and money. Subsidies, annuities, and treaty payments aside, the campaigns to suppress them cost the United States government millions upon millions of dollars (it was estimated that it cost the United States Army $1,000,000 to kill a single Indian). Any people less hardy, less courageous, and perhaps, above all, less greedy would have flinched in the face of such determined resistance, but not the settlers, miners, or emigrants who year after year poured into Indian country at the risk of their possessions and, not infrequently, their lives. They literally bet their lives on the fact that the United States government, however it might warn, discourage, or outright forbid them to venture onto Indian land, must in the end extend its protection over them and undertake to punish those tribes that—whatever their justification—murdered the intruders.

The killing of Crazy Horse was not, of course, the end of the tragedy of the Plains Indians. A few months after his death, one of the most unhappy episodes involving Indians and whites took place with the Nez Percé, a northwestern tribe that was proud of never having killed a white man or having had any but peaceful relations with the settlers who pressed constantly on its lands. With an ancient and sophisticated culture of their own, the Nez Percé, like so many other tribes, had been seduced by the opportunities presented by the horse culture and had ventured over the Cascades and the Bitterroot Range into what is today Idaho and western Montana to hunt buffalo. Their most famous chief had been Chief

Joseph, a convert to Christianity, who had guided his people with extraordinary tact and diplomacy through their initial contacts with the whites. On his death his mantle had fallen on his son, Hinmaton-Yalatkit, or Thunder Rolling Down the Mountain, also called Young Joseph. Under the reservation policy, the Wallowa Valley in northeastern Oregon was designated as Nez Percé country, but the pressure of settlers who coveted the beautiful valley caused the government to declare the area open to homesteaders. Joseph's father had told him in his dying hours: "This country holds your father's body. Never sell the bones of your father and mother."

An army commission that included General Oliver Otis Howard had met with Joseph to try to persuade him to sell the land. The commissioners were clearly impressed by Joseph's presence and by the quiet but determined skill with which he defended the right of the Nez Percé to their homeland.

> If we ever owned the land we own it still, for we have never sold it. . . . In the treaty councils the commissioners have claimed that our country has been sold to the government. Suppose a white man should come to me and say, 'Joseph, I like your horses, and I want to buy them but he refuses to sell.' My neighbor answers 'Pay me the money and I will sell you Joseph's horses.' The white man returns to me and says, 'Joseph, I have bought your horses and you must let me have them.' If we sold our lands to the government, that is the way they were bought.

The decision of the commissioners was that Joseph's Nez Percé should be required to join the other Nez Percé on the Lapwai Reservation by persuasion or force. Howard, who was in charge of the territory that included the Lapwai Reservation, gave Joseph a month to bring his tribe, which numbered fewer than a hundred warriors, into the reservation. Joseph protested that the Snake was too high for his band to cross safely, but Howard refused to allow him more time. After the Nez Percé band had crossed the river a group of young braves, who were not members of Joseph's band

and were furious at being forced onto the reservation, broke out in an orgy of killing. It was a classic Indian uprising, triggered by a profound sense of grievance and frustration and fueled by traders' whiskey. Before they were through, some twenty whites had been killed, with farms burned and women raped.

Howard started out from the Lapwai Reservation immediately with 110 soldiers and volunteers. The soldiers came up to Joseph's small band and, rejecting the offer of a truce, attacked its camp in White Bird Canyon. Although outnumbered, the Nez Percé, led by Joseph, killed thirty-four soldiers and wounded four, administering a severe defeat to Howard's small force. Howard began to round up a larger contingent of troops, and, since nothing succeeds like success, Joseph found his own band augmented by other discontented groups of Indians spoiling for a fight. Howard, now with 400 soldiers and 180 Indian scouts, surprised Joseph's party, which now included five other bands of Nez Percé, on the Clearwater River, in early July. The first warning the Indians had was the fire from Howard's howitzer and Gatling guns from a bluff above their camp. The Indians rallied, and once more Howard suffered a humiliating setback. The Nez Percé chiefs believed that if they could get over the Bitterroot Mountains into Idaho, they would be safe from pursuit. In a remarkable hegira, herding along several thousand horses as well as children, the sick, and those wounded at the Clearwater River, they reached western Montana, where they found their path blocked by some thirty-five army infantrymen. The Nez Percé made their way around the soldiers and stopped at Stevensville, where they bought much needed supplies from the townspeople. After crossing the Continental Divide, they made camp in the Big Hole Valley, near the present-day town of Dillon, Montana. There Colonel John Gibbon, veteran of the fighting against Crazy Horse and the Sioux, came on the camp and caught the sleeping Nez Percé by surprise in a dawn attack. Men, women, and children were killed indiscriminately. Once more the warriors rallied and gave such a good account of themselves that Gibbon's larger force soon found itself on the defensive (the Nez Percé were noted for being the finest marksmen of all the Indian tribes). Gibbon lost thirty-three dead and as many wounded, and his command may well have been saved from Custer's fate only by the arrival of Howard. The Nez Percé lost eighty-nine, most of them apparently women and children and old men. Among the Nez Percé dead were two of their most noted warriors, Rainbow and Five Wounds. The Nez Percé buried their dead before abandoning their camp, but the Bannock scouts dug up the bodies and scalped them.

What was most notable about all the engagements involving the Nez Percé was that the outnumbered Indians inflicted a series of defeats on superior forces of, in the main, army regulars. There was no parallel in all the years of fighting to the "victories" (victories in the rather modest sense of avoiding annihilation and inflicting heavier casualties than they suffered) of the Nez Percé over their pursuers, led by two of the ablest and most experienced Indian fighters in the West. By the time of the Big Hole Battle, the attention of the nation had become fixed on the dramatic odyssey of the Nez Percé. Chief Joseph, although only one among equals and not, in fact, the most accomplished of the Nez Percé leaders, was credited with the victories and became an instant hero. Indeed, it is safe to say that, Montana and Idaho settlers aside, there were more Americans rooting for Joseph and "his" Nez Percé than for Howard and the United States Army. Never able to resist a military hero, whatever the color of his skin, Americans elevated Joseph to that pantheon of Indian heroes that included Tecumseh (the middle name of William Sherman, commanding general of the United States Army, was Tecumseh), Black Hawk, Osceola, and, more recently, Crazy Horse and Sitting Bull.

Fleeing from Howard's implacable pursuit, the Nez Percé passed through Yellowstone Park, which was already attracting tourists. They had hoped to find refuge among the Crow, allies from other days against the Sioux and Cheyenne, but they found that the Crow were not only at peace with the whites but acting as army scouts. It was decided to press on to Canada, as the remnants of the Sioux under Sitting Bull had recently done, but in camp not far from the border they were overtaken by Nelson Miles, who had been called up from Fort Keogh with six hundred soldiers, including part of the Seventh Cavalry. Miles ordered a charge that was stopped with heavy casualties; twenty-four officers and men were killed, and another forty-two wounded. The Nez Percé, after four months of fighting against three different expeditions dispatched against them in a journey that had covered more than 1,300 miles, were still dangerous. Some of the Nez Percé women and children, among them Joseph's twelve-year-old daughter, escaped but the remaining warriors—some 120—found themselves besieged by Miles's much larger force. A few days later Howard arrived with more troops, ending all hope of escape. Joseph persuaded the remaining warriors, cold and hungry, to surrender. He sent his message of surrender to Howard by way of Captain John, a Nez Percé interpreter, who wept as he delivered it:

> Tell General Howard I know his heart. What he told me before I have in my heart. I am tired of fighting. Our chiefs are killed. Looking Glass is dead. . . . The old men are all dead. It is the young men who say yes and no. He who led the young men is dead.

> It is cold and we have no blankets. The little children are freezing to death. My people, some of them, have run away to the hills, and have no blankets, no food; no one knows where they are—perhaps freezing to death. I want to have time to look for my children and see how many I can find. Maybe I shall find them among the dead. Hear me, my chiefs, I am tired; my heart is sick and sad. From where the sun now stands, I will fight no more forever.

From Chief Logan, mourning the murder of his wife and children by renegade whites almost a hundred years earlier, to the words of Chief Joseph, there had been the same refrain of unfathomable sadness by Indian chieftains caught in the web of an inexorable fate.

Joseph rode into the lines of the soldiers and handed his gun to Miles. Of the handful of Nez Percé who escaped to Canada, some were killed by the Assiniboine and Hidatsa. Joseph's six children survived. Miles did what he could to assist those who surrendered, some four hundred in all. They were taken by train to Bismarck on the way to Fort Abraham Lincoln, and there they were greeted by the citizens of that frontier Indian-hating town as heroes, showered with gifts of food and clothing. Joseph and other chiefs were given a dinner by the women of the town. But the reservation they were placed on was hundreds of miles from the land where their ancestors were buried; they were moved from the luxuriant forests and clean winds to an area of malarial dampness. Within a few months a fourth of their number was dead from disease (among them all of Joseph's children), some doubtless from heartbreak. "I will fight no more forever," became a kind of epitaph for the American aborigines.

The heroic story of Chief Joseph and the Nez Percé put the Indians once more on the front pages of the nation's newspapers, with public sentiment overwhelmingly in favor of the aborigines. Chief Joseph was brought to Washington to experience another of those strange orgies of public adulation by now so familiar a part of the relationship between the aborigines and their white supporters.

Although few historians have taken notice of Grant's efforts on behalf of the Indians, for his reform-minded contemporaries it was the most notable achievement of his administration. A grateful Bishop Whipple wrote the president in 1875: "No act of any President will stand out in brighter relief on the pages of history than your kindness to a perishing race. When this change was made an honest agent was a rare exception. . . . For all this you are held in esteem by thousands of the best men in America. I cannot find words to express my own deep sense of obligation for your perseverance when a less brave man would have faltered." But within a year the Sioux were once more on the warpath, Custer and his men were dead, and the peace policy on which so much hope had been placed was in jeopardy. It was increasingly difficult to answer the charges of the Westerners that its principal effect had been to encourage and indeed to reward Indian recalcitrance. E. L. Godkin announced the failure of the policy in the *Nation*: "Our philanthropy and our hostility tend to about the same end, and this is the destruction of the Indian race . . . the missionary expedient may be said to have failed." But the reformers were far from ready to concede defeat. They reiterated all the familiar arguments. The bad behavior of the Indians had been provoked by the whites. Now, above all, was the time for forbearance. Others took the line that while it was evident that the Sioux must be brought to account, public indignation should not be allowed to prejudice the cases of those tribes that had remained peaceable. Still others took the occasion to reiterate that the army was the problem, not the Indians.

The election of Rutherford Hayes to the presidency in 1876 brought with it a new secretary of the interior, Carl Schurz. While sympathetic to the calls for fair dealing with the Indians, Schurz was determined to replace Grant's Quaker policy—a heavy dependence on the denominational churches for the actual management of the Indian agencies—with a more orthodox bureaucratic arrangement. Meanwhile, the debate over the Indian policy grew, if possible, more intense. The country seemed filled with self-appointed experts recommending one or another solution, ranging, at the most extreme, from turning the Great Plains and Rocky Mountain West into a vast Indian reservation to blueprints for turning Indians into white men. In his first annual message to Congress, Hayes came out strongly in support of a "just and humane policy" that would lead to citizenship for all Indians who could be prevailed upon to abandon their tribal alliances. The issue of transference, of placing the responsibility for Indian welfare under the War Department rather than the Department of the Interior, was perhaps the most bitterly debated issue of all. A move in that direction by Congress brought out the full force of the embattled reformers, and after a struggle that lasted for several years it was beaten back.

There was at least one more excruciating chapter to be written. At the end of the Sioux war, the band of Cheyenne under the leadership of Dull Knife had been placed on the reservation of the Southern Cheyenne and Arapaho in the Indian Territory. There they grew increasingly restless and dissatisfied, both with their surroundings and with the failure of the government to deliver the food and supplies it had promised. In 1878 they announced that they were determined to go home. Troops were summoned from Fort Reno and their camp was surrounded, but during the night some seventy warriors and their wives and children slipped away and headed northwest to their home range, pursued by U.S. cavalry and fighting a number of skirmishes as they went, replenishing their herds from ranches along the way. With hundreds of soldiers spread out to intercept them, they crossed three railroad lines and continued their flight toward the sand hills in northern Nebraska. In a snowstorm Dull Knife ran into two companies of cavalry. As the two parties parleyed, more and more soldiers arrived until finally Dull Knife felt he had no recourse except to surrender and agree to go to Camp Robinson on the White River near the Dakota–Nebraska boundary. Pressed to return to the reservation in the south, Dull Knife declared, "We will not go there to live. That is not a healthful country, and if we should stay there we will all die. We do not wish to go back there and we will not go. You may kill me here, but you cannot make me go back."

The sympathy that had been roused by the dramatic journey of the Nez Percé was again manifest for the plight of the Cheyenne. Even the editor of the *Omaha Herald* urged that they be allowed to remain in the country that they knew and loved. To take them back would mean starvation. "I implore you," he addressed the Indian Bureau, "for justice and humanity to those wronged red men, let them stay in their own country." The authorities in Washington were adamant, however. Amid a storm of public protest the order came to return the Cheyenne to the southern reservation lest their example encourage other tribes to leave the reservations assigned to them. The Indians repeated that they would rather die where they were than return. The officer in charge tried to force compliance by withholding food and then water. They refused to budge. Finally, when the officer in charge had tricked two of their principal warriors into a parley and put them in chains, the remaining warriors retrieved rifles that they had hidden under the barracks where they were quartered and prepared to fight to the last. At nightfall they broke out of their quarters and fled for the hills, with soldiers close on their trail. A number were killed or wounded in the escape. Others, fighting off their pursuers, pushed on for ten days until, surrounded and vastly outnumbered, they were driven to earth and killed or wounded. Dull Knife and his family made their way to the Pine Ridge Reservation, where friendly Indians concealed them. Of those who had broken out of the barracks, all who survived, some fifty-eight, were allowed to go to the Pine Ridge agency. Seven leaders were tried for killing white settlers in the course of their flight; but the cases were dismissed and they, too, joined the remnant of the band at Pine Ridge. Public feeling rallied so strongly now to the Cheyenne cause that soon all the Northern Cheyenne who survived were gathered on the Tongue River Reservation in the heart of the country they knew and loved.

The plan for the removal of the Indians to reservations and plans for civilizing them and bestowing citizenship on them willy-nilly went on much as before. Now attention came to focus on the unhappy plight of the Poncas.

The Ponca, related to the Omaha, had been living peacefully, if sordidly, on the southeast corner of an area claimed by the Sioux. The Sioux raided and pillaged the Ponca while complaining of their presence, and the Department of the Interior, anxious to placate the more active and dangerous tribe, undertook to move the Ponca to another reservation. The Ponca, rather to everybody's surprise, refused, but, faced with the threat of forcible removal, a portion of the tribe began what proved to be a terribly arduous trek to the new reservation. Many fell ill along the way, and a number died. The man who took up their cause and focused national attention on it was skillful journalist and propagandist Thomas Tibbles. Tibbles soon had the attention of the Eastern press focused on the desperate situation of the Ponca. A delegation of Ponca was given an audience with President Hayes and it asked, reasonably enough, that the tribe be sent back to its old reservation or to Nebraska, where the main body of Omaha lived. Once again the legions of reform rallied to the Indian cause. President Hayes admitted publicly that an injustice had been done to the Ponca, and Congress passed a bill for their relief. Meanwhile, their chief, Standing Bear, seeing the members of his band dying off from disease—primarily malaria— gathered the survivors together and headed for the Omaha reservation. Now the Eastern reformers, joined by a number of white residents of the Dakotas and Nebraska, drafted petitions asking that they be allowed to remain. Encouraged by white supporters, Standing Bear went so far as to bring suit for habeas corpus in a U.S. circuit court to prevent the return of the tribe to the malarial reservation from which it had fled. In May, 1879, Judge Elmer Scipio Dundy ruled that "in time of peace no authority, civil or military, exists for transporting Indians from one section of the country to another, without the consent of the Indians. . . ." Any Indians confined for the purpose of removal would be released on habeas corpus. Encouraged by the court victory, the friends of the Ponca renewed the right. Tibbles organized an extensive lecture tour featuring Chief Standing Bear and an attractive, missionary-school– educated young Omaha woman, Susette La Flesche, whose Indian name was Bright Eyes. The tour "opened in Boston" to enthusiastic audiences. Tibbles raised some $7,000 to carry on a legal battle for the Ponca. Carl Schurz, to his indignation, found himself squarely in the center of the battle. A Boston woman, Martha Goddard, was typical of those who took him to task for not responding generously enough to the plight of the Ponca. The condition of the Indians, she wrote him, was "the great question now, and you would be surprised if you knew how much people here think about it & care for it, not passionately, or with any political afterthought, but earnestly, and as a matter of humanity & justice & national honor, as they cared for the emancipation of the slaves."

The most formidable recruit to the Ponca cause was a Colorado woman, Helen Hunt Jackson, who, visiting Boston, heard Tibbles, Standing Bear, and Susette La Flesche and discovered the cause that was to obsess her for the remaining years of her life. While

Wendell Phillips, under a pseudonym, produced a tract called *The Ponca Chiefs*, which charged the government with being "incompetent, cruel and faithless," thereby earning "the contempt and detestation of all honest men and the distrust and hate of the Indian tribes," Mrs. Jackson began work on what was to be the most devastating indictment of the treatment of the Indians yet written—*A Century of Dishonor.* The marriage of Thomas Tibbles and Susette La Flesche added a decidedly romantic note to the three-year-long campaign on behalf of the Ponca.

Justice, so far as that was possible—legal justice at least—was finally done for the Ponca or what remained of them: somewhat more than six hundred members of the tribe. Congress voted $165,000 to compensate them for their losses, and they were given the choice of living either on their old reservation or with the Omaha. All in all, the Ponca controversy was one of the more remarkable episodes in American history. With the Indian wars finally at an end and the Indian "problem" to all intents and purposes "solved," with the vast majority of the Indians settled on reservations and presumably involved in the process of being "civilized," the nation indulged itself in a final orgy of guilt over the Indian question. Seen in this light, the Ponca affair, involving a small, obscure tribe that most Americans had never even heard of, set off rites of expiation designed, quite unconsciously, to ease a bad collective conscience. If the Ponca in the end could be treated justly and humanely, the books might be closed on the extended tragedy of the aboriginal Americans. During the Ponca controversy a number of the antislavery old guard, among them the greatest spirits of the age, died— William Lloyd Garrison in the spring of 1879, Lydia Maria Child and Lucretia Mott the following year.

The Apache under Geronimo continued to disturb the Southwest, and the Ghost Dance uprising would flare up into a bloody finale in the 1880s; but with the surrender of the Sioux and the Cheyenne the Indian wars were basically over. They had entered the realm of mythology and become as much a part of the nation's collective memory as the Trojan War for the Greeks, the material of countless romances and innumerable "Westerns," told and retold, interpreted and reinterpreted. But somehow the truth remained as elusive as ever. The issue became polemical rather than tragic. The government erected historical markers along busy, traveled roads, which told the brief and unrevealing facts. "Near here Crazy Horse and his Sioux warriors were defeated by. . . ." "At this spot, Chief Joseph surrendered to Colonel Nelson Miles." But sadness haunted the land. We have had occasion to say, "America was full of heartbreak." Nowhere more so than in the story of the confrontation between the aboriginal peoples of America and the white intruders on their lands.

By 1881 the Indians had 155,632,000 acres allocated to them. Indians on reservations and in the Indian Territory numbered 189,447. In addition, 117,368 white men and women lived in the Indian Territory and on reservations, as did more than 18,000 blacks, most of them former slaves of the Civilized Tribes.

In 1885, Grover Cleveland returned some of the Indian lands that his predecessor, Chester Arthur, had taken from the Indians, and three years later he reported to Congress that "over 80,000,000 acres have been arrested from illegal usurpation, improvident grants, and fraudulent entries and claims to be taken for the homesteads of honest industry. . . ." Nonetheless, Indian lands were whittled away until by 1900 only 84,000,000 acres were still reserved. But all such statistics are, in a sense, beside the point. Whether the approximately 200,000 Indians scattered on some three hundred reservations from Maine to Florida and from New York to Oregon had been on 20,000,000 acres (with an allocation of one hundred acres for each Indian, man, woman, and child) or on 200,000,000 (with one thousand acres for each member of every tribe) in the long run would have made no difference. As tribal people they lived in a world without any conception of "work," and they lived in the midst of a society in which "work" was only slightly less venerated than "property."

The organizations dedicated to the welfare of the Indian did not diminish in numbers or ardor. Rather the reverse. The last decades of the century saw the establishment of a journal devoted to progressive improvement in the condition of the Indian called *Council Fire*, edited by Alfred Meacham until his premature death—which was caused by wounds he received at the hands of Captain Jack and his Modoc chiefs. The Boston Indian Citizenship Committee, as its name indicated, was devoted to the cause of winning citizenship for the Indians. The Women's National Indian Association of Philadelphia was organized in 1879 and counted among its more prominent members Mrs. John Jacob Astor. In a few years it had sixty chapters, the most active being the Connecticut Indian Association, of which Harriet Beecher Stowe was vice president. Inspired by Helen Hunt Jackson's *A Century of Dishonor*, Herbert Welsh founded the Indian Rights Association in 1883. Together the various organizations contributed sums in excess of $100,000 a year to support educational programs on the various reservations. Perhaps most important was their watchdog role. They kept, through their agents and through the numerous missionaries to the Indians, a close eye on the government's dealings with the tribes and were ready at any moment to step forth to try to right a wrong or repair an injustice.

The passage of the Dawes Act in 1887 was the culmination of almost eighteen years of agitation on behalf of the Indian, and it also might be taken as the last nail driven into the coffin of tribal culture of the North American Indian. The committee that proposed the bill had in mind that "the sun dance shall be stricken down, and that in its stead we shall have industrial schools; that the commune shall give way to the dignity and rights of American citizens; that the heathen idols shall give place to the Christian altars, and that the tribal organization shall be broken up and the individuality of the Indian encouraged and developed, and the lands unnecessarily reserved for them opened to the pioneer, that intelligence and thrift may find lodging there." At last, we might say, Thomas Jefferson's program for civilizing the Indians was to be given practical effect. Such sentiments are, of course, uncongenial to the more anthropologically enlightened consciousness of today, but they were the best that the age could come up with; they were, in any event, the very opposite of "extermination," although it could well be argued that they killed the spirit if they left the body intact.

What the most enlightened and humane reformers and friends of the Indian could not, of course, understand was the power of "culture" over "civilization." In any serious contest between culture and so-called civilization for the soul of a people, culture must win even if winning means dying. As we have tediously reiterated, there were no "Indians" in the Americas; there were hundreds of tribes of aborigine that ranged from the "civilized" Cherokee, with their sophisticated agricultural–hunting mode of life, to the Ute of the Great Desert Basin, whose existence was as marginally human as any on this planet. Between the more highly developed tribes and the more primitive, there was a vaster difference than between a British lord and a Cherokee chief (who, it might be argued, were in fact, quite similar). What all those several hundred astonishingly diverse peoples shared was a common tribal consciousness, and to that tribal consciousness or culture they clung with a tenacity that confused, bewildered, and demoralized the exponents of civilizing the Indian, from Thomas Jefferson to the most recent twentieth-century authority on the subject. Tribal culture could not survive intact, and the aborigines could not wholly abandon it. They had to, perforce, live in a limbo.

If money and good intentions could have solved the "Indian problem," it would certainly have been solved early in the history of the Republic. By 1823 the federal government had spent more than $85,000,000 on Indian affairs—treaties, subsidies, gifts (not, of course, to mention the uncounted millions spent killing recalcitrant Indians). The total sum appropriated to pay for Indian lands and to pay the Indians subsequently to live on them would amount to billions of dollars. But buying off the Indians was simply another way of killing them. They were made dependent wards of the government, living, for the most part, in idleness and squalor.

It is a truism to say that the Indians were robbed of their lands, but even if a fair market value had been put on every acre of land purchased from the Indians, it would, in the long run, have done them little good. They had no use for or understanding of money. Their land had no value that could be equated with money for them. It was their life.

In addition to money (uncounted millions more were contributed through private philanthropy), thousands of white Americans devoted some or all of their lives to trying to "raise up" the Indians, to educate, Christianize, "civilize" them. But no one found a way to "empower" the Indians. The powerless are always, with the best of intentions, exploited by the powerful because those with power must treat them as wards, as dependents with no real control over their own destinies. So, as it turned out, everything done for the American aborigines made their situation worse. The reservations, which began at least in part as a way of protecting tribes from avaricious whites and, equally important, from each other, became a prison of the spirit. Better, by far, Richard Pratt's notion—eccentric as it was—of parceling out the aborigines all over the United States, ninety to a county, to be taken in by good Christian families. But it is doubtful that the Indians themselves would have taken kindly to such a solution. America indeed may be full of heartbreak: violent deaths in lonely places, wasting disease in malarial lowlands, the desperate life of the city poor, defeated hopes and frustrated expectations, truncated youth and barren old age, a kind of cosmic homesickness when home was so often so far away—all part of the price of being an American—a price that, generation after generation, millions of people seemed willing, indeed eager, to pay. But the aborigine had no choice. The limitless and incommensurable sadness was that he was dispossessed from the earth he loved by forces he could not comprehend. He had no choice in the matter. Civilization swallowed up culture, and, turn one way and another as we may, it is hard to see how it could have been otherwise. A far more exact justice might, indeed, have been done, but considering the ways of conquering peoples with the conquered in the long record of history, there turns out to have been much that was done or that at least was tried in the best spirit. But, as E. L. Godkin pointed out, the good and the bad seemed to have much the same result. If we could have repaired all the instances of bad faith and broken treaties, would not the outcome have been the same—the remnants of once–proud tribes living hopeless lives on reservations?

Beyond the endless drama, the scenes so vividly painted in words and on canvas, beginning with James Fenimore Cooper and extending to the most recent novels and historical and anthropological studies, there was above everything else the ineffable sadness of the destruction of tribal societies that, with all their cruelty and violence, contained much beauty. In every generation and perhaps none more than the present, the American aborigines have found their champions and admirers, men and women who, if they often shamelessly romanticize Indian life, nonetheless adore an essence of tribal experience beside which the corruptions and falsities of civilization have been constantly contrasted.

Finally, we are prone to overlook the fact that tens of thousands of Indians did indeed become "civilized." The greater number of those who did entered into the white man's culture by the only sure door open to them—through his religion. They thus adopted a new and larger cosmology and simply disappeared, were assimilated, so that their descendants were proud to say, "My grandmother [it was grandmother generally rather than grandfather since women assimilated more readily than men] was a Cherokee" or Sioux or Cheyenne or Navajo. Certainly those Indians who "passed" or amalgamated gave ample evidence that there was no "racial" or genetic inferiority in the American aborigines. They proved what the abolitionists claimed: that men, "primitive" as they might be, were in an astonishing (and, in Darwinian terms, inexplicable) degree "equal" for all practical purposes.

One thing is clear: However the great majority of Americans may have been caught in the terrible and unremitting sin of racism in regard to black Americans, it was not racism per se that cast such a dark cloud over the red–white clash. John Rolfe's marriage to Pocahontas was the unshakable symbol of that fact. In the first place, the American aborigines were not "Indians," were not a *race* in any rational meaning of that dangerously elusive word. They were innumerable tribes, some "noble," some "degraded," all "aboriginal" for want of a better word. Thousands of "white" men, or more accurately, men ranging in complexion from pink to swarthy, married thousands of aboriginal women without experiencing more than a modicum of hostility from their fellow whites. Often the reverse.

A handsome Indian woman was an object, certainly in the higher social circles, of fascinated attention, just as the appearance of a famous Indian chief would turn out the citizenry by the thousands wherever he appeared in the "civilized" world. To mix "racism" in with the jumble of catchwords and clichés through which we must hack our way in order to even approach the truth is, in my opinion, to hopelessly compromise the whole issue. We have enough to answer for in the *bona fide* area of racism. Certainly, settlers and other Americans unsympathetic to the Indians did not hesitate to speak of them as a "savage and degraded race," but worse things were said of the Irish, the Italians, and the Poles.

Wendell Phillips liked to pair the problem of the treatment of the Indians and the Chinese immigrants. But few took up the analogy; it was far too eccentric. Phillips's point, of course, was that both Indians and Chinese, each so different, were part of a common human brotherhood and must be so perceived and so treated. The pairing of the two "races," one a genuine race, the other a category, had the actual effect of highlighting the difference between the two issues. The Chinese were, from the moment they arrived on the American shores, the victims of flagrantly racist attitudes. That was never the Indian problem. We could do worse than leave the last word to the Reverend David Macrae, the touring Scottish minister. Many Americans expressed a sincere desire, he noted in 1854, to "improve" the Indian, i.e., make him more like a white man. "Before there is time to civilize him, he is likely to be improved from the face of the earth," Macrae wrote. "American civilization is impatient, and cannot wait for him. People who eat their meals in four minutes and half, and push railway lines across the prairie at the rate of two miles a day, cannot wait a hundred years to give the Indian time to bury his tomahawk, wash his face, and put on a pair of trousers." Especially if the Indian had no interest in such a transformation.

CHAPTER XXI

AFTER WOUNDED KNEE

It was certainly an unhappy circumstance that Wounded Knee was the last act in the almost three-hundred-year-long encounter between whites and Indians. First of all, it was a profound tragedy for the Indians themselves. In addition, it cast a dark shadow over the whole strange drama of Indian–white relations. It took on a symbolic character; it stood for all the suffering that the American aborigines had suffered at the hands of the intruders and, in doing so, helped to obscure a far more complex story, a story of perpetually defeated hopes, of violence and cruelty almost beyond the telling of it.

The cruelty of the Indians toward the whites and, even more, their cruelty to other tribes, was an integral part of tribal life. Many tribes, and especially those most often engaged in warfare with whites, lived to fight and raid and could not live without that endless rhythm of violence. It was their culture, their nature. But for the whites who were caught up in reciprocal violence it was a degradation, for their religion professed at least to teach them gentleness and peace.

At the time of the Dawes or General Allotment Act in 1887, the various tribes held title to some 137 million acres of land, the greater part of it in the states of South Dakota, Montana, Wyoming, Idaho, Utah, and Colorado. It might be argued that the fact that the tribes held 137 million acres of reservation weighed little against the fact that a few hundred years earlier the whole continent had been "theirs," but the fact remained that while it was far less land than the tribes needed to preserve their "wild" ways, it was, by the same token, far more than they could "use," far more than they needed to sustain themselves in a settled agricultural life. To the average American, with his Protestant ethic of thrift, piety and hard work, the un- or under-utilized land of the tribal reservations was both a temptation and a reproach to his most basic values.

Under the terms of the General Allotment Act, the Indians were encouraged to sell or lease those tribal lands that remained after each member had been allotted 160 acres, hopefully to cultivate and thereby make him independent.

The General Allotment Act was administered by the Bureau of Indian Affairs and each reservation was run, in effect, by an Indian agent. The agents' powers were considerable and, not surprisingly, were frequently abused, especially in regard to what they considered their primary responsibility—"detribalizing" their charges. On some reservations Indian children were punished for speaking the language of their tribe.

With the passage of the General Allotment Act, the Indians largely faded from public consciousness. It was largely assumed that the Act had initiated a process of assimilation that would in time "solve the Indian problem." Sequestered on reservations, the tribes entered a long period of degradation and neglect. After obsessing the imagination of the nation since the beginning of the republic, they virtually disappeared, living in a kind of limbo, neither tribes in a real sense nor functioning members of the larger culture that, for the most part, they disliked and distrusted.

Many Indians, appalled by conditions on the reservations, left to seek their fortunes elsewhere but most preserved a strong sense of their tribal identity as Sioux or Hopi or Shoshone and returned periodically to their home reservations. There was much intermarriage with whites, especially on the part of Indian women, so that some reservations had individuals claiming membership in the tribe who only had one-sixty-fourth Indian blood. Most tribes today require proof of one-quarter blood for membership but the fact that so many "genetically marginal" men and women claimed tribal ties should prove a conclusive argument against the notion that white attitudes toward the aborigines were "racist." There were, of course, practical considerations as well. All those who could claim tribal connections could participate in whatever monetary benefits might come from government coffers or from the sale or lease of tribal lands.

By the early decades of the twentieth century, reformers, dismayed by the conditions on the reservations, were pressing for a complete turnabout in Indian policy. The fight was led by the Society of American Indians, made up of non-Indians dedicated to preserving tribal culture. The Society had strong support from the Women's Clubs of America. The most articulate and resourceful advocate of Indian rights was John Collier. Armed with a report from the Brookings Institution on the shameful conditions of Indian life and with the support of Montana's Burton K. Wheeler, who made the Indian cause his own, Collier proposed an array of reforms. Franklin Roosevelt, who shared his countrymen's and -women's fascination with the Indians, appointed Collier Commissioner of Indian Affairs in 1933 and a year later the Wheeler–Howard Bill or Indian Reorganization Act, was passed and hailed as a "New Deal" for the American Indian.

Because, under the terms of the General Allotment Act, tribes had been able to sell off reservation lands, tribal reservations had shrunk from 137 million acres to fewer than 55 million at the time of the Act. Not only had the hopes for assimilation failed, tribal land holdings had shrunk by considerably more than half. All that could be said with confidence was that the reservations, however diminished in size, had survived. In the words of former BIA

Commissioner Philleo Nash: "The reservation system, with all its faults, is an integral part of Indian continuity, for it is the reservation that gives the tribes territoriality in the modern world." And it is this "territoriality" that constitutes what remains of tribal consciousness.

The high hopes that attended the passage of the Indian Reorganization Act were soon dashed. Among other things, the Act was sharply criticized for having failed to involve the tribes themselves in drafting the legislation. This was more easily said than done. As the white man was alleged to "speak with a forked tongue," the Indian spoke with many tongues. Indeed, individual tribes were often bitterly divided among themselves.

When a number of tribes protested portions of the bill, it was amended to give each tribe the right to accept or reject various provisions; and the federal government, in the person of the Bureau of Indian Affairs, set out on a protracted campaign to win tribal support. After more than five years of discussion and debate, 189 tribes accepted the terms of the Indian Reorganization Act and 77 rejected them. It seems safe to say that while, at least for some tribes, the Wheeler–Howard Act represented a modest step forward, it proved little more efficacious than its much-maligned predecessor in solving the major problems of the tribes. Once more, Indians drifted to the back of the public consciousness. Out of sight, out of mind.

The absence proved, as it had before, only temporary. In the mid-1960s, many young middle-class men and women began to lament the fact that they were not Indians. One of the most striking features of the so-called counterculture was its absorption with Indians, that is to say, with tribal life. Without much knowledge of real Indians, past or present, they "imagined" Indians and endowed them with the attributes they found missing in the "other" culture, their culture. Young men and women of the counterculture further invented an Indian history to go with their idealized vision of Indian life. In this history the American aborigines had been peacefully and harmoniously enjoying the sacred land of their ancestors when that land was invaded by alien conquerors bent on extermination ("genocidal criminals" one writer recently termed the invaders (us)). However muddled and moony, this rediscovery had an important social and cultural function. It drew attention once more to the existence of the Indians.

This interest was dramatically reinforced in the winter of 1973 when a group of militant Indians converged on Wounded Knee. Barricading themselves in reservation buildings, they held a force of law officers and FBI agents at bay for some sixty-eight days.

In the sporadic fighting that followed the occupation, two FBI agents were killed. The prolonged siege and the accompanying media attention made the situation of the tribes once more the focus of widespread concern. Moreover, the obsession of the counterculture with forms of tribal life gave a philosophical, psychosocial dimension to the issue.

If we are puzzled at the infatuation of the counterculture with tribal life, we might do well to recall that since the rise of civilization, the lives and practices of primitive peoples have had a strong attraction for the so-called civilized. This is especially true, of course, in romantic eras (such as the late 1960s and early '70s). When civilization and its discontents become too much to bear we yearn for the fancied innocence and simplicity of tribal life. At the dawn of the Age of Reason, John Locke and Thomas Hobbes crossed swords over the character of primitive life. Was it nature "red in tooth and claw," or was it marked by a rational choice to give up a degree of freedom for a compensatory degree of security? Locke, considered by many philosophers and political theorists as the "Father of Democracy" because of his "compact" theory of the origin of social life, argued that early man, "in a state of nature," as an isolated individual was subject to so many dangers and hazards that he decided to band together with other individuals. In so doing, the primitive man agreed to surrender certain natural rights he had enjoyed as an "individual" in order to lay the foundations for a more secure and orderly existence. But these rights or freedoms were only provisionally ceded. If the compact was violated, if the authority exercised in the name of the group became arbitrary or repressive, individuals had the inherent and inalienable right to withdraw their support. Hence the dissolution of the compact. Hence the theoretical justification of the American Revolution.

In every age the admirers of tribal life (or the despisers of civilized life) have used idealized versions of primitive or aboriginal life as a club with which to belabor their own societies and expose "falsehoods and hypocrisies." In the aftermath of our own revolution, Tom Paine argued that "civilization" could never consider itself superior to the world of the aborigines unless, or until, those individuals at the bottom of civilized social and economic orders were at least as well provided for as the members of tribal societies. Paine's yardstick is still a good measure to keep in mind when one talks of tribal and post-tribal cultures.

The tribe in its almost infinite variations was, after all, the primary and in some ways the most enduring form of social organization. The tribe invented marriage and burial or the ceremony of the dead. The tribe perceived the world as sacred and tribes developed rituals often so similar that, as we noted earlier, Lewis and Clark were convinced that the Indians were the Lost Tribes of Israel because some of the Indian rituals that they observed were like those described in the Old Testament. Present-day Orthodox Jews preserve classic elements of tribal life in the form of taboo foods and the ritual preparation of food. Indeed, it could be argued that all the great world religions contain residues of the sacred rites that lay at the core of tribal culture.

I have argued elsewhere in this work that tribes in their complete dependence on the natural world by no means lived the idyllic existence that their modern admirers imagine. The "escape from nature" was one of the great liberations of the race. While it is true that the Fall was from innocence into sin, from "good conscience" into the bewildering ambiguities of "civilized" man, there were considerable compensations. For the tribe, every other tribe was a potential enemy, a victim or a conqueror. The word for "human being" in Sioux was "Sioux." The tribe, by definition, was locked into its own consciousness and had no notion of larger human unities other than those that might be achieved by alliance or conquest.

Civilization brought with it the dream of a universal order. In the Judeo-Christian system, the Lord made "of one blood all the nations of the earth." This is a vision *beyond* the tribe. Marshall McLuhan spoke of the modern world with its system of instant communication as a "global village." Perhaps it would be better to think of it as a "global tribe." That is to say that unity of mankind may require that we retrieve some of the most basic elements of tribal consciousness in a post-tribal world. Such as a sense of the sacredness of all life, of food, of the natural world, of human relationships, most especially of marriage, of respect for the ancestors, of the importance of common rituals and ceremonies, of inspired play.

I BELIEVE THAT THE STORY or, more accurately, the almost infinite number of different stories of the hundreds of tribes of American aborigines and their encounters with the European intruders, remains the most tragic, dramatic and enthralling story in our history, the freeing of the slaves always excepted. The hopeful aspect of our present relationship with our brothers and sisters, the Indians of America, is the growth of their pride and our new appreciation of their cultures. That seems to me a genuine gain. In every past generation—as I trust this work has demonstrated—there were tens of thousands of white Americans who were charmed by what appeared to them the romance of Indian life, but it occurred to relatively few of them that there were elements of tribal life superior to the ways of civilization.

We cannot, however much we may wish, escape back into the tribe. The desire to do so is a measure of the psychic burdens carried by modern men and women. What it seems to me we can and mayhap do is translate the powerful and enduring elements of tribal consciousness into forms accessible to the post-tribal world. The time may be especially propitious for such a task. The Enlightenment

Dream in its various forms—Rationalism, Scientism, Darwinism, Marxism—which has dominated our lives for some two hundred years, has proved illusory. The counterculturists, were, it turns out, the first to perceive this fact.

Obviously, there are many obstacles to such a transformation. One of the principal ones is the disposition of the tribal enthusiasts to cast the issue in terms of conflict and recrimination. Such statements as "The Euro-Americans committed criminal genocide against Native Americans" make intelligent discourse impossible. Post-tribal consciousness is, as we have seen, everywhere and is always fascinated by tribal consciousness. To make that fascination bear fruit, a strong dose of reality is essential.

And something more. Thomas LaForge, the "White Crow," tells us of a Crow injunction, when quarrels threatened to break out among members of the tribe: "Keep your heart good." It is an admonition that we would do well to attend to in those areas of our common life where anger and vindictiveness seem so often substituted for good faith and mutual respect.

May the words of the Crow prevail here.

APPENDIX

(Note: Census numbers and other particulars here were compiled by Page Smith in 1989 as he prepared this text.)

Article 1, Section 8 of the Federal Constitution states: "Congress shall have the power . . . to regulate commerce with foreign nations, among several states, and with the Indians."

Even before the drafting of the Constitution, the Northwest Ordinance, passed by the Confederation Congress in 1787, stated: "The utmost good faith shall always be observed towards the Indians: their land and property shall never be taken from them without their consent and in their property, rights, and liberty, they shall never be invaded or disturbed . . . , but laws founded in justice and humanity shall from time to time be made for preventing wrongs being done to them, and for preserving peace and friendship with them."

That was the ideal. Needless to say, it was more honored in the breach than the observance but it is certainly important to note that the intention was there, embedded in the law of the land, entirely consistent with the spirit of "an enlightened and progressive people."

The Bureau of Indian Affairs was founded in 1824 and placed under the jurisdiction of the War Department seven years later (1831). Federal statutes specify that the Bureau must serve "any Indian tribe, band, nation, rancheria, pueblo, colony or community."

What follows is the Bureau's account of the services it provides. Though tribal self-determination and Indian economic development are today's focus at the BIA, policies have varied from removal to assimilation since the bureau's beginning in 1824. President Ronald Reagan, however, declared in 1983 that the United States will support a policy of tribal self-determination, which encourages and supports tribal efforts to govern themselves.

Contracting BIA programs is the primary means by which tribes take control of their own affairs. In 1974, when contracting was first allowed, tribes contracted for a total of just eight hundred programs. During fiscal year 1988 it is estimated that 345 tribes and groups will enter into nearly 1,500 contracts for a total of nearly $300 million.

The BIA is headquartered in Washington, D.C. but most of its employees work in 12 area offices, 84 agencies, and 180 schools throughout the country. The enormous range of their work is divided into four major areas—education, tribal services, trust responsibility/economic development, and BIA operations.

The Office of Indian Education provides funding for both public and private schools. It reaches more than 200,000 Indian students each year. The BIA runs 180 elementary and secondary schools, three post-secondary schools and hundreds of adult education classes where Indian students can earn their high school diplomas. In addition, 10,000 Indians receive BIA higher education scholarships and 177,000 others benefit from Johnson–O'Malley funding, a program that offers supplemental monies to public schools with large Indian populations.

If the BIA is a microcosm of the federal government, the Office of Tribal Services is a cross between the Health and Human Services, Labor, Justice, and Housing and Urban Development Departments. It pays welfare to the needy. It provides job training to 4,000 Indians. The office operates 19 special federal courts and funds 127 tribal courts. It pays for more than 1,000 uniformed police officers. During 1988 it will rehabilitate around 3,000 Indian homes.

The Office of Trust and Economic Development manages some 53 million acres of land held in trust by the United States for Indians. It is designed to help tribes not only protect but also develop their forest, water, mineral, and energy resources. Additionally, the bureau spends more than $10 million a year to develop Indian business enterprises.

The following list of tribes served by the bureau is taken from the Federal Register of "Indian Tribal Entities within the contiguous states recognized and eligible to receive services from the United States Bureau of Indian Affairs." Since the story of "Alaska Natives" is a very different one from that of the tribes of the "lower forty-eight" they have been omitted from this survey. (As of 1988 they number 91,106, living, for the most part, in native villages).

- Absentee-Shawnee Tribe of Indians of Oklahoma
- Agua Caliente Band of Cahuilla Indians of the Agua Caliente Indian Reservation, California
- Ak Chin Indian Community of Papago Indians of the Maricopa (Ak Chin) Reservation, Arizona
- Alabama-Coushatta Tribes of Texas
- Alabama-Quassarte Tribal Town of the Creek Nation of Oklahoma
- Alturas Rancheria, of Pit River Indians of California
- Apache Tribe of Oklahoma
- Arapaho Tribe of the Wind River Reservation, Wyoming
- Assiniboine and Sioux Tribes of the Fort Peck Indian Reservation, Montana
- Augustine Band of Cahuilla Mission Indians of the Augustine Reservation, California
- Bad River Band of the Lake Superior Tribe of Chippewa Indians of the Bad River Reservation, Wisconsin
- Bay Mills Indian Community of the Sault Ste. Marie Band of Chippewa Indians of the Bay Mills Reservation, Michigan
- Berry Creek Rancheria of Maidu Indians of California
- Big Lagoon Rancheria of Smith River Indians of California
- Big Pine Band of Owens Valley Paiute Shoshone Indians of the Big Pine Reservation, California
- Big Sandy Rancheria of Mono Indians of California
- Big Valley Rancheria of Pomo & Pit River Indians of California

- Blackfeet Tribe of the Blackfeet Indian Reservation of Montana
- Blue Lake Rancheria, California
- Bridgeport Paiute Indian Colony of California
- Buena Vista Rancheria of Me-Wuk Indians of California
- Burns Paiute Indian Colony, Oregon
- Cabazon Band of Cahuilla Mission Indians of the Cabazon Reservation, California
- Cachil DeHe Band of Wintun Indians of the Colusa Indian Community of the Colusa Rancheria, California
- Caddo Indian Tribe of Oklahoma
- Cahto Indian Tribe of the Laytonville Rancheria, California
- Cahuilla Band of Mission Indians of the Cahuilla Reservation, California
- Cahto Indian Tribe of the Laytonville Rancheria, California
- Campo Band of Diegueno Mission Indians of the Campo Indian Reservation, California
- Capitan Grande Band of Diegueno Mission Indians of California (Barona Group of the Barona Reservation, California; Viejas Group of the Viejas Reservation, California)
- Cayuga Nation of New York
- Cedarville Rancheria of Northern Paiute Indians of California
- Chemehuevi Indian Tribe of the Chemehuevi Reservation, California
- Cher-Ae Heights Indian Community of the Trinidad Rancheria, California
- Cherokee Nation of Oklahoma
- Cheyenne-Arapaho Tribes of Oklahoma
- Cheyenne River Sioux Tribe of the Cheyenne River Reservation, South Dakota
- Chickasaw Nation of Oklahoma
- Chicken Ranch Rancheria of Me-Wuk Indians of California
- Chippewa-Cree Indians of the Rocky Boy's Reservation, Montana
- Chitimacha Tribe of Louisiana
- Choctaw Nation of Oklahoma
- Citizen Band Potawatomi Indian Tribe of Oklahoma
- Cloverdale Rancheria of Pomo Indians of California
- Coast Indian Community of Yurok Indians of the Resighini Rancheria, California
- Cocopah Tribe of Arizona
- Coeur D'Alene Tribe of the Coeur D'Alene Reservation, Idaho
- Cold Springs Rancheria of Mono Indians of California

- Colorado River Indian Tribes of the Colorado River Indian Reservation, Arizona and California
- Comanche Indian Tribe of Oklahoma
- Confederated Salish & Kootenai Tribes of the Flathead Reservation, Montana
- Confederated Tribes of the Bands of the Yakima Indian Nation of the Yakima Reservation, Washington
- Confederated Tribes of the Chehalis Reservation, Washington
- Confederated Tribes of the Colville Reservation, Washington
- Confederated Tribes of the Coos, Lower Umpqua and Siuslaw Indians of Oregon
- Confederated Tribes of the Goshute Reservation, Nevada and Utah
- Confederated Tribes of the Grand Ronde Community of Oregon
- Confederated Tribes of the Siletz Reservation, Oregon
- Confederated Tribes of the Umatilla Reservation, Oregon
- Confederated Tribes of the Warm Springs Reservation of Oregon
- Confederated Tribes of the Bands of the Yakima Indian
- Cortina Indian Rancheria of Wintun Indians of California
- Coushatta Tribe of Louisiana
- Covelo Indian Community of the Round Valley Reservation, California
- Cow Creek Band of Umpqua Indians of Oregon
- Coyote Valley Band of Pomo Indians of California
- Creek Nation of Oklahoma
- Crow Tribe of Montana
- Crow Creek Sioux Tribe of the Crow Creek Reservation, South Dakota
- Cuyapaipe Community of Diegueno Mission Indians of the Cuyapaipe Reservation, California
- Death Valley Timbi-Sha Shoshone Band of California
- Delaware Tribe of Western Oklahoma
- Devils Lake Sioux Tribe of the Devils Lake Sioux Reservation, North Dakota
- Dry Creek Rancheria of Pomo Indians of California
- Duckwater Shoshone Tribe of the Duckwater Reservation, Nevada
- Eastern Band of Cherokee Indians of North Carolina
- Eastern Shawnee Tribe of Oklahoma
- Elem Indian Colony of Pomo Indians of the Sulphur Bank Rancheria, California
- Elk Valley Rancheria of Smith River Tolowa Indians of California
- Ely Indian Colony of Nevada

- Enterprise Rancheria of Maidu Indians of California
- Flandreau Santee Tribe of South Dakota
- Forest County Potawatomi Community of Wisconsin Potawatomie Indians, Wisconsin
- Fort Belknap Indian Community of the Fort Belknap Reservation of Montana
- Fort Bidwell Indian Community of Paiute Indians of the Fort Bidwell Reservation, California
- Fort Independence Indian Community of Paiute Indians of the Fort Independence Reservation, California
- Fort McDermitt Paiute and Shoshone Tribes of the Fort McDermitt Indian Reservation, Nevada
- Fort McDowell Mojave-Apache Indian Community of the Fort McDowell Indian Reservation, Arizona
- Fort Mojave Indian Tribe of Arizona
- Fort Sill Apache Tribe of Oklahoma
- Gay Head Wampanoag Indians of Massachusetts
- Gila River Pima-Maricope Indian Community of the Gila River Indian Reservation of Arizona
- Grand Traverse Band of Ottawa & Chippewa Indians of Michigan
- Greenville Rancheria of Maidu Indians of California
- Grindstone Indian Rancheria of Wintun-Wailaki Indians of California
- Hannahville Indian Community of Wisconsin Potawatomie Indians of Michigan
- Havasupai Tribe of the Havasupai Reservation, Arizona
- Hoh Indian Tribe of the Hoh Indian Reservation, Washington
- Hoopa Valley Tribe of the Hoopa Valley Reservation, California
- Hopi Tribe of Arizona
- Hopland Band of Pomo Indians of the Hopland Rancheria, California
- Houlton Band of Maliseet Indians of Maine
- Hualapai Tribe of the Hualapai Indian Reservation, Arizona
- Inaja Band of Diegueno Mission Indians of the Inaja and Cosmit Reservation, California
- Iowa Tribe of Kansas and Nebraska
- Iowa Tribe of Oklahoma
- Jackson Rancheria of Me-Wuk Indians of California
- Jamestown S'Klallam Tribe of Washington
- Jamul Indian Village of California

- Jicarilla Apache Tribe of the Jicarilla Apache Indian Reservation, New Mexico
- Kaibab Band of Paiute Indians of the Kaibab Indian Reservation, Arizona
- Kalispel Indian Community of the Kalispel Reservation, Washington
- Karuk Tribe of California
- Kashia Band of Pomo Indians of the Stewarts Point Rancheria, California
- Kaw Indian Tribe of Oklahoma
- Keweenaw Bay Indian Community of L'Anse and Ontonagon Bands of Chippewa Indians of the L'Anse Reservation, Michigan
- Kialegee Tribal Town of the Creek Indian Nation of Oklahoma
- Kickapoo Tribe of Indians of the Kickapoo Reservation in Kansas
- Kickapoo Tribe of Oklahoma (includes Texas Band of Kickapoo Indians)
- Kiowa Indian Tribe of Oklahoma
- Klamath Indian Tribe of Oregon
- Kootenai Tribe of Idaho
- La Jolla Band of Luiseno Mission Indians of the La Jolla Reservation, California
- La Posta Band of Diegueno Mission Indians of the La Posta Indian Reservation, California
- Lac Courte Oreilles Band of Lake Superior Chippewa Indians of the Lac Courte Oreilles Reservation of Wisconsin
- Lac Vieux Desert Band of Lake Superior Chippewa Indians of Michigan
- Las Vegas Tribe of Paiute Indians of the Las Vegas Indian Colony, Nevada
- Los Coyotes Band of Cahuilla Mission Indians of the Los Coyotes Reservation, California
- Lovelock Paiute Tribe of the Lovelock Indian Colony, Nevada
- Lower Brule Sioux Tribe of the Lower Brule Reservation, South Dakota
- Lower Elwha Tribal Community of the Lower Elwha Reservation, Washington
- Lower Sioux Indian Community of Minnesota Midewakanion Sioux Indians of the Lower Sioux Reservation in Minnesota
- Lummi Tribe of the Lummi Reservation, Washington
- Makah Indian Tribe of the Makah Indian Reservation, Washington
- Manchester Band of Pomo Indians of the Manchester-Point Arena Rancheria, California
- Manzanita Band of Diegueno Mission Indians of the Manzanita Reservation, California
- Mashantucket Pequot Tribe of Connecticut

- Menominee Indian Tribe of Wisconsin
- Mesa Grande Band of Diegueno Mission Indians of the Mesa Grande Reservation, California
- Mescalero Apache Tribe of the Mescalero Reservation, New Mexico
- Miami Tribe of Oklahoma
- Miccosukee Tribe of Indians of Florida
- Middletown Rancheria of Pomo Indians of California
- Minnesota Chippewa Tribe, Minnesota (Six component reservations: Bois Forte Band [Nett Lake], Fond du Lac Band, Grand Portage Band, Leech Lake Band, Mille Lacs Band, White Earth Band)
- Mississippi Band of Choctaw Indians, Mississippi
- Moapa Band of Paiute Indians of the Moapa River Indian Reservation, Nevada
- Modoc Tribe of Oklahoma
- Mooretown Rancheria of Maida Indians of California
- Morongo Band of Cahuilla Mission Indians of the Morongo Reservation, California
- Muckleshoot Indian Tribe of the Muckleshoot Reservation, Washington
- Narragansett Indian Tribe of Rhode Island
- Navajo Tribe of Arizona, New Mexico and Utah
- Nez Perce Tribe of Idaho
- Nisqually Indian Community of the Nisqually Reservation, Washington
- Nooksack Indian Tribe of Washington
- Northern Cheyenne Tribe of the Northern Cheyenne Indian Reservation, Montana
- Northfork Rancheria of Mono Indians of California
- Northwestern Band of Shoshoni Indians of Utah (Washakie)
- Oglala Sioux Tribe of the Pine Ridge Reservation, South Dakota
- Omaha Tribe of Nebraska
- Oneida Nation of New York
- Oneida Tribe of Wisconsin
- Onondaga Nation of New York
- Osage Tribe of Oklahoma
- Otoe-Missouria Tribe of Oklahoma
- Ottawa Tribe of Oklahoma
- Paiute Indian Tribe of Utah
- Paiute-Shoshone Indians of the Bishop Community of the Bishop Colony, California

- Paiute-Shoshone Indians of the Lone Pine Community of the Lone Pine Reservation, California
- Paiute-Shoshone Tribe of the Fallon Reservation and Colony, Nevada
- Pala Band of Luiseno Mission Indians of the Pala Reservation, California
- Pascua Yaqui Tribe of Arizona
- Passamaquoddy Tribe of Maine
- Pauma Band of Luiseno Mission Indians of the Pauma & Yuima Reservation, California
- Pawnee Indian Tribe of Oklahoma
- Pechanga Band of Luiseno Mission Indians of the Pechanga Reservation, California
- Penobscot Tribe of Maine
- Peoria Tribe of Oklahoma
- Picayune Rancheria of Chukchansi Indians of California
- Pinoleville Rancheria of Pomo Indians of California
- Pit River Tribe of California (includes Big Bend, Lookout, Montgomery Creek & Roaring Creek Rancheria & XI Ranch)
- Poarch Band of Creek Indians of Alabama
- Ponca Tribe of Indians of Oklahoma
- Port Gamble Indian Community of the Port Gamble Reservation, Washington
- Potter Valley Rancheria of Pomo Indians of California
- Prairie Band of Potawatomi Indians of Kansas
- Prairie Island Indian Community of Minnesota Mdewakanoa Sioux Indians of the Prairie Island Reservation, Minnesota
- Pueblo of Acoma, New Mexico
- Pueblo of Cochiti, New Mexico
- Pueblo of Isleta, New Mexico
- Pueblo of Jemez, New Mexico
- Pueblo of Laguna, New Mexico
- Pueblo of Nambe, New Mexico
- Pueblo of Picuris, New Mexico
- Pueblo of Pojoaque, New Mexico
- Pueblo of San Felipe, New Mexico
- Pueblo of San Ildefonso, New Mexico
- Pueblo of San Juan, New Mexico
- Pueblo of Sandia, New Mexico
- Pueblo of Santa Ana, New Mexico

- Pueblo of Santa Clara, New Mexico
- Pueblo of Santo Domingo, New Mexico
- Pueblo of Taos, New Mexico
- Pueblo of Tesuque, New Mexico
- Pueblo of Zia, New Mexico
- Puyallup Tribe of the Puyallup Reservation, Washington
- Pyramid Lake Paiute Tribe of the Pyramid Lake Reservation, Nevada
- Quapaw Tribe of Oklahoma
- Quartz Valley Rancheria of Karok, Shasta & Upper Klamath Indians of California
- Quechan Tribe of the Fort Yuma Indian Reservation, California
- Quileute Tribe of the Quileute Reservation, Washington
- Quinault Tribe of the Quinault Reservation, Washington
- Ramona Band or Village of Cahuilla Mission Indians of California
- Red Cliff Band of Lake Superior Chippewa Indians of Wisconsin
- Red Lake Band of Chippewa Indians of the Red Lake Reservation, Minnesota
- Redding Rancheria of Pomo Indians of California
- Redwood Valley Rancheria of Pomo Indians of California
- Reno-Sparks Indian Colony, Nevada
- Rincon Band of Luiseno Mission Indians of the Rincon Reservation, California
- Robinson Rancheria of Pomo Indians of California
- Rohnerville Rancheria of Bear River or Mattole Indians of California
- Rosebud Sioux Tribe of the Rosebud Indian Reservation, South Dakota
- Rumsey Indian Rancheria of Wintun Indians of California
- Sac & Fox Tribe of the Mississippi in Iowa
- Sac & Fox Tribe of Missouri in Kansas and Nebraska
- Sac & Fox Tribe of Oklahoma
- Saginaw Chippewa Indian Tribe of Michigan, Isabella Reservation
- Salt River Pima-Maricopa Indian Community of the Salt River Reservation, Arizona
- San Carlos Apache Tribe of the San Carlos Reservation, Arizona
- San Manuel Band of Serrano Mission Indians of the San Manuel Reservation, California
- San Pasqual Band of Diegueno Mission Indians of California
- Santa Rosa Indian Community of the Santa Rosa Rancheria, California
- Santa Rosa Band of Cahuilla Mission Indians of the Santa Rosa Reservation, California

- Santa Ynez Band of Chumash Mission Indians of the Santa Ynez Reservation, California
- Santa Ysabel Band of Diegueno Mission Indians of the Santa Ysabel Reservation, California
- Santee Sioux Tribe of the Santee Reservation of Nebraska
- Sauk-Suiattle Indian Tribe of Washington
- Sault Ste. Marie Tribe of Chippewa Indians of Michigan
- Seminole Nation of Oklahoma
- Seminole Tribe of Florida, Dania, Big Cypress & Brighton Reservations
- Seneca Nation of New York
- Seneca-Cayuga Tribe of Oklahoma
- Shakopee Mdewakanton Sioux Community of Minnesota (Prior Lake)
- Sheep Ranch Rancheria of Me-Wuk Indians of California
- Sherwood Valley Rancheria of Pomo Indians of California
- Shingle Springs Band of Miwok Indians, Shingle Springs Rancheria (Verona Tract), California
- Shoalwater Bay Tribe of the Shoalwater Bay Indian Reservation, Washington
- Shoshone Tribe of the Wind River Reservation, Wyoming
- Shoshone-Bannock Tribes of the Fort Hall Reservation of Idaho
- Shoshone Paiute Tribes of the Duck Valley Reservation, Nevada
- Sisseton-Wahpeton Sioux Tribe of the Lake Traverse Reservation, South Dakota
- Skokomish Indian Tribe of the Skokomish Reservation, Washington
- Skull Valley Band of Goshute Indians of Utah
- Smith River Rancheria of California
- Soboba Band of Luiseno Mission Indians of the Soboba Reservation, California
- Sokaogon Chippewa Community of the Mole Lake Band of Chippewa Indians, Wisconsin
- Southern Ute Indian Tribe of the Southern Ute Reservation, Colorado
- Spokane Tribe of the Spokane Reservation, Washington
- Squaxin Island Tribe of the Squaxin Island Reservation, Washington
- St. Croix Chippewa Indians of Wisconsin, St. Croix Reservation
- St. Regis Band of Mohawk Indians of New York
- Standing Rock Sioux Tribe of North & South Dakota
- Stockbridge-Munsee Community of Mohican Indians of Wisconsin
- Stillaguamish Tribe of Washington
- Summit Lake Paiute Tribe of Nevada

- Suquamish Indian Tribe of the Port Madison Reservation, Washington
- Susanville Indian Rancheria of Paiute, Maidu, Pit River & Washoe Indians of California
- Swinomish Indians of the Swinomish Reservation, Washington
- Sycuan Band of Diegueno Mission Indians of California
- Table Bluff Rancheria of Wiyot Indians of California
- Table Mountain Rancheria of California
- Te-Moak Tribe of Western Shoshone Indians of Nevada
- Thlopthlocco Tribal Town of the Creek Nation of Oklahoma
- Three Affiliated Tribes of the Fort Berthold Reservation, North Dakota
- Tohono O'odham Nation of Arizona (formerly known as the Papago Tribe of the Sells, Gila Bend & San Xavier Reservation, Arizona)
- Tonawanda Band of Seneca Indians of New York
- Tonkawa Tribe of Indians of Oklahoma
- Tonto Apache Tribe of Arizona
- Torres-Martinez Band of Cahuilla Mission Indians of California
- Tule River Indian Tribe of the Tule River Reservation, California
- Tulalip Tribes of the Tulalip Reservation, Washington
- Tule River Indian Tribe of the Tule River Reservation, California
- Tunica-Biloxi Indian Tribe of Louisiana
- Tuolumne Band of Me-Wuk Indians of the Tuolumne Rancheria of California
- Turtle Mountain Band of Chippewa Indians of North Dakota
- Tuscarora Nation of New York
- Twenty-Nine Palms Band of Luiseno Mission Indians of California
- United Keetoowah Band of Cherokee Indians, Oklahoma
- Upper Lake Band of Pomo Indians of Upper Lake Rancheria California
- Upper Sioux Indian Community of the Upper Sioux Reservation Minnesota
- Upper Skagit Indian Tribe of Washington
- Ute Indian Tribe of the Uintah & Ouray Reservation, Utah
- Ute Mountain Tribe of the Ute Mountain Reservation, Colorado, New Mexico & Utah
- Utu Utu Gwaitu Paiute Tribe of the Benton Paiute Reservation, California
- Walker River Paiute Tribe of the Walker River Reservation, California
- Washoe Tribe of Nevada & California (Carson Colony, Dresslerville, & Washoe Ranches)
- White Mountain Apache Tribe of the Fort Apache Reservation, Arizona
- Wichita Indian Tribe of Oklahoma

- Winnebago Tribe of Nebraska
- Winnemucca Indian Colony of Nevada
- Wisconsin Winnebago Indian Tribe of Wisconsin
- Wyandotte Tribe of Oklahoma
- Yankton Sioux Tribe of South Dakota
- Yavapai-Apache Indian Community of the Camp Verde Reservation, Arizona
- Yavapai-Prescott Tribe of the Yavapai Reservation, Arizona
- Yerington Paiute Tribe of the Yerington Colony & Campbell Ranch, Nevada
- Yomba Shoshone Tribe of the Yomba Reservation, Nevada
- Ysleta Del Sur Pueblo of Texas
- Yurok Tribe of the Hoopa Valley Reservation, California
- Zuni Tribe of the Zuni Reservation, New Mexico

Additions:

- Coquille Tribe of Oregon (6/28/89)
- Kickapoo Traditional Tribe of Texas (7/11/89)
- Ponca Tribe of Nebraska (10/31/90)
- San Juan Paiute Tribe of Arizona (3/28/90)

These reservations make up in excess of 53,000,000 acres of land. The Navajo Reservation extends over some 16,000,000 acres of land in Utah, Arizona and New Mexico. The extent of a particular reservation is determined by terms of the treaty between the government and a particular tribe negotiated at a certain time (at least ten "tribes" are presently applying for recognition, which brings with it access to a wide range of government benefits).

According to census statistics, Indians are our fastest growing non-immigrant minority. The Census Bureau informs us that the number of Indians in the United States in the census of 1980 was 1,513,195, an increase of 71 percent over the census of 1970. The Bureau is uncertain of the cause of such a large increase. Some of the reasons suggested are that the census of 1980 was more thorough in gathering statistics. Another explanation is that the recent general interest among non-Indians in Indians has encouraged Americans of Indian ancestry to identify themselves more readily as "Indians." The definition of what constitutes an "Indian" varies widely from one-fourth to one-sixth. Some tribes have accepted individuals with one-sixteenth "tribal" blood as bona fide members although most tribes now require one-fourth. On some reservations as few as ten percent of the tribe are "pure blood," the rest "mixed bloods."

There is often tension between the "pure bloods" and the "mixed bloods" and I have heard "pure bloods" express strong resentment at the fact that many if not all of the leaders in the American Indian Movement are "mixed bloods" who presume to speak for the "real" Indians.

Thirty-one of fifty states have "reservation" Indians living within their boundaries. The numbers vary widely from Connecticut with 80 to Oklahoma with 231,952. The five states with the largest Indian population on reservations are, besides Oklahoma, Arizona with 165,385, New Mexico 126,346, South Dakota 58,201, Washington 40,893, and Montana 34,001. California with 28,815 is a special case because of the large number of small tribes living in the area prior to the arrival of the Spanish.

In that state, Indians of 87 tribal groups live on what are called "rancherias," a carry-over from Spanish days. Many tribes are divided between "Mission Indians" and "Wild Indians." The Spanish did their best to "civilize" the California Indians by per-suading (or often forcing) Indians of particular tribes to live in mission compounds. Those tribal members who resisted the mis-sionary efforts often felt more hostility toward those who became "mission Indians" than toward their traditional enemies. Thus the "Wild" Hoopa live on a separate reservation (or rancheria) from the "Mission" Hoopa. And the same kind of separation persists among a number of California tribes. One of the larger California tribes, the Karoks were estimated to have numbered some 2,700 living in a hundred or so villages prior to the arrival of white settlers. By the 1950s there were estimated to be no more than 500 tribal members left. But by the census of 1980 more than 1,000 Karoks were living on a rancheria of 242 acres with 400 living nearby. By contrast, the Morongo Band of Mission Indians, affiliated with the Cahuilla, have some 500 members on a reservation of 33,361 acres with 493 living adjacent to the reservation. The Agua Caliente band of Cahuilla Indians has a reservation of 23,173 acres with 103 Indians living on the reservation and 141 adjacent.

In 1988 Congress granted 10,000 acres along the Klamath River to the Yurok. The Hoopa, one of the largest tribes in pre-Spanish California, has a reservation of 147,740 acres and, within or near the reservation, over 4,000 members, again a substantial increase over the population forty years ago.

The ten largest tribes in 1980 were Cherokee (232,080), Navajo (158,633), Sioux (78,608), Chippewa (73,602), Choctaw (50,220), Pueblo (42,552), Iroquois (38,218), Apache (35,861), Lumbee (28,631), and Creek (28,278).

Fifty-six percent of Indians age 25 and over were high school graduates, versus 66 percent of the total U.S. population. Among the ten largest tribes, the proportion of high school graduates was above 50 percent for all tribes except Navajo (40 percent) and Lumbee (38 percent). The highest proportion was 65 percent for Creek.

Married couples comprised 72 percent of all American Indian families in 1980, compared with 83 percent for the national population. Among the ten largest tribes, at least seven in ten families were married-couple families for Choctaw, Creek, Cherokee, Lumbee, and Sioux.

Among Indians age 16 and over, 59 percent were in the labor force compared with 62 percent for the total U.S. population. Roughly 60 percent of each tribe's population (except for the Pueblo, Sioux, and Navajo) was in the labor force. Navajo was lowest at 48 percent.

Twenty-eight percent of Indians aged 15 and over were below the poverty level in 1979, compared with 12 percent for the total population. Among the ten tribes, the rate ranged from 46 percent for Navajo to about 20 percent for Choctaw, Iroquois, Cherokee, and Creek. According to the 1980 census, the median income of Indian families was $13,680 in 1979, compared with the national median of $19,920. Among the tribes, Creek had the highest at $15,290 and Navajo had the lowest at $9,900.

DOCUMENT 1

REPORT OF THE UNITED STATES
COMMISSION ON CIVIL RIGHTS

CONSTITUTIONAL STATUS
OF AMERICAN INDIANS

INTRODUCTION

A thorough treatment of the constitutional status of American Indians would involve a complete analysis of the unique and complex field of Federal Indian law which cannot be adequately described merely by reference to the numerous treaties, statutory enactments of Congress, and court decisions or Federal administrative decisions. The legal and political status of Indian tribes, the relationship of Indians to their tribes and to their States, and the relationship of tribes to the States and to the United States Government have long been issues of controversy. Tribes have traditionally been viewed by Federal courts as dependent or "tributary" nations possessed of limited elements of sovereignty and requiring Federal protection.

Congress has alternatively viewed tribes as sovereign political entities or as anachronisms which must eventually be extinguished. The result has been two conflicting Federal policies—separation and assimilation, one designed to protect Indians from the rest of society and to leave them with a degree of self-government within their own institutions, and the other calculated to bring Indians within the mainstream of American life by terminating special Federal trust relationships and Federal programs and services. Termination reached its aegis during the Eisenhower Administration of the 1950s. The current Administration [Nixon Administration] has taken a strong stand against termination; in his message on Indian affairs, July 13, 1970, President Nixon said:

> Because termination is morally and legally unacceptable, because it produces bad practical results and because the mere threat of termination tends to discourage greater self-sufficiency among Indian groups, I am asking the Congress to pass a new concurrent resolution which would expressly renounce, repudiate and repeal the termination policy as expressed by the House Concurrent Resolution 108 of the 83rd Congress. This resolution would explicitly affirm the integrity and rights to continued existence of all Indian tribes and Alaskan Native governments, recognizing that cultural pluralism is a source of national strength. It would assure these groups that the United States Government would continue to carry out its treaty and trusteeship obligations to them as long as the groups themselves believed that such a policy was necessary or desirable. [It would] affirm for the Executive Branch . . . that the historic relationship between the Federal Government and the Indian communities cannot be abridged without the consent of the Indians.

SOURCES OF FEDERAL POWER

The historic relationship to which the President refers has a somewhat confusing background. The Federal Government has exercised plenary power over Indians for almost 100 years. This power emanates from three sources. First, the Constitution grants to the President and to Congress what have been construed as broad powers of authority over Indian affairs. Second, the Federal courts have applied a theory of guardianship and wardship to the Federal Government's jurisdiction over Indian affairs. And, finally, Federal authority is inherent in the Federal Government's ownership of the land which Indian tribes occupy. In *Worcester v. Georgia* Chief Justice John Marshall recognized that the aforementioned powers plus the power of war and peace "comprehend all that is required for the regulation of our intercourse with the Indians."

The treaty power was the traditional means for dealing with Indian tribes from the colonial times until 1871, when recognition of Indian tribes as sovereign nations for this purpose was withdrawn by the Indian Appropriation Act, which provided that " . . . here-after, no Indian nation or tribe within the territory of the United States shall be acknowledged or recognized as an independent nation, tribe or power with whom the United States may contract by treaty. . . ." Treaties made before 1871 were not nullified by that Act, but remain in force until superseded by Congress. It is a well established principle of constitutional law that treaties have no greater legal force or effect than legislative acts of Congress, and may be unilaterally abrogated or superseded by subsequent Congressional legislation. Until so abrogated, however, treaties with Indian tribes are part of the law of the land and are binding on the Federal Government. In carrying out its treaty obligations the Federal Government occupies a trust relationship which, according to the Court in *Seminole Nation v. United States*, "should be judged by the most exacting fiduciary standards." As part of the law of the land treaties cannot be annulled in their effect or operation by the acts of State governments.

TRIBAL SOVEREIGNTY

In considering the constitutional status of American Indians a distinction must be made between tribal entities and individual citizens. As stated before, the legal status of Indian tribes has vacillated throughout this Nation's history in the eyes of the Federal Government. The numerous treaties made with Indian tribes recognized them as governments capable of maintaining diplomatic relations of peace and war and of being responsible, in a political sense, for their violation. When engaged in war against whites, Indians were never treated as rebels, subject to the law of treason, but, "on the contrary, were always regarded and treated as separate and independent nations, entitled to the rights of ordinary belligerents and subject to no other penalties." Hostile Indians surrendering to armed forces were subject to the disabilities and entitled to the rights of prisoners of war.

Tribal sovereignty was originally formally recognized by Chief Justice Marshall in *Worcester v. Georgia*: "The Constitution, by declaring treaties already made, as well as those to be made, to be the supreme law of the land, has adopted and sanctioned the previous treaties with the Indian nations, and consequently, admits their rank among those powers who are capable of making treaties." That position, which determined the Federal Judiciary's basic policy toward Indian tribes throughout the nineteenth century may be contrasted with the attitude of later court decisions such as *Montoya v. United States*, wherein the court concluded that "the word 'nation' as applied to the uncivilized Indians was little more than a compliment."

Today, the concept of tribal sovereignty is widely misunderstood and can only be meaningfully discussed with regard to specific attributes or powers. Clearly, tribal governments are not on the same legal footing as independent nations; on the other hand, they are widely recognized as political units with governmental powers which exist, in some sense, on a higher level than that of the States. The contemporary meaning of tribal sovereignty is defined in *Iron Crow v. Oglala Sioux Tribe of Pine Ridge Reservation* as follows:

> It would seem clear that the Constitution as construed by the Supreme Court, acknowledges the paramount authority of the United States with regard to Indian tribes but recognizes the existence of Indian tribes as quasi-sovereign entities possessing all the inherent rights of sovereignty except where restrictions have been placed thereon by the United States, itself.

In his 1940 edition of Federal Indian law, Felix Cohen summarized the meaning of tribal sovereignty in the following manner:

> The whole course of judicial decision on the nature of Indian tribal powers is marked by adherence to three fundamental principles:
> (1) The Indian tribe possesses, in the first instance, all the powers of any sovereign state.
> (2) Conquest renders the tribe subject to the legislative power of

the United States, and, in substance, terminates the external powers of sovereignty of the tribe, e.g., its power to enter into treaties with foreign nations, but does not, by itself, affect the internal sovereignty of the tribe, i.e., its power of local self-government.

(3) These powers are subject to qualification by treaties and by express legislation by Congress, but, save as thus expressly quali- fied, full powers of internal sovereignty are vested in the Indian tribes and in their duly constituted organs of government.

POWERS OF TRIBAL SELF-GOVERNMENT

Indian tribes are recognized in Federal law as distinct political communities with basic domestic and municipal functions. This includes the power to adopt and operate under a form of gov- ernment of the tribe's choosing, to define conditions of tribal membership, to regulate domestic relations of members, to pre- scribe rules of inheritance, to levy taxes, to regulate property within the jurisdiction of the tribe, to control the conduct of members by tribal legislation, to administer justice and provide for the punishment of offenses committed on the reservation. Although Indian tribes began their relationship with the Federal Government as sovereign governments recognized as such by treaties and in legislation, the powers of tribal sovereignty have been limited from time to time by the Federal Government. It should be noted, however, that the powers which tribes cur- rently exercise are not delegated powers granted by Congress but rather, are "inherent powers of a limited dependent sovereignty which had not been extinguished by Federal action. What is not expressly limited often remains within the domain of tribal sov- ereignty simply because State jurisdiction is Federally excluded and governmental authority must be found somewhere. That is a principal to be applied generally in order that there shall be no general failure of governmental control."

The powers of self-government are normally exercised pursu- ant to tribal constitutions and law and order codes. Normally, these powers include the right of a tribe to define the authority and the duties of its officials, the manner of their appointment or election, the manner of their removal, and the rules they are to observe. This right, as with the exercise of all functions of tribal sovereignty, is subject to Congressional change. For example, Federal law has removed from some tribes the power to choose their own officials and has placed the power of appointment in the President and the Secretary of Interior.

Indian tribes, having the power to make laws and regulations essential to the administration of justice and the protection of persons and property also have the power to maintain law enforcement departments and courts to enforce them. Some smaller tribes have no courts at all or maintain very traditional customary courts which lack formal structure. Larger tribes, such as the Navajo, maintain quite advanced law and order systems with well-equipped police departments, modern tribal codes and a hierarchy of trial and appellate courts overseen by a tribal supreme court. Generally, the jurisdiction of Indian courts is exclusive as to matters involving tribal affairs, civil suits brought by Indians or non-Indians against tribal members arising out of matters occurring on the reservation, and the prosecution of violations of the tribal criminal code. Tribal jurisdiction operates to the exclusion of Federal and State authority. Federal courts are without jurisdiction over matters involving violations of tribal ordinances, as are State courts. With regard to cases within their jurisdiction tribal courts are courts of last resort. Their decisions are appealable to neither State nor Federal courts.

Several important limitations have been placed by Congress on tribal jurisdictions. Under the 1968 Indian Civil Rights Act tribes may not exercise jurisdiction over criminal offenses punishable by more than a $500 fine or 6 months in jail. Federal courts have jurisdiction to try and punish certain major offenses such as murder, manslaughter, rape, etc., pursuant to the Major Crimes Act. In certain instances, Congress has provided that the criminal laws and/or civil laws of a State shall extend to Indian reservations located in the State. States which have assumed responsibility for the administration of justice on Indian land are commonly referred to as "Public Law 280 States."

HUNTING AND FISHING RIGHTS

A current major issue arising from the limitations on State authority due to quasi-tribal sovereignty is the hunting and fishing rights controversy in the Northwest. It is well settled that a State cannot enforce its game and fish laws within the boundaries of an Indian reservation. However, the issue of State control over on-reservation hunting and fishing should be distinguished from the question of the extent to which treaty rights prohibit States from interfering with hunting and fishing by Indians off reservations. In a confusing decision the United States Supreme Court recently held that treaty rights to "fish at all usual and accustomed places" may not be qualified by a State but that the exercise of such rights is subject to reasonable State conservation legislation.

DOMESTIC RELATIONS

Indian tribes exercise a wide latitude of power over the domestic relations of tribal members. Tribes normally conduct marriages and grant divorces to the exclusion of State law even though the Indians concerned are also citizens of the State. Indian customary marriage and divorce has generally been recognized by State and Federal courts. Tribes also have complete and exclusive authority to define and punish offenses against the marriage relationship, although, as with other civil matters, Congress may make State law applicable.

TAXATION

An important power essential to the maintenance of governmental functions is the power of taxation. In *Buster v. Wright*, it was held that the Creek Nation had the power to impose a license fee upon all persons, Indian and non-Indian, who traded within the borders of that Nation. Tribal authority to levy a property tax on all property within the reservation was upheld in *Morris v. Hitchcock*.

Indian tribes are currently recognized by the United States as "units of local government" for the purpose of receiving Federal revenue funds pursuant to the Revenue Sharing Act of 1972.

As a general matter, then, Indian tribes are recognized by Federal law as governmental units exercising a wide variety of governmental functions, limited only by the assertion of Congressional plenary power over Indian affairs. Outside of the scope of this memorandum is a discussion of the wide spectrum of Federal administrative powers currently exercised over Indian affairs.

LEGAL STATUS OF INDIAN INDIVIDUALS

By virtue of the Indian Citizenship Act of June 2, 1924, all Indians born in the United States are citizens of the United States. As such, they are also citizens of the State in which they live, even though they may reside on a reservation. Although many Indians acquired citizenship prior to 1926, pursuant to various Federal statutes, it was early held that the provision of the 14th Amendment of the United States Constitution conferring citizenship on "all persons born or naturalized in the United States, and subject to the jurisdiction thereof" did not confer citizenship on Indians. State and Federal citizenship and tribal membership are not incompatible: Indians are citizens of three separate political entities. As citizens of the Federal Government they are subject to the laws of the Federal Government no matter where they may be located. As citizens of the tribal government they are subject to the civil and criminal laws of the tribe when they are on the reservation and within its jurisdiction (except, as stated above, in Public Law 280 States). They are subject to the laws of the States while off the reservation.

PROTECTIONS IN THE TRIBAL SETTING— CONSTITUTIONAL IMMUNITY

In their relationship with the tribe, Indians are normally protected by a wide variety of criminal due process, civil rights and civil liberties protections contained in the tribal constitution and the tribal law and order code. By their own weight the Bill of Rights and the 14th Amendment to the United States Constitution do not impose limitations on tribal action and thus, do not confer protections on tribal members. In the case of *Talton v. Mayes* for example, the Supreme Court refused to apply the Fifth Amendment to invalidate a tribal law that established a five-man grand jury. In *Glover v. United States*, the court stated that "the right to be represented by counsel is protected by the Sixth and 14th Amendments. These Amendments, however protect . . . this right only as against action by the United States in the case of the . . . Sixth Amendment . . . and as against action by the States in the case of the 14th Amendment, Indian tribes are not States within the meaning of the 14th Amendment."

Again, in the case of *Native American Church v. Navajo Tribal Council*, it was held by implication that a tribal Indian cannot claim protection against illegal search and seizure by tribal officials. In 1954, an attempt to redress tribal invasions of religious freedom arose in a suit against the James Pueblo Tribal Council and governor by Pueblo members, charging that they had been subjected to indignities, threats and reprisals solely because of their Protestant faith and that the tribal council had refused to permit them to bury their dead in the community cemetery and to build a church on tribal land. The court acknowledged that the alleged acts represented a serious invasion of religious freedom but concluded that the acts were not taken "under color of any statute, ordinance, regulation, custom or usage of any State or Territory" and thus no cause of action arose either under the Federal Constitution or under Federal civil rights acts. In *State v. Big Sheep*, the Tenth Circuit refused to concede the application of First Amendment protections through the Fourteenth Amendment to Indian tribes:

> No provision in the Constitution makes the First Amendment
> applicable to Indian nations nor is there any law of Congress
> doing to. It follows that neither, under the Constitution or the
> laws of Congress, do the Federal courts have jurisdiction of tribal

laws or regulations, even though they may have an impact to some extent on forms of religious worship.

1968 INDIAN BILL OF RIGHTS

These cases illustrate what the Constitutional Rights Subcommittee of the Senate Committee on the Judiciary saw as a "continued denial of Constitutional guarantee" to American Indians, on the ground that tribes are quasi-sovereign entities to which general provisions of the Constitution do not apply. In 1961 that Subcommittee instituted a lengthy investigation of the legal status of American Indians and the problems they encounter when asserting their Constitutional rights in their relations with the State, Federal and tribal governments. This effort, largely engineered by Senator Sam Ervin, Chairman of the Subcommittee, culminated in the passage of the Civil Rights Act of 1968, Title II of which constitutes a bill of rights for American Indians. It provides that Indian tribes exercising powers of self-government shall be subject to many of the same limitations and restraints which are imposed on Federal, State and local governments by the United States Constitution. Two major exceptions are that the Indian Bill of Rights provides the right to counsel before tribal courts only at the defendant's "own expense" and, although, religious freedom is protected, the Act does not contain a prohibition against the establishment of religion by a tribal government.

RIGHTS AND PRIVILEGES OF STATE CITIZENSHIP

While off their reservations, Indians are subject to the same laws, both Federal and State, as are other citizens. When brought before State or Federal courts they are entitled to the same Constitutional protections as other defendants. As a general matter, Indians are also entitled to the same Federal and State benefits, programs and services as other State and Federal citizens. From time to time, however, States have attempted to deny Indians participation in State programs on the grounds that their entitlement to special Federal programs made them ineligible. A law of the State of California, for example, declared that a local public school board could exclude Indian children from attending if the United States Government maintained a school for Indians within the school district. The California Supreme Court held that the law violated the State and Federal constitutions.

One justification commonly used by States for excluding Indians from participation in State programs and State services has been that Indians do not pay taxes. The restricted status of Indian land renders it immune from State and local taxation and, with certain statutory exceptions, income derived from the land is likewise nontaxable. Other local, State and Federal taxes commonly paid by citizens, including sales taxes, are paid by Indians. Indians pay State taxes on all non-trust property and are obligated for all fees and taxes for the enjoyment of State privileges, such as driving on State highways, and all other taxes which reach the entire population.

All attempts to treat Indian citizens differently or to exclude them from State and local programs raise clear Constitutional questions. As the Chief Counsel of the Bureau of Indian Affairs stated in a memorandum dated July 8, 1953, concerning the refusal of the State of North Dakota to admit and care for feebleminded Indian children in State schools under the same rules and conditions applicable to the admission and care of non-Indians, "such refusal [by the State] to treat Indians in the same manner as non-Indians would appear to deprive the Indians of equal protection of the laws guaranteed by the Fourteenth Amendment to the Federal Constitution."

WARDSHIP

There has been some confusion regarding the status of American Indians because of the common notion that Indians are "wards" of the Federal Government. The Federal Government is a trustee of Indian property, not the guardian of individual Indians. In this sense, the term "ward" is inaccurate. Indians are subject to a wide variety of Federal limitations on the distribution of property and assets and income derived from property in Federal trust. Land held in trust for an Indian tribe or for an Indian individual may not be sold without prior approval of the Secretary of the Interior or his representative (the Bureau of Indian Affairs). Related restrictions limit the capacity of an Indian to contract with a private attorney and limit the heirship distribution of trust property. Many Americans erroneously believe that as wards of the Federal Government Indians must stay on reservations and that they receive gratuitous payments from the Federal Government. Indians do not in fact receive payments merely because they are Indians. "Payments may be made to Indian tribes or individuals for loss which resulted from treaty violations. . . . [i]ndividuals may also receive government checks for income from their land and resources, but only because the assets are held in trust by the Secretary of the Interior and payment for the use of the Indian resources has been collected by the Federal Government."

Like other citizens, Indians may hold Federal, State and local office, are subject to the draft, may sue and be sued in State courts, may enter into contracts, may own property and dispose of property (other than that held in trust) and, as stated before, pay taxes. The large number of Federal and State laws and provisions which in the past denied Indians political rights and public benefits have either been legislatively repealed, ruled invalid by the Judicial branch or remain unenforced.

DOCUMENT 2

LAW AND ORDER ON INDIAN RESERVATIONS

BUREAU OF INDIAN AFFAIRS SUMMARY

HOW DID THE PRESENT INDIAN CRIMINAL JUSTICE SYSTEM DEVELOP?

Indian governments that existed since before the coming of the Europeans began to break down in the nineteenth century as tribes were confined to reservations. Indian agents established police forces among the tribes they supervised to maintain order and to control the sale of liquor.

In 1884, the Secretary of the Interior established Courts of Indian Offenses and promulgated regulations to govern the conduct of the courts and police. The following year, Congress gave the Federal courts jurisdiction over certain major offenses involving Indians on reservations. Those crimes were murder, manslaughter, rape, assault with intent to kill, assault with a dangerous weapon, arson, burglary and larceny. Amendments over the years have added the offenses of carnal knowledge, assault with intent to rape, incest, assault in serious bodily injury and robbery.

After the passage of the General Allotment Act of 1887, Indians who received allotments were made subject to State Civil and Criminal jurisdiction. In Oklahoma, the Curtis Act of 1898 abolished the Indian courts and police of the Five Civilized Tribes.

In 1907, Congress authorized the employment of Special Officers and Deputies to suppress liquor traffic in Indian country. Unlike the Indian police, the Special Officers reported directly to the Commissioner of Indian Affairs.

After the passage of the Indian Reorganization Act of 1934, many tribes established tribal courts, employed tribal police and enacted tribal ordinances. Tribally established courts and police were supported by tribal funds. Some tribes passed ordinances but relied on the Federally supported police and courts to enforce them. More tribes established and funded their own police and courts during the Second World War when Federal funding was curtailed.

In 1949, the Special Officers were assigned to individual reservations. Some of the reservations to which they were assigned had BIA police. Some had tribal police and still others had both. The Special Officers became the supervisor of any BIA police on the reservation. In some places the Special Officer also supervised tribal police. On others, tribal and BIA police continued to operate independently of each other.

In 1953 Congress passed Public Law 83-280, which gave States Criminal and Civil jurisdiction over Indian communities in Alaska, California, Minnesota, Nebraska, Oregon and Wisconsin, the only exceptions were the Warm Springs Reservation in Oregon, the Bad Lake Reservation in Minnesota.

The Indian Civil Rights Act of 1968 permits states to give up jurisdiction they had previously assumed under P.L. 83-280. Some States at the urging of individual tribes have returned jurisdiction.

In 1964 the BIA began to contract with tribes to provide part of the reservation criminal justice services. This approach made possible the combination of tribal direction of Federal funding.

In States that have assumed jurisdiction under P.L. 83-280 and in New York, Iowa, and Kansas State and Federal laws apply in Indian communities the same as they do anywhere else.

On Federal Indian reservations in other States the crimes listed in the Major Crimes Act are tried in Federal court applying Federal law if an Indian is involved. Violations of State laws that are not also punishable under Federal law are tried in Federal court applying State law when an Indian is involved. Violations of State law committed on a reservation but not involving an Indian will be tried in State court. General Federal laws apply on Indian reservations the same as they do elsewhere.

Tribal courts have jurisdiction over violations of tribal, civil and criminal codes committed by Indians on the reservation. The 1968 Indian Civil Rights Act limits the penalties tribal courts can impose to six months in jail and/or $500 fine. Tribal courts generally have civil jurisdiction over suits between tribal members. Judges for tribal courts are chosen either by the Tribal Council or by tribal election. Currently there are 73 such courts.

Twenty reservations have CFR courts established under the authority of the Secretary of the Interior and governed by the provisions of Title 25 of the Code of Federal Regulations. The BIA appoints judges for these courts subject to the approval of the tribal council. The jurisdiction of these courts is the same as that of the tribal courts.

An Indian convicted of a violation of a tribal code or the Code of Federal Regulations is lodged in one of 67 jails. There are 26 tribally owned jails and 19 county or city jails. The county and city jails provide detention facilities under contract with a tribe or the BIA.

The Indian Police Academy in Brigham City, Utah, provides a 600-hour basic training course for new police recruits and an 80-hour course for supervisors. The Center also provides a complete range of specialized training for all criminal justice personnel. Some advanced training is provided by the FBI National Academy, Quantico, Virginia and Criminal Investor Training, Treasury Department Combined Law Enforcement Training, Glynco, Georgia.

The rate of major crimes on Indian reservations, according to 1978 data, is about 2,100 per hundred thousand population, compared to a rate of 2,000 per hundred thousand population in all of rural America. The incidence of homicide (non-negligent) is nearly nine times higher than small cities under ten thousand population, eight times higher than cities of ten to twenty-five thousand population, and four times higher than all of rural America.

DOCUMENT 3

BUREAU OF INDIAN AFFAIRS SUMMARY OF TRIBAL CLAIMS AGAINST THE UNITED STATES

Until 1946 Indian tribal claims against the United States could be heard only under special legislation enacted on a tribe-by-tribe basis. A law was enacted on August 13, 1946, creating the Indian Claims Commission with authority to determine tribal claims that accrued up to the date of the Act. All tribal claims had to be filed with the Commission by August 13, 1951. The same Act authorized the Court of Claims to determine tribal claims that accrue after August 13, 1946.

Each tribal claimant hires one or more attorneys of its own selection to prosecute its claims. Neither the Bureau of Indian Affairs nor the Department of the Interior has authority to select or hire attorneys for tribes. However, tribal contracts with attorneys are subject to approval by the Secretary of the Interior.

Both the Court of Claims and the Indian Claims Commission are independent agencies of the Federal Government. They are not a part of the Bureau of Indian Affairs or the Department of the Interior. Neither the Bureau nor the Department participate in the litigation of the claims.

Claims filed with the Indian Claims Commission before August 13, 1951, were placed in 617 dockets. As of June 30, 1977, 484 dockets (78 percent) had been completed—284 with awards totaling nearly $669.1 million and 200 by dismissal. The remaining 112 claims (22 percent) are pending in various stages of litigation.

Most of the claims filed with the Commission are for fair payment of tribal lands taken many years ago—usually by treaty or agreement. Land claims are prosecuted in stages. First, the tribe must prove that it owned land when it was taken. If so, determinations are made in the next stage of the acreage taken, the value of the land at the time of taking, and the amount already paid for it. Offsets are determined in the final stage. Offsets are expenditures made for the benefit of the tribe by the United States when it was under no fixed obligation to do so. The case is then complete unless an appeal is filed.

Most of the claims filed with the Court of Claims under the 1946 Act have been for mismanagement of tribal trust funds and property. Other tribes believe that they may have good claims. They will be filed after an investigation has been made by the tribes and the claims are identified.

Decisions in tribal claims cases are subject to appeal. Decisions of the Indian Claims Commission are subject to appeal to the Court of Claims. Court of Claims decisions are subject to appeal to the Supreme Court. The appeal procedure adds assurances for settlement of claims with fair and just decisions.

It takes about thirteen years, on the average, to hear and determine a tribal claims case. Many issues are involved. The work includes researching records that may be more than 130 years old, preparing for and attending hearings, filing of motions and briefs, and disposing of appeals. Settlement of claims may be speeded up by compromise. The attorneys for both parties negotiate a proposed settlement; the tribe votes on it; and, if approved, the proposed settlement is processed for entry of a final award.

When a claim is settled with an award, Congress is requested to appropriate funds to cover the award. A law enacted October 19, 1973, provides for the Secretary of the Interior, after consultation with the Indians involved, to prepare and present a plan to both Houses of the Congress that sets out the purposes for which the award money is to be used. The plan goes into effect sixty Congressional working days after it is presented, if neither House of Congress adopts a resolution disapproving the plan. If the plan provides for a per capita distribution of the award money, a roll of the persons eligible to share in the distribution is prepared by the tribe or the Bureau of Indian Affairs. Each person who desires to share in the distribution must furnish satisfactory proof during a designated enrollment period that he is eligible to have his name included on the roll.

A tribe with both land and resources may elect to spend judgment funds in projects to bring long-range benefits to the tribe and its members. Such projects are planned by the tribe. They may include housing, sanitation, employment and educational opportunities, investment, and other enterprises which will increase the tribal income or improve the social conditions of the tribal population.

The 1946 Act provides only for settlement of tribal claims. It does not cover claims of individual Indians such as those arising from failure to be enrolled, failure to receive an allotment, injuries suffered in massacres, or arrest or imprisonment. Further, the 1946 Act provides only for money awards. It does not authorize the Indian Claims Commission or the Court of Claims to restore land or property to tribal ownership.

The Act of October 8, 1976, PL 94-465, 90 Stat. 1990, extended the life of the Commission to September 30, 1978, and directed that no later than December 31, 1976, the Commission was to transfer to the U.S. Court of Claims all cases which it determined it could not adjudicate by September 30, 1978; twenty-one such cases were transferred to the Court of Claims for completion.

One of the bitterest disputes over Indian land is not between the Federal Government and a particular tribe but between members of rival tribes. The dispute between the Hopi and the Navajo tribes has been described as "the Middle East of American Indian diplomacy." Ever since President Chester Arthur granted a 2.4 million-acre tract to "the Hopis and other Indians" in 1882, the Hopis, numbering some ten thousand people, have been at odds with the much larger Navajo tribe (some 119,000) over what the Hopis claim are Navajo encroachments on their land.

The Bureau of Indian Affairs estimates the Federal Government has spent $300,000,000 since the 1960s to try and resolve the dispute. There is now hope for resolving the hundred-year-old feud by giving the Hopis $15,000,000 and a large tract of public land.

Another pending Indian land claim is that of the Abnaki and Passamaquoddy tribes, numbering somewhat less than a thousand members. The tribes are suing the state of Maine for more than a million acres of land.

It should be noted that there are deep divisions in many tribes over a wide range of issues, including such relatively trivial ones as the use of Indian names and symbols for "non-Indian" sports teams (Atlanta Braves, Washington Redskins, etc.).

Individual Indians and tribes are by no means of one mind on these or many other very important issues.

3 1170 00995 9820